The New Nation

THE NEW NATION

A History of the United States During the Confederation 1781–1789

by Merrill Jensen

with a foreword by Richard B. Morris

A Classics Edition
NORTHEASTERN UNIVERSITY PRESS
Boston 1981

FIRST NORTHEASTERN EDITION, 1981
Northeastern University Press

Library of Congress Cataloging in Publication Data

Jensen, Merrill
The new nation.
Reprint of the 1st ed. published by Knopf, New York.
Bibliography: p.
Includes index.
1. United States—History—Confederation, 1783-1789.
I. Title.
E303.J45 1981 973.3'18 80-39976
ISBN 0-930350-15-4 (cloth)
ISBN 0-930350-14-6 (paperback)

Library of Congress Number 80-39976

PRINTED IN THE UNITED STATES OF AMERICA

To Edward McMahon

Professor Emeritus of American History

University of Washington

Foreword

A LITTLE MORE than thirty years since its publication, Merrill Jensen's *The New Nation* has assumed its rightful place as a classic. When it first appeared it was welcomed by the historical profession as a brilliant refutation of the traditional picture of the years preceding 1787, long regarded as a period of stagnation, ineptitude, and corruption. Jensen's was the most effective reply to an older classic, *The Critical Period of American History,* a book by James Fiske, the immensely popular lecturer-historian. The title of his work accurately defines its thesis.

Jensen thought that Fiske's book, stressing as it did the "chaos-and-patriots-to-the-rescue interpretation" of the Confederation years, had "no value as either history or example." In *The New Nation,* Jensen dismisses Fiske's thesis that the economic depression of the 1780s was sufficiently serious to justify supplanting the weak federal system then in operation by a stronger central government, and in any event, finds that a business upturn occurred prior to May of '87, when the Framers convened at Philadelphia to write the Constitution. The persuasive case he makes for the competence of the separate states in handling their internal domestic affairs rests on impressive research and buttresses the thesis of Allan Nevins' *The American States During and After the Revolution,* published some two decades earlier. Nevin postulates that the states had already made long strides toward fiscal solvency under "the First Constitution" and in advance of Hamilton's assumption measure. Further documentation in support of this position has since been provided in E. James Ferguson's *The Power of the Purse.*

The American Revolution was far more than a movement for independence; as the author demonstrates it was a creative movement, animated by a spirit of optimism, by a view of America as a refuge for the oppressed of the Old World and as a home for the achievement of social equality. The years of the Confederation that Jensen discusses witnessed a people on the move. Immigration from Europe poured into the port cities while, as John Jay observed with some of that Easterners' alarm, "a rage for emigrating to the western country prevail[ed]." At the same time, eastern cities grew at an unprecedented pace, while the growth of families, disrupted by the war, had an enormous demographic impact. That combination of uncurbed expansion of the frontier and a rapidly rising population spelt changing values for American society.

The people Jensen portrays were industrious, enterprising, and innovative. They dug canals, built bridges, improved roads, and founded newspapers and magazines at a rate undreamt of before the war. Historians, poets, satirists, inventors, scientists, philanthropists, penal reformers all testify to what Jensen has called "the enthusiasm with which the citizens of the new nation worked at altering the pattern of society that it had inherited from colonial times."

The New Nation marks a turning point in the treatment of the states' rights particularists, popularly known as "anti-federalists," who in Jensen's book are treated as constructive statesmen. Jensen prefers to call them "federalists" as opposed to the "nationalists," or centralists, who pressed for a new constitution. Impressive research undertaken since the appearance of *The New Nation,* and indubitably sparked by its revisionist thesis, has served to sharpen the definition of the party conflict between the "agrarian-localist" blocs in the states and the "commercial-cosmopolitans," which Jackson Turner Main denominates the antifederalists and their opponents. For the profound ideological difference between the parties we are indebted to Gordon S. Wood's insightful work, *The Creation of the American Republic, 1776–1787*, which delineates the evolution of a distinctive republican polity, with its strong moral overtones. Most recently, Pauline Maier probes the roots of antifederalism among the radical politicians, whom she calls the "old Revolutionaries," a group of very effective revolutionary organizers that faded rapidly, to be displaced by the more durable Founding Fathers.

The New Nation makes no pretense of relating the history of the Confederation "in all its fullness," as Merrill Jensen points out in his preface. His evidence on the degree of the Post-Revolutionary

War recession and its turning point is not conclusive and the data at hand is conflicting. In fact, the only economic index that showed an upturn during the Confederation years was that for foreign trade, for in commerce the worst of the depression set in a bit earlier than in all other lines and showed a more complete recovery by 1788. In the meantime, commodity prices continued to drop. They were to decline thirty percent between 1785 and 1789; farm wages were shrinking and fell to a low of forty cents a day by 1787. In central and western Massachusetts, mortgage foreclosures and judgments for debts, as David Szatmary has recently reminded us, reached an all-time high, (a factor indubitably contributing to Shays' Rebellion) and in the Valley of Virginia executions on judgments more than doubled between 1784 and 1788. The pattern of recovery varied from region to region, it is true, but Jensen tends to lean too heavily, perhaps, on the more roseate view of conditions that such leading statesmen as Benjamin Franklin and Thomas Jefferson were voicing to foreigners to reassure friends and well-wishers abroad that this country was not headed for collapse.

Having treated the Articles of Confederation in depth in an earlier monograph, Jensen treads lightly in the constitutional arena. *The New Nation* ends before the movement for a federal convention gets seriously under way, but the book does raise some interesting questions about why the effort to amend the Articles was aborted. Nor does *The New Nation* pretend to deal in depth with evolving American foreign relations during the Confederation years. Nonetheless, the world of historical scholarship owes a lasting debt to the author for subsequently assuming the editorship of the initial volumes documenting the ratification of the Constitution in the states, a notable documentary conception and one being impressively carried forward.

To the nationalists, then, and to many scholars today it is the inability of the Confederation government to deal effectively with the former enemy, Great Britain, its ally France, and its formidable neighbor Spain, which justifies considering the Confederation era "critical" for the destiny of the American nation. With the Spaniards blocking American shipping in the lower Mississippi and conspiring with Western secessionists and the Indian tribes of the Southwest; with the British tenaciously holding on to their frontier posts and arming the Indians of the Northwest, while declining to liberalize their Navigation Laws which were so restrictive of

American trade; with most of the Barbary states still preying on American commerce and still snatching hostages, the dangerous weakness and incapacity of the central government was apparent to European observers as well as to most of the major Founding Fathers.

In short, *The New Nation,* while providing us with a healthy corrective of the traditional view of the incapacity of the states to deal with many domestic issues constructively in the Confederation years, does not pretend to cover all the ground or give us all the answers. With characteristic modesty the author concedes that "much work still needs to be done."

Since the publication of *The New Nation,* new documentation has enriched the ore that may be mined in this area. The past generation has seen letterpress editions completed or in well-advanced stages for such major political figures as Jefferson, Hamilton, Madison, Robert Morris, George Mason, John Jay, and John Marshall, among others. In-depth studies on individual states are facilitated by W. S. Jenkins's compilation of reels of state legislative journals and laws. The operations of the Confederation government are further illuminated by the available microfilm sets of the Papers of the Continental Congress and the new more thorough-going edition of the correspondence of members of the Congress now in progress. Historians are bringing a statistical methodology to tax and price lists, vital statistics, shipping records, and business and farm ledgers, which offers promise of resolving some of the moot economic and demographic issues of the period. In sum, for those who have pursued the leads of this seminal work, and for their successors, *The New Nation* will remain a landmark work, challenging historical stereotypes and offering fresh insight.

RICHARD B. MORRIS

Gouverneur Morris Professor of History Emeritus
Columbia University

Preface

The Confederation Period in American History

THIS BOOK is an account of the first years of the new nation that was born of the American Revolution. Like every other segment of time, the history of the United States from 1781 to 1789 was an integral part of the past in which it was rooted and of the future into which it was growing. It was a time when men believed they could shape the future of the new nation, and since it was also a time in which they disagreed as to what that future should be, they discussed great issues with a forthrightness and realism seldom equalled in political debates. The history of the Confederation is therefore one of great inherent importance for the study of human society if for no other reason than that during it men debated publicly and even violently the question of whether or not people could govern themselves.

Aside from its inherent importance, the history of the Confederation has been of enormous significance to one generation of Americans after another in the years since then. Repeatedly Americans have turned to that history in the course of innumerable social and political struggles. They have done so because it was during those years that the Articles of Confederation were replaced by the Constitution of 1787. In order to explain their Constitution, Americans have appealed to the history of the period out of which it came. In the course of such appeals, sometimes honestly for light and guidance and sometimes only for support of partisan arguments, Americans have usually found what they sought. As a result the "history" has been obscured in a haze of ideas, quotations, and assumptions torn bodily from the context of fact that alone gives them meaning. Again and again political opponents have asserted that the founding fathers stood for this or that, while their writings have stood idly and helplessly in volumes on shelves or have lain buried in yellowed manuscripts and newspapers.

Since the founding fathers themselves disagreed as to the nature of the history of the period and as to the best kind of government for the new nation, it is possible to find arguments to support almost any interpretation one chooses. It is not surprising therefore that conflicting interpretations have filled thousands of pages and that all this effort has never produced any final answers and probably never will, for men have ever interpreted the two constitutions of the United States in terms of their hopes, interests, and beliefs rather than in terms of knowable facts.

The conflict of interpretation has been continuous ever since the first debates over the Articles of Confederation in the summer of 1776. Men then differed as to the kind of government which should be created for the new nation. They continued to debate the issue during the 1780's. The members of the Convention of 1787 differed as to the need for and the amount of constitutional change. When the Constitution was submitted to the public in October 1787 the controversy rose to new heights. Men talked in public meetings and wrote private letters and public essays in an effort to explain, justify, or denounce what the Convention had done. They disagreed as to what had happened since the war. Some said there had been chaos; others said there had been peace and prosperity. Some said there would be chaos without the new Constitution; others that there would be chaos if it were adopted.

Once it was adopted Thomas Jefferson and Alexander Hamilton, with two opposed ideals of what the United States should be, laid down two classic and contradictory opinions of the nature of the Constitution. These two basic interpretations may be simply stated. Jefferson held that the central government was sharply limited by the letter of the Constitution; that in effect the states retained their sovereign powers except where they were specifically delegated. Hamilton argued in effect that the central government was a national government which could not be restrained by a strict interpretation of the Constitution or by ideas of state sovereignty. These rival interpretations did not originate with

Hamilton and Jefferson, for they had been the very core of constitutional debate ever since the Declaration of Independence, and even before it, for that matter.

Jefferson and his followers used the states rights idea to oppose the plans of the Federalists when they passed the Alien and Sedition Acts in 1798. But when Jefferson became president and purchased Louisiana, he justified his actions by constitutional theories that even Hamilton hardly dared use. Meanwhile Jefferson's opponents seized upon his earlier theories in a vain attempt to block the expansion of the United States. They did so again during the War of 1812 when the Federalists of New England became out-and-out exponents of "states rights" and threatened secession because they were opposed to the war.

In the decades before the Civil War, Daniel Webster and John C. Calhoun carried on the dispute, each having changed sides since his youthful years in politics. Webster, who had been a states rights spokesman during the War of 1812, became the high priest of nationalism, while Calhoun, a leading nationalist in 1812, became the high priest of the states rights idea which he elaborated to defend the slave-owning aristocracy of the South.

The Civil War itself was the bloody climax of a social conflict in which the ultimate nature of the Constitution was argued again and again in seeking support for and arguments against antagonistic programs. But even the Civil War did not finally settle the constitutional issue. The stresses and strains that came with the rise of industrial and finance capitalism produced demands for social and regulatory legislation. The passage of such legislation by the states involved the interpretation of the nature of the Constitution, for business interests regulated by state governments denied their authority and appealed to the national courts. Those courts soon denied the power of regulation to state legislatures. Then, when regulatory laws were passed by the national government, the regulated interests evolved a "states rights" theory that limited the power of the central government, and the national courts once more agreed.

Throughout American history the courts have drawn boundary lines between state and national authority. The pose of judicial impartiality and finality assumed by the courts cannot hide the fact that they have shifted those boundary lines with the shifting winds of politics, and always with sufficient precedents, if not with adequate grace. As a result they had created by 1900 a legal and constitutional no man's land in which all sorts of activity could be carried on without effective regulation by either state or national governments.

The crash of American economy in 1929 once more posed in imperative terms the problem of the nature of the Constitution. How should it, how could it deal with the potentiality of chaos inherent in unemployment, starvation, and bankruptcy, and ultimately, the loss of faith in the utility of the economic and political foundation of the society itself.

As the national government began to act where, plainly, state and local governments had failed to or were unable to act, the question of constitutionality was raised. For a time the courts once more listened to and heeded states rights constitutional theories which were expounded by opponents of the New Deal. New Deal lawyers, in turn, adopted as weapons John Marshall's nationalistic interpretations of the Constitution for ends which Marshall himself would have fought to the death. President Roosevelt, in his fight on the Supreme Court, declared that the Constitution was not a lawyer's document; yet some of the ablest lawyers who ever lived in America wrote it. New Deal publicists wrote tracts in the guise of history to prove that there had been a "national sovereignty" in the United States from the beginning of the Revolution. Therefore, they argued, the courts could not stop the New Deal from doing what needed doing by following a strict interpretation of the Constitution. Both the New Dealers and the Republicans insisted that they were the sole heirs of the legacy of Thomas Jefferson, while Alexander Hamilton went into an eclipse from which he has not yet emerged.

The most recent appeal to the history of the Confederation Period has come from those who support some form of world government. Adequate arguments for such a government can be found in twentieth-century experience, but, like most men, its backers turn to history for analogies and lessons.

When the League of Nations was set up at the end of the First World War men turned to American history after the American Revolution as a parallel experience. At that time books were written to show the "chaos" of the Confederation Period and the happy solution that came with the Constitution of 1787. Among them was a book by a great authority on international law with the title *James Madison's Notes of Debates in the Federal Convention of 1787 and their Relation to a More Perfect Society of Nations.* The book was widely distributed by the Carnegie Endowment for International Peace. This and other books like it had little relation to the realities of world politics in the 1920's and 1930's, but despite this supporters of the United Nations and of various plans of world government have again turned to the history of the American states after the American Revolution.

The most notable appeal has been that of Clarence Streit. In his book *Union Now* he analyzes the history of our past as he sees it. He calls the Articles of Confederation a "league of friendship." He says, paraphrasing John Fiske, that by 1786 there was universal depression, trade had wellnigh stopped, and political quackery with cheap and dirty remedies had full control of the field. Trade disputes promised to end in war between states. Territorial disputes led to bloodshed. War with Spain threatened. The "league" could not coerce its members. Secession was threatened by some states. Congress had no money and could borrow none. Courts were broken up by armed mobs. When Shays's Rebellion came, state sovereignty was so strong that Massachusetts would not allow "league" troops to enter the state, even to guard the "league's" own arsenal. Streit goes on to say that the idea of turning a league into a union was not even seriously proposed until the Convention opened in May 1787. And then, he says, within two years the freedom-loving American democracies decided to try out this invention for themselves. Streit goes on to argue that it would be just as easy to secure union of the democracies now as it was for the American democracies to achieve a union then. Some things made it difficult then; some make it so now. Some made it easy then; some make it easy now.

Many men have followed in Streit's footsteps. His book was first published in 1939. In 1940 Federal Union Incorporated published a pamphlet called *It Must be done Again; the Case for World Federal Union . . . illustrated by excerpts from John Fiske's Critical Period, etc.*

In the February issue of 1945, the *Reader's Digest* published an article called "Our Post War Problems of 1787" which was still another summary of John Fiske's *The Critical Period of American History*. In May 1945, the *Saturday Review of Literature* had an editorial called "Where do we go From Here?" They urged John

Fiske's *Critical Period* as timely reading for the constitutional convention of the United Nations then meeting in San Francisco. The *Review* argued that American experience in the eighteenth century was analogous, despite those who pointed to the disparities. It declared that the crucial lesson offered by American experience was that unified government is not created by similarities, but by differences. But the *Review* was willing, for the sake of argument, to agree that even if the American colonies (it called them that instead of states) offer no valid parallel, even then the basic question is how to control differences. The answer, said the *Review*, is that the historical fact remains that "only government has been able to control war."

One more example will suffice, not only to show how the proponents of world government continue to use what they call "history," but to show how they too swing with the tide. On 12 March 1948 Federal Union took a full page in the *New York Times* to advertise this proposition in a headline: "By Hamilton's 'Stroke of Genius' Plan . . . we can stop Stalin Now . . . and avert Freedom's suicide." Hamilton's plan was "boiled down" to the following statement: "Unite democracies by federal union and have the Union not only replace their currencies with its currency but assume each democracy's public debt." The advertisement goes on to give the traditional story of how Hamilton saved public credit, saved money, cut government expenses, and so on. Thus a litter of ideas, fathered by hope and ignorance, are set before the public as historical fact.

Even if it can be granted that most appeals to the history of the Confederation have been sincere, let it also be said that they have seldom been infused with any knowledge of the period or its problems. The result has been the drawing of lessons the past does not have to teach. This is a luxury too expensive in an age when men have discovered how to unhinge the very force that holds matter itself together but have advanced very little beyond cave men in their notions of how to live peacefully with one another.

Yet it is little wonder that such false lessons have been drawn in the twentieth century because most of them have come from John Fiske's *The Critical Period of American History*, a book of vast influence but of no value as either history or example. Fiske, a philosopher and popular lecturer, wrote the book "without fear and without research," to use the words of Charles A. Beard. As long ago as 1905, Andrew C. McLaughlin, an impeccably conservative historian of the Constitution who wrote a far better book on the same period, said that Fiske's book was "altogether without scientific standing, because it is little more than a remarkably skilful adaptation of a very few secondary authorities showing almost no evidence of first hand acquaintance with the sources."

The story told by Fiske and repeated by publicists and scholars who have not worked in the field—and some who have, for that matter—is based on the assumption that this was *the* "critical period" of American history during which unselfish patriots rescued the new nation from impending anarchy, if not from chaos itself. The picture is one of stagnation, ineptitude, bankruptcy, corruption, and disintegration. Such a picture is at worst false and at best grossly distorted. It is therefore important to attempt a history which makes an effort to examine the sources, which is concerned with the nature of political and economic problems rather than with proving that one side or another in the innumerable political battles of the period was "right" or "wrong." Nothing is to be gained by following a "chaos and patriots to the rescue" interpretation. We have too long ignored the fact that thoroughly patriotic Americans during the 1780's did not believe there was chaos and emphatically denied that their supposed rescuers were patriotic. The point is that there were patriots on both sides of the issue, but that they differed as to desirable goals for the new nation. At the same time, of course, there were men as narrow and selfish on both sides as their political enemies said they were.

If one approaches the history of the Confederation in this way, if one tries to see it as men who lived in it saw it and to write of it in their terms, one may achieve some semblance of reality. It is not the task of the historian to defend or attack the various groups of men whose conflicts were the essence of the period, but to set forth what they believed and what they tried to achieve. This can be illustrated no better than in the definition of terms. Throughout this book the words "federalist" and "nationalist" are used to describe two opposed bodies of opinion as to the best kind of central government for the United States. In so doing I have followed the members of the Convention of 1787. Those men believed that the Articles of Confederation provided for a "federal" government and the majority of them wanted to replace it with a "national" government. The fact that the men who wanted a national government called themselves Federalists after their work was submitted to the public is relevant to the history of politics after 1787, not to the discussion of the nature of the central government prior to and during the Convention of 1787.

Whatever the confusion since then, there was none at the time. Gouverneur Morris stated the issue concisely in the Convention when he "explained the distinction between a federal and a national, supreme government; the former being a mere compact resting on the good faith of the parties; the latter having a complete and compulsive operation." This explanation was in answer to those members of the Convention who wanted to know what Edmund Randolph meant in his opening speech when he spoke of the "defects of the federal system, the necessity of transforming it into a national efficient government. . . ."

The issue was not, as has been argued from time to time, whether there was a "nation" before the adoption of the Constitution of 1787. That was not the question at all during the 1780's. There was a new nation, as the men of the time agreed: they disagreed as to whether the new nation should have a federal or a national government. They did so from the outset of the Revolution and men have continued to do so ever since. The Constitution of 1787 was, as Madison said, both national and federal. And while this fact has led to innumerable conflicts of interpretation, it has also been a source of strength; for as one political group after another has gotten control of the central government it has been able to shape the Constitution to its needs and desires. Thus with the single exception of the Civil War, peaceful change has always been possible, and as long as Americans are willing to accept the decisions of ballot boxes, legislatures, and courts, the Constitution will continue to change with changing needs and pressures.

The history of the writing and ratification of the Constitution of 1787 is not included in this book. If both it and the history of the Confederation were to be in one volume, one story or the other would have to be slighted and both are too important for such treatment. Yet despite the length of the present book, it would be immodest and inaccurate to say that the history of the Confederation had been told in all its fullness. Much work still needs to be done. The history of almost every state needs re-study. The history of the evolution of the central government during the 1780's is virtually an untold story. In such matters, as in others, the following pages point to areas where further research will yield much that is significant for the understanding of the foundations of the new nation.

My debt of gratitude to those who have helped me in the preparation of this book is very great indeed, although my acknowledgment here is necessarily inadequate. I am indebted to the Social Science Research Council, the John Simon Guggenheim Memorial Foundation, and the Research Committee of the Graduate School of the University of Wisconsin for financial help. The keepers of manuscripts at the New York Public Library, the New York Historical Society, the Pennsylvania Historical Society, the Philadelphia Free Library, the Library of Congress, the National Archives, the Yale University Library, the Harvard University Library, and the Massachusetts Historical Society have been both helpful and patient. The librarians of the State Historical Society of Wisconsin have been unfailingly tolerant of the incessant checking of references and quotations. During the past four years three assistants at the University of Wisconsin, Whitney Bates, Eric Polisar, and Walter Congdon have given intelligent help with endless details. James Ferguson of the University of Maryland has read portions of the manuscript and saved me from many a slip, as has Dr. Fulmer Mood of the University of California. Mrs. Elsie B. Crabb has typed and re-typed page after page with unfailing good temper. Lastly, my wife has watched over all with a cool eye, scholarly judgment, and tactful firmness.

MERRILL JENSEN

The University of Wisconsin

Contents

The New Nation

PART ONE

The Winning of Independence

THE WINNING of independence was slow and torturing labor for those Americans who believed in it. At times it seemed to civilians and soldiers alike that they could go on no longer. Whatever ideals they had seemed drowned in the indifference of fellow Americans, defeat at the hands of the enemy, and corruption, speculation, and money grabbing by those who seized on war's opportunities to enrich themselves without regard for the public good. Yet enough civilians and enough soldiers kept slogging along bitter month after bitter month, and endless year after endless year to keep the movement alive. From time to time their hopes were raised by events like Burgoyne's surrender, the French Alliance, or the battle of Cowpens. At other times they drooped in utter despair. The year 1780 was blackness itself. Soldiers mutinied, officers struck for higher pay, inflated prices destroyed the power to purchase supplies with paper money, and steadily the British crunched northward from the South across the Carolinas and into Virginia.

But the next year was the turning point of the war. In March of 1781 the Articles of Confederation were ratified, after five years of wrangling shot through with high purpose and low motives. The administration of public affairs was reorganized and new drive was given by new men coming into power. Then, in October, a French and American army penned up Lord Cornwallis at Yorktown in Virginia. On 19 October 1781 Cornwallis surrendered with all his men. News of the surrender gave Americans new courage and it brought about the fall of Lord North's cabinet in England. The Rockingham-Shelburne Whigs, friendly to peace and independence, took office, and negotiations with the waiting Americans in France got under way.

Thus ended six years of fighting. The Americans had failed many times. They had lost most of the battles. They were often helpless, but they won the war. The British were often as helpless as the Americans, especially when they went inland, away from their sea-borne supplies. The corruption and inefficiency of their supply system make American problems seem small by contrast. After Yorktown, British military men gave up. The southern posts were abandoned in 1782. Clinton retained only New York. There he remained while the peace negotiators carried on their work which ended in the signing of preliminary articles of peace in the fall of 1782.

As the war ground to an end American political leaders tried to solve what seemed to be insoluble problems. The army was discontented, for promises had not been kept and it was not likely that they would be, once peace was a fact. Some means of paying the national debt needed to be worked out but politicians could not agree on how to do it. Despite the adoption of the Articles of Confederation, American political leaders remained divided as to the future shape and power of the central government. One group was made up largely of the revolutionary leaders who had willingly faced the fact of war to achieve independence. The Articles of Confederation embodied their conviction that the greatest political gain of the Revolution was the independence of the several states. These men were the "federalists" of the Confederation period. Opposed to them was a group of men who, on the whole, had been reluctant revolutionists. Most of them believed that the new nation should have a central government with power to coerce the state governments and their citizens. This group got control of Congress in 1781 and held it until the end of the war. These men were the "nationalists" of the Confederation period. They were convinced that their best hope of achieving the government they wanted was the continuance of the war. Beyond this they believed, as did the "federalists," that the means used to pay the national debt would in large measure determine the extent of the power of the central government.

All these issues came to a head in the spring of 1783. Discontented army officers sent a delegation to Congress; public creditors clamored within and without its doors. But Congress lacked the means to satisfy either group. There were plots and rumors of plots which culminated in a scheme to unite the army and the public creditors to achieve by force that power which persuasion had not gained. At this dramatic moment the news of the preliminary articles of peace arrived in America, and within a few short months the nationalist leaders returned to their states and the federalist leaders were once more in control of the central government.

I

War and Peace

The Making of Peace

THE WAR for independence began when the British government tried to suppress local rebellions in some of Britain's American colonies; it ended as a world war in which France, Spain, and Holland were fighting Britain while the rest of the world looked on happily. France wanted to regain her leadership in Europe, even if it meant bankruptcy. She welcomed any trouble England might have with her colonies. Therefore, when they revolted she gave secret aid, and after it appeared they might actually succeed, she declared war officially. She agreed to stay in the war until Britain recognized the independence of the United States. This alliance was a marriage of convenience for France, and of necessity for America, hence neither party looked upon the union as one of trust and love. Spain declared war in 1779, but with great reluctance, for the idea of colonial independence was a horrible one which she did not care to have spread among her own vast and discontented dominions in the new world. She refused to join the Franco-American Alliance or to recognize American independence. Instead, she busied herself with taking West Florida and in besieging Gibraltar, which France promised Spain should have before France would quit the war. The Dutch came in even more unwillingly. They grew fat on the profits of war trade as the years went by. They sent naval stores to France. They helped to get English goods to America and American goods to England. Their West India island of St. Eustatius was one of the busiest way stations between Europe and the United States.

Merchants from everywhere, including England, came there to trade. The English demanded that such trade be ended and pointed to the terms of the treaty between the two countries. The Dutch listened and argued but kept on trading, so England at last declared war in 1780. Thus the Dutch, quite unwillingly, found themselves fighting for American independence, although their help was primarily financial and came mostly after the war was over.

It was with three such strangely assorted, differently motivated, and not too willing partners that the United States fought toward peace and independence. It was this, plus the fact that various neutral nations dabbled in peacemaking for reasons entirely unconcerned with American independence, that made the American position very dangerous. In the early part of the war Britain had offered peace of a kind. The Howe brothers in 1776 and Lord North in 1778 offered everything except the crucial thing—independence. Thereafter one outside power after another stepped in. In 1779 Spain offered to mediate but Britain refused to accept, although if she had she would have been in a far better position than at the final peace. Next, Austria and Russia proposed to act as mediators. If they had succeeded, the war might have ended with Britain in control of large parts of the coastline of the United States and the Americans helpless to do anything about it. And this might have happened had it not been for the victory at Yorktown and the change of British government which followed, a change that made peace negotiations possible and put independence within reach.

While the giants tossed about the fate of the tiny American states, almost unaware of their existence except as an irritant to Britain, members of Congress were developing their own ideas of what they wanted of the world of diplomacy. In 1779, as a result of the Spanish offer of mediation, John Adams was sent to Europe to negotiate peace. But Spain got into the war, so there was nothing official for him to do. Nevertheless, this farmer's son from Massachusetts, who had taught himself medieval Latin so he could study law properly, made no bones about letting Europeans know exactly what his kind of American wanted of the war. Perhaps he, as much as any other American, helped free the United States from the dilemma of the French Alliance. They were damned without it and damned with it. Without French help they could not win, yet France was helping the United States for French, not American, purposes. Vergennes would have been willing to end the war with the British in possession of parts of the United States if the mediation of Austria and Russia had gone through, and John Adams knew it. He countered such scheming with the knotty independence he had shown ever since the beginning of the war. In 1776 he had insisted that Americans could fight the war without foreign alliances. So when Spanish mediation failed, he proposed that the British be asked to make peace anyway, and thus put on them the responsibility for continuing the war if they refused. As far as the French Alliance was concerned, he told Vergennes that it was as important to France as to the United States. Moreover, he would refuse to enter into any peace conference unless all comers recognized American independence first. It is not strange that Vergennes soon developed a distaste for John Adams and came to the conclusion that he was not a proper diplomat, especially when compared to the agreeable Franklin. Vergennes wanted a stooge, not an independent and equal negotiator. Therefore he urged Congress to recall Adams and to send someone more likely in his place.

When France entered the war in 1778 she wanted her ally, Spain, to enter as well. But Spain was dubious about the creation of a new nation so near her own vast domains in the new world. Therefore Spain made demands. She owned everything west of the Mississippi; she now asked for everything east of it up to the Alleghenies, and the surrender of any claim to a "right" to navigate the Mississippi as the price of entering into a treaty with the Americans. It was up to France to get the Americans to agree. Conrad-Alexandre Gérard arrived in Philadelphia in July 1778 as the first envoy of France to the United States. He had no specific instructions regarding Spanish demands but he knew that France wanted Spain in the war and that it was up to him to look out for Spain's interests. When he arrived he found a situation ready-made for intrigue: the thirteen states were at loggerheads over the control of the very trans-Allegheny region that Spain demanded.

The conflict arose from the fact that eight of the states had claims to the trans-Allegheny west which were based on their colonial charters. The other five states—Pennsylvania, Maryland, New Jersey, Delaware, and Rhode Island—had no such claims, but instead had definite boundaries. During the twenty-five years before the Revolution, speculators in the "landless" colonies had created land companies. These companies had tried to establish claims within the bounds of the landed colonies by means of treaties with the Indians and appeals for grants from the British government. Their strongest opponent was Virginia, the largest and most powerful claimant to the region west of the Alleghenies.

The struggle continued without a break after the start of the Revolution. It affected the fighting of the war. It was a major issue in creating the Articles of Confederation and delayed their ratification for years. It warped the course of diplomacy. It shaped a good deal of the political and constitutional history of the Confederation. The landless states demanded that the landed states give up their charter rights to the nation except for the areas claimed by the land companies controlled by their citizens. In time the landed states agreed to cede the West to the United States, but Virginia insisted that the claims of the land companies be declared void before her cession became final. The speculators, organized as the Indiana and Illinois-Wabash companies, fought this requirement in Congress and out of it with all the means in their power.[1]

When Gérard arrived, he soon learned of the jealousies that existed and took sides. He became a share-holder in the Illinois-Wabash Company and thus joined the landless states in their fight against Virginia, a fight which he used to further the diplomacy of France and Spain. He urged Congress to assure Spain that the United States had no desire for an empire in the West. He asked Congress to pass a resolution declaring any state which tried to extend its boundaries beyond specified limits was an enemy of the Confederation. This met with the favor of several members of Congress, particularly those from the landless middle states. Those who opposed the claims of Virginia, and the representatives of the mercantile interests of Philadelphia and New York, swung very early to the support of Gérard's program. Some of the leaders of this group were John Jay, Robert Morris, Gouverneur Morris, and Daniel of St. Thomas Jenifer. Their attitude was a complex of inconsistent elements. In it there was much of the timidity which such men had shown in 1776 when they op-

[1] Merrill Jensen: "The Cession of the Old Northwest," *Mississippi Valley Historical Review*, XXIII (1936), 27–48.

posed a declaration of independence on the ground, among others, that it was first necessary to secure foreign aid. They continued to be frightened of the possible consequences of failure, and hence spared no effort to bring Spain into the war. At the same time they wanted to control the trade of the West, and this would be denied them, they felt, if the Mississippi were open to western trade. They believed that only by closing the river could western commerce be forced eastward across the mountains. Still other easterners were afraid that the West would develop rapidly, draw off the laboring population of the East, and thus raise the price of labor.

The political and economic implications of agrarian expansion westward were alarming to certain mercantile interests in the East who feared the loss of their political and economic control of an expanding America. True, the opposition to western expansion was inconsistent with the larger interests of that class and section, but economic "vision" is as often determined by remembrance of the past as by vision of the future. The merchants and their associates faced across the Atlantic with their backs to the West. Most of them could not realize that the future of the United States for a century to come had its brightest hope in the expansion of its people westward.[2] The rise of agrarianism made the years of the American Revolution unpleasant for more than one merchant. The plaint of Samuel and Robert Purviance is characteristic. They wrote to Robert Morris (who was engaged in privateering) that they were trying to formulate a plan to check privateers, for the matter had been utterly neglected by the various assemblies, especially that of Virginia. This neglect, they said, must be attributed to "the small representation of the mercantile interest in the respective assemblies" and "the unaccountable the universally prevailing prejudice of the planters & farmers against the trading interest." Matters were no better in Pennsylvania "where the interests of trade have ever been the principal care of government, we are sensible how little can be expected from them in the present state of things." [3]

Gouverneur Morris told Gérard that he and some of his col-

[2] Paul C. Phillips: "American Opinions Regarding the West, 1778–1783," Mississippi Valley Historical Association *Proceedings*, VII (1913–4), 286–305; also his *The West in the Diplomacy of the American Revolution* (University of Illinois Studies in the Social Sciences, XI, nos. 2 and 3, Urbana, 1913).

[3] Robert Morris Papers, Library of Congress.

leagues were impressed with the necessity of preventing any additions to the states already in the union. He believed that if Spain were given control of the Mississippi, the immense population which would form along the river could be held in subjection by the eastern states. But if the population of the West were in control of the Mississippi and the St. Lawrence, then it would dominate the eastern states.

Opposed to such politics were the states of Virginia and Massachusetts whose leadership was summed up in the term the "Lee-Adams junto." They opposed giving the West to Congress on terms whereby some of the best of it would go to land speculators from the middle states. They opposed the surrender of that same West to Spain and of the "right" to navigate the Mississippi. In 1779, despite the objections of the French minister and his congressional followers, they and their followers wrote instructions outlining the terms of a proposed treaty and the boundaries of the United States. Those, they said, should run westward from the St. John River in the northeast (more or less along the present northern boundary of New England and New York) to the St. Lawrence at the 45th parallel. Thence it was to run in a straight line to the southern end of Lake Nipissing and from there to the as yet unknown source of the Mississippi River. The Mississippi was to be the western boundary as far south as the 31st parallel. The southern boundary (between the United States and the Floridas) was to follow the 31st parallel eastward to the St. Mary's River and down that river to the Atlantic. In this and other matters, the commissioner to be appointed was to be guided by the French Alliance and by French advice, but also by his "knowledge of our interests, and by your own discretion, in which we repose the fullest confidence." [4] John Adams was elected commissioner to carry out these instructions while John Jay, his rival, was sent to Spain.

The men who wrote the instructions in 1779, the Lee-Adams junto, were out of power by 1781 and their old political enemies were in control. La Luzerne, the new French minister, claimed that he managed the election of Robert R. Livingston of New York as secretary of foreign affairs. He boasted that his loans of money to General John Sullivan of New Hampshire brought about

[4] *Journals of the Continental Congress, 1774–1789* (Library of Congress Edition, 34 vols., Washington, 1904–37), XIV, 960.

the rewriting of the instructions for peacemaking in accordance with the wishes of Vergennes. In June 1781, John Adams was surrounded by four other men: Franklin, John Jay, Henry Laurens, and Thomas Jefferson. Their new instructions required them to demand only independence. In all other matters they were to be subject to the guidance and control of the French. They could even yield on the boundaries demanded in the instructions of 1779.[5]

Thus it was that in the dark days before Yorktown the fate of the United States was handed over to France by one group in Congress: the merchants of the middle states and their political allies. Had it not been for John Jay, whose two and one half years in Spain brought a change in heart, and for John Adams, who had never had any illusions about European altruism, the war might have ended very differently for the United States.

Fortunately men and events in Europe, rather than congressional instructions, determined the writing of the peace. Yorktown in October 1781 gave Lord North's opposition the weapon it needed to overthrow him. The news of the disaster reached London late in November. By the end of February 1782 a resolution was carried through the House of Commons declaring that any minister in favor of carrying on the war was an enemy of his country. In the middle of March a vote of confidence was lost and on the twentieth Lord North resigned. The Rockingham ministry which came in was tied together only by its dislike of the North ministry. Charles James Fox, as secretary of state in charge of foreign affairs, wanted the recognition of American independence to come before peace negotiations. If this were done, he would control peacemaking. Lord Shelburne, his rival, was secretary of state in charge of the colonies. As long as the Americans were "colonists," however technical the status, dealings with them would be under the control of his office. Rockingham settled the dispute by dying. Shelburne became prime minister and at once took charge of the negotiations already under way.

The first approach was made to Franklin in Paris. For a time he was the only American commissioner there. John Jay had not yet arrived from Madrid. John Adams was completing a loan

[5] 6–15 June, ibid., XX, 602–55; Edmund C. Burnett, ed.: *Letters of Members of the Continental Congress* (8 vols., Washington, 1921–36), VI, 112–22, for the same dates, has much material. See particularly the speech of John Witherspoon on the appointment of new plenipotentiaries, 115–8.

from the Dutch and did not arrive until October. Henry Laurens got out of the Tower of London on parole but did not enter into the negotiations until the very last for reasons at best uncertain. Thomas Jefferson never left America. The British sent Richard Oswald to negotiate. Oswald, now grown old and philosophic, had made a fortune as an army contractor and slave trader, in which latter business Henry Laurens had once been his agent and partner.

In their first and strictly unofficial talks, Franklin and Vergennes made it plain to Oswald that there could not be a separate peace without France. Once this was understood, Vergennes turned over the discussion of British and American details to the two parties immediately concerned, an act he later had cause to regret. Franklin let Oswald know what he felt were the terms on which they could negotiate. He divided them into "necessary" and "desirable." First on the list of necessary terms was the recognition of American independence and the removal of British troops. The borders of Canada were to be moved back at least as far, if not farther, than at the time of the Quebec Act. The "right" of fishing on the Newfoundland banks was to be acknowledged. As "desirable" terms Franklin suggested a fat money indemnity for damage done by the British in America, an acknowledgment by act of Parliament that the British had been wrong in fighting the Americans, provision for equality of treatment of the ships of both parties in each other's ports, and the surrender of all of Canada to the United States. In making these suggestions, Franklin covered his tracks so well that it could not be proved that the suggestions came from him, nor did he tell Vergennes anything about them.

With such suggestions in hand, Oswald then got a formal commission to treat with the Americans. But the commission did not recognize the United States nor the American commissioners as plenipotentiaries. It spoke of the "colonies" and authorized Oswald to treat with any of them or any persons appointed or to be appointed by them. Vergennes and Franklin agreed that such a commission would be adequate, but John Jay would have none of it. He had come to Paris with a fine suspicion of the French and the Spanish, although earlier while in Congress, he had played their game in opposition to the Lee-Adams junto. He had then been as willing to give the trans-Allegheny region to Spain as he was in 1786 to sell out that region in exchange for privileges for east coast merchants. But it is said his suspicions were "fired" when the French proposed to restrict the United States to the Alleghenies in order to appease Spain, once again losing hope of regaining Gibraltar.[6] Certainly his suspicions of French and Spanish motives were thoroughly justified. But perhaps it is legitimate to suspect that Jay, whose sense of his own importance was as great as that of John Adams, was moved as much by anger at cool treatment by the Spanish as by real concern for the territorial extent of the United States. Whatever his motives, he insisted that there must be recognition of independence before the writing of a treaty. He realized that if there were no such recognition, and the negotiations fell through, Britain would have given and the Americans would have gotten exactly nothing. As it was, the British cabinet was willing to make the grant of independence if the Americans insisted. But the Americans did not insist, for Jay backtracked and agreed that it would be enough if Oswald were empowered to treat with them as plenipotentiaries of the United States. Franklin agreed to it readily enough, and naturally the British went no further than they had to.

Willingness to engage in double-dealing was characteristic of all parties. Vergennes allowed the British to find out that he had no desire to support the Americans in everything they wanted, such as the "right" to fish in British waters. John Jay sent an emissary to Shelburne to make it plain that he preferred American to French interpretations of the obligations of the Franco-American Alliance of 1778. The English were pleased at such evidence of division but were seemingly unable to make real use of it.

Because of Franklin's illness, Oswald and Jay carried on the negotiations that resulted in blocking out the treaty in its first rough form. By October 1782 they had a preliminary draft ready, although they agreed that hostilities should not end until preliminary articles had been agreed to between France and Britain. Most of the detail went back to the previous summer when Franklin and his friend Oswald had talked unofficially. The draft treaty written by Jay and Oswald contained Franklin's "necessary" articles, and in addition, an article guaranteeing freedom of navigation and commerce on the Mississippi, and on all the other waters

[6] Samuel F. Bemis: *The Diplomacy of the American Revolution* (New York, 1935), 220. This is the most thorough account to date of the peace negotiations.

of the world belonging to either party, to the citizens of both countries. British merchants were to have the same rights in the United States ports that Americans had, and American merchants were to have the same rights and privileges in British ports that British merchants had.

When this draft was submitted to the British cabinet it at once demanded changes. Compensation should be made for the confiscated property of the Loyalists. Pre-war debts to British citizens should be paid in cash. The Americans should be kept out of the fisheries of British North America. The Canadian boundary should be moved southward. The result of these demands was more wrangling. John Adams arrived and at once put up a tough fight for the "right" to fish in British waters. His instructions back in 1779 had ordered him to get a cession of Canada and Nova Scotia and "more particularly" to get a guarantee of the "common right" of Americans in the fisheries.[7] As a good New Englander he knew where the fish were and how important they were to New England economy. Furthermore he was backed up by his state. In December 1781, the Boston town meeting, after long debate, voted to instruct the Massachusetts delegates in Congress not to conclude any peace unless the "eastern states" got a free right in the fisheries.[8]

John Adams drew up a proposed article which granted the "right" of Americans to fish in the waters they had always fished in and the "liberty" to dry those fish on the unsettled shores of Nova Scotia, Labrador, and the Magdalen Islands. The British insisted on the word "liberty" to fish. They said their instructions did not allow them to grant the "right" to fish. John Adams told them to send a messenger to London to get their instructions changed. Here the British commissioners fell down. They were unwilling to ask for new instructions for fear, as one of them said, that to lay all before Parliament would be "going to sea again."

The Americans at once grabbed fair opportunity. Franklin suggested that if a messenger were sent to ask about the fisheries question, he should also ask about another disputed point. Since the British were demanding compensation for the Loyalists, what about compensation for Americans who had suffered at British

[7] *Journals*, XIV, 956–60.

[8] John R. Livingston to Robert R. Livingston, Boston, 13 Dec. 1781, Robert R. Livingston Papers (Bancroft Transcripts), New York Public Library.

and Loyalist hands? What about the goods that had been carried off from Boston, Philadelphia, and the Carolinas? What about the towns that had been burned? Why even his own library had been stolen by the British. John Adams jumped in with the tale of Gage's "atrocities." Henry Laurens told how the British had plundered Carolina of its Negroes and silver plate. John Jay added a few other details.

This was too much for the British. They retired from the room and when they returned they agreed to give in on the fisheries issue. They later explained to the British government that they feared any further delay would have put the Americans in such bad humor as to make them suggest new and even more embarrassing demands than those for a "right" in the fisheries. So far as the Loyalists were concerned, the British commissioners likewise agreed that Congress should "recommend" to the states some form of compensation for the confiscated property of those who had remained loyal to Great Britain.

On the issue of the debts owing British creditors from before the American Revolution, quite a different attitude was shown by the American commissioners. British creditors were insistent, and British politicians correspondingly urgent. Even before Shelburne took office sixty-six Glasgow merchants and companies sent him a petition in which they asked that in any peace negotiations, their property and money in the United States be made secure. They said their trade before the war was mainly with Virginia and Maryland and that £1,300,000 sterling was still owing to them from their citizens. Other merchants asked that Shelburne make it his "peculiar care" to guarantee them their legal demands as creditors.[9]

It was easy enough for men like Jay, Adams, and Franklin to agree that the pre-war debt should be paid. The great bulk of this debt was owed by the planters of the southern states. The American commissioners were from the commercial towns of the North, and even Henry Laurens from Charleston was as much merchant as planter in outlook. As representatives of the commercial towns these men knew that it was to the advantage of most merchants to have regular payment on mercantile debts.

[9] Memorial of Glasgow Merchants to the Earl of Shelburne, 30 May 1782; Memorial from "Merchants in behalf of themselves and others interested in North American trade previous to the year 1776," Shelburne Papers, vol. 87, Clements Library.

They knew that the trans-Atlantic trade was dependent on the smooth flow of debit and credit across the Atlantic. If the planter interest had been represented at the negotiations, had Thomas Jefferson arrived, the story might have been different. It was agreed in the treaty that creditors on both sides of the Atlantic should meet with no lawful impediment to the recovery of debts. The provision, however, did not settle the issue which long remained a storm center in American politics.

The question of boundaries was settled by men who drew lines here and there on John Mitchell's map of North America without knowing very much about the geography they thus disposed of so lightly. The boundaries demanded in John Adams's instructions in 1779 were dropped from the instructions of 1781, but Franklin and Adams in their different ways wanted to push out the boundaries as far as possible. Even John Jay had changed and demanded far reaches for America. Thus the American commissioners agreed that French and Spanish notions of limitation should be ignored. So the boundaries agreed on in the preliminary articles were pretty much those of John Adams's instructions of 1779. The inclusion of an agreement for the freedom of navigation and commerce on the Mississippi River in the first draft committed both the United States and Great Britain to that river as the western boundary, although in the end only the idea of free navigation was retained. The cession of Canada, which Franklin was so anxious to get, was simply dropped by John Jay, who wanted to make sure of British support for the Mississippi as a western boundary. It was agreed that the boundary on the north should be either the 45th parallel or approximately the present St. Lawrence River-Great Lakes boundary from the point where the 45th parallel strikes the St. Lawrence. The 31st parallel was to be the southern boundary, but a secret article provided that if the British held West Florida after the war, the boundary should be 32°28′ to the Yazoo River rather than the 31st parallel.

The idea of complete commercial reciprocity between the two nations, which Franklin had been anxious for, and which was included in Jay's first draft early in October, disappeared from the final draft. Commercial relations were left to future negotiations, and the problem of commerce, like that of the Loyalists and the debts, was to plague American politicians and Anglo-American relations for years to come.

These preliminary articles, with some minor changes, were agreed to by the negotiators on 3 November 1782. They were then taken to England where the Shelburne cabinet authorized Oswald to sign them finally if, after trying, he could not get a few more concessions for English creditors and the Loyalists. On 30 November the articles were signed by the British and American delegations, although they did not go into effect until France signed preliminary articles of her own with Great Britain. This happened 20 January 1783. An armistice was at once declared. The final treaties of peace were signed in September 1783, the one between the United States and Great Britain remaining the same as the preliminary articles of 30 November 1782 despite many discussions of possible changes.

The American commissioners, in getting their treaty, had disregarded their instructions from Congress. Those instructions had left them in the power of the French. They waited until the preliminary articles were signed before informing Vergennes. Even then he was slow to wrath, slower in fact than some members of Congress who failed to appreciate the great and lasting triumph of Adams, Franklin, and Jay: "the greatest victory in the annals of American diplomacy. . . ." [10] The language of the scholar is clear; that of the participant is life itself. John Adams, with the treaty at last complete, wrote in triumph to his friend: "Thanks be to God, my dear Gerry, that our Tom Cod are safe, in spite of the malice of enemies, the finesse of Allies, and the mistakes of Congress." [11]

The First Constitution of the United States

While armies struggled on the fields of battle, conflicts of as great seriousness and of at least equal bitterness took place on the fields of politics. No issue was more fought over than that of the nature of the central government to be created by the thirteen states. The Articles of Confederation were written in 1776 and

[10] Bemis: *Diplomacy*, 256.

[11] John Adams to Elbridge Gerry, Paris, 14 Dec. 1782, William Smith Mason Collection, Yale University Library.

1777, but they were not adopted until March 1781, as the war was coming to an end. This first constitution of the United States lasted only eight years, but it has an importance that transcends its duration as a framework of government.[12]

Americans began disputing the problem of a central government long before independence, and they continued to dispute it without a break during the war itself. The revolutionary groups that grew up in the colonies after 1763 focused their antagonism on the centralizing policies of Great Britain. Most Americans could and did agree on resistance to such policies, but they could not agree on how far to carry it. This division among Americans became more rather than less sharp as the British made it plain that they intended to rule the colonies with the brute power of an army if necessary. By the time the First Continental Congress met in 1774, two groups were struggling for control of policy. The radical wanted independence in fact, if not in name, and it won adherents steadily during 1775 and 1776 as its predictions of British tyranny were borne out one by one. The conservative group was determined, as the dispute between Britain and the colonies verged rapidly toward armed conflict, to stay within the British Empire no matter what the cost to colonial self-government. For a time they blocked a declaration of independence in the Second Continental Congress. But eventually repeated acts of British aggression convinced many of them that Britain had disowned the colonies and large numbers became revolutionists. However, they did not alter their political behavior or their political ideas. Thus, after independence as before it, there was a struggle within the revolutionary group—that is, among the Patriots—for control of the governments of the various states and of the United States.

It is this continuity of conflict that gives coherence to the political history of the age of the American Revolution. Otherwise many men and events must be ignored, or their significance distorted, if they are fitted into a pattern that assumes a sharp break in political history in 1776. The roots of this struggle lay deep in colonial history. In the course of a century and a half colonial society had grown into broad social groupings based on specific

[12] The following account is based in part on Merrill Jensen: *The Articles of Confederation: An Interpretation of the Social-Constitutional History of the American Revolution, 1774–1781* (Madison, 1940), and on Merrill Jensen: "The Idea of a National Government During the American Revolution," *Political Science Quarterly*, LVIII (1943), 356–79.

economic and political conditions. Along the narrow strip of tidewater from Georgia to New Hampshire lay most of the colonial cities. Dominating these cities were the colonial merchants who had grown to power as exporters of colonial farm produce, timber, furs, and fish, and as importers of manufactured goods from Europe, tropical goods from the West Indies, and slaves from Africa. These merchants were middlemen, they were bankers, and they were land speculators. Their economic power was paralleled by their political power. In the southern colonies the planters who raised tobacco, rice, and indigo, and who owned thousands of acres of land and hundreds of slaves formed the dominant social group. These two social groups dominated the older areas of the colonies and their governments. The ordinary citizens of the colonial towns did little to disturb aristocratic control of government.

The great majority of the American people were small farmers owning their own land, and for the most part they were voters in a society which insisted that only the propertied had any stake in a government whose chief purpose was the protection of property. Nevertheless these small farmers did not exercise power in proportion to either their numbers or their property. Most of them lived west of the tidewater and had settled their lands during the first half of the eighteenth century. As the wilderness to the westward was settled and cleared, its people applied to the colonial governments located along the coast for organization as townships and as counties and for representation in the colonial legislatures. But those legislatures were controlled by the colonial aristocracies and were slow to set up new western counties. When they did they made them very large and gave them but few representatives. Thus, despite the fact that by the time of the Revolution the "back-country" farmers were far more than half of the total population, they could do but little to achieve their ends in most of the colonial legislatures.

There was no legal way of defeating minority control and the occasion might never have arisen if the planter and merchant aristocracies had invariably ruled in the public interest. But, safe behind a barrier of farmers and frontiersmen, they were slow to vote money for frontier defense against the Indians. Merchants interested in the fur trade were rather more concerned with protection of the Indian than of the frontiersman. As dominating figures in colonial legislatures, planters and merchants had enormous advantages in the business of land speculation which engrossed so many Americans in the eighteenth century. They grabbed land everywhere, calmly indifferent to fraud and corruption as a method of acquisition, and then demanded strict legality in payments from the settlers to whom they sold it. Seated as they were near the coast and waterways, most of the planters and merchants were slow to vote the roads and bridges so needed by backcountry farmers to get their crops to market.

The back countrymen fought off land speculators, refused payment of rents, and from time to time were attacked by troops sent out by the colonial governments to maintain "law and order." The back countrymen were of many religious sects, and while perhaps not tolerant by conviction, they were so of necessity on the frontier where so many religious groups were settled. Hence, they opposed established churches and the payment of taxes to support them. They objected to the taxes levied by colonial legislatures for other purposes. They knew full well what taxation without representation meant when it was used by members of the colonial aristocracy to argue against the Stamp Act in 1765. All these things and more were expressed in petition after petition to colonial legislatures, but the redress of grievances asked for was seldom granted.

The result was that colonial history was punctuated by rebellions against minority rule. There had been Bacon's Rebellion in 1676. There was the Regulator Movement in the Carolinas a hundred years later. There were tenant farmer rebellions in New York and New Jersey. There was the recurrent demand for paper money which threatened to break out in rebellion when debtor farmers were defeated by their creditors in the legislatures. There was discontent with religious life which expressed itself so eloquently in the "Great Awakening" in the middle of the eighteenth century. What was true of the farmers was true also of the townspeople. They too had cause for discontent and from time to time they rioted, sometimes because of real distress, sometimes perhaps, merely because of boredom.

The focus of social tensions in colonial society was the governments of the colonies. Aristocratic control of those governments was challenged repeatedly. Various members of the aristocracy fought for control among themselves, as did the Livingstons and the De Lanceys of New York and the planters of the James and of the Potomac river valleys of Virginia. But in general the minority was agreed that it, rather than the small farmer and mechanic and artisan classes, should rule the colonies, and it had the support of British power. It was horrified by anything that smacked of "democracy." The term was little used of course, but the program of the discontented was essentially democratic in content, involving as it did a far wider participation in government than was the practice. There was no question here of a propertied versus propertyless struggle. The farmers were as property conscious as the planter and merchant aristocracies: it was simply that their economic, religious, and sectional interests clashed.

During the years of peace, depression, and increasing British interference in colonial affairs after 1763, the conflict between rival social groups grew more bitter. The governing classes naturally objected to British interference with their rule quite as much as they objected to farmer and artisan interference. But their constitutional arguments against Britain were of little effect, so they sought the help of farmers and artisans. The merchant aristocracy of the towns encouraged popular riots to give point to constitutional theories about the right of self-government. Thus they were able to prevent the Stamp Act from going into effect. But such theories also fitted the American scene too closely for comfort. Soon, popular leaders sprang up voicing popular grievances against merchants and planters. Men like Samuel Adams and Patrick Henry attacked merchants and planters for their half-hearted opposition to British policies. They cloaked themselves, some sincerely and some not, in the mantle of patriotism. They sought places of power in colonial governments, some with programs of reform and some with none whatever. But mixed and various as were the motives of revolutionary leaders, there grew up in most of the colonies effective revolutionary organizations. In the North these were largely confined to the towns, though gradually they spread out into the country. In the South they were centered in the legislatures.

It is this complexity of American society and the political attitudes arising from it that gives content to the political history of the revolutionary generation. There was demand for change within the American colonies. Britain was bent on imposing change from the top. The colonial aristocracies argued for the right of self-government in opposing Britain at the same time that they denied it at home, and in time were caught in a web spun from their own contradictions.

As they were swept in the direction of independence they realized that one result might well be social revolution within the American states. Some realized it earlier than others and gave up all opposition to British measures, preferring the certainties of British rule to the uncertainties of a future in which small farmers and artisans might speak with a far louder voice. Others realized it and yet continued to oppose British measures. Thus there was little agreement among the conservative groups as to how to maintain power. In New York in 1774, Gouverneur Morris declared that if the disputes with Britain continued, the aristocracy would be ruled by a riotous mob. Therefore reunion should be sought with the parent state. In Pennsylvania, Joseph Galloway worked out a plan for a constitutional union between the colonies and Great Britain with the same end in view. Morris became a Patriot and Galloway a Loyalist but their views on the nature of government were essentially alike: they believed in the need of coercive, centralized government. They did not need the experience of the Revolution to demonstrate what were for them the benefits of such a government. The idea was expressed before the First Continental Congress met. In that body Joseph Galloway gave it precision. He argued that if the colonies denied the authority of Parliament they would be in a "perfect state of nature" in their relations with one another. Civil war would break out among them; in fact it was at the moment prevented only by the presence of British power. Some central government must have the power to regulate trade because the colonies could not do it for themselves. Such arguments were not those of future Loyalists alone. Men like James Duane, John Dickinson, and Robert Morris were in complete agreement. Such men fought off independence as long as they could, and then, when it could no longer be avoided, they demanded prior creation of a central government. They argued eloquently for the need of sovereign authority over the states-to-be.

People who thought thus dominated the committee that wrote the first draft of the first constitution of the United States. Led by John Dickinson as chairman they wrote articles of confederation and gave them to Congress in July 1776. It was a constitution with great possibilities for centralization, for it contained few limitations on the power of Congress and no guarantees of power to the states. Congress was given wide power over state boundaries and western lands, one of the most bitterly contested issues of the day and one that was to be the chief source of delay in establishing government under the Articles of Confederation. States with definite western limits, like Pennsylvania and Maryland, had long been bitterly opposed to Virginia whose claims to what most eighteenth century men believed to be the "golden west" were well-nigh unbounded. The citizens of the landless states wanted a share in the wealth that was hoped for from the sale of western lands. Before the Revolution they had appealed to Great Britain to force Virginia to disgorge. Now they appealed to Congress. Only by appealing to or creating an authority sovereign over the states could their hopes be realized. The landed states led by Virginia wasted little time in removing this sweeping grant from the proposed Articles. Furthermore they added to them a specific provision that no state could be deprived of its territory without its consent.

Another dispute concerned the way the states should vote in Congress: that is "representation." The first Congress had decided that each state should have one vote and the Dickinson draft agreed. But here lines formed differently, for the states with large populations, Virginia, Massachusetts, and Pennsylvania, united to demand that voting be according to population. The smaller states objected to this, as did the men who opposed a central government freed from state control. It was obvious to them that the very nature of the central government would be different if units of population rather than state governments were represented. These men were the true "federalists" as the eighteenth century understood the term. They believed that the central government should be created by and always be kept subordinate to the states, each of which retained its sovereignty and independence. Thus they united with the small states who feared their large neighbors, and established the equality of the states in the Articles of Confederation.

With some exceptions the conservative group wanted a "national" government. In the Convention of 1787 James Wilson declared that Dickinson's draft of the Articles of Confederation was designed to provide for such a government. Wilson was one of the leaders in the debates in 1776. He argued that Congress represented the people, not the states, and that all Americans were one nation. His implication was that the government should be a national government. At first this was not clearly realized for the Dickinson draft was written by a man who was a master of legal subtleties; with a mind capable of argument, in Carl Becker's words, "subtle but clear, deriving the nature of an act from the intention of its makers, and the intention of its makers from the nature of the act. . . ." [13]

The Articles were dropped in August 1776 after a month's debate and not taken up again until April 1777. By that time the more obvious issues were settled and men like James Wilson were arguing for the establishment of precedents from which might be deduced the supremacy of Congress over the states. Men like Thomas Burke of North Carolina were truly alarmed. He saw at once when he came to Congress that the landless states were trying to create a central government powerful enough to take land away from the other states. He believed sincerely that unlimited power was not to be safely trusted to any man or set of men on earth. Thus when the Articles were again taken up he realized that the Dickinson draft was full of potential danger to the independence of the individual states, particularly the third article, which in Burke's words, "expressed only a reservation of the power of regulating the internal police, and consequently resigned every other power." He therefore proposed an amendment to the Articles which stated that all sovereign power was in the states separately; that Congress could exercise only those powers delegated to it by the states. Burke was so convincing that Congress supported him overwhelmingly and an amendment was added to the Articles of Confederation stating this point of view with complete precision.

The Articles of Confederation, when completed and sent to the states for ratification in November 1777, left ultimate power in the hands of the states. The central government was given specific and sharply circumscribed powers. And most important of all, the states retained for themselves that vast area of unspecified, unenumerated powers, the twilight zone wherein constitutional governments function most largely. Soon all the states except Mary-

[13] Carl Becker: *The Eve of the Revolution* (New Haven, 1918), 133.

land had ratified the Articles. Maryland demanded that control of the West be given to Congress for "the good of the whole," but from this she made a significant exception: all lands in the West that had been granted before the Declaration of Independence. Thus would be guaranteed the claims of the Indiana, Illinois, and Wabash companies in which men like Governor Thomas Johnson of Maryland, James Wilson, Robert Morris, Benjamin Franklin, and many other leaders from the middle (and landless) states were interested.

The Virginians knew perfectly well the cause of Maryland's opposition. At once the Virginia government examined and voided all such claims to western lands. The land companies then petitioned Congress, sent members to Congress, and bribed Virginians to argue their cause. So the argument went on while Virginia took further steps to consolidate her control of the West. But by 1780 it was felt generally that if only the Confederation were completed, somehow it might help in fighting the war. Furthermore, there were a good many Virginians, particularly the group centering around Thomas Jefferson, who had a vision of the West divided into free and independent states. Such men were willing to give up Virginia's western claims for the "good of the whole," but to make sure of it they insisted on attaching conditions to an act of cession before it could become final. The most important condition was one providing that Congress must declare void all the deeds that had been given by the Indians in the region to be ceded to the United States. There was a bitter dispute over this in Congress. The delegates from the landless states insisted successfully that Congress make no such promise. Despite this, Virginia went ahead and ceded the land to Congress, carefully attaching the requirement that all Indian deeds must be declared void in the region before the land could pass finally from Virginia to Congress. New York had already ceded her claims so there was little left for Maryland to do but to ratify the Articles of Confederation and this her delegation did formally on the first of March 1781.

At last the United States had a central government with a legal foundation and a constitutional method of procedure. The *Pennsylvania Packet* described the high hopes produced by:

This great event, which will confound our enemies, fortify us against their arts of seduction, and frustrate their plans of division, was announced to the public at twelve o'clock under the discharge of the artillery on the land, and the cannon of the shipping in the Delaware. The bells were rung, and every manifestation of joy shown on the occasion. The *Ariel* frigate, commanded by the gallant Paul Jones, fired a *feu-de-joye*, and was beautifully decorated with a variety of streamers in the day, and ornamented with a brilliant appearance of lights in the night.

At two o'clock in the afternoon his excellency the president of Congress received the congratulations of the legislative and executive bodies of this state, of the civil and military officers and many of the principal citizens, who partook of a collation, provided on this happy occasion. The evening was ushered in by an elegant exhibition of fireworks.

Thus has the union, began by necessity, been indissolubly cemented. Thus America, like a well constructed arch, whose parts, harmonizing and mutually supporting each other, are the more closely united the greater the pressure upon them, is growing up in war into greatness and consequence among the nations.[14]

[14] 3 March 1781.

2

The Politics of War and Finance

THE PROBLEMS of the peace were many. Some had long-range consequences that lasted far beyond the years of the Confederation. Others had immediate impact. Of this latter kind, the two most important were the demobilization of the army, and the payment of the war debt. Both had widespread political implications and were the subject of sharply differing opinions. Both were rooted in the years of war and continued into the years of peace, but the coming of peace itself brought them to a sharp and sudden crisis which threatened a political revolution before they could be solved, or at least evaded by the passage of time.

The Army at the End of the War [1]

The story of the battles, marches, and counter-marches of the revolutionary armies is a simple one compared with other problems which plagued the country before and after the war and

[1] Various problems of the army are treated in the following: Louis C. Hatch: *The Administration of the American Revolutionary Army* (Harvard Historical Studies, X, New York, 1904); Charles K. Bolton: *The Private Soldier Under Washington* (New York, 1902), gives much detail concerning the life of the ordinary soldier. The only recent study of the problems of supply is Victor L. Johnson: *The Administration of the American Commissariat During the Revolutionary War* (Philadelphia, 1941). The kind of life the officers led is detailed in some length by Harry E. Wildes: *Anthony Wayne: Trouble Shooter of the American Revolution* (New York, 1941). Infinite detail is to be found in many of the biographies of Washington, and above all, in his writings. The most unusual account, and one worthy of careful study, is that of Bernhard Knollenberg: *Washington and the Revolution: A Reappraisal* (New York, 1941).

affected the policies of both state and central governments. Ultimate power in military affairs lay with Congress which elected and dismissed officers, laid down policies for supplying the army, and from time to time determined military objectives. Congress was damned by the officers and soldiers as the chief root of evil and has been so damned ever since. Some of this blame is rightly placed, but experience with later wars would indicate that the problems are always the same. Everyone makes mistakes, but too few men are big enough to acknowledge them. Congress kept the military under close control because Americans did not trust armies of any kind. They had inherited the English fear of a standing army; they had experienced British determination to use an army to rule them in the years before the Revolution, and they would have none of it. Sam Adams expressed that feeling to James Warren in 1776 when he said that a "standing army, however necessary it may be at sometimes, is always dangerous to the liberties of the people. Soldiers are apt to consider themselves as a body distinct from the rest of the citizens. They have their arms always in their hands. Their rules and their discipline is severe. They soon become attached to their officers and disposed to yield implicit obedience to their commands. Such a power should be watched with a jealous eye." [2] John Adams was more succinct. He told Horatio Gates that Congress had made him dictator of Canada for six months, and then said "we don't choose to trust you generals, with too much power, for too long time." [3]

Such feeling was common among the men who began the Revolution, and close control was the result. Congress elected generals and fired them at will. Political groups formed behind rival generals as the inevitable battles among officers followed one after another during the course of the war. It was perhaps an inefficient way of conducting affairs, but the present age, which saw a politically unhampered army send snowplows to the tropics and desert equipped and trained divisions to Alaska, should at least temper criticism of the Continental Congress with the realization that the grant of arbitrary power to military men does not inevitably result in efficiency.

Congress had a tremendous problem; it had to fight a war with-

[2] 7 Jan., *Warren-Adams Letters* (2 vols., Massachusetts Historical Society *Collections*, LXXII, LXXIII, Boston, 1917, 1925), I, 197–8.

[3] 18 June 1776, Burnett, I, 497.

out money and without the power of coercion over either the states or their citizens. Congress worked badly, haltingly, and inefficiently, but it did manage to run the war despite all the obstacles. Throughout the war it supported Washington, although at times with hesitation, and for good reason. Perhaps few generals in history have been so often defeated and still retained their commands. The continuous support of Washington by Congress did give the military policies of the Revolution a kind of coherence that made it possible to win through to independence in the end.

When one turns from Congress to the army itself it becomes obvious that Congress was not alone to blame. To begin with there were fourteen armies: the thirteen state militias and the Continental Army. Americans were so sensitive about the dangers of uncontrolled military power that it was difficult to establish a permanent organization such as the Continental Army even long after the need for it was imperative, and once established, continued trouble was inevitable. Continental and state troops were paid differently and were enlisted for different terms and the advantage was usually with the state troops. Officers were jealous of one another, and sometimes to a ludicrous degree as in the story of two colonels at the funeral of a brother officer. Each was to act as a pallbearer. Colonel Crafts of the militia insisted on walking first because he was the older man; Colonel Jackson of the Continentals insisted that he go first because he was in the Continental Army. The dispute ended when Colonel Crafts and his friends left the house in a huff and the corpse to the continental officers.[4]

As a group, the officers were enormously concerned about their honor. It was always being smirched. They quarreled over precedence, which likewise involved their "honor." Many of them would rather quit the army than fight without proper promotions. Their quarrels over such matters drove Washington and Congress to distraction and lent weight to John Adams's statement to General Greene that "honor" was one of the most "putrid corruptions of absolute monarchy . . . the honor of preferring a single step of promotion to the service of the public, must be bridled." [5]

The wholesale grant of commissions to foreign officers early in

[4] Hatch: *Revolutionary Army*, 36.

[5] Charles Francis Adams, ed.: *The Works of John Adams* (10 vols., Boston, 1850–6), I, 263.

the war was a genuine source of discontent and of mixed advantage. Some of them were good; some of them were bad; all of them caused trouble. Horatio Gates and Charles Lee, two retired British army officers living in America, were put high in the army almost at once because of their past experience. To this day it is impossible to evaluate the services of either of them fairly. The average Frenchman was bad. Washington denounced them in no uncertain terms when he described them as men of "a little plausibility, unbounded pride and ambition, and a perseverance in application not to be resisted but by uncommon firmness, to support their pretensions; men, who, in the first instance, tell you they wish for nothing more than the honor of serving so glorious a cause as volunteers, the next day solicit rank without pay, the day following want money advanced to them, and in the course of a week want further promotion, and are not satisfied with any thing you can do for them." [6]

There were exceptions, of course. Lafayette was the best of the lot, although the honors and distinctions given him caused heart-burning throughout the army. Congress made him a major general at the age of twenty, largely because of his family and political connections in France. Washington's personal fondness for him made him an untouchable throughout the rest of the war and brought him continued distinctions of command. But Lafayette was sincere and he had great courage and enthusiasm. Perhaps his greatest service was in bridging partially the gap between the Americans and the so recently detested French. "Baron" Steuben, who as drillmaster really created an army out of the continental troops, and who knew how to save supplies, was probably as nearly indispensable as any man in the army except Washington.[7] The "Baron" Kalb was an honest, experienced fighting man; Kosciusko, the Polish patriot, was still another. But the bulk of foreign officers might well, for the good of the American cause, have stayed at home.

From the beginning of the war the officers wanted special concessions in the way of pay. They got a pay increase in 1776. Then they demanded half pay for life after the war was over, the prac-

[6] To Gouverneur Morris, 24 July 1778, John C. Fitzpatrick, ed.: *The Writings of George Washington From the Original Manuscript Sources, 1745–1799* (Bicentennial ed., 39 vols., Washington, 1931–44), XII, 226–7.

[7] See Richard Peters to General Horatio Gates, 23 Feb. 1784, Emmet Collection, no. 8729, NYPL.

tice in European armies. Washington at first set himself against the idea but eventually he told Congress the very life of the army depended on it. One group in Congress objected to half pay persistently. Throughout the North and particularly in New England, it was believed, and rightly, that this would create a favored class in society such as America had not had before. But in 1778 despite such opposition, Congress was forced to grant half pay for seven years after the war to those officers who agreed to serve for the duration. Noncommissioned officers and privates were to have a bounty of eighty dollars, one year's pay.

The agitation for half pay for life continued. Washington finally told Congress that officers were resigning and spreading sedition throughout the army. Finally, in the fall of 1780 with the war at its lowest ebb, Congress gave in. Officers had been resigning at an alarming rate since the first of the year and the army promised to disintegrate by that route, if no other. Then too the changing political complexion of Congress had its effect. Unlike the old revolutionary group, the group now coming into power had no distrust of distinctions in society; they wanted them. They had no objection to a standing army if they controlled it. The result was that on 21 October 1780 Congress promised the officers half pay for life.[8]

The discontent of the common soldier was as great as that of the officers and was at least as justified. At the beginning of the war many a man had joined the army to fight for freedom and equality: the principles of the Declaration of Independence. As time went on it grew more and more difficult to get men to join the army, and once in it, to stay there. The states and Congress were forced to give cash bounties, then land bounties, and then larger cash bounties to induce men to enlist. Why this happened has many explanations. The war was long and bitter and most men lost their early enthusiasm and were content to drop back into the anonymity from which they had come. Those who had joined to fight for freedom and equality found precious little of it in the army to start with, and less and less of it as the Continental Army was organized and drilled. The army needed discipline, it is true, but most of the common soldiers were free Americans: farmers and their sons and the independent mechanics and artisans of the towns. Their officers, especially those from the

[8] *Journals*, XVIII, 958–9.

colonial aristocracy, often treated them as if they were the riff-raff that made up the European armies of the day.

Punishments were brutal beyond reason or necessity. Washington's whippings were so severe that Congress had to step in and limit the number of lashes that might be laid on a man's bare back. Too often the officers were men the soldiers could not respect. When a general like Lord Stirling got drunk every day, he went unpunished, while privates were whipped for the same thing. While officers struck for higher wages and quit the army if they did not get them, privates were whipped or shot for desertion.

Certainly for those ordinary men who believed and could be moved by Thomas Paine's appeal not to be summer soldiers and sunshine patriots on the bitter eve before Trenton—for these there was too little to keep idealism alive. The result was that men deserted and threatened mutiny, and tension increased until in January 1781 even the dependable Pennsylvania line mutinied. They had wanted to know the precise terms of their enlistment but their officers refused to tell them. They claimed that the officers treated them brutally and tricked them when they sought information. Then early in January 1781, Pennsylvania recruiting agents arrived in camp. They offered twenty-five dollars in coin to six months troops who would re-enlist for the remainder of the war. This was too much for the veterans who had gone unpaid for months. They united and demanded a redress of grievances and particularly some statement as to just how long they were supposed to stay in the army. So good was their cause, and so weak the force of those officers who preferred shooting to negotiation and redress of grievances, that justice was at last done them. Thereafter there were a few attempts at mutiny by other troops before the end of the war, but these were put down firmly and their leaders were executed.[9]

Back of the discontent of both officers and soldiers lay the everlasting problem of pay and supply. During the early years of the war, state and continental paper money served a real purpose, but as prices rose and rose the money men got meant less and less. In time it was valueless and the army entirely dependent on the commissary and quartermaster general departments. Food, clothing, and ammunition were always scarce and sometimes non-

[9] Carl Van Doren: *Mutiny in January* (New York, 1943); Hatch: *Revolutionary Army*, ch. vii.

existent, or at places far from the army. As paper financing failed, Congress adopted the policy of calling on the states for specific supplies. From the beginning of 1780 until the middle of 1781 this method was depended on with results that were at times disastrous and at no time satisfactory. When Robert Morris took over as superintendent of finance in 1781 he was given absolute control. He at once adopted the European method of supplying the army by using private contractors.

The system of private contracts brought as many complaints as the old system of specific supplies, and the still earlier one of direct government purchases. The contractors profiteered. They squabbled over rations to be allowed. Washington denounced Comfort Sands, the chief contractor, as a practitioner of "low dirty tricks." Sands's contracts were voided and other men took over. Fortunately the fighting ended with Yorktown and the supply problem was lessened if not entirely solved. So the army at the end of the war was at least well fed. It was likewise well clothed, although the problem of clothing, like that of food, had plagued everyone from Congress and Washington to the lowliest private ever since the beginning of the war. By the spring of 1783 Washington could report that the troops were "better covered, better clothed, and better fed than they have ever been in any former winter quarters." [10] In the South, troops were helped only by the milder climate. Otherwise General Greene's letters give a picture as black as anything said of Valley Forge: naked troops, men on the march fainting from starvation, maggot-riddled meat when there was any at all, and a total lack of rum.[11] But here too, as in the North, the end of active fighting solved the worst problems of supply, although it did not ease the feelings of the men who had suffered so much.

Who was to blame? Officers blamed Congress. Congress blamed officers. Both blamed public indifference. Everybody, beginning with Washington, blamed speculators as a class.[12] Congress appointed quartermaster and commissary generals, and then restricted their power. Congress has been blamed for this, yet there

[10] To Major General William Heath, 5 Feb. 1783, *Writings*, XXVI, 97.

[11] To Robert Morris, 22 April 1782, Greene Papers, CL.

[12] See for instance Hamilton's essays, signed "Publius," which were printed in the *New York Journal* in the fall of 1778. They are reprinted in John C. Hamilton, ed.: *The Works of Alexander Hamilton* (7 vols., New York, 1850–1), II, 156–63.

was justice in the distrust Congress showed. That there was corruption is evident. How widespread it was is difficult to say. Even when there was no corruption there was a lack of ethical standards in the way the business was handled. Thomas Mifflin, an able quartermaster general, resigned toward the end of 1777. He was in time succeeded by General Nathanael Greene. Greene insisted on appointing his own business partners as deputies. Joseph Trumbull was succeeded by Jeremiah Wadsworth as commissary general. They were given complete control and a commission of one per cent on everything they spent—an eighteenth century version of the cost-plus contract. They were as expensive then as now but the army was better off for a time at least.

Characteristic of business ethics was the fact that Greene and Wadsworth went into secret partnership with Barnabas Deane in 1779. They put up most of the money and he acted as manager. Whether the firm sold much to the army does not appear. But Greene and Charles Pettit, one of his deputies, were also in partnership in an iron works, the products of which were sold to army contractors from whom they in turn, in their official capacity, bought the goods. Whether or not corruption was involved is unknown. But the suspicion of it in this and many other cases was ever in the minds of members of Congress and explains, as much as any propensity to meddle, the close attention Congress paid to the details of supply.

As the war came to an end the crucial problem was that of pay. Effectively the war was over with Yorktown, but officially it dragged on as the peace commissioners argued back and forth. The officers grew more desperate as they waited, for with a treaty of peace, the need for them, and hence their influence, would diminish if not vanish entirely. They had just grounds for complaint. Nothing had been done about the half pay promised them in 1780 and it looked as if nothing would be done as state after state made it plain that it was opposed to the plan. Their regular pay was hopelessly in arrears. Massachusetts officers decided to appeal to their legislature for compensation: if not half pay, then a lump sum payment. A committee with a memorial went to Boston in September 1782. Rufus Putnam wrote Samuel Adams, then president of the Massachusetts senate, that if the memorial was not acted upon, the army ought not to be trusted with arms.[13]

[13] 18 Oct. 1782, Samuel Adams Papers, NYPL.

Governor John Hancock promised support, but the legislature balked. In the senate, dominated by the mercantile interest along the coast, a majority was willing; but in the house, dominated by its country members, the majority against any grant was four to one. The whole thing was dropped when one of the members of Congress informed the legislature that Congress would take up the whole question early in 1783, and furthermore, that Congress now regarded the grant of half pay as too great a concession.

The Massachusetts committee returned to camp at Newburgh on the Hudson and took the lead in preparing a list of grievances to send to Congress. Unrest grew as the rumor spread that Congress had no intention of making good on the earlier promise of half pay. Various means of putting pressure on Congress were suggested. Some of the officers wanted to resign as a group, an effective and drastic proposal, since officially the war had not ended. Washington stayed in camp and used his vast prestige to bring about a milder form of protest. Regiments were invited to present lists of grievances. A memorial to Congress was drawn up in which the officers stated their case: short rations, inadequate pay and depreciation of paper money, lack of proper clothing. On the question of half pay they were willing to compromise: they were willing to take a flat sum. They asked also that some means be established to pay the common soldiers the eighty dollar bounty promised those serving to the end of the war. They concluded by pointing to the great and growing discontent in the army and urged Congress to convince the army and the world that the independence of America was not to be accomplished by the ruin of one class of her citizens.

A committee of three: Major General McDougall, Lieutenant Colonel Brooks, and Colonel Ogden were chosen to carry the memorial to Congress. When they got to Philadelphia, they were caught up in a scheme for a political revolution which had its roots in another problem of the war; that of finance and the payment of the war debt.[14]

[14] Hatch: *Revolutionary Army*, 151–2. See *post* ch. iii.

The Financial Dilemma at the End of the War

Congress financed the American Revolution by capitalizing its only asset: the hope of winning independence. Congress could not levy taxes, but even if it had had the power, there was little money in the country that could be gotten that way. At first Congress could not borrow money, for the Americans were colonists until 1776, and even after the Declaration of Independence, France wanted to be sure that they would continue to fight before lending them money. Congress did the one thing it could do and which Americans had been doing for nearly a century: it issued paper money. Congress began in 1775 and by 1779 had issued approximately $200,000,000. The various states issued untold sums in addition.

All too often this issuance of paper money has been damned as unsound economics, and even as immoral practice. But many contemporaries understood the necessity and inevitability of doing what was done. "Is there any principle of religion or morality which forbade a weak and infant nation, driven into war for the avoidance of slavery, to arm itself by the best means in its power?" Thus asked Edmund Randolph as he looked back at the financing of the Revolution. He went on to say that it was "scarcely possible indeed, that depreciation should not be foreseen. The degree of it and its havoc, probably were not. Yet to stop would have been political suicide. Thus what in established governments might have been fraud, in ours, which without final success must have been annihilated, was explained, nay justified by its situation." [15]

The depreciation of paper money during the Revolution—that is, the rise in prices people asked for articles when selling them for paper—was the most obvious fact of Revolutionary finance. The causes of that rise are not as simple as a "quantity" theory of money would have one believe. The quantity issued was important, but contemporaries believed that there were other explanations. Everyone united in damning the "speculators"—the eighteenth century war profiteers—not only for profiteering, but for inflating the currency as well. They operated in many ways,

[15] "Edmund Randolph's Essay on the Revolutionary History of Virginia, 1774–1782," *Virginia Magazine of History and Biography*, XLIV (1936), 36.

but Michael Hillegas, treasurer of the United States during the Revolution, described the usual method. He agreed that high prices were in part the result of the quantity of money in circulation but that another cause was "a scarcity of foreign articles (and which scarcity was by the traders made somewhat artificial by secreting the goods we really had). This the retailers as well as the importers availed themselves of, and continued to raise in their prices (till lately) higher and higher. This same spirit of avarice soon got among the farmers, particularly those who were disaffected, who in turn when they were asked the prices of necessaries of life &c., they had for sale would naturally in justification of their demands plead the high prices they were obliged to give for salt, sugar, rum, coffee and all kinds of European goods." [16] Thus the combined forces of greed and the quantity of paper kept the spiral of inflation going at an ever-increasing rate. Things were bad in 1778, but as Hamilton realized, paper money could "draw out the resources of the country a good while longer. . . ." [17]

Congress continued to issue more and more money until 1780. Meanwhile it borrowed money. First it borrowed the paper money it had issued, which, by the end of 1776, had passed largely into the hands of the merchants through whom the bulk of the war supplies came to American troops. In October 1776 Congress offered four per cent interest for $5,000,000. Little came in, for the interest rate was felt to be too low. Then early in 1777 Congress decided to borrow $15,000,000 and raised the interest rate to six per cent. Furthermore it agreed that the interest should be paid in bills of exchange drawn on the American commissioners in France who were expected to borrow money in France. By the end of the war Congress had borrowed a total of over $67,000,000 of the money it had issued. This paper figure was reduced to a specie value of about $11,500,000 in June 1780.

A third variety of domestic debt was created by the quartermasters and commissaries of the army. These men were authorized to issue certificates in exchange for supplies. Such certificates were issued without much supervision by either Congress or the officials immediately responsible. No one knows how much was

[16] Michael Hillegas to Benjamin Franklin, York Town, 17 March 1778, *Pennsylvania Magazine of History of Biography*, XXIX (1905), 233–4.

[17] Hamilton to ——— ———, Headquarters, 8 Nov. 1778, *Works* (Hamilton ed.), I, 70–2.

thus distributed, but as late as February 1781, after the states had been collecting such certificates as taxes and turning them over to Congress for over two years, there were still nearly $100,000,000 face value outstanding. Congress estimated that they were worth about $850,000 market value, so greatly had they depreciated.[18]

An increasingly important means of financing the war was the money Congress got in Europe. France began with a secret gift of a million livres in 1776 and followed this with further gifts amounting to a total of almost $2,000,000 by the end of the war. Spain too, unwilling partner though she was, gave nearly $400,000 before the end of the war. More important than gifts were the loans. These began in 1777 with a loan of a million livres from the Farmers General of France. Eighteen million livres were borrowed in 1778, ten million livres in 1781 and six million in 1783. France thus loaned the Americans a total of approximately $6,352,000 during the war. Spain loaned an additional $248,098. The money was handed over to the United States partly in cash and partly in supplies and was an indispensable part of financing the Revolution. The Dutch loans came later and were as important in financing the Confederation as they were in financing the national government after 1789.[19]

But the most difficult problem facing Congress was the ever-increasing depreciation of its paper money, quartermaster and commissary certificates, and loan office certificates. Congress issued money faster and faster. At the beginning of 1779 the official rate of exchange was eight dollars of continental paper money for one of specie. By summer it was twenty to one, and by the end of the year, forty to one, and the market value was perhaps one hundred to one for "the merchants and traders, taking advantage of the depreciation raised the price of their commodities to an enormous degree, so that the Commonwealth lay like a ship stranded. . . ." [20]

Congress turned this way and that in a vain effort to solve an insoluble problem. It asked the states to give up their own paper money which, like that of Congress, had depreciated. It asked them to furnish $6,000,000 a year for fifteen years so that the

[18] *Journals*, XIX, 165.
[19] Bemis: *Diplomacy*, 93, and the preceding discussion of loans.
[20] Charles Thomson to John Jay, 12 Oct. 1780, Burnett, V, 418.

public would take continental bills at a higher rate. Finally it pledged itself never to issue more than $200,000,000 in paper money, a top limit it had almost reached when it made the pledge. This was in effect a surrender of power, for as long as Congress could get its money accepted, at however low a rate, it was by that much independent of the states. The fact that Congress, through the first years of the war, had been able to finance itself, gave it an independence it was not to have again until it got ready to sell western lands. The members of Congress realized exactly what they were doing but, as Madison said, "to continue to emit *ad infinitum* was thought more dangerous than an absolute occlusion of the press." [21]

Congress meanwhile had declared that it would never repudiate the paper money it issued, but once more the facts of the market place dictated action, for the people long since had repudiated the currency. Therefore in March 1780 Congress accepted public judgment of its finances and ordered that its old paper issues should be valued at forty dollars of paper to one dollar of specie—an overvaluation, even then. In place of the old money, 10,000,000 of new dollars were to be issued. This money was to be backed by the states and to bear interest. As the old bills came into the state treasuries they were to be replaced by this new issue. Congress was to get four tenths of the money and the states six tenths.

This act was followed by another in June by which Congress decided to liquidate all loan office certificates according to a scale of depreciation it established. Since the loan office certificates had been sold for depreciated paper money, this action was a simple recognition of the fact.

The whole scheme that Congress thus proposed failed of any real result. To begin with, Congress, even at forty to one, overvalued its own currency which was selling in the market at prices ranging upwards of fifty to one, and in some cases as a result of manipulation of the merchants of Philadelphia, at one hundred and fifty to one. The states had problems enough with their own paper money and did not want to issue that of Congress and take responsibility for it. Some states filled their quotas of congressional requests for old continental currency by buying it in other states where it was cheaper. Elbridge Gerry told Robert Morris that

[21] To Joseph Jones, [24] Oct. 1780, ibid., V, 427–8.

if the merchants of Philadelphia and Boston would get behind the currency and support it, they could do more than the legislatures of their respective states.[22] But the merchants refused. They could make more money by depreciating the currency still further and this they proceeded to do by raising prices despite all efforts of state governments to regulate them or to force the acceptance of paper money in payment of debts. An example occurred in Philadelphia in December 1780. The Pennsylvania legislature called in leading merchants and asked them to form an association to stop the depreciation of continental currency which at the time was selling at seventy-five to one. The merchants agreed to stabilize the price at that figure which delighted both the assembly and Congress; but no sooner had the merchants returned to their shops than they promptly doubled the specie prices of the articles in them. The result was to double the depreciation of the continental currency. It was a kind of "patriotism" which one member of Congress said he hoped would not spread to his state.[23]

The result of such actions by men in positions of economic power was to complete the destruction of paper finance as a means of fighting the war. By March of 1781 when the Articles of Confederation went into effect, Congress was advising the states to do away with their legal tender laws. Shortly thereafter it advised them to do away with paper money entirely. By the end of 1781 paper currency had stopped circulating as money. Some states were still collecting it as taxes and turning it over to Congress for destruction, and some speculators still toyed with it, but the financial and political importance of continental money was forever ended.

Such was not the case with the rest of the public debt, particularly the loan office certificates, which were to be the center of political struggles until well into the 1790's. The debt represented by paper currency, quartermaster and commissary certificates had been spread widely among the people. As it passed from hand to hand depreciating as it went, it acted as an effective

[22] 11 June 1780, ibid., V, 205–6.

[23] John Sullivan to Meshech Weare, 3 Dec. 1780, ibid., V, 473. In a memorial to Joseph Reed, President of Pennsylvania, 7 May 1781, Joseph Reed Papers, New York Historical Society, several citizens of Reading attacked the "lawless proceedings of the merchants and traders of Philadelphia in depreciating our state money" and offered to support the government.

though rough form of taxation, as Gouverneur Morris explained to Washington in 1778.[24] Once these forms of debt had passed from circulation they ceased to be of political interest, or at least their holders were without political influence. But the loan office debt was the crucial debt of the Revolution. By the end of the Revolution it was concentrated in one section. In 1783 Hamilton said that four fifths of it was in Pennsylvania and the states to the north.[25] By 1790 it was said that almost forty per cent of it was held in Pennsylvania. This was natural enough, for Philadelphia was the economic center of the United States during the war and the loan office debt was held mostly by the mercantile class which had acquired it in the course of trade and army supply. There were a few, of course, who had invested in such funds during the war and who held them until they were paid in the 1790's, but this was a relatively small group.

The public creditors, western land speculators, merchants, and ordinary investors wanted, first of all, interest on their holdings, and ultimately the principal. Located near the centers of political and economic activity, they were in a position to voice their demands effectively and they did so ever more loudly as congressional finance staggered toward complete collapse. The holders of the public debt joined with other groups such as the land speculators and the army officers in demanding that something be done for them. They found willing listeners and often fellow members among the men in Congress, particularly among those who had been arguing since the beginning of the Revolution for the creation of a centralized government—a national government—with coercive authority over the states and their individual citizens. Their plans and the measures they took, shape much of the history of the years 1781 to 1783, and frustrated though they were as the treaty of peace was proclaimed, their program for the future was revealed almost in its entirety. It had as its chief end the destruction of that self-government within the states which the separation from Great Britain made possible.

[24] 26 Oct. 1778, Jared Sparks: *The Life of Gouverneur Morris* (3 vols., Boston, 1832), I, 175.

[25] To Governor George Clinton, 14 May 1783, *Works* (Hamilton ed.), I, 366–8. Robert Morris wrote to Nathaniel Appleton, Massachusetts loan officer, that a "very great proportion" of the public debt was due to the citizens of Massachusetts, 22 Jan. 1782, Balch Papers (Bancroft Transcripts), NYPL.

They looked upon that self-government as an evil, an evil which they described as "democracy."

The Demand for a National Government

The men who wrote the Articles of Confederation created a federal government wherein the state governments retained sovereign power and the central government was their creature. They had done this in spite of the determined opposition of those members of the colonial ruling classes who had chosen independence but who wanted along with it a centralized government with independent power and coercive authority. These men chose independence but they did not surrender the ideals of government they expressed during the debates from 1774 onward. Their experience with revolutionary enthusiasms and more democratic forms of state government confirmed them in the fears they had expressed before the Declaration of Independence. Hence, their desire for a "national" government was intensified rather than diminished, and they showed no more intention of accepting the Articles of Confederation as a permanent constitution than they did of accepting the more democratic constitutions adopted by some of the states. Edward Rutledge expressed their attitude early in the war when he wrote to John Jay in the fall of 1776 urging Jay to provide for a strong executive in the proposed constitution for New York, for he said, "a pure democracy may possibly do, when patriotism is the ruling passion; but when the state abounds with rascals, as is the case with many at this day, you must suppress a little of that popular spirit." [26]

For a time the Revolution swept many of the men who believed thus from positions of effectiveness, although enough remained in legislative seats to voice from time to time the demand for centralized authority. They could not change the Articles of Confederation, now before the states for ratification, but they could and did seek to establish precedents upon the basis of which they

[26] 24 Nov. 1776, Henry P. Johnston, ed.: *The Correspondence and Public Papers of John Jay* (4 vols., New York, 1890–3), I, 94.

could argue the sovereignty of Congress. Gouverneur Morris had favored such strategy as early as 1775 when he heard that Congress might consider the case of James Rivington, the Tory printer in New York City. Morris declared that such action by Congress would give it judicial power just as the Association of 1774 had given it legislative power. The canny Morris was keenly appreciative of the importance of precedent. "The power of government, as of man," he said, "is to be collected from small instances; great affairs are more the object of reflection and policy. Here both join." [27]

Time and again the minority of "nationalists" who remained in Congress after 1776 tried to "collect" the power of government "from small instances." One such instance was the report of a price-fixing convention in New England in 1777. The report was laid before Congress. James Wilson and others argued that the approval of Congress was necessary. Benjamin Rush stated flatly that this meeting had usurped the powers of Congress. The "long metaphysical debate" continued, for many of the revolutionary group were as well aware as the nationalists of the subtle power of precedent. So the real "federalists"—Sam Adams, Richard Henry Lee, and Thomas Burke—opposed Wilson and Rush. Adams insisted that the right to assemble and discuss was the privilege of freemen and feared only by tyrants. Richard Henry Lee drove home the point that it was the unconfederated Congress itself that had no legal power.[28]

In addition to those men who argued in general for a central sovereign authority, there were particular interests that stood to gain by the creation of such authority. The most persistent and pervasive were the land companies centering in the landless middle states: the Indiana, the Illinois, and the Wabash companies. They had appealed to centralized government (Great Britain) before the Revolution; they appealed to Congress once war began, and they got what they wanted in the Dickinson draft of confederation, only to have it removed. They appealed also to Virginia. They were, in fact, ready to uphold either national or state sovereignty if by either means they could get the land they wanted. When Virginia's actions finally made it plain that there

[27] Gouverneur Morris to Richard Henry Lee, May 1775, Peter Force, ed.: *American Archives* (4th and 5th ser., 9 vols., Washington, 1837–53), 4th ser., II, 726.

[28] Jensen: *Articles of Confederation*, 170–2.

was little to be gained from her, representatives of these land companies evolved tenuous theories in support of the sovereignty of Congress in general, and over western lands in particular. An Indiana Company memorial in 1779, for instance, declared that the West had been set up as a separate government under the sovereignty of the king, and that now the jurisdiction over that land was in the hands of "the whole United States in Congress assembled, in whom the sovereignty is now vested."[29] Other memorials were even more explicit. One of them declared that "all the rights and all the obligations of the Crown of Great Britain respecting the lands and governments devolve upon the United States and are to be claimed, exercised and discharged by the United States in Congress assembled."[30]

This subtle doctrine of the devolution of sovereignty was the creation of the nationalists, for such men as James Wilson and Robert Morris were leading members of the land companies. But no such doctrine, however subtle, could mislead the representatives of the landed states. And when Virginia denied all jurisdiction of Congress in such matters, William Trent replied for both the Indiana and Vandalia companies with utter frankness that the "question of the jurisdiction of Congress" was the very essence of their claims, and that it was "of infinite consequence to the American union as well as to your memorialists."[31]

The second group supporting the demand for a strong national government were the public creditors—an ever more vocal interest group created by the Revolution. Great riches for them lay in the mass of depreciated paper used to finance the war if Congress could get and enforce the power of taxation. Despite the difficulties involved, the nationalist group did not look upon the debt as a handicap, but agreed with Hamilton who declared in 1781: "A national debt, if it is not excessive, will be to us a national blessing. It will be a powerful cement of our union."[32] There was no novelty, even then, in this concept of a creditor group as a powerful nationalizing force. As early as May 1775 the New York Provincial Congress had concerned itself with currency problems and accepted a report drafted by Gouverneur Morris.

[29] Papers of the Continental Congress, no. 77, ff. 234–45, LC.

[30] Walpole Company Memorial presented by William Trent, 11 Sept. 1779, PCC, no. 41, X, ff. 79–86, LC.

[31] 13 Oct. 1780, PCC, no. 77, ff. 230–3, LC.

[32] Hamilton to Robert Morris, 30 April, 1781, *Works* (Hamilton ed.), I, 257.

This report declared that Congress should control all currency. It went on to argue "that whenever a paper currency has been emitted, and obtained general credit, it will be a new bond of union to the associated colonies. . . ." [33] And as the war neared its end Gouverneur Morris, assistant superintendent of finance, wrote to John Jay, "finance, my friend, the whole of what remains of the American Revolution grounds there." [34] To Nathaniel Appleton in Massachusetts, Robert Morris declared that "a public debt supported by public revenue will prove the strongest cement to keep our confederacy together." [35]

It is thus evident that men saw a connection between centralization and the public debt during the Revolution. It is also evident that some of them looked upon the public debt and debt funding as involving more than economics or justice. Hamilton and Gouverneur Morris early realized that the creditor group might be consolidated behind a movement for the imposition of a national government upon the states.

The demand for centralized power grew stronger as money depreciated ever more rapidly, and the army grew more desperate and discontented because of lack of supplies and pay. It was not long before the notion was abroad in the land that what the country needed was a dictator. In the spring of 1780 it was proposed in Congress that a committee be sent to the army to share with Washington "a kind of dictatorial power, in order to afford satisfaction to the army, and to arrange the great departments thereof." [36]

When the committee got to the camp at Morristown, New Jersey, it went to work busily but secretively. "Great things are in contemplation," wrote General Greene to Joseph Reed, "but the means of execution concealed." So far as Washington was concerned, Greene did not think "the great man" knew what was going on. "He has strange notions about the cause, and the obli-

[33] "Report of the Committee on the expediency of a Continental Paper Currency," Force: *American Archives*, 4th ser., II, 1262–4.

[34] Sparks: *Morris*, I, 234. Robert Morris wrote to Hamilton, 2 July 1782, that "what remains of the war, being only a war of finance, solid arrangements of finance must necessarily terminate favorably. . . ." *Works* (Hamilton ed.), I, 285.

[35] 16 April 1782, Balch Papers (Bancroft Transcripts), NYPL.

[36] Philip Schuyler to Hamilton, Philadelphia, 8 April 1780, *Works* (Hamilton ed.), I, 135–6.

gation there is for people to sacrifice fortune and reputation in support thereof, if it shall become necessary for the common good. Little does he know of the feelings, and great principles which govern human nature in the wide field of politics. I shall not combat his opinions; but leave time and future events to effect what reason will have no influence upon." [37]

As things grew worse during the summer "the necessity of appointing General Washington sole dictator of America" was talked of more and more.[38] The only way to stop such talk was to get money from the states and this the opposition realized. Or else, as one of them said, "we must expect frequent maggots about creating omnipotencies." [39] "We must have money at all adventures. Nothing else is wanting to raise us again into reputation, and prevent stupid plans of creating absolute dictators to get supplies without paying for them." [40]

The opposition thus aroused was strong enough to bring the congressional committee back from camp. But once back in Congress John Mathews of the committee made a motion to give to Washington absolute power to choose his own means to bring an army of 25,000 men into the field, to clothe, arm and equip that army, to appoint all its officers and to try them and sentence them; to call on any state militia he might want. In addition to all this he was to be vested with power "to do all such other matters and things as shall appear to him necessary to promote the welfare of these United States," and to draw on the treasury of the United States for such sums of money as he needed to carry out such powers. Furthermore Congress should agree to ratify everything he did. The only limitation on this breath-taking proposal was that the powers would end 1 December 1781.[41]

The revolutionary group still in Congress fought this whole scheme with all their old-time fervor and shelved it without even

[37] Morristown, 20 May 1780, Joseph Reed Papers, NYHS. Washington wanted more power for Congress but there is considerable doubt that he wanted the role of dictator. See Joseph Reed to General Greene, 8 Sept. 1780, Joseph Reed Papers, NYHS. Greene's preferences are indicated by a letter to him from James Varnum, 26 March 1780, *Magazine of History*, XXIII (1916), 246–7.

[38] Ezekiel Cornell to Gov. William Greene of Rhode Island, 1 Aug. 1780, Burnett, V, 305.

[39] James Lovell to Elbridge Gerry, 5 Sept. 1780, ibid., V, 361–2.

[40] James Lovell to Samuel Holten, 5 Sept. 1780, ibid., V, 362–3.

[41] James Lovell to Elbridge Gerry, 20 Nov. 1780, ibid., V, 451–2.

submitting it to a committee. Mathews was given such a verbal beating as he had never experienced before. He declared that, "such an insult I never saw offered to any member of Congress," and that although he had heard a good deal and had seen something of "the rancour of these demagogues," he had never seen it rise to such a height.[42]

The attempt to do anything within the framework of Congress thus failed for the moment, but on the outside there was even more activity. A convention met at Boston with merchants and lawyers from Massachusetts, Connecticut, and New Hampshire in attendance. Rhode Island appointed commissioners who did not arrive. The delegates were instructed by their state governments to advise and consult on the problem of winning the war. They met and resolved that the balance of state troops requested by Congress should be raised; that state purchasing agents should correspond with one another as to purchases and prices paid; that the states should transport to places directed their own quotas of supplies for the army. They should empower the chief American officer with the French troops to prevent frauds by provision sellers, and to induce people to bring plentifully and sell reasonably. The states should repeal embargoes on articles transported by land. They should pay the old continental debt by taxation as far as possible. They should take measures for the support of new bills. They should issue no more money of their own. The soldiers and sailors of one state falling sick in another should be cared for by local selectmen and overseers who should charge the expense to the state to which the sick belonged. The public credit and the powers of Congress should be fixed on a solid foundation and "the important national concerns of the United States be under the superintendency and direction of one supreme head. . . ." The states should confederate with whatever states were willing. Proper boards and officers should be established by Congress for the regulation of the several departments so that proper estimates of public wants could be made and enough money provided by the states or by foreign loans. In case Congress did not take steps to fill magazines and raise troops by January 1781, the states should do so anyway. Finally, in order to secure uniformity, it was recommended that the commissioners meet again at Hartford

[42] To Washington, 15 Sept. 1780, ibid., V, 372–4.

in November and that New York and other states be invited to join them there.[43]

The resolutions of the Boston convention met with hearty approval in New York. Some members of the legislature were for "appointing a dictator, with a vice dictator in each state, invested with all the powers conferred formerly by the Roman people on theirs." General Schuyler fully expected to go to Hartford "with instructions to propose that a dictator should be appointed." [44]

The Hartford convention of November did not name names, as Schuyler and others were doing in their letters, but it did urge that Washington be given power to collect supplies from the states and that Congress be given the power of taxation in order to pay the interest on the public debt. It declared that the lack of coercive power was the greatest defect in the "general government of the continent." To remedy this the idea of implied powers was set forth. The powers of Congress had never been defined, said the convention, but there was a "necessarily implied compact" among the states at the beginning of the war. From this it "may be certainly inferred that Congress was vested with every power essential to the common defense. . . ." However, the convention was willing to waive argument on this point. The important thing was to exercise power now, and though the idea might seem harsh, a weak and inefficient government could never answer the ends of society. These ends the convention defined as defense against foreign invasion.[45]

Such ideas were startling to men like James Warren, who wrote to Sam Adams:

> If one of them [the resolutions] does not astonish you I have forgot my political catechism. Surely history will not be credited when it shall record that a convention of delegates from the four New England states and from the next to them met at Hartford in the year 1780 and in the height of our contest for public liberty and security solemnly resolved to recommend to their several states to vest the military with civil powers of an extraordinary kind and where their own interest is concerned, no

[43] Franklin B. Hough, ed.: *Proceedings of a Convention of Delegates From Several of the New England States, Held at Boston, August 3–9, 1780. . . .* (Albany, 1867), 35–52.

[44] Schuyler to Hamilton, Poughkeepsie, 10, 16 Sept. 1780, *Works* (Hamilton ed.), I, 182–3, 184–5.

[45] "Proceedings at a Convention . . . holden at Hartford . . . the eighth day of [November] . . . 1780," *Magazine of American History*, VIII (1882), 688–98.

less than a compulsive power over deficient states to oblige them by the point of a bayonet to furnish money and supplies for their own pay and support.[46]

The outstanding expression of the nationalists' political philosophy in 1780, the program they wanted, and the methods they were ready to use to establish themselves, came not from such conventions but from the pen of Alexander Hamilton. He presented his program of action in the form of a letter to James Duane, one of the most consistent nationalists, who was once more a member of Congress.

The root of evil, said Hamilton, is that Congress lacks the power to act upon the states collectively. To get around this fact he conjured up the idea that Congress should use "undefined powers." Such powers could be limited only by the object of the establishment of Congress. This object Hamilton defined as the freedom and independence of America. The Confederation should be ignored since it had not been ratified, and furthermore, it was defective because of the idea it contained of the "uncontrolled sovereignty in each state over its internal police. . . ." Congress must perform innumerable acts for the general good which would interfere with this power of the states.

There were two ways to get power. The first was to assume that Congress had once had and used discretionary power limited only by the end for which it had been organized. Hamilton was too realistic to suppose that such an assumption would be accepted by "the generality of Congress," and his second proposal showed that the nationalists had learned much from radical tactics. Hamilton proposed that a convention be called and that it be given power to draw up and adopt a new government without reference to Congress, the states, or the people. This government would be a "solid, coercive union" with "complete sovereignty" over the civil, military, and economic life of the thirteen states. Its economic power was to be assured by permanent revenues in the form of land taxes, poll taxes, duties on trade, and the ownership of all unoccupied western lands.

In the meantime Congress must take immediate steps to secure power. The committees in charge of foreign affairs, war, marine, trade, and finance must be replaced by single executives who should be "men of the first abilities, property, and char-

[46] Plymouth, 4 Dec. 1780, Samuel Adams Papers, NYPL.

acter, in the continent. . . ." Another step was for Congress to consolidate behind it the power of the army, which, like the creditors, Hamilton described as an "essential cement of the union. . . ." The army should be reformed. Hamilton said it was "a mob rather than an army; without clothing, without pay, without provisions, without morals, and without discipline." Congress could attach the army to it by providing clothing and by giving the officers half pay for life. "Congress would then have a solid basis of authority and consequence; for, to me, it is an axiom, that in our constitution, an army is essential to the American Union." [47] Hamilton's readiness to use the force provided by the creditors and the army to achieve political ends foreshadows the attempted *coup d'état* of 1783, and is of a piece with the willingness of some of the nationalists to use force to obtain their ends in 1787.[48]

By the end of 1780 the nationalist group was once more in a position to influence the working of the central government in a significant fashion. The stresses of that year gave them the political justification for return to power in the states where they had lost control or been weakened. The war was going from bad to worse as the British marched northward relentlessly. Paper finance was at last brought to an end. The army had to depend on specific supplies from the states, and these were inadequate. The demand for strong men and strong measures grew more and more plausible as the hopes of Americans grew darker and darker. Men of mercantile connections and interests now came to the fore in greater numbers than at any time since 1776. Congress and the states were poverty-stricken but men like Robert Morris had made fortunes out of the war. They controlled warehouses, goods, ships, credit, and good hard cash in abundance as a result of their privateering and the purchase and sale of war supplies to Congress and the states. Such men denounced their political enemies in power as corrupt and inefficient, and the voters, who saw the

[47] Hamilton to Duane, 3 Sept. 1780, *Works* (Hamilton ed.), I, 150–68.

[48] See the letter of Benjamin Rush to Richard Price, Philadelphia, 2 June 1787, "Richard Price Letters," MHS *Proceedings*, 2nd ser., XVII (1903), 367–9. Rush said that time, necessity, and reason would wear down the opposition to the constitution when it appeared, but that if those failed "*force* will not be wanting to carry it into execution, for not only all the wealth but all the military men of our country (associated in the Society of the Cincinnati) are in favor of a wise and efficient government."

surface but not the deeper issues, voted into office the men of property and power who had been successful, as the men in office had not. In Pennsylvania the "Republican" party dominated by the Philadelphia merchants won the elections in the fall of 1780. In 1780 Massachusetts got a constitution which threw much power into the hands of the coastal merchants. In 1781 Thomas Jefferson was replaced as governor of Virginia by Thomas Nelson who had opposed independence, and above all, any change in the established order in Virginia.

These changes were reflected in Congress where the Lee-Adams leadership was at last fading. New men came to Congress and nationalist leaders were re-elected. Richard Henry Lee went back to Virginia and for the next two years the tone of the Virginia delegation in Congress was set by James Madison who, in this period of his life, was ardent in behalf of centralized power. James M. Varnum, an out-and-out believer in dictatorship, came to Congress from Rhode Island. James Duane and Robert R. Livingston were back in Congress by 1780. Alexander Hamilton came in 1781; James Wilson returned in 1783. General John Sullivan from New Hampshire was no follower of the Lee-Adams group either, so that by the fall of 1780 Harrison was able to report to Hamilton that "our friends Sullivan and Carroll . . . have contributed immeasurably, by their independent conduct, to destroy the Eastern Alliance. . . ." [49]

As the complexion and leadership of Congress thus changed, the attitude of the one-time minority changed too. Where once they had damned Congress for its weakness, they now thought it a respectable body. Now in power themselves, they declared that party spirit had been forced to hide its head, and that public-spirited men devoted to the public interest were now at the helm.[50]

"Leonidas," in the *Pennsylvania Gazette*, extolled the "Patriots" now in power. He blamed most of the existing evils on the Patriots of 1775 and 1776 who, he said, had more of passion than of principle. Our troubles have been left us by "the disaffection of some of them, by the timidity of others, and by the ignorance of them all." The men who began the present revolution may be compared

[49] 27 Oct. 1780, *Works* (Hamilton ed.), I, 192–3.

[50] Ezekiel Cornell to William Greene, 29 Aug. 1780, Burnett, V, 347, and by way of contrast see Hamilton to Governor George Clinton, 12 March 1778, Henry Cabot Lodge, ed.: *The Works of Alexander Hamilton* (2nd ed., 12 vols., New York, 1903), IX, 127–31.

with the light infantry who gave notice of the enemy's approach but who fell back when the battle thickened. The heavy troops have now come forward and have turned the battle from the gates. Thus in heavy metaphor did the nationalists find support in the public press as well as in legislatures.[51] They had, in a measure, the acquiescence if not the approval of some of the most ardent of the believers in the sovereignty of the states. Even men like Sam Adams could say that "we have often a choice of difficulties." Therefore he accepted such schemes as a permanent army and the proposal for a heavy tax by Congress.[52]

Yet they did not change their opinions of their enemies. General Gates urged Sam Adams to stay in Congress for if "our best Republicans quit the field to the rapacious graspers of power and profit, what will become of that liberty we have suffered so much to obtain; proud aristocratic men and avaricious merchants are the last of mankind, to whose hands our government should at this critical hour be committed." [53] Gates was perhaps insincere for he played fair with every side, but he did express the views of the revolutionary group, now losing control, a loss for which they were partly to blame. They had not used their influence to strengthen the hand of Congress where it was needed the most, so fearful were they of the loss of the principle of state sovereignty. Too late they learned the lesson that the only way to save a greater part of that autonomy was through a partial surrender of power. When the grant of power did come, it was to do away, in legal terms at least, with most of what they had fought for since before the Revolution.

[51] *Pennsylvania Gazette*, 17 July 1782.
[52] To Samuel Cooper, 7 Nov. 1780, Burnett, V, 440.
[53] 1 July 1779, Samuel Adams Papers, NYPL.

3
The Politics of Demobilization

The Nationalists, Congress, and the Army, 1781–3

IN 1781 the nationalist group bid for power within the framework of the Articles of Confederation. It is significant that talk of revolutionary action died down as they gained control of Congress. "The day is at length arrived," wrote James Duane to Washington, "when dangers and distresses have opened the eyes of the people and they perceive the want of a common head to draw forth in some just proportion the resources of the several branches of the federal union. They perceive that the deliberate power exercised by states individually over the acts of Congress must terminate in the common ruin; and the legislature, however reluctantly, must resign a portion of their authority to the national representative, or cease to be legislatures." [1] General Sullivan was more precise when he declared that "Congress and assemblies begin to rouse from their slumber and individuals are now alarmed for the public safety who have for years past been employed in amassing wealth." [2] And John Mathews, who had wanted to make Washington dictator in the fall of 1780, now wanted Congress to be given dictatorial powers by the states.[3]

Their program was stated clearly by James Duane. "There are," he wrote Washington, "some political regulations . . . I have exceedingly at heart and which are now drawn near to a

[1] 29 Jan. 1781, Burnett, V, 551.

[2] To Washington, 29 Jan. 1781, ibid., V, 548.

[3] To Nathanael Greene, 20 May 1781, ibid., VI, 93–4.

conclusion . . . the principal measures to which I allude are the establishment of executives or ministers in the departments of finance, war, the marine and foreign affairs, the accomplishment of the Confederation: and procuring to Congress an augmentation of power and permanent revenues for carrying on the war." [4]

This program was carried out with smoothness and precision. The ideas expressed in newspaper essays, private letters, and the Hartford convention, were adopted in some detail. For years the nationalist group had insisted that the various departments should be headed by single individuals outside Congress rather than by standing committees of members of Congress. The revolutionary group had insisted on committees. It was basic in their political thinking that power could not be trusted to individuals for any length of time. Their fear of dictatorship was very real and was based partly on their reading of history and partly on their knowledge of the desires and intentions of the nationalists. Their convictions were sincere for they put limitations on their own officeholding. Most state elections were annual. No man could be a member of Congress for more than three out of any six years.

By 1781 the revolutionary group was outnumbered and worn down by defeat. The best it could do was to fight for some of the offices created.[5]

On the 10th of January 1781 Congress created the "Department of Foreign Affairs" with a "Secretary for Foreign Affairs." He was to run the department and handle correspondence with foreign ministers and American emissaries abroad; attend Congress to keep in touch with domestic affairs, and to explain the reports he might make from time to time. Here was the beginning of a form of ministerial responsibility, since the secretary was elected by Congress, held office at its pleasure, and must explain his actions before it. In February, Congress established the post of "Secretary of War." He was to make reports and keep records of the armed forces, prepare estimates of supplies needed, and transmit the orders of Congress to the land forces of the United States. It was decided that the secretary should be a general officer of the army. On the same day Congress established the "Department of Finance." This became the keystone in the arch

[4] 29 Jan. 1781, ibid., V, 551.

[5] The best account of the establishment of these offices is in Jennings B. Sanders: *Evolution of Executive Departments of the Continental Congress, 1774–1789* (Chapel Hill, 1935).

of "executivism" under Robert Morris, who in time became the all-powerful force in every department, in Congress, in the army, and wielded more power in the United States than any man had yet done.

In the election of men to fill the posts thus created, the old revolutionary group made a last stand. Seven months passed before Robert R. Livingston was elected secretary of foreign affairs. His chief opponent for the post was Arthur Lee of Virginia, brother of Richard Henry and William Lee, arch foe of Franklin, Morris, and the whole nationalist group of the middle states. At first he got the votes of more states than Livingston. On a second vote his own state was induced to "throw away" its vote. New Jersey changed its vote and Smith of Pennsylvania was carried in on his sick bed to swing his delegation in favor of Livingston. Behind the scenes was the hand of the Chevalier de la Luzerne, the minister of France, who took entire credit for the victory as he did later for running the affairs of the office. Luzerne, like Vergennes, had no use for the independent Lee-Adams group and he spared nothing, including the cash of his royal master, to elect Livingston. Bribery of and loans to members of Congress by a foreign power were effective in the election of the first secretary of state of the United States.

It took eight months to elect a secretary of war. The leading candidate at first was General John Sullivan of New Hampshire, but he was bitterly opposed by Sam Adams and his cohorts for they looked upon Sullivan as a traitor to their cause, as indeed he was. He had borrowed money from Luzerne who was highly purposeful in the making of such loans. It was not until the fall of 1781 that Congress finally made a choice. Sullivan had dropped from sight and Generals Knox, Greene, and Lincoln were nominated. To everybody's surprise, Benjamin Lincoln got the job. His generalship in the South had been so bad that the British had captured his whole army without any particular effort on his part to save it. In fact, the only successful military exploit he ever engaged in was during Shays's Rebellion when he marched mercenary troops against his fellow citizens in western Massachusetts. His conquest of the disorganized farmers who lived there was an unquestioned victory.

Despite an undercurrent of opposition Morris was elected unanimously. He said he did not want the post and he laid down certain conditions that Congress must meet before he would accept it. He must be allowed to continue his own private business; he must appoint all officers in the department; he must have absolute power to appoint and dismiss anyone having anything to do with the spending of money. Unless he had such powers he insisted that "the business of reformation" could not be managed. Furthermore, he demanded control of the financial affairs of the quartermaster, commissary, and medical departments of the army. Morris's supporters insisted that public necessity demanded so sweeping a grant of power, and Congress finally agreed to all the conditions. Morris himself denied that he liked power for its own sake, while his friends hailed him as the savior of the country.

His enemies did not agree. They had opposed his business practices since the beginning of the war; they opposed him now; they continued to fight him with ever greater violence until his resignation in 1784. They saw in him the spearhead of a movement to overthrow the federal government and to establish a dictatorship. His fulsome protestations of disinterested patriotism did not convince his enemies, nor even many of his friends. In fact only his later biographers, who have lacked both the knowledge and realism of his contemporaries, have ever accepted Morris at his own evaluation. They, too, are the creators of the myth that Robert Morris financed the American Revolution, a myth absurd if for no other reason than the fact that he did not take office until the Revolution was virtually over. Throughout the war he made money as an owner of privateers and as an international merchant, selling goods at high prices on both sides of the Atlantic. At the end of the Confederation, it was a matter of newspaper comment that he still owed money to the United States. Here commentary coincided with fact, for the books of the treasury in 1790 showed him to be the government's largest individual debtor.[6]

Morris did not take office when elected in February 1781. He was a member of the Pennsylvania legislature, then controlled by his group, and he wanted to stay there until legal tender laws were repealed and others providing for taxation in specie were passed.

Meanwhile, it was obvious that the new paper money plan proposed by Congress in March 1780 had failed. Congress finally gave

[6] War Records, Army Branch, Revolutionary War Documents, no. 28,793, National Archives.

up paper money as a means of financing itself and began to struggle with the problem of getting an independent income. Congressional committees met, talked, reported, and then met to talk and report again. Scheme after scheme was proposed. In November 1780 a long committee report indicated the various ideas afloat. It was suggested that Congress call on the people to lend at interest all the coined silver and gold and plate they could spare. Some argued that if such metal could be gotten, it should be deposited in a bank. This bank should be set up by Congress which would appoint its manager. The bank would issue paper money backed by the metal so deposited. Others objected to such a bank. Still others suggested that there be several banks. Most agreed that Congress should ask the states for an impost law which would allow it to levy duties on imports for the purpose of carrying on the war and paying the debts of the United States. One member went so far as to insist that Congress should control all ports. One other potential source of revenue was the sale of western lands, once they were ceded to Congress.[7]

The result of these discussions and of the desperation of Congress was the adoption of an amendment to the Confederation which was submitted to the states for ratification. This was the "Impost of 1781." In February, Congress asked to be allowed to levy a duty of five per cent on the value of all goods imported into the United States. The revenue was to be applied to the discharge of the principal and interest on debts arising from the war. The amount asked for was limited, but the grant was to be of indefinite duration.[8] Twelve states ratified in a short time. Rhode Island alone, in November of 1782, flatly refused to do so.

Meanwhile, the Articles of Confederation were ratified but the nationalists were not overjoyed. Hamilton declared that it would be a happy event if the people did not believe that the Confederation gave Congress enough power and refused to give it more. If that happened ratification would be an evil: "the republic is sick and wants powerful remedies." [9] A writer in the *Pennsylvania Gazette* chimed in with the same sentiment. "These covenants or confederations on paper, are of no consequence, unless they are supported by virtue and honor." He went on to argue

[7] Proceedings and Observations of the Committee of Finance, Nov. 1780, Burnett, V, 464–72.

[8] *Journals*, XIX, 102–3, 110, 112–3.

[9] To ——— ———, Headquarters, 7 Feb. 1781, *Works* (Lodge ed.), IX, 230–1.

in a series of essays that Congress was bad and getting worse.[10] Even sober Joseph Jones agreed that the Articles were defective, that "amendments and additional powers are necessary. . . ." [11]

The result was that as soon as the Articles were ratified, a committee of three outstanding nationalists—James M. Varnum, James Duane, and James Madison—was appointed to prepare a plan to give Congress the power for "carrying into execution in the several states all acts or resolutions passed agreeably to the Articles of Confederation." [12] The report they brought in was clearer evidence of their desires than of the political realities of the moment, for, short of revolutionary action, the Articles of Confederation could not be changed except by unanimous consent of the states. The committee used the idea of implied powers differently than Hamilton and the Hartford convention had used it the year before. They insisted that the Confederation itself gave Congress "a general and implied power" to carry the Articles into effect, but that since there was "no determinate and particular provision" to that effect, there needed to be a specific amendment. The amendment they proposed would allow Congress to use the army and navy to enforce its decisions upon the states, seize their vessels, and prohibit their trade. Seven years before, Great Britain had tried this in Massachusetts. The memories of living men were short, but not that short. The report was handed over to another committee and suppressed. Eventually that committee asked to be discharged on the interesting ground that any exposition of the Confederation would be coextensive with its subject. If they omitted to enumerate any congressional powers it would at once be an argument against their existence. It was soon enough to enumerate such powers after they had been used. In other words, use power and argue about it afterwards.[13]

But from 1781 to 1783 such doings and resolutions in Congress were not as important as those of a single man, Robert Morris. It was around him, his satellites, and their activities that the

[10] "An Independent American" to the People of America, *Pennsylvania Gazette*, 14, 28 March, 4, 11 April 1781. Contemporaries thought the writer was Sir James Jay who was venting his spleen because Congress had refused to offer him a job. See Thomas Bee to [John Laurens], 28 March 1781, Emmet Coll., no. 1206, NYPL.

[11] To Washington, 27 Feb. 1781, *Letters of Joseph Jones of Virginia, 1777–1787* (Washington, 1889), 70–2.

[12] 6 March, *Journals*, XIX, 236.

[13] PCC, no. 24, ff. 49–51, LC; *Journals*, XX, 469–71, 773.

government really revolved. Morris's power was described by Joseph Reed when he said that "Mr. Morris was inexorable, Congress at mercy" and since his appointment "the business of that august body has been extremely simplified, Mr. Morris having relieved them from all business of deliberation or executive difficulty with which money is in any respect connected, and they are now very much at leisure to read dispatches, return thanks, pay and receive compliments, &c. For form's sake some things go thither to receive a sanction, but it is the general opinion that it is form only." [14]

While Morris had been elected in February and accepted the post in May 1781, he did not take over the office officially until September, about a month before Yorktown. Meanwhile, Congress handed over one portion of sovereign power after another to the superintendent of finance. In May it authorized him to establish a bank; in June it placed in his hands all the money borrowed in France during 1781 and all the unsold bills of exchange; in July it gave him power to import and export goods on the account of the United States. In July and later, Congress placed the whole department of marine under his control. At the same time he was authorized to supply the army by means of private contracts and to dispose of specific supplies received from the states as he saw fit. In October he was authorized to correspond with the foreign ministers of the United States, and thus, in effect, a separate department of foreign affairs was set up under his control.[15]

For all practical purposes Morris was made dictator by Congress. Joseph Reed called him a "pecuniary dictator" and said that the qualities required for the job were "ability of mind, some money in hand, and a private credit for more." [16] As superintendent of finance and private business man at one and the same time, Morris's chief concern was with providing Congress with funds. His first proposal was the organization of a bank. There had been much talk of such a bank, with the Bank of England as an

[14] Reed to General Greene, Nov. 1781, William B. Reed, ed.: *Life and Correspondence of Joseph Reed* (2 vols., Philadelphia, 1847), II, 374–5; Joseph Reed Papers, NYHS. See also General William Irvine to Walter Stewart, Carlisle, 26 Aug. 1782, Walter Stewart Papers, NYHS.

[15] *Journals*, XIX, 290–1, 432–3; XX, 545–8, 597–8, 721, 723, 724–5; XXI, 943, 1070.

[16] Reed: *Reed*, II, 374.

example. Some men wanted a bank owned and operated by the government. Morris's plan involved government support but not government control, except so far as he personally was the government.

Three days after he accepted office he presented his scheme for the Bank of North America to Congress. The bank's stock was to consist of $400,000 in specie divided into shares of $400. When the full amount was subscribed, Congress would give the bank a charter, and it was to operate under close supervision of the superintendent of finance. The bank would carry on private business but would also loan money in the form of bank notes to Congress. Thus it would provide the circulating medium of the country, not Congress and the states, which had done so from 1775 to 1780. The beginning was to be a small one, but in time Morris hoped that it would be expanded greatly and that the stock would some day be £400,000 or more.

Morris was convinced that the bank, once established, would be the first really sound achievement of the Revolution, an attitude, to say the least, divergent from that of the founding fathers of 1776. In a circular letter to men of property urging them to buy shares, he expressed the hope that the bank would last as long as the United States, be as useful in peace as in war, and predicted that in the end it might "prove the means of saving the liberties, lives, and property of the virtuous part of America." Once started, the benefits would be so obvious that it would be necessary to appeal only "to the interest of mankind which in most cases will do more than their patriotism. . . ." [17] To individuals he was more specific. To one Robert Smith he promised dividends of from eight to ten per cent. To John Jay he expressed the hope that in time much of the private property of America would be dependent on the bank.[18] William Duer wrote Morris that his letters to the public had not been very specific as to the advantages of the bank. He agreed that this would have been imprudent, but he assumed that Morris was "more minute" in his explanations "to the principal gentlemen of monied interest, in the different states." [19] Morris had done this and more. He explained to Jay

[17] 11 June 1781, Francis Wharton, ed.: *The Revolutionary Diplomatic Correspondence of the United States* (6 vols., Washington, 1889), IV, 494–5.

[18] Ibid., IV, 581–4, 567.

[19] Robert A. East: *Business Enterprise in the American Revolutionary Era* (New York, 1938), 289.

that one strong motive was "to unite the several states more closely together in one general money connection and indissolubly to attach many powerful individuals to the cause of our country by the strong principle of self-love and the immediate sense of private interest." [20]

Despite such appeals it was difficult to interest men of property in the bank. Morris got his partners and friends to help sell the stock. They sent agents to the army but they met with little success, for the officers and even Washington were too poor to buy shares. Morris took his newly founded Bank of Pennsylvania into the scheme by exchanging its shares for shares in the new bank. Agents abroad were urged to get specie loans. Still not enough money could be raised to start the bank.

Then in September, John Laurens returned from Europe with nearly a half million dollars in cash he had borrowed for Congress. Morris, as superintendent of finance, had absolute control of this money. He had to spend some of it for other purposes, but he used a quarter million dollars of it to buy 633 shares of the bank's stock. At last the conditions had been met. Congress passed an ordinance chartering the bank on the last day of 1781.[21] The bank was thus made possible by funds borrowed by Congress but it was entirely under the control of a close-knit group of Morris's friends and partners. Thomas Willing, William Bingham, and John Swanwick were his partners, and William Smith and Jeremiah Wadsworth were close business and political allies. At one time this small group held more than half the bank's stock.

There was as much doubt in 1781 that Congress had the power to incorporate the bank as there was ten years later. When the request was first made for a charter, the prospect was so distant that Congress made the promise without too much concern about its propriety. In the fall of 1781 the issue was again raised: nowhere in the Articles of Confederation was such a right given to Congress. The promises of one Congress were binding on another, argued supporters of the bank. More to the point was Morris's argument that without the bank he could not pay the army. So Congress yielded, "some of those who voted in the affirmative thinking themselves obliged by the engagement in May, others contending for a constitutional power in these cases, and others

[20] Wharton, IV, 562–3.
[21] *Journals*, XXI, 1186–90.

assenting to it from absolute necessity."[22] And the consciences of those who doubted the power of Congress were salved by an appeal to the states to incorporate the bank.

The Bank of North America rendered important services to the United States during the years Morris was superintendent of finance. From 1782 to 1784, Morris the superintendent borrowed a total of about a million and a quarter dollars from Morris the banker. In addition, the bank discounted bills of exchange drawn on Morris as superintendent. In time the directors of the bank decided that enough money had been loaned to Congress. So Morris, as financier, sold $200,000 par value of the government's shares in the bank for $300,000 and reduced the debt by that amount. The next year he sold the remainder to Dutch investors. By the time he retired from office the debt of Congress to the bank had been paid and Congress was no longer a stockholder. In that year, 1784, the bank declared dividends of fourteen per cent on its stock.[23]

The bank never assumed the great place Morris hoped for it, either as an economic power or as a supporter of centralized government. Its failure was in part due to the return to power of its political enemies, both in Congress and in the state of Pennsylvania, in part due to too heavy loans to some of its friends, and in part to the failure of the nationalists to secure permanent revenues for Congress. They hoped that a permanent revenue, pledged to pay the interest on the national debt, would center the political and economic interests of important Americans on the central government rather than scatter them among the states. The bank, acting as agent for the government, would be the practical focus of political and economic power. Since the nationalists of 1781 had no more intention of paying the national debt than the "Federalists" of the 1790's, they looked forward to a long and profitable future.

Yet for a time it seemed that the nationalists would succeed. Morris put steady pressure on state governors and state legislatures for the grant of the Impost of 1781. The necessity was real, and by the fall of 1782 all the states except Rhode Island had ratified. At first it seemed that she might fall in line, for her delegates, James M. Varnum and Ezekiel Cornell, were both army

[22] Madison to Edmund Pendleton, 8 Jan. 1782, Burnett, VI, 289–90; Virginia Delegates to the Governor of Virginia, 8 Jan. 1782, ibid., VI, 288–9.

[23] Joseph S. Davis: *Essays in the Earlier History of American Corporations* (2 vols., Cambridge, Mass., 1917), II, 36–40.

men and nationalist-minded. Then in the summer of 1782 Rhode Island underwent a political revolution and sent new men to Congress: David Howell, Jonathan Arnold, and John Collins. Howell in particular was in the Sam Adams tradition, and he became a leader in the war against the "aristocratical schemes" of Robert Morris and his followers.

All the forces of propaganda at the command of the Morris group were brought to bear on Rhode Island. Morris secretly hired Thomas Paine to write letters against the iniquities of Rhode Island and these appeared in the newspapers.[24] Morris himself told the governor of Rhode Island that the impost was the only suitable form of taxation and that the United States had to have an income in order to borrow money abroad.

To this the Rhode Islanders replied that Congress had borrowed and was borrowing money abroad without the impost. And why not accept Virginia's cession of her western claims and sell the land? Congress was asking Rhode Island to give up her revenue from impost duties while other states were selling their western lands. Above all, argued Rhode Island, the impost was unconstitutional. The states would have no control over the income it would produce. The term of its duration was unlimited. Its collection would be an entering wedge for the central government to act directly on individuals, whereas by the Confederation it could act only upon the states. This issue was thus clearly joined and recognized by most of the participants. The United States had a federal government. The nationalists wanted a national government.

Morris found it difficult to answer Rhode Island so he took refuge in what were, for him, uncommonly abstruse arguments. He told the governor of Rhode Island, who had insisted that even the request for the impost amendment was contrary to the Confederation, that "if a thing be neither wrong nor forbidden it must be admissible"; that the requisition was not forbidden and certainly not wrong for "it can not be wrong to do that which one is obliged to do, be the act what it may." And even if one admitted that the request was contrary to the Confederation, the Confederation itself was created by general consent and by general

[24] These have been printed in Harry Hayden Clark, ed.: *Six New Letters of Thomas Paine: Being Pieces on the Five Per Cent Duty Addressed to the Citizens of Rhode Island* (Madison, 1939). Only Gouverneur Morris, Robert R. Livingston, and Washington were told of this.

consent might be altered. "The requisition therefore, if complied with, will by that very compliance become constitutional." [25]

Congress decided to send a delegation to Rhode Island. Before the men got off, Rhode Island sent a flat refusal. The governor of the state enclosed the unanimous resolutions of the Rhode Island assembly. These declared that (1) the impost would be unequal, bearing hardest on the commercial states; (2) it was against the constitution of the state, introducing as it did, officers unaccountable to it; (3) by granting to Congress for an indefinite time an indefinite quantity of money, Congress would "become independent of their constituents; and so the proposed impost is repugnant to the liberty of the United States." [26]

Despite this refusal, the delegation set forth. After a half day's journey one of the men remarked casually that Virginia had repealed its ratification, whereupon the delegation at once started back to Philadelphia. There, they found that Madison had a private letter from Virginia which he now read to Congress. Soon official word was received from Governor Benjamin Harrison, an old business partner of Morris. He was bewildered by the act of repeal of which he had heard nothing until it was put before him after the assembly session. Other supporters of Morris among the Virginians were equally at a loss. Some thought that Arthur Lee might have been responsible for it, but he denied this, and it was admitted by his enemies that it was done too quietly for him to have had a hand in it. Edmund Randolph reported that he found it almost impossible to get any clear notion of the motives involved. Some men said the act of ratification had been passed without thought during the alarms of war; others that Congress should have revenue only as provided by the Confederation. The confusion was great, but the fact remained that Virginia had repealed her act. Randolph's only suggestion was that perhaps the previous approval of the impost had deprived "this state of the power of revocation, until Congress should release it from the grant." [27]

Virginia's repeal was a stunning blow to the nationalists. There was now no hope of forcing Rhode Island into line, much less

[25] 24 Oct. 1782, Wharton, V, 830–2.

[26] 30 Nov. 1782, *Journals*, XXIII, 788–9.

[27] To Madison, Richmond, 13 Dec. 1782, Madison Papers, LC. See also Governor Harrison to the Virginia Delegates, 4 Jan. 1783, Burnett, VII, 20, n. 19; Madison to Randolph, 22 Jan. [1783], 4 Feb. 1783, ibid., VII, 21–2, 31.

mighty Virginia. Their despair once more produced a plan for revolutionary action. The nationalists had realized ever since the battle of Yorktown that the end of the war would mean an end of their greatest hope for constitutional revolution. Their arguments for centralization and the supposed efficiency and economy that would result depended heavily on the continuation of the war, and they knew it. Shortly after Yorktown, Gouverneur Morris wrote General Greene that the acquisition of power by Congress was a difficult matter, but that "to reinforce the reasonings, to impress the arguments, and to sweeten the persuasions of the public servants, we have that great friend to sovereign authority, a foreign war." But if the war were to stop he said that he had little hope that the "government would acquire force."[28] Robert Morris was in precise agreement. He would welcome peace in order to be rid of his job, but if he were to speak as a Patriot, he would wish the war to continue until the central government could get more power.[29] Washington, too, was aware of this current of thought. He said that the continuation of the war might result in the realization of the centralized power which he had so long desired, but at the same time he hoped for peace.[30]

The failure of the Impost of 1781 and the approach of peace was a blow to such hopes. As plans failed, one by one the nationalists once more took refuge in talk of conventions. In July 1782 the New York legislature adopted a recommendation drafted by Hamilton for a national convention to give Congress both power and money.[31] Public creditors in New York held a meeting in September 1782 and talked of a creditors' convention for the state, and even of one for all the states.[32] Hamilton told Governor Clinton of New York that because Congress had the power to determine how much money should be paid into the

[28] Philadelphia, 24 Dec. 1781, Sparks: *Morris*, I, 239–40.

[29] To Matthew Ridley, 6 Oct. 1782, *The Confidential Correspondence of Robert Morris* (Stan. V. Henkels, Catalogue no. 1183), 41.

[30] To the Rev. William Gordon, 23 Oct. 1782, *Writings*, XXV, 287–8.

[31] Hamilton to Robert Morris, Poughkeepsie, 22 July 1782, *Works* (Lodge ed.), IX, 264–6.

[32] Hamilton to Robert Morris, 28 Sept. 1782, ibid., IX, 293. A meeting of lesser creditors is reported in *Pennsylvania Gazette*, 1 Jan. 1783. A group met at the house of Thomas Carpenter at East Bradford, Chester County, in November 1782, and protested the failure to pay interest and to liquidate their accounts for supplies furnished. They insisted that those in charge of public monies had embezzled them, and that state officers got too high salaries.

public treasury, it had the constitutional power of taxation.[33] Such arguments and theories reveal more of the desires and hopes of the men who used them than they do of the nature of the constitution which they tried to shape to their program.

But they did more than theorize and plan conventions. Some of them believed they had at hand the means, desperate though they were, of achieving their political ends. As we have seen, the discontent of the army mounted as the year 1782 wore on, with the result that a delegation of three officers headed by General Alexander McDougall was sent to Congress. When they arrived early in January 1783, they were involved in a scheme for uniting the army officers and the public creditors in a movement to establish by force what argument and persuasion had not achieved. Though the scheme was abortive, as we shall see, it revealed much of the opposing forces in the new nation. Within its limits are to be found the basic political divisions of the decade of the 1780's.

Peace, Finance, and Demobilization, 1783

The expectation of news of peace overshadowed most moves in Congress during the early part of 1783. For months only rumor told what was going on across the Atlantic, and suspense mounted ever higher. Would war continue? Should another campaign be planned, and if so, with what? What would be the effect of peace on the army, plans for finance, politics? On 11 March, Madison wrote that yet another week had passed and that there was no relief from the suspense—the latest official information was five weeks old. Then the very next morning Captain Barney arrived from France on the *Washington* with dispatches announcing the signing of the preliminaries on 30 November. The ship belonged to Robert Morris, and his bitter enemy Arthur Lee said that the sailors were not allowed to land and that Morris ordered the dispatches taken to him before they were delivered to Congress. Lee said that Congress had not yet heard from Morris but that "when his speculations are settled we shall be favored with the news." [34]

[33] 24 Feb. 1783, *Works* (Lodge ed.), IX, 315.
[34] To James Warren, 12 [March 1783], Burnett, VII, 77.

The relief from suspense was soon followed by a new fear and then anger at the peacemakers who had ignored the French. The war could not end until preliminaries between France and England had been signed. Many members of Congress thought the French would be angry, and that if the war continued the Americans would be left at the mercy of the British. It was therefore proposed to censure the commissioners and to inform the French of the displeasure of Congress. Meanwhile Washington was told the news confidentially in the hope that it would not get out, especially to the discontented army.

The idea of censure was soon squelched by the arrival of a ship on 23 March. It had been sent out by Lafayette with the news of the signing of the preliminary articles between France and England on 20 January. On 25 March this news got into the Philadelphia newspapers, although no official word had been received. But this came too, and on 11 April Congress proclaimed the end of hostilities.[35]

Once the terms of peace were published in the papers, the joy of the public was great indeed! The public celebration anticipated in Philadelphia was such that a "True Whig" pleaded with officials and the populace to restrain themselves during the course of the "illumination of the city." [36]

Public joy was soon tempered by concern over specific terms of the treaty. The item of debts owing British creditors stood first in the minds of many. In Philadelphia, "the property of the Whigs being in public funds," they could not realize cash on it, and they were afraid they would be ruined if they had to pay up immediately.[37] In Virginia there was opposition among the more radical, or at least more debt-ridden, citizenry. "Some ill digested minds are daily belching out crude invectives and determinations to oppose the collection of British debts," reported Edmund Randolph. The "moderates" deplored the article, but they declared they would abide by the treaty.[38] Such reactions were scattered, however, and it took time for the antagonisms engendered by the

[35] *Journals*, XXIV, 238–40. On the question of censure see for instance Madison to Edmund Randolph, 18 March 1783, Burnett, VII, 89–90.

[36] *Pennsylvania Gazette*, 9 April 1783.

[37] Elias Boudinot to Franklin, 28 April 1783, Burnett, VII, 152–3.

[38] To James Madison, Richmond, 15 May 1783, Madison Papers, LC; George Mason to [Col. William Cabell], 6 May 1783, Emmet Coll., no. 9540, NYPL.

treaty to become a serious political issue. Most people were delighted with independence and some were astounded by the size of the territory ceded to the United States.[39]

Meanwhile Congress continued to wrangle over finance, an argument given new fervor by "the memorial from the army." [40] Other public creditors had been growing ever more insistent that Congress do something for them. One member of Congress wrote that "Congress are, and have been exceedingly embarrassed by the urgent, and reiterated demands made upon them by the public creditors, holding certificates, and liquidated accounts." [41]

It was into this situation that General McDougall and his fellow officers walked early in January 1783, bearing the complaints of the army officers. Those who had rung loud changes on the need of congressional funds to fight the war and to pay the public creditors now bolstered the argument for "general funds" by pleading the case of the army, and the danger of mutiny if Congress did not secure such funds. The delegation from the army was given an official hearing before Congress, but it also engaged in unofficial meetings with some of the nationalist politicians, including Robert Morris, Gouverneur Morris, Alexander Hamilton, and James Wilson. Such men saw in the clamors of the creditors, and the discontent of the officers, an opportunity to unite the two groups to secure national revenue, and even, perhaps, the kind of government they had been unable to get by either constitutional amendment or interpretation.[42]

As a result of the unofficial negotiations, the army committee was convinced that it should throw in its lot with Congress rather than turn to the states for a settlement of accounts—a step which many officers were prepared to take.[43] A delegate was sent back

[39] William Paterson to his brother, 12 May 1783, William Paterson Papers (Bancroft Transcripts), NYPL.

[40] Madison to Edmund Randolph, 28 Jan. 1783, Burnett, VII, 25.

[41] Samuel Wharton to the Delaware Council, 6 Jan. 1783, ibid., VII, 2–4.

[42] There are but two accounts of this scheme worthy of attention. The oldest is that of George Bancroft: *History of the Formation of the Constitution of the United States of America* (2 vols., New York, 1882), I, ch. v, "A Plan to Force a Stronger Government." Within the limits of his materials Bancroft does a much better job than subsequent historians who have covered the same ground. The other account is that of John Corbin: *Two Frontiers of Freedom* (New York, 1940), ch. iii, "Fascism—1783."

[43] Gouverneur Morris to General Greene, 15 Feb. 1783, Sparks: *Morris*, I, 250–1.

to the army officers at Newburgh, apparently with instructions to keep Washington in the dark.[44] General McDougall was perfectly frank in reporting the situation to General Knox. He listed all the difficulties in the way of securing a settlement and then asked: "Under these apprehensions, as well as others of general concern to the Confederacy, what if it should be proposed to unite the influence of Congress with that of the army and the public creditors to obtain permanent funds for the United States which will promise most ultimate security to the army?" [45] Meanwhile Gouverneur Morris was predicting, prematurely but revealingly, that "much of convulsion will ensue" and that it "must terminate in giving to government that power, without which government is but a name." No grant of funds would be made by the states, he said, unless the army united with the other public creditors to obtain it.[46] To General Knox he wrote that the only thing the army could do was to unite with creditors of every kind, both foreign and domestic, and urge the granting of permanent funds to Congress. "The army may now influence the legislatures and if you will permit me a metaphor from your own profession, after you have carried the post the public creditors will garrison it for you." [47] Another man, signing himself "Brutus," wrote Knox that the army should prepare for the worst that could happen to it.[48] Knox declared that if promises to the army were kept, the soldiers would return to their homes, "the lambs and bees of the community," but if they were disbanded before a settlement, they would be so stung by ingratitude as to "become the tigers and wolves." [49]

Arthur Lee told Sam Adams that "the terror of a mutinying army is played off with considerable efficacy." [50] James Madison

[44] John Armstrong, jr. to General Gates, Philadelphia, 29 April 1783, Burnett, VII, 155, n. 3. This letter, written after the failure of the scheme, predicts that civil war will follow.

[45] 9 Jan. 1783, ibid., VII, 14, n. 2. See also McDougall's letter of 19 Feb., ibid., VII, 50, n. 3, and McDougall and Ogden to Knox, 8 Feb., ibid., VII, 35–6, n. 3.

[46] Morris to John Jay, 1 Jan. 1783, Sparks: *Morris*, I, 249.

[47] 7 Feb. 1783, Knox Papers, MHS.

[48] 12 Feb. 1783, Knox Papers, MHS. "Brutus" appears to have been General McDougall and he kept Knox fully informed. See William Johnson: *Sketches of the Life and Correspondence of Nathanael Greene* (2 vols., Charleston, 1822), II, 394, n.

[49] To General Lincoln, 3 March, Knox Papers, MHS.

[50] 29 Jan. 1783, Burnett, VII, 27–8.

reported the gossip in more detail: the discontents and designs of the army were growing more serious daily; it was whispered that they would not lay down their arms until justice was done, and that a public declaration saying so would be made; it was said that Washington was losing his influence with the army and that there was a plan to put some "less scrupulous" guardian in his place.[51]

Despite such gossip, and far more of it went on in Philadelphia than in the army, the key figure in any plan, however vague, was Washington. Hamilton undertook to sound him out but he did so circuitously. Washington's reactions were not to be predicted in spite of his reiterated demands for a stronger central government. Hamilton said that the army could expect little help from Congress; that it would have to support itself if the war went on; and to continue to support itself to secure justice if peace were declared. Only Washington could keep a suffering army in bounds. He should take direction of the army's efforts to obtain redress, and he should endeavor to retain the confidence of the army without losing that of the people. Hamilton insinuated that Washington was suspected of not being sufficiently interested in the welfare of the army. He concluded by saying that the "great *desideratum* . . . is the establishment of general funds, which alone can do justice to the creditors of the United States. . . . In this the influence of the army, properly directed, may co-operate." [52]

Washington refused to accept the responsibility. He refused to believe that the discontent of the army was as serious as the politicians in Congress said it was. He said flatly that he did not believe the army would exceed "the bounds of reason and moderation, notwithstanding the prevailing sentiment in the army is, that the prospect of compensation for past services will terminate with the war." [53] And finally he charged that the whole affair was a plot of politicians in Philadelphia, a charge that was sound, for the army officers alone would not have planned, or even dreamed of carrying out such a scheme, nor had that been their intention when they sent the delegation of three to Congress.[54]

[51] To Edmund Randolph, 25 Feb. 1783, ibid., VII, 57–8.

[52] 7 Feb. 1783, *Works* (Lodge ed.), IX, 310–3.

[53] To Hamilton, 4 March 1783, *Writings*, XXVI, 185–8.

[54] To Joseph Jones, 12 March 1783, ibid., XXVI, 213–6; to Hamilton, 12 March, ibid., XXVI, 216–8. Once the plot had failed, Hamilton denied that he had ever contemplated the use of force, although he admitted that he considered it would be well to unite the army and the creditors. To Washington, 17 March, *Works* (Lodge ed.), IX, 326.

Washington was either unaware how far the plans had gone among his officers at Newburgh, or else he chose to ignore them until anonymous petitions were circulated. These urged the officers to refuse to fight if the war should continue and to refuse to lay down their arms if peace should be declared, unless their accounts were settled. Washington then took charge, and in a dramatic speech to the officers he defeated the scheme, for without him and the officers who were sure to follow him, nothing could be done.[55]

The army discontent and the political schemes that led to the climax at Newburgh gave new urgency to the debates over financial policy in Congress. The army delegation had demanded an advance on back pay, some provision for the payment of the remainder due, and above all, some settlement of the promise of half pay for life to the officers, which had been made in the dark days of 1780. Most members of Congress agreed that the soldiers should have back pay, but there was bitter opposition to the half pay promise. The officers recognized this and were willing to accept some other form of payment: that is, "commutation." Although there was strong feeling against any payment at all on the part of some members, the discontent of the army was so alarming, or was made to appear so, that Congress finally agreed to "commute" the half pay for life to full pay for five years after the war.[56]

It was one thing to promise payment to the army, but quite another to get the funds. Robert Morris declared at the outset that he had no money to pay the army.[57] And if funds were to be raised to pay all the creditors, should they be raised by Congress independently of the states and paid directly to the creditors; or should the funds be raised by the states and paid over to Congress; or, most importantly, should the entire national debt be apportioned among the states? These were the basic issues of policy which underlay the debates in Congress in the spring of 1783.

The nationalist group led by Hamilton, Madison, and James Wilson, and by Robert and Gouverneur Morris in the office of

[55] The Newburgh proceedings are in the *Journals*, XXIV, 291–312. Washington's account of this affair is to be found in his letters to the President of Congress, 18 March, *Writings*, XXVI, 229–32, and to Joseph Jones, ibid., XXVI, 232–4.

[56] *Journals*, XXIV, 145–50, 207–9.

[57] Madison: Notes of Debates, 7 Jan. [1783], ibid., XXV, 847.

superintendent of finance, insisted that the national debt must be funded and paid by Congress from its own revenues. They argued that the debt was a "cement" of the union and that without independent funds for Congress, the union would collapse. The anti-nationalist group led by Richard Henry Lee, John Rutledge, and John Mercer, insisted that the debt must be divided among the states. They agreed with the nationalist argument that the debt was a "cement" of the union, but they objected to the kind of union that would result if Congress became independent of the states. They went even further. They attacked speculation in the national debt, and demanded that distinctions be made between the original holders of the debt and the speculators in it.[58] They demanded that the soldiers be sent back to the states to be cared for. John Mercer of Virginia expressed their views most clearly. He was opposed to commutation by Congress "as tending in common with the funding of other debts, to establish and perpetuate a monied interest in the United States; that this monied interest would gain the ascendance of the landed interest, would resort to places of luxury and splendor, and, by their example and influence, become dangerous to our republican constitutions." But even Mercer agreed that opinions in Congress were so indecisive, and its opinions so various, that something must be done—that it would even be better to "new-model the Confederation" than to do nothing at all.[59]

Despite the bitterness of the opposition, and yet partly because even it agreed that Congress must act, those in favor of national revenues could control the votes of seven states during the spring of 1783. They won a victory in the commutation scheme. They continued to plan a new revenue program to be laid before the states, despite the defeat of the Impost of 1781. The argument was endless, although the issues were clear. The Articles of Confederation provided that expenses of the central government should be distributed among the states according to the value of the lands in each state and the improvements upon them. Yet salt taxes, poll taxes, direct land and house taxes were all proposed and then abandoned for the obvious reason that Congress had no power to levy such taxes.

[58] For examples of arguments see Madison: Notes of Debates, 18–20 Feb., ibid., XXV, 899–905.

[59] Madison: Notes of Debates, 27 Feb. 1783, ibid., XXV, 916.

But sectional interests and state prejudices continued to clash over the method laid down by the Articles. As the North Carolina delegates put it, "the rule was good and plain," but the application was difficult. If the individual states fixed the value of their land, the result would be unequal and unjust. Land in Virginia was rated one third higher for taxation purposes than in Pennsylvania, and yet it was believed that Pennsylvania land was one third more valuable than Virginia's. If a group of commissioners could value all the land in all the states, justice might be had, but "it would be an even chance which would come first, the fixing the quotas or the day of judgment." The "eastern" states wanted to base quotas on population as they had when the Articles of Confederation were written. But here the problem of slaves came up. The easterners said they would make an allowance for slaves, excluding those under sixteen years, but the southerners felt that if they agreed to this, the easterners would soon say that a slave was equal to a white man.[60] The southerners won out for the moment and on 17 February Congress agreed on a plan for the valuation of land.[61] This was in keeping with the Confederation, and with the ideas of those opposed to an independent income for Congress, but their victory was only momentary.

The advocates of an independent income for Congress would not give up. Early in March a committee dominated by the nationalists submitted a report to Congress which embodied most of their ideas but also some concessions. They proposed that Congress have the power to levy a five per cent impost on all foreign goods at the time and place of importation, and in addition, specific duties on salt, wines, rum, brandy, sugar, and tea; that the states raise a million and a half dollars a year for twenty-five years; that the states which had not ceded their western land should do so, and that others should revise the cessions already made. Congress should assume the debts the states had incurred in fighting the war. And once more they proposed an amendment to the Articles of Confederation making population, rather than land values the basis for apportioning expense among the states.

The nationalists agreed to limit the grant of an impost to

[60] To the Governor of North Carolina, 24 March 1783, Burnett, VII, 97–9. See also the New York Delegates to the Governor of New York, 5 March 1783, ibid., VII, 66, for the "eastern" view.

[61] *Journals*, XXIV, 133–7; James Madison to Edmund Randolph, 18 Feb. 1783, Burnett, VII, 49.

twenty-five years and to apply it only to the interest and principal of the debt. They also agreed that the collectors of revenue should be appointed by the states, but they must also be acceptable to and removable by Congress. The revenues would be credited to the states in which they were collected, and would be adjusted from time to time according to the quotas allotted to the states. Finally, all the states must agree to all these measures before they could go into effect, but once agreed to, they would comprise an irrevocable compact.[62]

This report was debated, amended, and re-amended week after week until 18 April when it was at last adopted. It was far more than an impost; it was a grab-bag of all sorts of ideas put together for the purpose of getting ratification one way or another. The impost and specific duties were included. The amendment to the Articles changing the basis of allotment of expenses from real property to population had been refined to take the form of the so-called three fifths compromise. It declared that the states should supply the common treasury in "proportion to the whole number of white and other free citizens and inhabitants, of every age, sex, and condition, including those bound to servitude for a term of years, and three-fifths of all other persons not comprehended in the foregoing description, except Indians not paying taxes, in each state. . . ." [63] The "deduction of ⅖," said Madison, "was a compromise between the wide opinions and demands of the southern and other states." [64] Dropped from the scheme was the article providing for the assumption of the war debts of the states, to the dismay of, among others, Thomas Jefferson, who declared that "the conversion of state into federal debts was one palatable ingredient at least in the pill we were to swallow." [65]

On the final vote only Alexander Hamilton stood solidly in opposition, for once united with the two delegates from Rhode Island. Madison said that Hamilton had a scheme which "he supposed more perfect." He was opposed to the limitation of the impost to twenty-five years, for he believed the debt would not be paid in that time; he objected because the scheme did not designate all the funds from which interest was to be paid; he did not

[62] 6 March 1783, *Journals*, XXIV, 170–4.

[63] Ibid., XXIV, 257–60.

[64] To Edmund Randolph, 8 April 1783, Burnett, VII, 127.

[65] To Madison, 7 May 1783, Albert E. Bergh, ed.: *The Writings of Thomas Jefferson* (20 vols., Washington, 1904–5), IV, 440–1.

like the appointment of collectors by the states for those states with "little interest in the funds, by having a small share of the public debt due to their own citizens" would appoint men little likely to collect the revenue. Despite such objections, he urged New York to adopt the plan, for he said that the share of the public debt due to her citizens was probably far greater than the state's share of that debt. There were also superior motives: "the obligations of national faith, honor, and reputation. . . ."[66]

Stephen Higginson described the scheme as an "artful plan of finance, in which are combined a heterogeneous mixture of imperceptible and visible, constitutional and unconstitutional taxes . . . no part of it is to be binding unless the whole is adopted by all the states. This connection and dependence of one part on another is designed to produce the adoption of the whole. The cessions are to serve as sweeteners to those who oppose the impost; the impost is intended to make the quotas more palatable to some states. . . ." But he did not think the scheme would work, and it did not, as the following years were to show.[67] It did not, because many believed with Jonathan Arnold of Rhode Island that the plan of revenue for Congress was a scheme to undo the Revolution. He had hoped, he said, that the end of the war would end the "formidable plea of necessity" but that "ideas of the necessity of forming a general system of finance (which will throw a share of the power and strength of government, now held by the states, into the hands of Congress) seems in the minds of some to prevail over every other consideration. . . ."[68]

Beyond the political desires of the nationalists and the pleas of the public creditors, the overpowering fact that drove Congress to adopt the new measures was the presence before it of the delegation from the army and the threat of an army-creditor combination that might result in no one knew what horrors. Congress had to get money from the states by persuasion or by force, and the majority preferred persuasion.

On the same day that Congress agreed to commutation of the half pay promise, Washington's report of his suppression of the

[66] Madison to Jefferson, 22 April 1783, Burnett, VII, 145–6; Hamilton to Governor Clinton, 14 May 1783, *Works* (Lodge ed.), IX, 340–1.

[67] Stephen Higginson to Theophilus Parsons, sr., April 1783, Burnett, VII, 123–4, and to Samuel Adams, 22 May, ibid., VII, 171–2.

[68] To the Governor of Rhode Island, 28 March, ibid., VII, 110–1.

threatened revolt at Newburgh got to Congress. He had done his part. He pointed out that it now remained for Congress to establish funds and actually pay the army.[69] This was precisely the problem, as one delegation reported. The passage of yet another resolution was no solution for "promises; even those which are most spacious, are found to be very light food." [70] Along with his letter, Washington sent the resolutions passed by the officers after his magnificent denunciation of the anonymous plotters at Newburgh. The officers expressed the hope that Congress would not disband the army "until their accounts are liquidated, the balances accurately ascertained, and adequate funds established for payment. . . ." [71]

This and the other papers were handed over to a committee which at once found itself so "embarrassed" that it wrote two private letters to Washington asking him what to do. Theodorick Bland said that it would be ruinous to keep the army in the field until all the accounts were settled and funds established for their payment. The result would be "clamors among the citizens" that would probably prevent Congress from carrying out its financial measures. What would Washington think of a declaration by Congress that it intended to do justice to the army and stating the means it intended to use? The general peace, announced in the newspapers that very day, made it imperative that something be done. Bland endorsed resolutions promising that Congress would do all it could to settle accounts, and promising not to disband the army until after the various lines had been marched to their respective states and their accounts settled there.[72]

Hamilton as usual went directly to the point. Congress could settle the accounts but it could not establish the funds. "They have no right by the Confederation to *demand* funds, they can only recommend; and to determine that the army shall be continued in service 'till the states grant them would be to determine that the whole present army, shall be a standing army during peace unless the states comply with the requisitions for funds." This would alarm the states, increase opposition to funding, in-

[69] To the President of Congress, 18 March, *Writings*, XXVI, 229–32.

[70] North Carolina Delegates to the Governor of North Carolina, 24 March, Burnett, VII, 98.

[71] *Journals*, XXIV, 310–1.

[72] 25 March, Burnett, VII, 106–8.

crease the debt even more, and furthermore, it was said "that there is danger in keeping the army together, in a state of inactivity. . . ." It had been suggested that the several lines return to their states where they might further the adoption of funds. Thus ran comment in Congress, according to Hamilton in his letter as a representative of the committee.[73]

But with this he sent another letter written "as a citizen zealous for the true happiness of this country—as a soldier who feels what is due to an army which has suffered every thing and done much for the safety of America." He stated flatly that the army's distrust of Congress was justified, that some men still wanted to use force, that he himself would be inclined to use it if he thought it would get results. The army must submit to its hard fate if the country is ungrateful. "Republican jealousy has in it a principle of hostility to an army whatever be their merits, whatever be their claims to the gratitude of the community. It acknowledges their services with unwillingness and rewards them with reluctance." If the army seeks redress by force of arms they will be ruined. It would moulder of its own weight for want of means of keeping together. The soldiers would desert their officers. "There would be no chance of success without having recourse to means that would reverse our revolution." Such observations are made to show why: "I cannot myself enter into the views of coercion which some gentlemen entertain, for I confess could force avail, I should almost wish to see it employed. I have an indifferent opinion of the honesty of this country, and ill-forebodings as to its future system." [74]

The committee asked for advice, which it got with fervor, indignation, and all the force which Washington could command when thoroughly aroused, and he wrote after he had consulted officers in whom he had confidence. He explained that the idea of keeping the army together until accounts were settled and funds established was expressed at a time when peace seemed distant. Now with peace near, the army had no such intention. They did not suppose "they could operate on the *fears* of the civil power or of the people at large. . . ." But, said Washington, certain things should be done. First of all, it was "an *indispensable*

[73] To Washington, 25 March 1783, ibid., VII, 103.
[74] To Washington, 25 March, ibid., VII, 104.

measure" that all accounts be settled before the army was disbanded. It was equally essential that this be done before the lines went back to their states. Even more important was the necessity of three months' pay after the accounts were settled and before the army was disbanded. Without such funds many would be unable to leave camp and the worst might be expected. The soldiers were in debt and if they were dismissed like a"Sett of Beggars" they would be in despair. A small amount would satisfy them and their creditors.[75]

To Hamilton, Washington was far more explicit. The picture in Hamilton's letters he viewed "with astonishment and horror . . . the idea of redress by force, is too chimerical to have had a place in the imagination of any serious mind in this army; but there is no telling what unhappy disturbances might result from distress, and distrust of justice." Both Washington and many of the officers were suspicious of the "politicians." Some of the leading officers were convinced that the army was being used "as mere puppets to establish continental funds. . . ." Robert Morris was suspected of being at the bottom of it. If such a suspicion became general in the army, it would oppose the whole scheme. The army, Washington warned, "is a dangerous instrument to play with." Its just claims should be settled and it should be disbanded without delay.[76]

Washington was truly alarmed at what might happen if the scheming continued between the group in Congress and his discontented officers. He was particularly suspicious of Gouverneur Morris whom he had blamed for the Newburgh affair, although he seems not to have suspected Hamilton and General Henry Knox, who were also involved. Like Knox, Hamilton disclaimed responsibility with an air of wide-eyed innocence. Hamilton was anxious to allay Washington's doubts and went at length into the politics of Congress. He defended Robert Morris against all charges. He insisted that it was the same old Lee-Deane factionalism at work and that Morris was hated because he had been on Deane's side. Then with entire truth he declared that "there are two classes of men sir in Congress of very different views—one attached to state the other to continental politics. The last have

[75] To Bland, 4 April 1783, *Writings*, XXVI, 285–91.
[76] 4 April, ibid., XXVI, 292–3.

been strenuous advocates for funding the public debt upon solid securities, the former have given every opposition in their power and have only been dragged into the measures which are now near being adopted by the clamours of the army and other public creditors." He summed up by assuring Washington that the men he suspected were "in general the most sensible the most liberal, the most independent and the most respectable characters in our body, as well as the most unequivocal friends to the army. In a word they are the men who think continentally." [77]

In this situation, already teeming with possible dangers, the news of peace could no longer be kept quiet. On 11 April Congress proclaimed an end to hostilities.[78] Congress sent the proclamation to Washington, but they told him nothing further about demobilization. Meanwhile, General Knox reported to Washington that the noncommissioned officers of the Connecticut line were uneasy because of the inequality of the proposed settlement: if the officers got five years' pay, the soldiers wanted it too. Knox said that this was a new claim and that others might spring up. The sooner the "war men," the men enlisted for the duration, were discharged, the better. The excuse could be given that many men wanted to hurry back to their farms in the spring. On the same day General Huntington expressed alarm at the temper of the "war men" and hoped for their discharge. Far to the south, General Greene reported that the news of discontent among the northern troops was spreading "and threatens a convulsion." What, he asked Washington, is the temper of the northern army, and what can be done? [79]

Washington, in turn, asked Congress what to do: the noncommissioned officers were making "new and unusual demands of compensation for their services." The soldiers enlisted for the duration of the war would instantly demand their discharges. Should the proclamation be issued in public orders, and if so, what should be done about discharges? [80]

At first Congress decided that men enlisted for the duration of the war could not be discharged until ratification of the definitive treaty of peace, but that Washington might grant furloughs or

[77] [9 April] Burnett, VII, 129–31.

[78] *Journals*, XXIV, 238–40.

[79] Knox to Washington, 16 April; Huntington to Washington, 16 April; Greene to Washington, 16 March 1783, Washington Papers, LC.

[80] 17 April 1783, *Writings*, XXVI, 328–9.

discharges as he saw fit.[81] Meanwhile, the common soldiers themselves were making it perfectly plain that all they wanted was to go home, whatever Congress, their officers, or Washington might think.

By the end of April, Washington reported that the soldiers were rioting and insulting their officers and demanding final discharges. "I believe," he wrote Hamilton, "it is not in the power of Congress or their officers, to hold them much, if any, longer; for we are obliged at this moment to increase our guards to prevent rioting, and the insults which the officers meet with in attempting to hold them to their duty. The proportion of these men amount to seven-elevenths of this army. . . ." Washington was convinced that all men should be discharged who were not to be kept on a peacetime establishment. Otherwise the problem would get worse, not better. He had just been handed a petition from the noncommissioned officers of the Connecticut line, but had turned it back because it did not come "through the channel of their officers." He expected more such attempts and he mentioned it to "show the necessity, the absolute necessity of discharging the *wars men* as soon as possible." [82]

By May it was reported that "the soldiers are loud and insolent, the officers broken, dissatisfied and desponding. The states obdurate and forgetful and Congress weak as water and impotent as old age." [83] The officers were desperate, for their accounts were still unsettled and they had been given no promise of pay. At last Congress acted. Robert Morris was instructed to give the soldiers three months' pay. Then on 26 May it instructed Washington to grant furloughs to those enlisted for the duration of the war.[84] Much bitterness still remained. One officer wrote that "the dissolution of our army was unexpected, as it was sudden, and I can assure you had you been a spectator of the scene, your heart would have bled for the poor fellows who were in so disgraceful a manner turned off. But as the step tends to economy, however villainous in itself; it will be generally approved and must be submitted to." [85] There were threats of mutiny. Officers sent a

[81] *Journals*, XXIV, 269–70.
[82] 22 April 1783, *Writings*, XXVI, 350–1.
[83] John Armstrong, jr. to General Gates, 9 May, Burnett, VII, 160, n. 3.
[84] *Journals*, XXIV, 364.
[85] Walter Stewart to General Gates, Camp Newburgh, 20 June 1783, Emmet Coll., no. 8028, NYPL.

bitter address to Washington, but he defended Congress as having done all that it could do.[86] His officers demanded that he keep the soldiers in camp until all their accounts had been settled, but he refused, and on 13 June 1783 most of the common soldiers, and many of the officers started for home without formality or farewell. Thus the army disappeared as a force to be reckoned with in politics and war.[87]

The nationalist failure to keep the army in being was part of their failure to establish a peacetime military establishment. James Madison, Hamilton, James Wilson, Samuel Osgood, and Oliver Ellsworth were appointed a committee to deal with such matters. Stephen Higginson reported that "there are those also among us who wish to keep up a large force, to have large garrisons, to increase the navy, to have a large diplomatic corps, to give large salaries to all our servants. Their professed view is to strengthen the hands of government, to make us respectable in Europe, and I believe, they might add to divide among themselves and their friends, every place of honor and of profit. But it is easy to see where all this will lead us, and Congress I think is not yet prepared for such systems." [88]

Higginson was an accurate reporter of congressional views. The committee submitted recommendations in June and they were ignored. The same committee turned over the same report in October. The report was a long argument that it was constitutional for Congress to maintain a standing army rather than for the states to do so, and it provided elaborate outlines for such a national army.[89] Meanwhile Congress made temporary provision to garrison the frontiers. The nationalists insisted that this was constitutional; that too great burdens would be placed on individual states if they had to provide for their own protection; that jealousies might be excited among states. But with the war over, and with nationalist leaders returning to their states one by one, there was little that could be done.

Madison was soon to complete the three years in Congress allowed by the Confederation and could not return until three

[86] Washington to Major General William Heath, 6 June 1783, *Writings*, XXVI, 472–5; Madison to Edmund Randolph, 17 June, Burnett, VII, 189.

[87] Hatch: *Revolutionary Army*, chs. viii–ix, is the best general account. The relevant documents are in Burnett, VII, and Washington, *Writings*, XXVI.

[88] To Samuel Adams, 20 May, Burnett, VII, 167.

[89] 23 Oct., *Journals*, XXV, 722–45.

more years had passed. Hamilton went to New York to practice law. Gouverneur Morris resigned as assistant superintendent of finance. Robert Morris finally resigned in 1784. Robert R. Livingston quit as secretary of foreign affairs and resumed the office of chancellor of New York. Thus, once more the wheel turned so that by 1785 Congress was back in the hands of the Lee-Adams junto, with Richard Henry Lee himself as president. His brother Arthur Lee was one of the three men who took over control of financial affairs from Robert Morris.

Congress itself collapsed for a time at the end of the war. Its collapse was symbolized, even made ludicrous, by the revolt of some Pennsylvania troops who surrounded the halls of Congress in June and scared its members half out of their wits. After spending the day cooped up, they at last emerged in the middle of the afternoon with as much dignity as they could muster. Thereafter they left Philadelphia, going first to Princeton, then to Annapolis, and finally in 1785 to New York, which remained the capital until after the end of the Confederation.

The collapse was natural enough at the end of a long, exhausting war and an equally long and exhausting political struggle. The nationalists who ruled Congress from 1781 to 1783 had not achieved their ends. Their constitutional theories, their proposed amendments, and even the desperate hope of actual military revolt had all been shattered by the winning of independence itself, without the adoption of any of the measures which they had insisted were indispensable for the winning of it. In a way, they had discredited Congress among the people by their insistence on gathering power to it. The people, so far as they had fought for independence, had not fought for the independence of a vague entity known as the United States, but for the independence of their own particular states. Nevertheless, they had created a new entity, for war had produced interests which transcended state boundaries, interests which demanded the creation of a central government superior to the state governments and with the power to act upon individuals everywhere, whatever their political allegiances.

Thus a large part of the history of the years after the Revolution is a history of continuous struggle between two groups: between those who wanted to retain the political essence of the Revolution, the federal government; and those who wanted to create a national government over the American states. This political struggle takes place against a complex background. There was a post-war depression; there were discontented groups of wealthy creditors on one hand, and of debtor farmers on the other; there were trade difficulties. Politically, there was the possibility of majority rule within state boundaries and its implications for various minority groups in American society.

PART TWO

The Fruits of Independence

IF WE look at the new nation only through the eyes of angry politicians and soldiers at the end of the war, we get a distorted concept of the spirit of the times. Yet the history of the period is too often written in terms of the shrill cries of politicians who were seldom easy when in office and who prophesied doom when their opponents won elections. But if we turn from such sources we see a spirit of exuberant optimism everywhere, a belief in the great destiny of the new nation, a conviction that Americans could do anything they wanted to, untrammeled by the traditions of the old world. The fact that dominated their thinking was that they were no longer colonists, that they could do as they pleased without outside interference. For nearly three centuries the western world had been in bondage to Europe. Now one portion was free, and within a few decades the vast dominions of Spain and Portugal would also be free. Although many Americans had doubted that the Revolution would succeed, and many others had hoped that it would not, most Americans were delighted and proud at the end of the war. Many Englishmen were embittered and sure that the new nation could not last, or that if it did, it would be a menace to the political institutions of Europe. But many Europeans, including Englishmen, looked upon the new nation and its political principles as the hope of the world.

The conflict of opinion as to the nature of this experiment, and its promise of good and bad, produced many books and pamphlets in Europe. These were read and praised, or condemned, according to their character or according to the preconceptions of the readers. From time to time such writings were used in American political debates to prove one argument or another. However, the citizens of the new nation were entirely capable of writing their own story, of pointing to their own promise, and of describing the golden destiny that was to be theirs. Whatever their religious or political beliefs, however they might differ as to the nature of the problems of the new nation and the means of their solution, they could all agree that power and greatness and the betterment of man's lot were to be the results of the American Revolution.

Their faith was expressed in many ways: in letters, in poems, in histories, in newspaper essays. Some of these outpourings were crass and boastful, others were defensive: evidence of a half-felt inferiority. But beyond all this was the fact that Americans had done what no other colonists had ever done—they had fought for and won their independence from the greatest empire the world had yet seen. They were now free, and that freedom found expression in many forms. Americans wrote histories of the war and of the individual states. They wrote geographies, grammars, and spelling books. They fought furiously in state politics for and against the democratization of political and social life. They organized societies for economic and social betterment. They dug canals, built bridges, and planned new roads to encourage the flow of goods and the making of profits.

Yet despite their concern with domestic affairs and their delight in independence, Americans had to face the fact that they were still a part of the world at large; that because of economic and political necessities they must live in a world dominated by empires. Hence some of the ablest men in the new nation—John Jay, John Adams, and Thomas Jefferson—walked on the world stage and achieved a measure of success, partly because of their own abilities, and partly because of international rivalries over which they had no control, but which they used to the advantage of the nation they had helped to found.

In their multitudinous activities, Americans usually combined idealism and enthusiasm with common sense. But sometimes their optimism led them into schemes so grandiose that they are rescued from the ludicrous only because they are such supreme evidence of the sublime faith of Americans in their destiny. It is important, therefore, to give some account of the American spirit as expressed in books and sermons and newspapers, of the day to day problems of government, of the movement of people, of their effort to improve their own lot and that of the less fortunate members of society, and of the role they had to play in the world at large. The history of these things is the history of the lives they led from day to day, whereas the history of their politics is one of crises in which politicians seldom predicted anything but catastrophe. The American people, unlike their political leaders, had a spirited faith in the future, a faith that, far more than the rhetoric of the politicians, gives us some conception of the fruits of independence.

4
The Spirit of the New Nation

THE SPIRIT and faith of the new nation were expressed variously, but no expression was more obvious and popular than that to be found in Fourth of July celebrations. In 1783 a Charleston paper reported: "Yesterday, the 4th of July, afforded a spectacle equally awful and grand. The inhabitants of the whole continent of America, eagerly devoted in commemorating the anniversary of the greatest revolution that ever took place—the expulsion of tyranny and slavery, and the introduction of freedom, happiness, and independency, throughout the greatest continent in the world." [1] Four years later, after a celebration of the eleventh anniversary of the Declaration of Independence, a Boston paper declared that the Revolution "has not only given the blessing of freedom to this western world; but has enlightened nearly all Europe, with respect to the natural rights of mankind." [2]

The news of Yorktown in 1781 had barely reached New England before doughty Timothy Dwight preached a sermon in which he summed up the experience of the past, the problems of the present, and the hopes for the future. His text was from Isaiah: "to the islands he will repay recompense. . . ." The Lord had humbled Britain for her cruelties in India and America, and Yorktown was the crowning victory. But the Americans had sins too: dissipation of thought, prostitution of reason, contempt for religion, disdain of virtue, deliberation in vice, and universal levity and corruption of soul. Skepticism was growing everywhere. But there is progress in knowledge. The present century is the most enlightened of any. The growth of knowledge

[1] *South Carolina Gazette, and General Advertiser*, 5 July 1783.
[2] *Massachusetts Centinel*, 14 July 1787.

has shown the ridiculousness of "popish ceremonial" and the folly of prescribing creeds. Even war may be ended, and kings walk in the way of science. As a result of "this convulsion," the American Revolution, "the world hath seen for the first time an extensive empire founded on the only just basis, the free and general choice of the inhabitants." In America the rights of human nature are unfolded. The church is free from control. Here society is friendly to genius. The "convulsion" has awakened a disposition to freedom of inquiry and to independence of decision. We may therefore hope for great advances in political and natural science and a most noble progress in theology. We may soon have arts hitherto without name and sciences besides electricity "deriving their birth from American genius." To this disposition we may soon owe new, improving, and enrapturing ideas of human nature and duty. "May we not in a word expect from this disposition a depth of research, a candor of debate, and a friendliness to truth, which shall exhibit a contrast to former prejudices, begin a new era in the progress of science, and attemper the mind to the easiest reception of the grace of gospel." [3]

Dwight's prophecies were echoed by many another, particularly in the rapidly growing number of newspapers. One writer said that the United States was "like the sun rising with brilliant radiance from the eastern ocean . . . in the infancy of their power, emerging from the tumultuous sea of warfare, and shining in the cultivation of arts and sciences. Genius is now fostered by the charitable hand of public munificence; and the man of invention reaps the benefit of his ingenuity. The states in general vie with each other in the encouragement and patronage of learning, and the polite arts." [4] Still another writer declared that it was difficult to conceive of the greatness or importance of North America within a century or two. "Agriculture, the basis of a nation's greatness" will probably "be raised to its pinnacle of perfection and its attendant, commerce, will so agreeably and usefully employ mankind, that wars will be forgotten, nations by a free intercourse with this vast and fertile continent, will again become brothers, and no longer treat each other as savages and monsters. The iron generations will verge to decay. . . ." To the west lies land of

[3] *A Sermon Preached at Northampton on the Twenty-Eighth of November 1781 Occasioned by the Capture of the British Army Under the Command of Earl Cornwallis* (Hartford, n.d.).

[4] *Massachusetts Centinel*, 27 March 1784.

"inexpressible beauty and fertility." There the trees are greater, there the rivers and streams fall into that "grand repository of a thousand streams the far famed Mississippi . . . this prince of rivers, in comparison of whom the Nile is but a rivulet, and the Danube a mere ditch. . . ." [5]

America's vastness was a continuous source of pride and wonder. Everything is on a larger plan than on the "eastern" continent. The mountains are a third larger and higher, the rivers and lakes are larger, and the five Great Lakes are like so many Baltics and Mediterraneans. It is reasonable to suppose that the sentiments of the mind bear some relation to the objects around it. Philosophers and poets declare that the natural course of improvement will lead to universal civilization and social happiness and that the millennium may actually commence in the territories of the United States. Here everything, like its mountains and rivers, is on a more liberal plan. "And this seems to be the reason why this country is reserved to be the last and greatest theater for the improvement of mankind, that the productions of nature, and the expansion of the human mind, should unite in completing the perfection of civil government and the happiness of society." The greatness of genius and the liberality of sentiment in America are such as no nation has ever equaled. "Many of the useful arts of life, as well as various branches of philosophy, such as electricity, mechanicks and astronomy, have received more improvements from our countrymen than they have from all Europe during the present century." [6]

Not only was America already the center of learning in the eyes of some of its citizens, it was to be a refuge for the oppressed of the world. The independency of the United States was in no one instance a greater blessing to the world "than in its being the asylum whither the indigent and oppressed, whom the lawless hand of European despotism would crush to the earth, can find succour and protection, and join common fellowship in a country,

> Where happy millions their own fields possess,
> No tyrant awes them, and no lords oppress." [7]

By 1786 the boasts and prophecies were bolstered by assertions of achievements. Franklin's philosophy was declared to have the

[5] Ibid., 11 Dec. 1784.

[6] *Massachusetts Centinel*, 25 Feb. 1786.

[7] *Pennsylvania Gazette*, 5 Oct. 1785.

unrivaled admiration of every country in Europe. The "moral scrutinies" of Jonathan Edwards had the applause of most Protestant countries, even of those opposed to his opinions. "The quadrant, injuriously called Hadley's, was the invention of Mr. Godfrey of Philadelphia; mercurial inoculation was the discovery of the late Dr. Muirson. . . ." Trumbull's *M'Fingal* was ranked along with *Hudibras* by the English reviewers. The painters Copley and West found little competition, even in Europe. The memorials of Congress were classed in Europe along with the best of their kind ever published. European praise of our military and political characters renders "our own applauses totally unnecessary to their glory. Of no other nation can so honorable things be mentioned, at so early a period of their existence." [8]

The following year "An Essay on American Genius" declared that the time had come to explode the European creed that "we are infantile in our acquisitions and savage in our manners; because we are inhabitants of a New World, lately occupied by a race of savages." The writer then proceeded to review the achievements of living Americans. He pointed to Ramsay's history of the Revolution in South Carolina as an example and urged further writing on the military history of the Revolution. The writer's main concern, however, was with the fine arts. Americans have a strong talent for painting. Benjamin West of Philadelphia is one of "the first historical painters of the age." John Singleton Copley of Boston, "in the same walk of genius, is not spoken of as second to any of the profession." John Trumbull of Connecticut, though a younger man, has "exhibited the happiest dispositions. . . ."

Yet the writer of the essay was forced to admit that "the age of ultimate refinement in America is yet to arrive." Most of the painters he had named could not have attained their fame and wealth if they had remained in America. Too much money was spent on vulgar amusement and some pains should be taken to "lead the taste of the nation to substitute, instead of the vulgar enjoyments of cock-fighting, gambling, and tavern haunting, pleasures of a more refined and innocent nature." He was convinced, however, that there was much less gaming, dissipation, and tavern haunting than before the war and that the future progress of wealth and population would be a source of improvement in "music, architecture, gardening, sculpture, and other

[8] Ibid., 17 May 1786.

elegant arts." As an example he pointed to the progress of poetry despite "many disadvantages, and notwithstanding some ungracious insinuations to the contrary. . . ." Perhaps the poets living in Connecticut were equal to any then writing. At least the question might be appealed to the "bar of critical taste." Joel Barlow's *Vision of Columbus* was in press, and when published it would give the "reader of discernment an exalted idea of American genius and refinement." [9]

Such boastfulness was the result of a pride that was not without solid foundation, a foundation that was laid by American writers, who, with great effort and little profit, sought to tell the story of the movement of which they had been a part and to give character to the new nation which they had helped create. Americans could turn to the newspapers and there read advertisements such as that of Benjamin Guild, who offered for sale at his Boston Book Store an assortment of books "among which are the following American productions, Memoirs of the American Academy of Arts and Sciences . . . Belknap's History of New Hampshire, Smith's History of New Jersey, Ramsay's Revolution of South Carolina, History of Connecticut, Ledyard's Voyage round the World, Adams' Defence of the American Constitutions, Chauncey's Universal Salvation, and other works, Barlow's Vision of Columbus, Humphrey's Poems." [10]

The list was heavily weighted with history, for the belief that the American Revolution was of world-wide significance drove men to write its history even as it was beginning. Educated men of the eighteenth century were steeped in history and they were keenly aware of the rise and fall of nations and empires. They believed that the British Empire was in the last stages of decadence. Americans of the revolutionary generation had before them an example of a modern American history: Thomas Hutchinson's *History of the Colony of Massachusetts Bay*. The first volume was published in 1764; the second in 1767 from a soiled manuscript picked up in the streets of Boston after its owner's house was destroyed by a revolutionary mob; but Hutchinson was a leader of the aristocratic forces in the Bay Colony and he had fled to England at the outbreak of the war. There he died in 1780 and the

[9] *The New Haven Gazette and the Connecticut Magazine*, 1 Feb. 1787.
[10] *Massachusetts Centinel*, 22 Aug. 1787.

third volume of his work was not published until long afterwards. It is good history, but the people of his day would not read it because his politics had been of the wrong kind.

The Reverend Jeremy Belknap was more fortunate. Like Hutchinson he was born in Boston, but his father was a leather dresser and furrier rather than a wealthy merchant. Belknap went to Harvard, and then taught school and studied for the ministry. In 1766 he became the pastor of the Congregational Church at Dover, New Hampshire. In time he became a strong supporter of the movement for independence, although he did not subscribe to the democratic ideas that were so much a part of it. Shortly after he went to New Hampshire he began work on a history of the colony. He stayed in New Hampshire until 1786. The next year he went to Boston as pastor of the Federal Street Church and remained there until his death in 1798. All his life he had an intense interest in history and politics. He helped found the Massachusetts Historical Society. He corresponded with influential politicians and his letters are a remarkable source for conservative political thinking. In 1783 the first volume of his history of New Hampshire was announced as ready for the press and people were asked to subscribe for it. An advertisement in the *Pennsylvania Gazette* declared "the vast importance of this rising empire renders the history of each part of it extremely interesting." [11] The first volume appeared the next year but the second and third did not appear until the 1790's.

State histories such as Hutchinson's and Belknap's had been inspired by colonial experience and the example of histories written in Europe in the eighteenth century, and cannot be attributed to the influence of the Revolution although each of the authors played roles in the movement.

The first Americans to write histories of the Revolution itself were Dr. David Ramsay of South Carolina, and the Reverend William Gordon of Massachusetts. Ramsay was born in Pennsylvania in 1749 and graduated from the College of New Jersey in 1765. He tutored and studied medicine and got a medical degree from the College of Philadelphia in 1772. He practiced in Maryland for a year and then moved to South Carolina in 1773 where he became a leading figure in its political life. His marriages were

[11] 3 Sept. 1783.

many and politically important: in turn he married a Charleston merchant's daughter, a daughter of his old college president, John Witherspoon, and a daughter of the great Charleston merchant, Henry Laurens. He was a friend of Dr. Benjamin Rush and other leading figures of the day. His medical practice was successful, but his time was spent mostly in politics. He represented Charleston in the South Carolina legislature from 1776 onward. He was a member of the Confederation Congress from 1782 to 1785, of the South Carolina house of representatives from 1784 to 1790, and from 1790 until he retired from politics in 1796 he was president of the South Carolina senate. He was unsuccessful only in business and in the writing of history. His speculations led him into bankruptcy in 1798 and he was forced to pledge his professional services to Charleston business men for years thereafter.

His interest in writing a history of the Revolution in South Carolina began while he and other South Carolina leaders were prisoners of the British at St. Augustine in 1780–81. His connections and experience gave him a unique opportunity to write of the Revolution. He finished his first book in 1784, and after many difficulties in finding a publisher, it appeared in December 1785.

The fact that Ramsay and Gordon were working on histories was known to the public, and their efforts were praised before either appeared in print. During the summer of 1785, New York and Philadelphia newspapers reported that "the new histories of America, which are already, in some measure, promised to the public, are looked for with great expectation by the literati in Europe; they are anxious to behold in what manner an historian will appear in a country where the press is really free, and not under the trammels of bigotry or ministerial influence." [12] Ramsay advertised his book, but it did not sell. Late in January 1786 he wailed that but four copies had been sold in Philadelphia. He sent copies to a friend John Eliot in Boston who thought that four dollars was too much for two volumes. Furthermore, the Reverend William Gordon was conducting an advance sale campaign for his unprinted work that caused Eliot to remark that Gordon was "in the zenith of subscription glory." But Ramsay was sympathetic with Gordon. He offered to help sell Gordon's work but warned him that there were no "brilliant pecuniary prospects," for the trade of author was a very poor one: "in point of pecuniary

[12] *Pennsylvania Gazette*, 27 July 1785.

interest I would exchange all my prospects for the profits of a few benefit nights of the New York theatre." [13]

Ramsay's difficulties got to the public by way of the newspapers. The *Massachusetts Centinel* told him that even if the sale did not pay his expenses, he would have the satisfaction of having "sacrificed to the encouragement of American arts, while he was endeavoring to present the rising generation with a faithful detail of what their fathers have done and suffered to secure for them the inestimable blessings of liberty and independence." [14]

Despite his failure in America, Ramsay hoped for sales in Europe. But he had said such forthright things about Lord Rawdon and Lord Cornwallis that his London agent refused to bind and sell the book for fear of mobs and the law officers of the Crown. The ex-spy, Dr. Edward Bancroft, was hired to cut out objectionable passages, but still the publisher hesitated to sell the book openly. Some copies were sold privately, some shipped to Holland, and still others were sent to Thomas Jefferson in France. Jefferson had denounced the revisions but despite all his efforts was able to sell but nine copies in two years.

Americans were furious with the British.[15] Philip Freneau, who had used his pen so ably during the war, once more denounced the British in forthright verse:

So the British, worn out with their wars in the west
(Where burning and murder their prowess confessed)
When, at last, they agreed 'twas in vain to contend
(For the days of their thieving were come to an end)
They hired some historians to scribble and flatter,
And foolishly thought they could hush up the matter.

But Ramsay arose, and with Truth on his side,
Has told the world what they labored to hide;
With his pen of dissection, and pointed with steel,
If they ne'er before felt he has taught them to feel,
Themselves and their projects has truly defined,
And dragged them to blush at the bar of mankind.

As the author, his friends, and world might expect,
They find that the work has a damning effect—
In reply to his Facts they abuse him and rail,
And prompted by malice, prohibit the sale.

[13] David Ramsay to Gordon, New York, 18 Jan. 1786, Myers Collection, no. 528, NYPL. Ramsay even saved his plates for Gordon's use.

[14] 4 March 1786.

[15] *Pennsylvania Gazette*, 2 Aug. 1786.

But we trust, their chastisement is only begun;
Thirteen are the States—and he writes of but one;
Ere the twelve that are silent their story have told,
The king will run mad, and the book will be sold.

Meanwhile Ramsay began work on a general history of the Revolution and finished it by 1788. He then waited to see if the Constitution of 1787 would be adopted for "the Revolution cannot be said to be completed till that or something equivalent is established." The book was published in 1789 with a repetition of all the old troubles. There were typographical errors; he could not sell enough to pay the printer's bills; and the British and the Irish pirated the book without benefit of royalties.[16]

While Ramsay was suffering all the pangs of authorship and the even worse pangs of an author who must pay for the publication of his own books, William Gordon of Massachusetts had even greater problems to solve. Gordon, an English clergyman, was sympathetic with the colonial cause. In 1770 he emigrated to Massachusetts where in 1772 he became pastor of the Third Congregational Church at Roxbury. He was a vigorous supporter of the revolutionary party and was rewarded with conspicuous posts. He was chaplain of the provincial congress that met at Watertown in 1775 and delivered the election day sermon before the General Court that year. He delivered the sermon commemorating the first anniversary of independence in 1777. He became an overseer of Harvard College. However, his relations with the Massachusetts government came to a sudden end when he attacked some provisions of the proposed constitution of 1778.

Early in the war he decided to write its history. In July 1775 he declared that he hoped there would not be a total separation from Great Britain. Nevertheless "there have been various special providences in our favor, which I have a design of writing down, to be thrown in order when time and circumstances will admit of it and however these things may lightly be accounted of by the profane, they will excite proper emotions in the breasts of the pious. May there be repeated interpositions of providence to make the chronicles of the American united colonies the favorite read-

[16] The above account of Ramsay including the quotations, except those from the newspapers and from the letter to William Gordon, are from Robert L. Brunhouse: "David Ramsay's Publication Problems, 1784–1808," *Papers of the Bibliographical Society of America*, XXXIX (1945).

ing of the godly in this new world till the elect shall be gathered in." [17]

As the Revolution continued, Gordon spent more and more time gathering materials. He wrote to everyone, went everywhere, and gossiped incessantly about political and military events. He knew generals, members of Congress, and business men. They wrote to him and sent him newspapers. When he saw them they told him their versions of passing events.[18]

After Yorktown Gordon started out for Virginia to satisfy his thirst for political knowledge, according to one of his friends.[19] Gordon himself said that he was seriously "historiographing." He looked for private papers and announced that he was convinced that precious few people had any "sterling patriotism." [20] He asked Washington for the use of his papers. Washington replied that it was "impracticable for the best historiographer living, to write a full and correct history of the present revolution" without access to the archives of Congress, of the states, of commanding officers, and of the commander in chief. Although Washington agreed that his papers were public property, Gordon could not see them until Congress gave permission.[21]

When the war was over Gordon once more asked Washington's permission [22] and once more Washington told him that no historian could write a "perfect history of the Revolution" if he did not have access to all the sources, and even then that "some things probably, will never be known." [23]

Congress soon agreed that Gordon could use any of its papers that were not secret, and also any papers that Washington thought could be "submitted to the eye of the public." [24] Armed with the confidence of Congress and Washington's permission, Gordon spent part of the summer of 1784 at Mount Vernon. He got "to Gen. Washington's by breakfast on June 2; when he had read the resolve of Congress he told me that he would make no re-

[17] To Mrs. Elizabeth Smith, 30 July 1775, Emmet Coll., no. 2847, NYPL.

[18] Horatio Gates to Gordon, 3 May 1779, Emmet Coll., no. 8158, NYPL; Gordon to Gates, 25 May 1781, Gates Papers, NYHS.

[19] Ebenezer Hazard to General Gates, 26 Oct. 1781, Gates Papers, NYHS.

[20] To Benjamin Rush, 9 Jan. 1782, Benjamin Rush Papers, Philadelphia Free Library.

[21] To Gordon, 23 Oct. 1782, *Writings*, XXV, 287–8.

[22] To Washington, 8 March 1784, Washington Papers, LC.

[23] 8 May 1784, *Writings*, XXVII, 398–9.

[24] 25 May 1784, *Journals*, XXVII, 427–8.

serve and keep no papers back, but should trust to my prudence for the proper use of them." Gordon went to work with a will, rising at daylight and continuing until far into the evening. He stopped only for meals and refused all invitations, which must have been difficult for the gregarious parson. By 19 June he had finished searching and "extracting" thirty-three volumes of copied letters and many bundles of private letters. He had labored hard but he said, "my gain of knowledge will amply compensate." [25] Even at that, when he got back home he found that one of his notes was incomplete and Washington cheerfully obliged by checking it for him.[26]

Gordon had no money to publish, so he sold advance subscriptions and finally decided to publish in England. Soon he was attacked in the newspapers. One "Jonathan Lumberwit" was said to have established an insurance office where subscribers, for a ninety-eight per cent premium, would be guaranteed the book or their money in forty years. But the "underwriters" refused to be liable for damages "arising from the history being disgusting to the Americans, abusive to particular characters, from inelegance of style, or want of taste in the author." [27] Soon it was reported that Gordon had cut out passages favorable to the United States.[28] Others argued that while he had been "squibbed, roasted, and basted on all sides," much that had been said against his history was untrue. However, he should have told people that he intended to publish in England. No one could blame him for wanting to make a fortune but in any other than the parson's profession the proposal would be "called by some a species of knavery. . . ." He had been a "most furious and flaming whig" and it had been known for years that he would be partial to one side or another. At any rate let him go to his native land in peace, and those who choose to, have the right to send their money with him.[29]

The attack on Gordon came perhaps because he was an enemy of John Hancock. As treasurer of Harvard, Hancock was reluctant to account for his use of its funds, and Gordon had been

[25] To General Gates, 31 Aug. 1784, Emmet Coll., no. 4369, NYPL.

[26] Gordon to Washington, 10 Jan. 1785, Washington Papers, LC; Washington to Gordon, 8 March 1785, *Writings*, XXVIII, 96–8.

[27] *Massachusetts Centinel*, 8, 18, 22 Feb. 1786.

[28] *Pennsylvania Gazette*, 8 March 1786.

[29] Ibid., 29 March 1786.

baying at his heels.[30] Gordon's friends stuck by him and declared him without blame as he left for England in the spring of 1786.[31] In England he had as much trouble as Ramsay: it was said that he was too friendly to Americans and made libelous statements about the English. Several clergymen revised the manuscript by cutting out much of his source material and copying in large chunks of the *Annual Register.* In 1788 the work appeared as *The History of the Rise, Progress and Establishment of the Independence of the United States of America.* An American edition appeared the next year. The *History* is in the form of "letters." The effort is made to give them the appearance of being contemporary with the events they describe. For long, the *History* was regarded as an authoritative source, as were the works of David Ramsay, although a modern scholar says that both are worthless because of plagiarism from the *Annual Register.*[32]

The charge of plagiarism is plainly true. Plagiarism of this kind was common practice in the eighteenth century. Virtually all writers copied documents and accounts of public events from such publications as the *Annual Register.* The significant thing about Ramsay, Gordon, and later John Marshall in his life of Washington, is not what they copied, but the particular contributions that they made themselves. These were the result of their own participation in the events they described. Such insights and interpretations are scanty but they are important.

While historians were busy recounting the events of the Revolution, other writers were equally active in the effort to picture the spirit of the new nation. An astonishing number of them were sons of Connecticut. Some of them came to be known as the Hartford, or Connecticut, Wits. Their leaders were John Trumbull, Timothy Dwight, David Humphreys, and Joel Barlow. Associated with them were men such as Theodore Dwight and the acidulous physician, Lemuel Hopkins. Most of them were brilliant under-

30 Gordon to Samuel Osgood, 25 Feb. 1786, Osgood Papers, NYHS.

31 Ebenezer Hazard to Gates, 11 July 1786, Emmet Coll., Misc., NYPL; 7 Dec. 1786, Emmet Coll., no. 6935, NYPL.

32 Orin G. Libby: "A Critical Examination of William Gordon's History of the American Revolution," American Historical Association *Annual Report* (1899), I, 367–88, and his "Ramsay as a Plagiarist," *American Historical Review,* VII (1901–2), 697–703.

graduates at Yale before the Revolution. John Trumbull and Theodore Dwight became lawyers; Timothy Dwight became a minister and in time, president of Yale. Humphreys was a soldier in the Revolution, then a diplomat, and eventually a manufacturer. Barlow became a land salesman and a wealthy man. Of the whole group he was the only one to turn away from conservative political ideas.

Trumbull won an early reputation. He entered Yale at thirteen, although he had passed the entrance examinations at the age of seven. He was graduated in 1767. In 1770 he got a master's degree and at that time gave an oration, an "Essay on the Use and Advantages of the Fine Arts," in which he sang of the future glories of America. As a tutor at Yale with Timothy Dwight, he attacked the conventional course of study. The immediate result of his venture as a curriculum reformer was a poem satirizing the whole business of college education: *The Progress of Dulness*. He then entered the law office of John Adams in Boston and was caught in a swirl of strictly non-academic activity in that whirlpool of revolution. The result was a poem in 1774 called *An Elegy of the Times*. He went back to Hartford to practice law and in 1775 he published the first part of *M'Fingal*, a satire on the Tories in the person of "M'Fingal" whose

> fathers flourished in the Highland
> of Scotia's fog-benighted islands;
> Whence gain'd our Squire two gifts by right,
> Rebellion, and the Second-sight.

In ancient days rebellion had gained the "noblest palm of praise." M'Fingal enjoyed the new rebellion, but he availed himself no less of the Scottish gift of second sight:

> Nor only saw he all that could be,
> But much that never was, or would be.
> Gazettes no sooner rose a lie in,
> But straight he fell to prophesying;
> Made dreadful slaughter in his course,
> O'er threw provincials, foot and horse,
> Brought armies o'er by sudden pressings,
> Of Hanoverians, Swiss and Hessians,
> Feasted with blood his Scottish clan,

And hang'd all rebels to a man,
Divided their estates and pelf,
And took a goodly share himself.

Thus Trumbull pilloried the opponents of independence and won fame for himself among the men of his generation. But, like his fellow "Wits," he did not like the democratic implications of the Revolution. He busied himself with law practice and wrote little more poetry, although when Shays's Rebellion came in 1786 he joined with his friends in writing *The Anarchiad*, a violent and scurrilous attack on democracy. He lived long beyond his generation and died in 1831 in Detroit, Michigan.

Timothy Dwight, who with Trumbull led the "Wits," became a preacher of Calvinism in religion and of conservatism in politics: "a walking repository of the venerable *status quo*."[33] His output was prodigious and almost uniformly lacking in the sprightliness of his friend Trumbull. As a chaplain during the Revolution he wrote the song *Columbia* which was sung everywhere. Once the war was over he wrote *The Conquest of Canaan*, a poem far more remote from the realities of the day than the writing of his friends. His great work was as president of Yale after 1795. From that post he fought a mighty battle against advancing democracy while at the same time he pioneered in modern education by promoting the teaching of science.

David Humphreys was an aide and friend of Washington during the war. At the end of it he celebrated independence and the future greatness of America in two poems of dubious merit but of great enthusiasm: *The Glory of America* and *A Poem on the Industry of the United States of America*. In the latter he urged home manufactures:

First let the loom each lib'ral thought engage,
Its labors growing with the growing age;
Then true utility with taste allied,
Shall make our homespun barbs our nation's pride.

He went on to urge the importation of merino sheep and the planting of hemp and flax. He besought "Columbian dames" to save their country from threatened fall and asked them if they would adopt from every zone,

[33] Vernon L. Parrington: *The Connecticut Wits* (New York, 1926), xl.

> Fantastic fashions, noxious in your own?
> At wintry balls in gauzy garments dressed,
> Admit the dire destroyer to your breast?

for if you do,

> Then death your doom prepares: cough, fever, rheum,
> and pale consumption nip your rosy bloom.

It is perhaps well for poetry that Humphreys gave it up for diplomacy. After years abroad and marriage to a wealthy Englishwoman, he returned to America in 1802 to become a manufacturer of the cloth he had urged on his fellow Americans in his poetry at the end of the war.

Joel Barlow was the least consistent and most exciting of all the "Wits." Like them he had faith in American destiny, and to begin with he had their vision of it. His friend Noah Webster said that in 1785 Barlow was the go-between for some rich merchants and military men in New England "to give a government to this country by force" in case of civil convulsion. Webster said that at the time Barlow was "ripe" for the establishment of a monarchy.[34] In 1787 he published his epic, *The Vision of Columbus*. In it he sang of the new nation and its opportunities in every field; of opportunities for education not only in its colleges but also:

> . . . and where rude hamlets stretch their inland sway,
> with humbler walls unnumbered schools arise,
> And youths unnumber'd seize the solid prize.
> In no blest land has Science rear'd her fane,
> And fixed so firm her wide-extended reign;
> Each rustic here, that turns the furrow'd soil,
> The maid, the youth, that ply mechanic toil,
> In freedom nurst, in useful arts inured,
> Know their just claims, and see their rights secured.

Like other American writers he made little from it. Richard Price wrote from England that no bookseller in England would dare to print it because of its dedication to the King of France and its praise of the American and French armies. David Ramsay in Charleston offered to try to sell twenty-five copies but doubted

[34] Noah Webster: *A Letter to General Hamilton* (1800), 5, cited by Harry R. Warfel, *American Literature*, VI (1934–5), 466.

that he could because "we have few readers here." Only people like Ramsay, who had published books, would be apt to buy it.[35]

In 1788 Barlow began a new career. He had been a chaplain during the Revolution, then a lawyer in Hartford, a dabbler in politics and poetry, and now he went to France as a land salesman for the Ohio Company. In France he became as enthusiastic for the French Revolution as his friends in Connecticut were horrified by it. With Thomas Paine he joined in the attack on Edmund Burke. His "Advice to the Privileged orders of Europe" was as much a manifesto of democracy as any of Paine's writings. It won him the enmity of the English government, but it also won him citizenship in the French Republic. In 1795 he was appointed United States consul in Algiers where he played an important part in settling difficulties with the Barbary States. In 1805 he came home to study and write and to urge national education. Then in 1811 James Madison appointed him minister to France. He died in Poland while on his way to meet Napoleon.

Still another Connecticut Yankee to write of and serve the new nation was Jedidiah Morse, the "Father of American Geography." He was graduated from Yale in 1783, decided to be a minister, and stayed on for two more years teaching and studying. Thereafter he went away to teach school, returned to Yale as a tutor, then preached in Georgia for a while, and finally, in 1789, went to Charlestown, Massachusetts, and was installed as pastor in a church where he remained for thirty years. Theologically he was an arch-Calvinist who campaigned against those tainted with Unitarian notions, and he helped to drive them out of the Congregational Church. Politically he was a Federalist who thundered against the iniquities of democracy and the French Revolution. He was a "Pillar of Adamant in the temple of Federalism." [36]

But his greatest fame was gained as a writer of books on American geography. He did not like European accounts of America, so in 1784 he published *Geography Made Easy*, a book that went through twenty-five editions in his lifetime. Meanwhile he wrote a far larger work, *The American Geography*, which was published in 1789. It went through many editions in America and Europe, and won him an honorary degree from Edinburgh

[35] Price to Barlow, 4 Feb. 1787, Ramsay to Barlow, 10 April 1787, Barlow Papers, Harvard University Library.

[36] A. Johnson and D. Malone, eds.: *Dictionary of American Biography* (20 vols., New York, 1928–36), XIII, 245–7.

University. He went on to write many other works, for he was, as his friend Timothy Dwight said, "as full of resources as an egg is of meat."[37]

His *American Geography* was far more than a geography. Morse wrote of politics, economics, and literature as well. The first fifth of the book, after a bow in the direction of geographical definitions, is taken up with a history of the United States from the founding of the colonies through the adoption of the Constitution of 1787. He believed that the "natural genius of Americans" had suffered from want of information "in the descriptions of some ingenious and eloquent European writers." He declared flatly that "the literature of the United States is very flourishing. Their progress in the art of war, in the science of government, in philosophy and astronomy, in poetry, and the various liberal arts and sciences, has, for so young a country, been astonishing."[38] He quoted at length from Jefferson's *Notes on Virginia* in defense of American genius, as well as of the size of American livestock. But he admitted that Americans had their faults and he lectured them like the stern parson he was. They drank too much; they imported too many manufactured goods; negro slavery was bad and carnal intercourse between whites and blacks was an abomination. Many Americans did not like to pay their taxes, and even worse, wanted paper money. This latter sinfulness, praise Heaven, had been stopped by the adoption of the Constitution. The rest of the book takes up the states one by one, with much commentary on character and government, and only a moderate amount of geography. Americans in general were good, but the New Englanders were by all means the best. Even of Vermonters, for whose ideas he could say little, he remarks: "It is sufficient to say they are New Englandmen."

The careers, the activities, and the influence of all these writers pale to nothing beside that of the greatest publicist of the age: for himself, for his books, and for the new nation—Noah Webster. He was born at West Hartford, Connecticut, in 1758, entered Yale in 1774 and was graduated in 1778. His father mortgaged the family farm to pay his college bills. Yale was disrupted by the war, but not Noah Webster. When he was called to serve in

[37] Ibid., XIII, 245–7.

[38] *The American Geography; Or a View of the Present Situation of the United States of America* (Elizabeth Town [N. J.], 1789), 63, 65.

the state militia he insisted that as a student he was a member of the corporate body of Yale and not subject to the draft.[39]

He studied law and was admitted to practice in Hartford in 1781. But lawyers were many and fees were small. He tried to start a school in Sharon, Connecticut, but failed. The next year he turned up at Goshen, New York, with seventy-five cents in his pocket and got a job teaching school. By this time he was full of a great desire to write textbooks extolling the American language in order to free Americans from dependence on English texts and to make money for himself. He planned three books: a speller, a grammar, and a reader, and he proposed to call them "The American Instructor." His plans were submitted to many people, among others Ezra Stiles, president of Yale, who talked him into calling the series "A Grammatical Institute of the English Language."

The speller was published in 1783. In its preface Webster wrote a manifesto in behalf of America in which he said:

"The author wishes to promote the honour and prosperity of the confederated republics of America; and cheerfully throws his mite into the common treasure of patriotic exertions. This country must in some future time, be as distinguished by the superiority of her literary improvements, as she is already by the liberality of her civil and ecclesiastical constitutions. Europe is grown old in folly, corruption and tyranny—in that country laws are perverted, manners are licentious, literature is declining and human nature debased. For America in her infancy to adopt the present maxims of the old world, would be to stamp the wrinkles of decrepit age upon the bloom of youth and to plant the seeds of decay in a vigorous constitution. American glory begins to dawn at a favourable period, and under flattering circumstances. We have the experience of the whole world before our eyes; but to receive indiscriminately the maxims of government, the manners and the literary taste of Europe and make them the ground on which to build our systems in America, must soon convince us that a durable and stately edifice can never be erected upon the mouldering pillars of antiquity. It is the business of *Americans* to select the wisdom of all nations, as the basis of her constitutions, to avoid their errours, to prevent the introduction of foreign vices and corruptions and check the career of her own, to promote virtue and patriotism, to embellish and improve the sciences, to diffuse an uniformity and purity of language, to add superior dignity to this infant Empire and to human nature." [40]

[39] Noah Webster Papers, NYPL.
[40] Harry R. Warfel: *Noah Webster* (New York, 1936), 59–60.

The grammar was published in 1784, the reader in 1785, and Webster was launched on a career as one of the most successful textbook writers in the history of the world. The speller was the most popular. In 1837 Webster estimated that 15,000,000 copies had been sold, by 1890 the number was 60,000,000, and happy publishers do not find it unsaleable even at present.

Meanwhile Webster pamphleteered for the congressional impost, the commutation of army pay, and judicial reform. In 1785 he published *Sketches of American Policy* in which he declared that representative democracy was the most perfect system of government. He demanded a "new model" central government with the power to make laws and force the states to obey them. Without such power the Confederation could never be more than "a burlesque on government." [41]

While he pamphleteered and worked on his texts, he continued to study law and for a short time had a scanty, unprofitable practice. He then set out on a tour of the United States to sell his books. In May 1785, aged twenty-seven, he left Hartford, carrying copies of his texts and of *Sketches of American Policy*. He traveled everywhere, met everybody of consequence, and sought testimonials for his works. He lobbied for copyright laws with an astonishing degree of success. Neither youth nor lack of experience could stop the busy Yankee peddler. He asked Washington to help introduce his texts in the South but Washington begged off as not being a good judge of such matters.[42] Later he talked Washington out of asking for a young Scotsman as a secretary, insisting that the northern colleges could supply a man. Webster offered to take the job but since he could not begin at once, Tobias Lear, another New Englander, got the post.[43]

When Webster got to Charleston he advertised his *Grammatical Institute* as "an attempt of an American to ascertain the pronunciation of the English language. . . ." He said that 20,000 copies had been sold in the northern states in the eighteen months since publication. Webster declared that his books "will encourage genius in this country, and the EMPIRE OF AMERICA will no longer be indebted to a foreign kingdom for books to learn the children

[41] *Sketches of American Policy* (Facsimile ed., New York, 1937).

[42] Webster to Washington, Baltimore, 18 July 1785, Washington Papers, LC; Warfel, 122.

[43] Ibid., 130–1.

their native language."[44] With canny practicality he gave several hundred copies of his speller and grammar to a committee engaged in the founding of a new college. The advertising and good will he got as a result made his books standard in South Carolina.[45]

He returned to Baltimore where he tried to start a school. When this failed he offered to teach singing. His success was so great that after his first public concert he got a large class. The life of a singing teacher was hopelessly frustrating for a man of Webster's ambitions. He now decided to become a lecturer in order to spread the gospel of an American language and to sell his books. He got the idea after listening to a blind man give a lecture on light. He wrote five lectures on the history of the English language, pronunciation, errors in pronunciation, errors in the use of words, and on education. In these lectures he urged the principles set forth in his texts and particularly the idea that popular speech and common usage should determine the rules rather than ideas taken from arbitrary, and particularly from English, compilers of dictionaries.[46]

Webster lectured in Philadelphia, Annapolis, and New York, and members of Congress and governors of states and lesser people turned out to hear him.[47] After his lectures in New Haven, the *New Haven Gazette* commented that they "command the attention and excite the speculations of our politicians as well as of the literati." Plans were on foot to reform the alphabet, giving each letter an invariable sound in order to make written language conform with the spoken.[48]

Webster was lecturing in Massachusetts at the outbreak of Shays's Rebellion. Once more he wrote essays for the newspapers. He denounced villainous legislatures and demanded law and order. He attacked schemes for paper money in New England and again urged a national union. Where a short year before he had praised representative democracy as the best of all forms of government, he now declared that people were too ignorant to manage their own affairs. "This is the misfortune of republican governments. For my own part, I confess, I was once as strong a

[44] *The State Gazette of South Carolina*, 30 June 1785.
[45] Warfel, 123.
[46] Ibid., 121, 124–9. The lectures were published in 1789 as *Dissertations on the English Language*.
[47] *Pennsylvania Gazette*, 18 Jan., 15 March 1786.
[48] 29 June 1786.

republican as any man in America. Now, a republican is among the last kinds of government I should choose. I would infinitely prefer a limited monarchy, for I would sooner be the subject of the caprice of one man, than to the ignorance and passions of the multitude."[49] Back in Hartford he was no longer popular, he was broke, and there was no room for more lawyers, so he set off for New York. From there he went to Philadelphia where he talked with Franklin about his schemes for simplified spelling. Although he could get no audiences for his lectures, he was in the thick of politics, now wholeheartedly on the side of the nationalists. He made only one error: he came out against the speculators in public funds. He thought that the original holders of public debt should be paid in full and that the speculators should get only what they had paid, plus interest. He was wildly accused of being a fomenter of rebellion, but he defended himself and republished his diatribes against paper money to show that he was "sound."[50]

Once the Constitution of 1787 was presented to the public, Webster pamphleteered for its adoption. He then decided to start a magazine. All the large towns except New York had one, so to New York he went and founded *The American Magazine.* It was soon one of the best. Webster's writing was vigorous, his interests were wide, and he was careless of the toes he trod on, but he lost money and within a year he went back to Hartford to practice law. At the age of thirty-one, after many failures as a suitor, he was married. Within a few years he was back in New York as a newspaper editor only to give it up and return once more to Connecticut. His name was known everywhere, but his great career was yet ahead of him. Once settled in New Haven he took up the study of language in earnest. The first result was a dictionary published in 1806 and the final outcome was the first edition of *An American Dictionary of the English Language* in 1828. His battles and projects continued to be many. Most of them are forgotten today, but no man could hope for more enduring monuments than the Blue Backed Speller and Webster's Dictionary.

The writers who were stimulated by the creation of a new nation made a vigorous contribution to the thought and life of the 1780's.

[49] *Connecticut Courant*, 20 Nov. 1786.
[50] Warfel, 160–1. See *post*, ch. xvi.

Most of them were dubious about, if not violently opposed to, the political democracy that was either expressed or implicit in the actions of the state governments. Yet they still believed in the promise made possible by independence. David Ramsay, in his *History of the American Revolution*, summed up those beliefs and analyzed the progress since the beginning of the Revolution. He decried democratic excesses, as did other members of his social group, and hailed the Constitution of 1787 as a check upon democratic action. He believed that the Revolution gave America virtues as well as vices. It broke down localism. When the war began, "the Americans were a mass of husbandmen, merchants, mechanics, and fishermen; but the necessities of the country gave a spring to the active power of the inhabitants, and set them on thinking, speaking and acting, in a line far beyond that to which they had been accustomed. The difference between nations is not so much owing to nature, as to education and circumstances." The "leading strings" of the mother country were broken at the outset and Americans then had to carry on the work of civil society by themselves. The Continental Army helped to break down barriers; intermarriages were taking place; bigotry was being destroyed by the disestablishment of state churches. Schools and colleges were closed by the war, yet many arts and sciences, such as geography, were promoted by it. The needs of defense resulted in the invention of a machine "for submarine navigation" and of "sundry other curious machines for the annoyance of British shipping." Surgeons had learned more in a day on the field of battle than they could in years of peace. The Revolution had diffused knowledge of the "science of government" among Americans. Mistakes were made but they had learned much, particularly of the "folly of unbalanced constitutions and injudicious laws."

In winning independence, the pen and the press were of equal merit with the sword. "As the war was the people's war, and was carried on without funds," it could not have been won by the army alone if the great body of the people had not been prepared and kept in constant opposition to Great Britain. To rouse them and keep them united for years was difficult work and was "effected in a great measure by the tongues and pens of the well informed citizens, and on it depended the success of military operations."

Without schools and colleges, which had trained the revolutionary leaders, the Revolution might have failed for the "union which was essential to the success of their resistance, could scarcely have taken place, in the measures adopted by an ignorant multitude." Ramsay insisted that it was the uninformed and the misinformed in places "never illuminated, or but faintly warmed by the rays of science" who had opposed independence.

Literature too had favored revolution and had in turn been promoted by it. Ramsay listed the writers who had supported the war and then went on to describe the increase of schools, colleges, and societies for human betterment, the last of which had been founded at a rate never equaled before the Declaration of Independence.

Yet all was not well, for the overturning of an established government "unhinges many of those principles which bind individuals to each other." Principles such as the right of a people to resist their rulers were necessary in 1775, but they are not favorable to "the tranquility of present establishments," especially when "recurrence is had to them by factious demagogues. . . ." The military, political, and literary talents of Americans were bettered as a result of the war, but their moral character was inferior to what it had been. It was therefore necessary for the friends of public order to do their utmost to extirpate vicious principles and habits which had taken deep root.

Thus Ramsay's summation of the results of the Revolution was an expression of his thoroughly conservative political philosophy. He was in harmony with most of the writers of the period who hoped to shape the destiny of the nation they had helped create. They urged their ideas with fervor and imagination and sometimes with literary merit. The nation, for which they wrote and to which they preached, often ignored them, for it was so busy with practical things that it neither bought their books nor read them. Yet even so, they mirrored a spirit of optimism that was characteristic of the most practical man. The majority shared the writers' beliefs in America's great destiny at the same time that it disagreed with them as to the nature of its political character.[51]

[51] David Ramsay: *The History of the American Revolution* (2 vols., Philadelphia, 1789), II, appendix 4.

5

The People and the Governments of the New Nation

THE NEW nation that was born into a world of empires stretched from the Atlantic Ocean on the east to the Mississippi River on the west, and from British Canada on the north to Spanish Florida on the south. In 1789 Jedidiah Morse, the "father of American geography," recorded that Thomas Hutchins, the first geographer of the United States, had measured the length, breadth, and extent of the new nation. There were a million square miles of it: 589,000,000 acres of land and 51,000,000 acres of water. Beyond the frontiers lay the Old Northwest, a vast public domain estimated at 220,000,000 acres. The states ceded it to the government of the United States. Thus, more than a third of the new nation was unoccupied, except by the Indians, and to it Americans could and did look for expansion, profit, and the payment of the national debt.[1]

The new nation had perhaps 3,000,000 people in 1775. Of these about a half million were Negroes, most of whom were slaves. Population increased astonishingly during and after the Revolution. The census of 1790 counted 3,699,525. This growth was the result of immigration and of natural increase, and was made up of "people of almost all nations, languages, characters, and religions." The greater part, however, was descended from English stock and "for the sake of distinction, are called Anglo-Americans." [2] Of the total population in 1790 nearly a sixth were Negro slaves, most of them living in the states south of Pennsylvania.

[1] *American Geography*, 35.

[2] Ibid., 63. Morse estimated the population at 3,083,600 in 1789.

Not counted, yet very much in evidence, were tens of thousands of hostile Indians on the northern, western, and southern frontiers. Their experience had built up within them a burning desire to exterminate all white men, and particularly the American variety. Most citizens of the new nation, in turn, had as ardent a desire to reduce the Indian population as rapidly as possible, by fair means or foul.

The vast majority of the white and black population of the United States lived in a narrow band of settlement along the Atlantic coast stretching from Maine to Georgia. As one moved westward from the ocean, people were fewer in number and settlements more and more scattered until one reached the western side of the Appalachian ranges. Only a few permanent settlers had ventured beyond the Alleghenies before 1783. But after 1783 people poured westward in such vast numbers that during the 1790's two new states were created in what had been wilderness only a few years before. The citizens of the new nation were tantalized by thoughts of a strange land and by visions of wealth in the West and the South. Most of those who moved were farmers, but with them went hunters, fur traders, and adventurers, and those men who wanted to and could escape from what seemed to them the drab reality of life along the coast.

Both Americans and Europeans were aware of the promise of the vast area of unoccupied lands in the Ohio Valley, and writer after writer told of the movement of people to the frontiers. Those who had fled from the frontiers at the outset of war started back on the news of peace. In April 1783 a report from Albany said that "the roads are daily filled with their removals." In the fall of the same year another report said that the "rage for land here exceeds all conception and the influx of people from the East is so great, that this kind of speculation is the object of every person who has the means to embark on it." [3] Dr. Edward Bancroft, renegade Yankee and British spy, wrote from Philadelphia late in 1783 that "multitudes of people are gone and going over the Allegheny Mountains, to settle near the Ohio. . . ." He expected great disorders "from the licentious, ungovernable temper of all the interior inhabitants of America." [4] A Frenchman described

[3] Marinus Willett to Washington, 14 April 1783, Washington Papers, LC; Robert S. Hooper to James Wilson, 27 Sept. 1783, James Wilson Papers, Pennsylvania Historical Society.

[4] To William Frazer, 8 Nov. 1783, Bancroft: *Constitution*, I, 333.

the same movement. The new westerners would form into "free societies" when there were enough of them and he doubted they would ever be subject to Congress. He saw no gain in the movement except for the "unhappy of Europe," and particularly those of Britain and Germany, who might succeed in escaping from government oppression and the burden of public debt.[5] A letter from Ireland said that a shipload of young fellows, mechanics, and artificers, was leaving because of heavier taxes, "too impatient to wait for better times at home. . . ."[6]

The "powerful emigrations" from states like Virginia to North and South Carolina, Georgia, and Kentucky alarmed men like Richard Henry Lee. He said the movement was the result of too heavy taxes and of the people's desire for land. As a remedy he proposed lower taxes and a reasonable debt-funding program.[7] The movement from eastern New England where those in control of governments were far less concerned with the plight of the farmers than the Virginia planters, was much more striking. Even in Rhode Island, which was looked upon by its neighbors as a heaven for debtor farmers, an English traveler reported "it's astonishing the number of people that have emigrated from this place to settle in different parts of New England and New York."[8] Another English traveler passing through upper New York and Vermont in 1785 said that the region was then "settling very fast by people from the eastern states."[9]

No one knows how many people moved westward year by year. One count was made at Fort Harmar where troops were stationed. From the tenth of October 1786 to the twelfth of May 1787, the adjutant of the troops counted "177 boats containing 2,689 souls, 1,333 horses, 766 cattle, 102 wagons and one phaeton; besides a number which passed in the night unobserved."[10] A letter from Fort Finney on the Ohio described the glories of the country and the "amazing emigration" that could no more be stopped than a

[5] Luzerne to Rayneval, 21 April 1784, ibid., I, 355–6.

[6] *The Pennsylvania Packet, and Daily Advertiser*, 29 April 1785.

[7] To James Madison, 20 Nov. 1784, James C. Ballagh, ed.: *The Letters of Richard Henry Lee* (2 vols., New York, 1911, 1914), II, 300.

[8] Robert C. Hunter, jr.: *Quebec to Carolina in 1785–1786* (Louis B. Wright and Marion Tinling, eds., San Marino, 1943), 119.

[9] Joseph Hadfield: *An Englishman in America, 1785* (Douglas S. Robertson, ed., Toronto, 1933), 23, 36–7.

[10] *Massachusetts Centinel*, 21 July 1787.

torrent of water. The population of Kentucky was 176 in June of 1779 and it was over 30,000 by December 1785.[11] This country, wrote Samuel Holden Parsons from the mouth of the Miami, is a "terrestrial paradise." The population exceeds belief and any man is better off with one fourth of his estate here than he would be with the whole of it in New England.[12]

John Jay, secretary of foreign affairs, did not trust his fellow Americans who were moving westward. Yet in 1785 he said that "a rage for emigrating to the western country prevails, and thousands have already fixed their habitations in that wilderness. The Continental Land Office is opened, and the seeds of a great people are daily planting beyond the mountains." [13] Two years later he wrote to Thomas Jefferson that "the enterprise of our countrymen is inconceivable, and the number of young men daily going down to settle in the western country is further proof of it." Yet he feared the "western country" would one day give trouble, and questioned whether the people there would be fit to govern themselves after two or three generations.[14] Robert Morris said that his acquaintances were of the opinion that "emigrations from the middle states to the western country are already so great as to be injurious" and therefore they did not want to encourage it in any way.[15]

The growth of population west of the Alleghenies was a source of wonder to men both east and west. One said there were 150 men but no women in Kentucky in 1775. By 1790 there were 73,677 people including 12,430 slaves and 114 free Negroes. Tennessee had a population of 7,700 in 1776 and 35,691 in 1790.

Even more striking was the movement down the mountain valleys into the back country of Virginia, the Carolinas, and Georgia. Virginia had 400,000 people in 1775 and nearly 750,000 by 1790. In 1775 South Carolina had 150,000, and 250,000 by 1790. Georgia had 50,000 at the beginning of the war and over 82,000 in 1790. At the same time New Englanders, who were pouring both west and south, were also pouring northward into Maine and Vermont. Vermont had 30,000 people in 1784, and

[11] *New Haven Gazette*, 2 March 1786.

[12] To [William Samuel Johnson?], 26 Nov. 1785, William Samuel Johnson Papers, LC.

[13] To William Bingham, 31 May 1785, *Correspondence*, III, 153–4.

[14] 24 April 1787, ibid., III, 245.

[15] To Winthrop Sargent, 12 May 1786, Winthrop Sargent Papers, MHS.

85,000 by 1790. Maine's population was a fourth of that of Massachusetts by 1790. Perhaps a hundred thousand people moved out of the four old states during the 1780's, fleeing from heavy taxes to lighter ones, and from poorer to better lands.[16]

The population that grew and thrust westward beyond the Alleghenies, southwestward down the mountain valleys, and northward into upper New England was made up mostly of farmers. But American cities also grew rapidly, some of them amazingly, despite the dislocation and destruction caused by war. Yet the war itself was partly responsible for the new growth. Merchants from smaller towns moved into larger ones and rapidly took the place of the Loyalist merchants who had left. Thus Stephen Higginson, Elbridge Gerry, the Cabots, the Lowells, and others moved from smaller Massachusetts seaports to Boston. Foreigners such as Stephen Girard and John Holker from France, and many more from England, Scotland, and Holland, moved to New York, Philadelphia, and other towns to take advantage of the opportunities that would be the fruits of independence.[17]

The five "great" cities of the United States were Philadelphia, New York, Boston, Charleston, and Baltimore. One can make only rough estimates of their population at the beginning of the war. Philadelphia, the metropolis of the mainland colonies, had at least 30,000 in 1776; New York perhaps 22,000; Boston 16,000; Charleston 14,000, and Baltimore 6,000.[18] During the 1780's various efforts were made to count the inhabitants of American towns. Newspapers reported the number of houses and then guessed at the number of people living in each.[19]

The census of 1790 is a clear index to the rapid growth of cities

[16] Lewis C. Gray: *History of Agriculture in the Southern United States to 1860* (2 vols., Washington, 1933), II, 614–5; Evarts B. Greene and Virginia Harrington: *American Population Before the Federal Census of 1790* (New York, 1932), *passim.* Most population figures before the census of 1790 are estimates which vary widely from source to source. The figures given are at best highly uncertain.

[17] East: *Business Enterprise*, 231–7.

[18] Stella H. Sutherland: *Population Distribution in Colonial America* (New York, 1936); Greene and Harrington: *American Population*, *passim.*

[19] *Pennsylvania Gazette*, 23 Aug. 1786 and *The Gazette of the State of South Carolina*, 14 Sept. 1786. In 1786 it was said that Philadelphia had 4,600 houses; New York 3,500; Boston 2,100; Baltimore 1,900; Charleston 1,540. Far behind them were Albany with 550; New Haven 400; Hartford 300; Wilmington, Del. 400; Annapolis 260; Frederick Town, Md. 400; Alexandria, Va. 300; Richmond 280; Petersburg 290; Williamsburg 230.

after 1775. It showed that Philadelphia and New York had grown by a third in fifteen years and that Baltimore had more than doubled.[20] Other American towns had grown proportionately. The accounts of house building during the 1780's are additional evidence of city growth. Baltimore was America's boom town. Before the war was over its citizens were concerned with its "notorious" unpaved streets and asked for advice on paving costs.[21] Three years later a British traveler reported that the "side pavement here is as convenient as at Philadelphia." He said that it was astonishing "what a stir there is in Baltimore." The houses were almost entirely of brick and they were "building away here in every corner of the town as fast [as] possible." [22] In Philadelphia building went on at an even more rapid rate. One proud citizen declared that no less than 600 brick houses were built in a single summer, and this fact alone he felt, was answer enough for those who thought that Philadelphia was declining because of the commercial depression.[23]

To the south, Charleston recovered slowly from the ravages of occupation. North Carolina towns were growing with expanding trade. Alexandria, Virginia, was made the sole port of entry for foreign shipping entering the Potomac in 1784, an effort of the Virginia planters to avoid the toll they must otherwise pay to the merchants of Baltimore and Philadelphia. In New England, which was hurt more by the commercial depression than the middle and southern states, there were similar developments. Robert Hunter reported that Providence, Rhode Island, was a town of 500 houses, 150 of which had been built after the end of the war. Rents were very high because many strangers always were in the town. President Stiles of Yale told Hunter that New Haven had 450 houses, fifty of which had been built in the past year.[24]

The rapid growth of cities led to many complaints and prob-

[20] In 1790 Philadelphia had a population of 28,522 plus 13,998 in the suburbs; New York 32,328 plus 803 in Harlem; Boston 18,038; Charleston 16,359; Baltimore 13,503.

[21] Samuel Purviance to George Bryan, 6 March 1782, George Bryan Papers, PHS.

[22] Hunter: *Quebec to Carolina*, 179–80. General Greene said that 300 houses were built in Baltimore during 1783. East: *Business Enterprise*, 234–5.

[23] *Pennsylvania Packet*, 29 April 1785.

[24] Hunter: *Quebec to Carolina*, 118, 154.

lems. Carpenters and masons were hard to get, and their wages were higher than they ever had been. Rents were so high as to be a scandal to the godly, a trial to tenants, and a source of joy to landlords. Franklin estimated that values of lands and houses had tripled between the time he left America before the war and the time he returned in 1785.[25] In Boston it was said that no house had ever rented for more than fifty pounds a year before the war but by 1786 they were renting for from eighty to a hundred and fifty pounds. Landlords were denounced for grinding the faces of the poor, exacting the last farthing from distressed tenants, and letting houses stand empty rather than lower their rents. Honest industry should not "suffer, to indulge these insatiable leeches, who fatten and are bloated by the blood of the honest mechanic, and hard working laborer." [26]

The rising cities had other problems. One ever old and ever new problem was that of prostitution. One citizen of Boston declared that the increase was "incredible" and unless stopped in the "embryo" would have pernicious consequences. Furthermore the officers of the town whose job it was to "confine those of that sect in the work house, are the very frequenters of their infernal habitations, and seem rather to encourage their diabolical proceedings than put a stop to them." [27]

Another ageless problem was that of garbage disposal. The street commissioners of Philadelphia tried to economize by getting farmers and others to clean the streets in exchange for manure. This was in January 1783. By the end of August the citizenry were denouncing the commissioners. The dirty streets were declared to be a principal source of disease: dead dogs, cats, fowls, and offal from the market place were the cleanest articles to be found in them. Never would they be cleaner as long as the farmers and gardeners were free to remove garbage when they pleased. The harassed street commissioners admitted, after a year's trial, that the plan had not worked, and once more hired "scavengers." The retreat was hurried by the publication of "Dialogues of the Dead" wherein a dead dog and a dead cat lying in the streets of

[25] To M. Le Veillard, 6 March 1786, John Bigelow, ed.: *The Complete Works of Benjamin Franklin* (10 vols., New York, 1887–8), IX, 300–1.

[26] *Massachusetts Centinel*, 12 April 1786.

[27] Ibid., 4 June 1785.

Philadelphia, discussed the past and the presumably unhappy future of the unhappy street commissioners.[28]

The nature of city government came in for heated discussion. Before the war both legal and informal town meetings had been a focal point of revolutionary activity. Now that the war was over, conservative-minded men sought to avoid further unpleasantness by doing away with town meeting government, substituting for it a corporate form whereby the towns could be governed by mayors and councils. Incorporation as means of escape from democratic town meetings had been proposed before the war by aristocratic leaders like Thomas Hutchinson. Of Boston he said, "this town is no corporation, but by virtue of several province laws all towns are empowered to meet for a few special purposes only" and are illegal when meeting for any other purpose. Yet, he said, most town meetings were held without legal authority and should be punished. But this could not be done except "by a legislative power superior to any within the province. . . ." He declared that "if the town was a corporation, much of the disorder would be prevented." [29]

The first town to be incorporated after the war was Charleston, South Carolina. The city was divided into wards, elections were held, and thereafter ordinances poured forth. They ranged all the way from one forbidding the killing of cattle within the city limits to regulations organizing the port. This was hailed as opening a new era in the history of the city, propitious for its rising glory, increasing commerce, and growing opulence.[30]

New Haven was incorporated shortly thereafter with a corporation consisting of "a mayor, aldermen and common council, officers hitherto unknown in the eastern states." This was the work of "five of the principal gentlemen" who had, according to the report, the unanimous support of the people. Every man, whatever his religion or politics, was to be a citizen. The corporation was to improve streets, plant double rows of elms, extend the pier, cut canals, and in general make the city a commercial center. The corporation was also reported to have in view "some literary establishments. . . . Thus, the enlightened patriotism

[28] *Pennsylvania Gazette*, 22 Jan., 27 Aug. 1783; 21 Jan., 10 March 1784.

[29] To John Pownall, 23 Oct. 1769, C. O. 5:758, Public Record Office, Great Britain. New York and Philadelphia were the only important American cities having a corporate form of government before 1776.

[30] *South Carolina Gazette*, 23–6 Aug. 1783, et seq.

of few will cause the prosperity of this new city; may it become rich and flourishing, as it is already the most salubrious and elegant on the continent." [31]

In New Jersey the merchants backed incorporation consistently in an effort to escape town meetings. Petitions for incorporation began coming into the legislature in 1784 and during that year New Brunswick, Perth Amboy, and Burlington were given charters.[32] The same movement went on even in Virginia.[33]

The attempt to incorporate Philadelphia and Boston met much more, and for a time, successful opposition. Philadelphia had been governed by a closed corporation before the war. From 1776 on it was in the hands of the executive council and the assembly. By 1781 certain citizens were demanding incorporation. During 1783 petitions both for and against incorporation were presented to the legislature. The division on the issue was a strict party one. The conservative, the "Republican" party, demanded a charter on the ground that the city needed better police protection and other regulations. The democratic forces, the "Constitutionalist" party, opposed it bitterly as an "aristocratical" scheme. They declared that since the proposed charter limited the vote to freeholders, three fourths of the population would be disfranchised. Not until 1789, when the Republicans were in complete control of the legislature, was Philadelphia incorporated. The new city government was at once put in operation with Samuel Powell, the pre-war mayor, as mayor once more, and with Benjamin Chew, the neutral, if not Loyalist, colonial chief justice, as a member of the council. The counter-revolution in Philadelphia was complete.[34]

The greatest battle came in Boston where the town meeting idea was so firmly imbedded that it could not be overturned for decades. The movement got under way early in 1784 and was backed by a "great number of very respectable gentlemen." [35] When the town met in May, the hall was packed. The governor, lieutenant-governor, and "several other gentlemen of distinction were present." A long debate was "not without a small degree of

[31] Letter from Hartford, *Pennsylvania Gazette,* 18 Feb. 1784.

[32] Richard McCormick: New Jersey in the Confederation (Ph.D. Thesis, University of Pennsylvania, 1946).

[33] John Dawson to Madison, 12 June 1787, Madison Papers, LC.

[34] Robert L. Brunhouse: *The Counter-Revolution in Pennsylvania, 1776–1790* (Harrisburg, 1942), 152–3, 184–5, 220–1, 247.

[35] *Massachusetts Centinel,* 28 April, 1 May.

tartness. . . ." Joseph Barrell, a wealthy merchant, talked at length on the need of incorporation. He declared that the police system was bad and could be improved only by handing the government over to a mayor, alderman, and councilmen. This would save both time and money, for the citizens had spent at least a tenth of their time in town meetings during the past eight years. He said that he had no self-interest in the matter but was concerned only for the good of his fellow citizens.

Sam Adams, for long the great leader and manipulator of the Boston town meeting, then rose to defend it in one of the few of his speeches of which we have a record. He denied that change was necessary. The "present constitution" of the town had more than a century of experience behind it. A change of measures rather than of government would take care of the grievances. The new plan carried with it the "appearance, and might in its consequences be instrumental to the introduction of aristocracy, a government of all others, he said, the worst." A love of novelty and the desire for change in other nations had been the avenue by which aristocracy had entered, and he cited the Greek and Roman republics as examples. There were men in America as well as in Europe who "continue such a hankering for the *leeks and onions* of Great Britain, that they leave no opportunity unoccupied for their introduction into this country." Adams declared that he was "too great a friend to democracy ever to wish they may succeed."

The issue was thus clearly defined. Others spoke. Those who supported the idea of incorporation repeated Barrell's ideas, while those who were opposed demanded the appointment of a committee to report at the next town meeting. Barrell demanded a vote then and there, but men like Stephen Higginson, as well as Sam Adams, would not have it. So it was agreed to appoint a committee to consider the petition for incorporation and to report on defects and the need for better police regulations. Both sides were represented on the committee, which included Sam Adams and Joseph Barrell.[36]

The fight was at once transferred to the newspapers. One moderate writer asked for more information from the supporters of the plan since the people in general did not have it, and especially because it was "allowed on all hands that the management of the affairs of the town, will, under the proposed form be less

[36] Ibid., 12, 15 May 1784.

popular. . . ." Another writer expressed the hope that at the next town meeting "Mr. Bluster" would allow the citizens to talk freely without branding them with the epithet "dirty dirty, fellow" if they did not agree with his dogmatic statements.[37] "An American" took a lofty tone. He decried the personalities which had appeared in the newspapers and declared that the demand for incorporation was for the benefit of the "mechanicks" who were starving because country people were competing with them in manufactures which could be kept out if a corporation government were set up.[38]

When the town met again on 4 June, two plans were presented by the committee. After a long debate it was voted to print the plans for the perusal of the citizens, and the meeting was adjourned to 17 June.[39] "An American" came back once more with a long "historical" argument citing examples as far back as the eleventh century to prove that law, police, and commerce are all improved when cities are incorporated. But such arguments were useless because the "mechanicks" were the "principal opposers." [40]

The movement was killed in 1784 but it rose again with new vigor in the fall of 1785. At a town meeting in October, a petition for incorporation with over 100 signatures was presented, but when the moderator asked its "fathers" to explain their object, no one appeared and there was a "buz." Some said the petition should be rejected, but a majority were for the appointment of a committee "to conjure up, (as a gentleman there expressed it) the end and aim thereof, and to report accordingly." A "Mechanick" sniffed that "the better sort" of people had revived the idea of incorporation. Another town meeting was called to consider the question while the debate went on in the press. "Old Whackum" declared that it was another attempt to deprive the people of their native rights and privileges and to set up an aristocratical power. He cited a letter of Edward Randolph, who had talked of the "better sort" and the "low folks," and a letter of Hutchinson in 1770, in which he described the selectmen as the creatures of the populace and said the town was ruled by the lowest sort of people.

"A Bostonian" declared that the Revolution had come from the

[37] Ibid., 19 May 1784.

[38] Ibid., 26 May 1784.

[39] Ibid., 5 June 1784. One was a plan for mayor, recorder, aldermen, and councilmen; the other for a president with a selectman from each ward.

[40] Ibid., 16 June, 10 July 1784.

town meeting and said that incorporation would put power in the hands of the few. "Publicola" saw "tyranny erecting its brazen front. . . ." There are those people who fondly think that the republican principles, which every native sucks in with his milk, and annual elections, "will effectually check the pride and power of the rich" and thus preserve equality. But the destruction of that equality is what "a few haughty, purse-proud *better sort of folks*, mortified that the poor should have equal liberty," have long wanted to achieve. Such people are like the "arch-fiend Hutchinson" and all their arguments are lies.

The opposition was so effective that at the next town meeting the petitioners for incorporation asked and were given leave to withdraw their petition. The meeting was adjourned to a later date for the purpose of adopting a code of bylaws and on 6 December 1785 this was done. Even the *Massachusetts Centinel*, which had been so heartily in favor of incorporation, greeted the decision with relief and declared that "at length the storm subsides, and the din of 'incorporation,' is no longer to assail our ears." [41]

Sam Adams had long since lost power in state politics, but in the Boston town meeting the old master was still supreme. Boston incorporation did not come until long after he was dead, and long after the growth of the town had rendered the town meeting system unworkable. But elsewhere the combined forces of urban growth and reaction in politics swept American cities in the direction of more formal governments less responsive to the will of the electorate. Only in rural areas did the citizens continue to meet and legislate in town meeting as they had done in colonial times.

The extraordinary increase of population in the new nation came first of all from the large American families that were to be found everywhere. It came also in part from renewed immigration after the war. To the oppressed of the Old World, the new world was a land of opportunity, as both advertising and their hopes had always caused them to believe.

No man knew better such hopes than Benjamin Franklin. As the most noted American in Europe at the end of the war, he was

[41] 19, 26, 29 Oct., 9, 30 Nov., 3, 7 Dec. 1785.

besieged by would-be immigrants. A calico printer of London asked advice on going to America because he wanted to better his family. A man who had come to London from the Palatinate ten years before, and who was a maker of organs, harpsichords, grand and little pianofortes, and piano harps, asked for Franklin's help. Owen Owen, curate of Stoke, near Coventry, told Franklin that he had risen as high as he could "where sychophants to great fortune are the men caressed nowadays." [42] Franklin explained that when he gave recommendations, and he was asked to give many, he gave merely dinner and advice. Many people wanted to go to America with romantic schemes but no money, and he tried to dissuade those without a useful trade.[43]

Men with useful trades had no difficulty in getting jobs. In Baltimore, for instance, jobs were so plentiful and wages so high that George Washington found it difficult to get men for work at Mount Vernon. Tench Tilghman, to whom Washington delegated the job, reported that a vessel with 450 on board had arrived. Only ninety of these were servants. There was one bricklayer who could not say much for himself, and the carpenters would not agree to a definite term nor would they take less than the "high daily wages given to such tradesmen here. Such is the demand for carpenters and masons, that the master builders in those branches who are settled here, in order to entice the newcomers to give them a preference, will agree to release a four years' indented servant at the expiration of one year and a half." Few people leave Baltimore except on such terms; there is something so alluring in a town to "people of that class" that they would prefer it even with disadvantages, to the country.[44]

There are no records of the number of immigrants. One estimate says that four thousand a year arrived in the United States between 1784 and 1794.[45] Yet one issue alone of the *Pennsylvania Gazette*, 28 July 1784, reported over 1,400 people arriving in Philadelphia within a week. A letter from Dublin declared that hundreds were offering to go to America as indentured servants,

[42] J. McIntosh, 18 March, J. Gerb, 25 March, Owen Owen, 11 June 1783 to Franklin, Bache Collection, American Philosophical Society.

[43] To [Mr. and Mrs. Richard Bache], Passy, 27 July 1783, Bache Coll., APS.

[44] Tench Tilghman to Washington, 15, 27 July 1784, Washington Papers, LC.

[45] William J. Bromwell: *History of Immigration to the United States* (New York, 1856), 13–4.

but that ship captains had so many passengers they were taking only those who could pay, or tradesmen of "a certain description." [46] In Massachusetts it was said that a million people were ready to leave Ireland. The banks of the Ohio and the Mississippi were ready to receive them. "Here you may enjoy inviolate your rights and properties—be instrumental in founding a mighty empire—help make America the garden of the world—and rear a paradise on its surface." [47] The immigrants coming to Pennsylvania promised to make her shortly "the most flourishing in the Union." [48]

This fact caused citizens of New England some concern. One writer declared in 1786 that Pennsylvania had gotten 20,000 German, Irish, and Scottish servants since the war and that Massachusetts had gotten but a hundred. It was "narrow policy" not to encourage immigration by freedom from taxes for a few years.[49] The *Massachusetts Centinel* denounced those who wanted to stop immigration because of economic difficulties in the state and declared that every novice in politics knows that "people constitute the real wealth of a country." [50] Later it reported the arrival in Philadelphia of 540 passengers from Holland, the arrival in New York of seventy people from Glasgow, including many mechanics, and the arrival in Portsmouth of fifty families of farmers and mechanics from Glasgow en route to Vermont. There, every opportunity was held out to them. Land was good and cheap and "the principles of democratical equality exist in their greatest force, it being hail fellow well met with them, from the chief magistrate down to the lowest plebeian." This was Vermont, but other parts of the United States too were open to the world. "The independency of the United States of America, is in no one instance, perhaps, a greater blessing to the world, than in its being the asylum whither the indigent and oppressed, whom the lawless hand of European despotism, would crush to the earth, can find succour and protection, and join common fellowship in a country,

[46] *Pennsylvania Gazette*, 4 Aug. 1784.

[47] *Massachusetts Centinel*, 7 Aug. 1784.

[48] *Pennsylvania Gazette*, 22 Sept. 1784.

[49] James Swan: *National Arithmetick or, Observations on the Finances of the Commonwealth of Massachusetts* (Boston, n.d.), 45–7.

[50] 20 July 1785.

Where happy millions their own fields possess,
No tyrant awes them and no lords oppress." [51]

The spirit of optimism, of belief in America as a refuge for the oppressed of the Old World, as a place of democratic equality, all show that the American Revolution, in result if not in origin, was far more than a movement for independence. Planted in it were seeds that promised the fruit of democracy. The breakdown of old political controls and the creation of new governments, however similar in form and substance to the old, carried with it the possibility of the democratization of American society. This democratic potential was a fact that all Americans were aware of, however much they might disagree as to its value. Some had wanted it and hoped to work it out within the bounds of the independent states. Others were frightened of it and even before the war was over had tried to create some form of dictatorship within the new nation. In time, others were to crave a return to a monarchical government from which they had fought to escape so shortly before. For such people it was plain that the chief result of the war for independence had been the creation of democracy, either as threat or as actuality. The American Revolution was something that was happening or might happen within the United States and they hoped either to prevent it in those states where it had not yet taken place, or to circumvent it in those states where it had.

In making the opening speech to the Constitutional Convention in 1787, Edmund Randolph told its members that the chief danger facing the country "arises from the democratic parts of our [state] constitutions." No member rose to deny this, while outside the hall General Henry Knox declared that the Convention had met to "clip the wings of a mad democracy." Once the Convention had presented its work to the public, James Madison argued that the Constitution was better than the Articles of Confederation because a "republic" was a better form of government than a "democracy." Since that day some writers have ignored the issue, or denied that "democracy" was involved in the disputes of the founding fathers. A few have faced the fact that the founding fathers who wrote the Constitution of 1787 were a quite different

[51] *Massachusetts Centinel*, 21 Sept. 1785. See also *ante* where the same sentiments were expressed in Pennsylvania.

set of men from those who signed the Declaration of Independence in 1776; that of the few signers of the Declaration who were in the Convention of 1787, Elbridge Gerry refused to sign the Constitution in its final form and Robert Morris and James Wilson had been bitter opponents of separation from Great Britain. Only crabbed Roger Sherman of Connecticut willingly agreed to and signed the Declaration of Independence, the Articles of Confederation, and the Constitution of 1787.

Whatever we may think today, the men of the eighteenth century thought that "democracy" was a vital force unleashed by the Revolution. Democracy as they saw it found expression in the Revolutionary constitutions of the states and in the refusal to grant coercive powers to a central government under the Articles of Confederation. The Revolution had altered the whole theoretical foundation of American government. The colonial governments, legally, were the creation of the Crown. All political authority was a grant that in theory, and sometimes in fact, could be and was changed by action of the Crown. On 15 May 1776 Congress resolved that "the exercise of every kind of authority under the said Crown should be totally suppressed, and all the powers of government exerted, under the authority of the people of the colonies. . . ." [52] The passage of the resolution was generally regarded as a declaration of independence. John Adams declared it was "the most important resolution that ever was taken in America." [53] The Declaration of Independence confirmed the resolution and elevated it to a philosophical level, and however often the theory has been disregarded since then, the idea that the people may create and destroy their governments at will has been the theoretical starting point for all governments in the United States. During the Confederation the practical application of the theory in the politics of the states was an ever present danger to those who disliked democracy.

A second result of the Revolution—of profoundest practical importance—was the removal from the American scene of a central government with coercive power: the British government. In most of the colonies the governors, the high courts, and the upper houses of legislatures were appointed by the British. In addition there was a horde of British appointed customs and fiscal

[52] *Journals*, IV, 357–8.
[53] To James Warren, 15 May, *Warren-Adams Letters*, I, 245.

officials. The laws of most colonial legislatures, once they had been approved by the governors who had absolute veto power, had to be submitted to England for approval before going into effect. Cases from colonial courts could be and were appealed to Britain for final decision. In theory the British Crown owned most of the land and more and more attempted to control the disposition of ungranted lands. After 1763 the navy was used to enforce the laws of trade, and a standing army was established. That army was, in part, for frontier defense, but as the revolutionary movement developed, more and more of it was moved to the densely populated centers of the colonies, there to be used in an effort to support British officials and to stamp out the revolutionary movement. Americans fought against and freed themselves from this coercive and increasingly centralized power. In winning independence they rid themselves of its officials, courts, army, and navy, and put an end to its power over the acts of American legislatures.

They did not create such a government when the Articles of Confederation were written, although there were Americans who wished to do so. In practice, whatever the theories, the separate American states were sovereign and independent. Within each of the states a majority of the voters could do as they pleased without interference from outside state borders.

In the writing of the revolutionary constitutions of the states, Americans put their experiences into a new balance within old constitutional forms. Where the royal governor had been all-powerful, at least in law, the new legislatures were made the dominant branch of the government. The governors were now elected either by the legislatures or by popular vote. They had little legal authority. Only in Massachusetts was a governor given a veto, and that could be overridden by a two thirds vote. The courts likewise were subordinated to the legislatures, for they were either elected by them or appointed by governors who in turn were responsible to the legislatures.

The Declaration of Independence declared that the purpose of government was to secure the "life, liberty, and the pursuit of happiness" of the governed, not to protect "life, liberty, and property." The attack on the notion that a man must own property before he could take part in government was well under way. Many more years were to pass before the majority of the voters was to be the same as the majority of the "people," but the start was made. Pennsylvania, Georgia, North Carolina, and New Hampshire wiped out the property qualification for voting: a man had only to be a taxpayer. A start was made at lowering the property qualification for office holding. Representation according to population was established in Pennsylvania and North Carolina.

There was strong opposition to any change in the old order from those members of the colonial ruling classes who became revolutionists. They put up a hard struggle in the writing of state constitutions and achieved a measure of success in states like Maryland, South Carolina, Virginia, New York, and Massachusetts. Even in those states, however, they fought against continuous and sometimes successful demands for social and political reform and economic relief measures such as paper money. In the states where they lost out in the writing of the state constitutions, as in Pennsylvania, they carried on a continuous political battle to get control of the governments. But elections were annual and the majority of the voters were farmers. The farmers by no means always voted against the American aristocracy, for many of them were equally conservative on many issues, but where agrarian interests were involved in such matters as local self-government, paper money, debt-collection policies, and taxation, they could and did outvote the minority. And in such cases, there was no central government to which a hard-pressed minority could appeal for help; the governors had no veto; the courts were weak. Thus the American Revolution made possible the democratization of American society by the destruction of the coercive authority of Great Britain and the establishment of actual local self-government within the separate states under the Articles of Confederation.[54]

[54] See the discussion of the revolutionary constitutions in W. C. Webster: "Comparative Study of the State Constitutions of the American Revolution," *Annals of the American Academy of Political and Social Science*, IX (1897), 380–420, and W. C. Morey: "The First State Constitutions," ibid., IV (1893–4), 201–32.

6

The Betterment of Humanity

THE POLITICAL upheaval and change that was an integral part of the American Revolution made possible other changes in American society: changes that were sometimes an answer to ancient grievances, and sometimes a response to new conditions. The deep-rooted antagonism to established churches was expressed in the revolutionary constitutions and in laws disestablishing or removing the special privileges of established churches. Negro slavery, long hateful to some, was attacked anew as inconsistent with the idealism of the Revolution, and several states (invariably where slavery was unimportant), abolished slavery and the slave trade. The criminal codes, long as merciless as England's, were revised in the direction of humaneness. Prison reform was advocated and conditions were improved.[1] The engrossment of the land was not stopped but the abolition of laws of entail and primogeniture did away with one legal foundation for great land holdings. British Crown lands and confiscated estates of Loyalists fell to the individual states and in turn were sold and granted, usually in smaller lots. In a measure, this contributed to the democratization of land holding, as did the opening up of the vast national domain west of the Appalachians.

On the practical side, Americans now got together as they had never done before in creating societies for social and economic improvement, digging canals, building bridges, and improving roads. They founded newspapers and magazines at a rate undreamed of before the war. All these and many more activities

[1] The best accounts of such matters are to be found in Allan Nevins: *The American States During and After the Revolution 1775–1789* (New York, 1924), ch. x, "Progress in Liberalism and Humanity"; J. Franklin Jameson: *The American Revolution Considered as a Social Movement* (Princeton, 1940).

were a reflection of the new spirit and the new opportunities which were the result of the successful outcome of the American Revolution.

Religion had been a basic part of American thought and feeling from the beginning, and so had controversy about it. Some believed in a theocracy, as did the Puritans of Massachusetts Bay. Others, like Roger Williams and William Penn, believed that men should be free to worship as they pleased, or not at all if such was their desire. But such men and the colonies they founded were exceptional. By the time of the Revolution most colonies had state-churches, established by law and supported by the taxation of all the people, whatever their personal religious beliefs. In New England, aside from Rhode Island, the Congregational Church was so privileged. To the south the Church of England was supported by law and public money in most of the colonies.

There was ever mounting opposition to this union of church and state during the eighteenth century. The back country was settled by a multitude of religious sects that objected ever more violently to paying taxes for the support of churches they did not believe in and often actively hated. In addition there was the growing influence of ideas which did battle with authoritarian ones. These ideas had various names at various times but basic to most of them was the belief that the individual had the right to decide for himself what religion, if any, he should have, and the corollary that no state could support and enforce any one religion in preference to any other. For the most part, though not invariably, men who believed thus were believers in democracy. Beyond this most of them, whatever their political beliefs, were subscribers to the religious belief known as Deism. Thus Thomas Paine, John Adams, Thomas Jefferson, and Benjamin Franklin was each in his own way a Deist. Years after, in *The Age of Reason*, Paine was to formulate that creed in its clearest form. It was stated in another way by George Mason in the Bill of Rights of the Virginia Constitution of June 1776. In it he declared that "that religion, or the duty which we owe to our Creator, and the manner of discharging it, can be directed only by reason and conviction, not by force or violence; and therefore all men are equally entitled to the free exercise of religion, according to the dictates of conscience; and that it is the mutual duty of all to practice Christian forbearance, love, and charity towards each other." John

Adams expressed their creed in a practical way when asked about the appointment of Anglican bishops in America after the Revolution. He saw no objection and thought it inconsistent with American character and the American constitution to raise political objections. He did not believe that "the Father of all" was confined by lines of distinction or differences of opinion. "When we can enlarge our minds to allow each other an entire liberty in religious matters, the human race will be more happy and respectable in this and the future stage of its existence." [2]

The attack on established churches took many forms. The clearest example of the combination of back-country opposition and a leadership moved by high ideals of human freedom came in Virginia. There the Presbyterians who had gotten a measure of tolerance were less opposed to the Anglican establishment than were the Baptists who carried on a long and heartbreaking struggle. Their preachers were persecuted and Patrick Henry won some of his early fame as a lawyer by helping Baptist preachers out of jail. The Revolution was for such people a great opportunity. In 1774 they circulated petitions demanding freedom of conscience and disestablishment of the Anglican Church. Since the Baptists and other dissenters were a majority of the population of Virginia, and the planter leaders of the revolutionary movement needed support, dissenting petitions were listened to as never before. Leaders such as George Mason and Jefferson, who believed in freedom of conscience as a matter of conviction rather than of expediency, thus got far more help than otherwise they would have had.

The framing of the Virginia constitution was followed by new attacks on the Anglican Church. The battle was long, for the majority of the legislature, unlike their constituents, were Anglicans who wanted no change in the old aristocratic order. But Mason, Jefferson, and Madison kept up the fight. First they repealed the law requiring dissenters to pay taxes for the support of the Anglican Church. Then, in 1779, Jefferson wrote a bill calling for the separation of church and state. This was countered by a proposal that the state take over the support of all churches within its bounds. Patrick Henry, who had won much fame in fighting established churches, was now equally ardent for the

[2] To Rev. William White, London, 28 Feb. 178 [4 or 5], Joseph Reed Papers, NYHS.

"establishment" of all churches in the state, and Jefferson's bill was defeated. The fight went on until 1786 when James Madison was at last able to steer Jefferson's bill of 1779 through the legislature.[3] The law was a striking achievement for its day and at the end of his life Jefferson regarded it as one of his three greatest services to his country.

The disestablishment of the Anglican Church in the remainder of the South was an easy matter, for it was a sickly institution. The laws favoring it were strong but the dissenters were vastly superior to the Anglicans in numbers, tenacity, and courage. There were only a half dozen Anglican ministers in North Carolina and most of them were Loyalists. The Constitution of 1776 declared that no church should be established in preference to any other and that no one could be compelled to pay for the upkeep of a church. The Georgia Constitution of 1777 provided religious freedom for all people in the state. The Anglican clergy in South Carolina were able men and most of them were Patriots, but there too the dissenters demanded and got the church disestablished. The Constitution of 1778 provided for civil and religious equality for all peaceable members of Protestant sects.

In New England the Congregational clergy had been leading propagandists for revolution. This gave them strength in maintaining their privileged position in Massachusetts, Connecticut, and New Hampshire. In Massachusetts the church was tax-supported by all citizens except Baptists, Quakers, and Episcopalians, who were required by law to support their own churches. Yet the Baptists led the opposition to this system. When the Constitution of 1780 was written it included an article dealing with religion that was confused if not self-contradictory. It declared that every man had the right to worship in the way and time most agreeable to his own conscience, and yet it insisted that all men must worship publicly at stated times. It declared that no sect should ever be subordinated to any other by law, yet it required that towns should tax for the support of ministers, leaving it up to the town fathers to grant taxes to dissenters for their own churches. The result was that the towns taxed one and all, and dissenters found it difficult to get their share. Congregationalist town fathers, especially in rural districts where Calvinist orthodoxy was to hold

[3] H. J. Eckenrode: *Separation of Church and State in Virginia* (Richmond, 1910), *passim.*

sway for many years to come, found it easy to avoid such payments. This was entirely in keeping with the narrow Calvinism of such men as Sam Adams who helped draft that part of the Constitution.

New Hampshire followed in the steps of Massachusetts, but Connecticut held out much longer against what its citizens regarded as the forces of iniquity. They allowed dissenters to escape payment of taxes to the established church if they presented the clerk of the local church with a certificate of church attendance signed by an officer of the dissenter's own church.

New York had a mixed lot of religious sects: Dutch Reformed, Presbyterian, Episcopalian, Quaker, Moravian, Baptist, and many others. The establishment of the Anglican Church was nominal at best, and disappeared with the outbreak of the war. The Constitution of 1777 made the break complete. New Jersey had no established church but had almost as many vigorous groups as New York, and its Constitution of 1776 provided for complete freedom of religion.

The situation in Maryland was unique. The Anglican Church was established by law. There were many dissenters, but there were also many wealthy Catholic leaders in the colony, and fear of the latter kept the dissenting sects quiet on the subject of the Anglicans, despite the fact that Anglican preachers in Maryland had a universally bad reputation. They were well paid out of public taxes, appointed by the governor, and often lived a life of riotous enjoyment. There was little objection to the disestablishment provided for by the bill of rights in the Maryland Constitution of 1776 which declared that no one could be compelled to go to other than a church of his own choice.

Despite the attacks on established churches and proclamations of religious freedom, many of the states were still much concerned with the maintenance of Christianity, particularly of the Protestant variety, and within it, of a belief in the Trinity. At the same time that Georgia and the two Carolinas refused clergymen seats in their legislatures, they limited governmental offices to Protestants. The New York Constitution of 1777 provided for freedom of religion but required that all foreigners who applied for citizenship must renounce allegiance to all foreign rulers in ecclesiastical matters as well as civil. Even in Pennsylvania, Delaware, and New Jersey, where there had always been religious freedom, holders of public office were required to measure up to certain religious marks. In Pennsylvania they were required to believe in the divine inspiration of the Old and New Testaments. Delaware barred Deists, Jews, and others by requiring all officials to believe in the Trinity. In New Jersey only Protestants could hold office.

The steps in the direction of religious freedom and the complete separation of church and state were thus halting, but the direction was sure and the purpose was clear. The multitude of dissenting sects and the liberal religious and political ideas of many revolutionary leaders did not disappear although often defeated in particular battles. It was perfectly plain by the end of the 1780's how much progress had been made. A bill of rights was a part of the price that had to be paid for the ratification of the Constitution of 1787. The first of those rights declared that Congress should never make any law "respecting an establishment of religion, or prohibiting the free exercise thereof. . . ." The orthodox were horrified of course. Many Americans then as now have never accepted the idea that people's minds should be and must be free.

There were forms of bondage other than spiritual from which some Americans of the revolutionary generation sought to free themselves or their fellow men. Negro slavery had long been opposed in the colonies. The Quakers had delivered the first protests against it. The independent small farmers in the South objected to a labor system with which they found it difficult to compete. Many planters such as William Byrd II, Thomas Jefferson, and others, objected to slavery although their way of life was in large part founded on it. Clergymen like George Whitfield preached against it and found support among the back countrymen. The equalitarian ideals of the Revolution itself caused more than one man to question their reality when faced with the fact of human bondage. Freedom from Britain made it possible to act, for the British government had consistently supported slavery and the slave trade. In the decade just before the Revolution several of the colonies, including some in the South, made serious efforts to stop the trade only to have all legislation vetoed in London. At the beginning of the war only Georgia and South Carolina were in favor of the slave trade, and in every colony there were believers in the abolition of slavery.

Within a few years after 1775, either in constitutions or in legislation, the new states acted against slavery. Within a decade all the states except Georgia and South Carolina had passed some form of legislation to stop the slave trade. Freeing the slaves was much more difficult except in those states where there were very few of them. Vermont abolished slavery in her Constitution of 1777. In 1780 the Massachusetts Constitution declared that all men were born equal and endowed with freedom. It was at once argued that this part of the bill of rights freed all the slaves held in the state, and the state supreme court agreed. New Hampshire followed this lead in its Constitution of 1784. Other states such as Connecticut, Pennsylvania, and Rhode Island passed acts for piecemeal abolition. There was no unanimity, however, even in New England. A writer calling himself "Not Adams" declared that ever since "that class of people called Negroes" began to imbibe the idea they were not slaves, they have been coming to Boston. This made it harder for the poor inhabitants of the town to make a living. No Negroes should be allowed in Boston, he said, except such as had been born there.[4]

The concern with slavery led to the creation of many organizations which were the forerunners of the abolitionist societies of a later age. The first abolitionist society in America was organized in 1774. As with most Philadelphia societies during his lifetime, Franklin was president.[5] Pennsylvania passed a law for the gradual abolition of slavery in 1780. This was largely the work of George Bryan, one of the democratic leaders in the state, and one of slavery's most tireless opponents. The law was evaded and when the Society re-emerged in 1784, it made prosecution of such evasion its main business. It was instrumental in having the law revised and for years was an active force in the abolition movement. By 1800 Pennsylvania had less than 2,000 slaves left, as a result of her gradual emancipation law and of the watchful vigilance of the Society.[6]

In New York the "Society for the Promotion of the Manumission of Slaves and Protecting such of them that have been or may

[4] *Massachusetts Centinel*, 18 Dec. 1784.

[5] *American Museum*, I, 388–9. The society disappeared during the war and was revived in 1784 under the name of "Pennsylvania society for promoting the abolition of slavery, and the relief of free negroes, unlawfully held in Bondage, and for Improving the Condition of the African Race."

[6] Edward R. Turner: "The Abolition of Slavery in Pennsylvania," PMHB, XXXVI (1912), 129–42.

be Liberated" was organized in 1785 with John Jay, a slaveholder, as president, and Alexander Hamilton, as secretary. There was strong anti-Negro feeling in New York where a good many slaves had always been held, and the Society was unable to secure passage of a bill for gradual abolition. It kept up its agitation, however. In 1788 it agreed that its members would boycott all auction masters who sold slaves and to give business only to those who "shall uniformly refrain from a practice so disgraceful and so shocking to humanity." [7] It likewise concerned itself with building a school for the children of free Negroes. But despite all its efforts there were more than 20,000 slaves in the state in 1790.[8]

The well publicized activities of the Philadelphia and New York societies led to the formation of others, usually with names as top-heavy. One was organized in Delaware in 1788 and between then and 1794 others were organized in Rhode Island, Connecticut, New Jersey, Maryland, and Virginia. Maryland had a very active movement for gradual abolition. A writer in Maryland declared that slavery was inconsistent with the principles of the Revolution and he pointed to the horrors of slavery in the South.[9]

There was important opposition to slavery in the South during and after the Revolution. Washington, Jefferson, Madison, and Patrick Henry all hoped that slavery could be ended in some fashion. They were in a minority, although Virginia did pass laws making it easier to free slaves. Farther to the south there was bitter opposition to the idea of abolition and to any restriction on the slave trade. Tolerance soon disappeared from Virginia as well, and the law making it easy to free slaves was repealed and petitions for abolition were ignored. Economics and idealism met head on and the former won an easy victory.

Still another institution that was a source of both labor supply and immigration to America was the system of indentured servitude. Tens of thousands had come to the new world in this way, and although it had offered them opportunity to escape from the evil of poverty in Europe, their lot as "servants" was not a happy one. Very few people either during or after the Revolution, except the German societies, seem to have shown much concern over

[7] *New York Journal, and Daily Patriotic Register*, 27 Nov. 1788.

[8] Evarts B. Greene: *The Revolutionary Generation, 1763–1790* (New York, 1945), 323.

[9] Nevins: *American States*, 449.

these people or the improvement of their lot. In New York an effort was made to get a group of citizens to liberate a shipload of white servants by paying their passage, taking in return small deductions from wages. It was argued that while immigration was necessary, the traffic in white people was contrary to the idea of liberty and to the feelings of many citizens.[10] However, the only laws passed during the 1780's were simply to clarify their status rather than to change it, and the system did not die out for decades.[11]

Americans were far more deeply concerned about their fellow men who lost their freedom through crime and debt. The accounts of the treatment of law breakers, the violence with which they were punished, and the jails into which they were thrown, have about them a nightmarish quality difficult to realize. This was as true in Europe as in America, and such conditions there brought about investigations and demands for reform which found their counterpart in America. The list of acts for which one could be punished was long and the penalties brutal. Death was common for robbery, forgery, housebreaking, and counterfeiting. In Pennslyvania in 1783, five men were put to death for one robbery. Two years later, a man in Massachusetts who made fifty counterfeit dollars, was set in the pillory, taken to the gallows where he stood with a rope around his neck for a time, whipped twenty stripes, had his left arm cut off, and finally was sentenced to three years' hard labor. Actually this was an improvement (from the public if not his point of view) for the usual punishment had been death.

Many Americans took such things casually. In 1787 Henry Jackson wrote to Henry Knox that one of his "late federal soldiers," only twenty-three years old, had been executed for burglary. He had thanked Jackson for his efforts to have him pardoned, insisted on his innocence to the last moment, and died with "astonishing firmness." [12] During the war Justice William Atlee of the Pennsylvania supreme court was riding circuit. He wrote to his wife of a man who had been sentenced to death for burglary. That did not bother him, but a case coming up the next

[10] Philadelphia *Freeman's Journal*, 4 Feb. 1784.

[11] William Miller: "The Effects of the American Revolution on Indentured Servitude," *Pennsylvania History*, VII (1940), 131–41.

[12] Boston, 25 Nov. 1787, Knox Papers, MHS.

day did. A woman was to be tried for killing her husband and Atlee feared it would go hard with her. He hoped that she would be acquitted "to save us the disagreeable task of ordering her to be burned. What affects me much is that her son, a likely young man of about eighteen or twenty is an evidence against her for the death of his father. We shall doubtless have a tender scene with her at the bar and her child giving the fatal testimony which may bring her to the stake." [13]

Such punishments were abhorrent to those who believed in "reason" as a guide to man's actions. Some writers attacked the "dark and diffuse" laws of England and said that Americans should burn the vast "load of legal lumber" and have concise, intelligible, and rational laws.[14] Others, like Jefferson, were more moderate in their demands for legal reform. In 1776 he undertook to bring Virginia laws into line with republican government. The law should be shaped, said Jefferson, with "a single eye to reason and the good of those for whose government it was framed." He revised the criminal code, abolishing all death penalties except for treason and murder. His revision was not passed and after the war it failed again. Not until 1796, twenty years after Jefferson had begun the work, was he able to get it adopted by the State of Virginia.

There was a sharp demand for reform of the laws of Pennsylvania. William Penn at the beginning of the colony had drawn up a humane code but it had been vetoed by the British government. For a time the legislature had stuck to Penn's ideas but eventually it gave in and followed the English code. The Constitution of 1776 demanded a revision, but the death penalty for such crimes as robbery was not repealed for ten years. The demand did not stop with this law. Men like Dr. Benjamin Rush and William Bradford continued to propagandize for more humane criminal laws. Year in and year out, they wrote and spoke against capital punishment with such effectiveness that in 1794 Pennsylvania made a sweeping revision of her whole code, retaining the death penalty only for wilful murder. This code was to be a model for other American states for years to come.[15]

One other side of the law in its relation to the individual gave

[13] William Atlee to Mrs. Esther Atlee, York, 23 April 1778, Atlee Papers, LC.
[14] Philadelphia *Freeman's Journal*, 11 Feb. 1784.
[15] *American Museum*, IV (July 1788), 78–81.

concern to Americans. No "tank" in a twentieth century American city, however bad, can equal the horrors of an eighteenth century "gaol." All ages, all varieties of criminals, and both sexes were crowded together in filthy, often unheated jails. Food was poor at its best and at its worst, rotten. Jailers were of the lowest kind and made money robbing the inmates of their clothing and selling liquor to those who had means to buy. So bad was the jail in Philadelphia, said a grand jury in 1787, that it had become "a desirable place for the more wicked and polluted of both sexes." [16] Investigations during the 1780's revealed conditions that were horrifying to some people. The infamous Newgate prison in Connecticut was established by thrifty Connecticut legislators. It was an old copper mine in which men lived in conditions that only a fevered imagination can visualize.[17]

Conditions in Philadelphia were so bad that they led to the formation of the "Philadelphia Society for Assisting Distressed Prisoners" in 1776. The Society bought covered wheelbarrows which it sent through the streets daily carrying a sign "Victuals for the prisoners." British occupation put an end to the Society but in 1787 "The Society for Alleviating the Miseries of Public Prisons" was organized. In it were men such as Dr. Benjamin Rush, Tench Coxe, and Bishop William White of the Episcopal Church, who was its president for forty years. This Society investigated the prisons and made suggestions for their improvement. It proposed that the sale of liquor be stopped, that men and women be separated, that rooms be washed with lime, and many other things.

The jailers naturally opposed interference with their prerogatives. They objected to inspections: they said the criminals were too desperate. Once when Bishop White visited the jail, the chief jailer put on a show. He started by asking the visitors to give him their valuables for safekeeping. The prisoners were lined up in the common room facing loaded cannon beside which men stood ready to fire. The prisoners, unfortunately for the chief jailer's purpose, were so struck by the proceedings that they were quiet and polite while the good bishop questioned them. The Society did much to bring about the adoption of the new penal code.

[16] *Pennsylvania Gazette*, 26 Sept. 1787.

[17] John B. McMaster: *A History of the People of the United States* (7 vols., New York, 1914), I, 98–102 for a description of prisons.

When regular prison inspectors were created by law in 1790, most of them came from its membership.[18]

Prison reform in New York took a different turn. There it was concerned with those imprisoned for debt. No people in eighteenth century society were more luckless than those imprisoned for debt, and they were an astonishingly large part of the jail population. The idea of imprisonment for debt seems completely irrational in an age which has different notions of what is reasonable, but it seemed logical enough in the "age of reason." People were put in jail for small sums. In Boston, for instance, a woman was jailed for four months for failing to pay a fine of sixpence.[19] No one ever explained how a debtor in jail was better able to pay his debts than a debtor out of jail and at work. But more and more people were questioning the sense of it all, particularly for people whose debts were small, and they demanded legislation to free debtors from jail sentences. In New York the "Society for the Relief of Distressed Debtors" was organized. Its twenty-four members were required to see that jailed debtors got food, fuel, and clothing to lighten the burdens of their stay in jail. Despite such activity and newspaper comment[20] on the idiocy of the practice, dominant opinion for some years to come was that of the creditors who could see no fallacy in jailing a man when he failed to pay his debts.

The organization of societies for the abolition of slavery, the improvement of jails, and of the lot of debtors, was not an isolated phenomenon in the years after the war. Immigrant aid societies had been organized in most colonial towns by Scotch, Welsh, Irish, English, and German immigrants to take care of those who followed them. Library societies were formed in Philadelphia, New York, Providence, and Charleston, and in smaller towns before the middle of the eighteenth century. Marine societies were organized in New England and other towns.

All told, some thirty-odd such societies were organized during the colonial era, most of them in the four urban centers of Philadelphia, New York, Boston, and Charleston. Philadelphia had at least eleven, Charleston eight, New York six, and Boston

[18] John T. Scharf and Thompson Westcott: *History of Philadelphia, 1609–1884* (3 vols., Philadelphia, 1884), I, 444–5; II, 1476–7.

[19] *Massachusetts Centinel*, 13 Aug. 1785.

[20] *Pennsylvania Gazette*, 25 Feb. 1784.

three or four. Most of these societies were small and exclusive and concerned more with social affairs than with practical ones, but they were a focus for humanitarian ideals and intellectual interests. Most of them suspended activity at the outbreak of the war, but before it was over they began to revive and new societies began to appear, five of them in Boston alone. Between 1783 and 1786, eleven pre-revolutionary societies got going again and no less than eighteen new ones were formed. Between 1786 and 1789 fourteen more new societies were formed and most of the rest of the pre-revolutionary ones were reorganized. This was extraordinary activity: more societies were organized between 1776 and 1789 than in the whole colonial period. They were much more active; their meetings were more regular; and their influence spread wider and wider as in the case of the abolition and prison reform groups.

Perhaps the most intriguing of the new societies were the "humane" societies: one in Boston and one in Philadelphia. Their main concern was the rescue of those suffering from "suspended animation": that is, those who appeared to be dead but actually were not. The primary cause of "suspended animation" was drowning, but hanging, sunstroke, lightning, drinking laudanum, drinking cold water when overheated, and so on, were also recognized as causes.[21]

These societies drafted first aid rules, published them in American papers, and posted them in likely spots. They offered rewards for lives saved. They provided special lifesaving equipment and stored it at wharves and taverns near the waterfront. Such equipment included bellows for inflating and deflating the lungs, drags, hooks, and medicines. An extraordinary device, long a favorite with the Massachusetts Humane Society, was the "fumigator," an instrument for pumping tobacco smoke into the rectum of a person supposed to be drowned.[22] In addition, the Massachusetts Society erected huts at spots along the coast where shipwrecks were likely. These were stocked with food and firewood and proved useful, although prowlers soon broke in and ate the food and used the wood.[23]

[21] *Massachusetts Centinel*, 8 March 1786.

[22] M. A. DeWolfe Howe: *The Humane Society of the Commonwealth of Massachusetts* (Boston, 1918), 7–23, 26.

[23] Ibid., 56–61; *New York Journal*, 1 Jan. 1788.

The marine societies cooperated closely with the humane societies during the 1780's. These organizations had appeared before the Revolution and had operated continuously. They were organizations of seamen, and particularly of pilots who were much concerned, not only with their present but their future. As early as 1786 it was proposed to build a hospital for disabled seamen in Boston and to place it under the direction of the marine society in that town. The marine society likewise worked with the humane society in the building of huts for the shipwrecked.[24] In Philadelphia there were two organizations: the "Society for the Relief of Poor and Distressed Masters of Ships, Their Widows and Children," and the "Society for the Relief of Widows of Decayed Pilots." In 1788 the legislature provided that the latter society should receive a quarter of the tonnage duties paid by shipowners.[25]

Societies for specifically charitable purposes were organized as well. One of the first was the "Massachusetts Charitable Society" which had roots before the war but was not incorporated until March 1780. It was religious in spirit but professed to be nonsectarian for it declared that "charity is a principle that no particular persuasion can monopolize. . . ." It was interested in general charities and tried to raise money for a girls' school.[26] A Black Friar's Society was organized in New York for both charitable and social purposes. In Philadelphia a "Corporation for the relief and employment of the poor" was organized. An "Amicable Society" was organized in Richmond for the purpose of relieving strangers in distress. As early as 1769 Charleston had a "Fellowship Society" which gathered funds, half for "the deplorable maniac" and the other half for the education of children.[27]

The beginnings of temperance organizations are also to be found, and this alone, if nothing else, is adequate testimony to the optimism of a period in which the per capita consumption of liquor was enough to win the admiration of all other ages. Dr. Benjamin Rush, one of the most optimistic of joiners, declared

[24] *Massachusetts Gazette*, 15 Dec. 1786.

[25] Scharf and Westcott: *Philadelphia*, I, 453; II, 1469.

[26] *Massachusetts Centinel*, 24 Aug. 1785; *Boston Gazette and Country Journal*, 9 Sept. 1782; *Massachusetts Gazette*, 15 Dec. 1786.

[27] *New York Journal*, 8 April 1788; *Pennsylvania Gazette*, 11 May 1785; *South Carolina Gazette*, 20–22 May 1784; David Ramsay: *The History of South Carolina* (2 vols., Charleston, 1809), II, 363.

in 1788 that now that traffic in slaves was over in Pennsylvania, his next task would be the correction of abuses of liquor.[28] The next year a temperance society was actually organized in Litchfield, Connecticut, where the forty members agreed not to use liquor in their business and to serve only beer and cider to workingmen.[29]

The immigrant aid societies were only partly humanitarian in purpose. They were also social clubs for immigrant groups. Inevitably they were political as well, for leading politicians in towns like Philadelphia made a point of belonging to all the groups, whatever the politicians' own origins might be. With few exceptions their activities were convivial. A French traveler in describing an initiation to the Irish Society of Philadelphia said that they were "initiated by the ceremony of an exterior application of a whole bottle of claret poured upon the head, and a generous libation to liberty and good living, of as many as the votary could carry off." [30] The chief exceptions were the societies organized by Germans in Philadelphia, New York, Charleston, and Baltimore. There were few social or political leaders among them and they had a pietistic streak that led some of them to forbid meetings in taverns. In Philadelphia the society demanded a bureau for the registration of German immigrants and the legislature set one up in 1785. For years thereafter it was manned by members of the society. They visited vessels coming into port to see that immigrants had not been mistreated; they got jobs for immigrants; they provided legal aid for indentured servants. They were concerned also with charity and education. They set up German language grammer schools and founded a library. They established scholarships to send poor German boys to the University of Pennsylvania and during the 1780's supported fifteen scholars in that school.[31]

The societies whose main interests were humanitarian in origin

[28] 6 May 1788, to Jeremy Belknap, "Belknap Papers," MHS *Collections*, 6th ser., IV, 403–4.

[29] John A. Krout: *The Origins of Prohibition* (New York, 1925), 68. As early as 1786 prohibitionists cited the fact that the citizens of the state were paying £80,000 a year for 400,000 gallons of rum which they could well do without. *New Haven Gazette*, 7 Dec. 1786.

[30] Marquis de Chastellux: *Travels in North America in the Years 1780, 1781, and 1782* (2 vols., London, 1787), II, 37–8, n.

[31] Erna Risch: "Immigrant Aid Societies before 1820," PMHB, LX (1936), 15–33.

were outweighed both in number and importance by organizations whose interest was in scientific investigation, the furtherance of knowledge, and in economic development. Important among these were the library societies, of which the oldest was the Library Company of Philadelphia, founded by Franklin in 1731. By the end of the Revolution it had 5,000 volumes and was open both to members and the general public. The Charleston Library Society was organized in 1743 and had an even bigger collection of books than the Philadelphia Company but all these were burned in 1778. It was reorganized in 1783 but it did not regain its former position for years. New England libraries found it difficult to get support. The Newport Library was burned; the Portsmouth Library gave up and sold its books in 1786. Others were too short of funds to perform any real service. Practically all of the library societies, except the one in Philadelphia, looked upon themselves as exclusive social clubs and had no desire to serve the public.[32]

Of the scientific societies, the one with the widest reputation during the 1780's was the American Philosophical Society. Philosophy in the eighteenth century had a very broad meaning: it included natural and physical science, social science, and theology; in fact it took all knowledge for its field. The Philosophical Society did little before the war and it was reorganized in 1780. The act incorporating it declared that it was interested in the improvement of agriculture, the development of trade, "the ease and comfort of life, the ornament of society, and the increase and happiness of mankind" to the end that prejudices might be abolished, a humane and philosophical spirit be cherished, and that youth be stimulated to a "laudable diligence and emulation in the pursuit of wisdom." [33] Despite its high ideals its meetings were poorly attended at first, its funds were small, and it owed most of its reputation to two men: Benjamin Franklin and David Rittenhouse. Not until Franklin returned from France in 1785 did the Society get going actively. Its first volume of transactions was

[32] Edward McGrady: *The History of South Carolina Under the Royal Government 1719–1776* (New York, 1899), 510–12; *South Carolina Gazette*, 27–30 Dec. 1783, 1 Jan. 1784; Horace M. Lippincott: *Early Philadelphia, Its People, Life and Progress* (Philadelphia, 1917), 129–34; Charles K. Bolton: "Circulating Libraries in Boston, 1765–1865," Colonial Society of Massachusetts *Publications* (1906–7), XI, 196–207.

[33] *Laws and Regulations of the American Philosophical Society . . .* (Philadelphia, 1866), 21.

published and Franklin promoted it with all his old skill. He distributed the volume and saw to it that important people in both America and Europe were invited to join.

The most active of the societies during the Confederation was the American Academy of Arts and Sciences which was founded in Boston in 1780. John Adams was the driving force behind its formation. In Europe he discovered the high reputation of the American Philosophical Society, which was doubtless at that time due more to Franklin's prestige and his gift for advertising than to its achievements. When Adams returned to America he was perhaps the chief architect of the Massachusetts Constitution of 1780, which included a clause calling for state encouragement of scientific associations.[34] With James Bowdoin as president, the American Academy got off to a flying start and published its first volume of *Memoirs* in 1785. It was concerned with both economic improvement and scientific investigation. James Bowdoin's political career has too long obscured the fact that he was one of the leaders in the scientific thought of his day and one of the few men who had the courage to dispute scientific points with Franklin, and the capacity to come off with at least even honors. Other such societies were attempted in New York, Connecticut, and elsewhere, but with little result.

At the same time there was a rapid development of medical societies which had both humanitarian and scientific interests. The first ones were organized during the 1760's in New Jersey and Connecticut and were concerned primarily with establishing standards for medical practice. But in medicine, as in so many other things, Philadelphia was the center.[35] The Philadelphia Hospital was founded in 1751. The American Medical Society was organized in 1773. Medical education began in 1765 when the College of Philadelphia, at the urging of Dr. John Morgan, began formal instruction in medicine. King's College in New York started medical training in 1767. Meanwhile, more and more American doctors were being educated in Europe, particularly at Edinburgh University. Between 1758 and 1788 no less than sixty-three Americans were graduated from it.[36] The Revolution itself gave doctors an opportunity to "practice" as they never had be-

[34] Greene: *Revolutionary Generation,* 294; Ralph S. Bates: *Scientific Societies in the United States* (New York, 1945), 9–10.

[35] Ibid., 11, 17–8.

[36] Greene: *Revolutionary Generation,* 88–9.

fore and, as Ramsay pointed out in his history, they learned more in one day on the battlefield than in months at home.

After the war Philadelphia continued to be a center of medical activity. The "Society for inoculating the Poor Gratis" had been organized in 1774 by doctors and others and was providing free vaccinations for all who applied at the state house. It disappeared during the war but in 1787 the dispensary was providing free medicine for the poor. During that year Brissot de Warville said that it had treated 1,647 people at a cost of £200.[37] During the 1780's the College of Physicians was formed. It met for discussion of medical research and took an active interest in improving public health in such matters as street cleaning, quarantines, and in the creation of a "contagious" hospital.

The doctors of Boston organized the Massachusetts Medical Society in 1781. It was interested in standardizing fees but also in medical research. It founded a library in 1782 and by the 1790's was publishing research papers. It was soon in competition with the new medical school which Harvard established. Harvard announced the appointment of three professors of medicine in the fall of 1783. A curriculum was outlined, and the whole story was sent forth to the newspapers of the United States and was printed in many of them.[38] Harvard and the Medical Society engaged in a bitter struggle over the examination and licensing of doctors to practice, but the competition seems not to have hurt either institution.

But great difficulties were encountered everywhere by medical schools in getting "materials" for training purposes. Adequate medical training called for the dissection of bodies, but the populace looked upon this as sacrilege. Antagonism developed until, in New York, it led to the "doctor's riots" of 1788 in which the militia was called out and several people were killed.[39] While great advances were made in medicine, even greater distances were yet to be traveled. As always, popular opinion and much medical opinion was opposed to the "radicals." Barbers, druggists, and dentists were "doctors" and still practiced on the citizenry and the citi-

[37] J. P. Brissot de Warville: *New Travels in the United States of America, performed in 1788* (2nd ed. London, 1794), 279; Scharf and Westcott: *Philadelphia*, II, 1475–6.

[38] See for instance *The Gazette of the State of South Carolina*, 27 Nov. 1783.

[39] E. Wilder Spaulding: *New York in the Critical Period 1783–1789* (New York, 1932), 43.

zenry still found quacks more appealing than scientists. A certain Reverend W. M'Kee announced that at last he had found the cure for cancer. He got testimonials for his product which he had tried on the helpless denizens of the Philadelphia almshouse. Not only would it cure cancer but ulcers, scurvy, ringworm, and other dread afflictions.[40] It was such charlatanry that led Dr. Lemuel Hopkins to write his biting ode to a man killed by a cancer quack:

> Here lies a fool flat on his back,
> The victim of a cancer quack;
> Who lost his money and his life,
> By plaster, caustic, and by knife.
> The case was this—a pimple rose,
> South-east a little of his nose,
> Which daily reddened and grew bigger,
> As too much drinking gave it vigor.
> A score of gossips soon ensure
> Full threescore different modes of cure;
> But yet the full-fed pimple still
> Defined all petticoated skill;
> When fortune led him to peruse
> A hand-bill in the weekly news,
> Signed by six fools of different sorts,
> All cured of cancers made of warts;
> Who recommend, with due submission,
> This cancer-monger as magician. . . .
> Go, readers, gentle, eke and simple,
> If you have wart, or corn, or pimple,
> To quack infallible apply;
> Here's room enough for you to lie.
> His skill triumphant still prevails,
> For death's a cure that never fails.

The Revolution had devastating effects on many established schools. School after school was abandoned, colleges were "purged" of those tainted with Loyalist sentiments, their endowments were ruined, and their student bodies decimated. Yet at the same time many revolutionary leaders were much concerned with the development of an educated people. Five of the new state constitutions declared that the state was responsible for education. John Adams said in his "Thoughts on Government" that "laws for the liberal education of youth, especially of the lower class of people, are so extremely wise and useful, that, to a

[40] *Pennsylvania Gazette*, 18 Oct. 1786.

humane and generous mind, no expense for this purpose would be thought extravagant."[41] Jefferson, believing in education as an indispensable basis for democracy, tried to establish a public school system in Virginia with his "Bill for the More General Diffusion of Knowledge,"[42] but could not get it passed. New winds blew through old halls when, under Jefferson's prodding, the College of William and Mary set up chairs of law and modern languages. Once the war was over, men like Jefferson, John Adams, Benjamin Rush, and, as we have seen, Noah Webster, preached the idea of public education. Various states, including New York, Georgia, and North Carolina, set up university organizations, at least on paper. Private academies were being founded in every state as well as private colleges, some of them with public support. In 1786 the *Massachusetts Centinel* applauded the "encouragement of literature, and diffusion of knowledge" in the southern states and cited the money and land given by the Pennsylvania legislature to Dickinson College, and the lands given for schools by North and South Carolina and Georgia.[43] Elaborate plans for a public school system in Pennsylvania were set forth to the readers of the *Pennsylvania Gazette*.[44]

In every other field concerned with the betterment of humanity, as with education, there was talk, argument, writing, and organization. No better example exists than in the concern of Americans with the improvement of transportation. Expansion westward before the Revolution produced demands for better means of getting back-country crops to market. Roads and bridges were an obvious answer that not everyone was willing to give. The first Americans had lived on or near water and waterborne transportation was an ideal they tried to project into the wilderness. Before the Revolution George Washington and his friend Thomas Johnson of Maryland made plans to clear the Potomac so that boats could go to and from the back country. The war was no sooner over than southerners once more took up the promotion of a water route to the West. Washington again led. Early in 1785 Maryland and Virginia gave identical charters to the Potomac Company. Virginia subscribed to a fifth of the

[41] Adams: *Works*, IV, 199.

[42] Paul L. Ford, ed.: *The Works of Thomas Jefferson* (12 vols., New York, 1904–5), II, 414–26.

[43] 14 Jan. 1786.

[44] 10 May 1786.

stock. Maryland too supported the project as the years went on. It was an enormous undertaking primarily because too few people had any technical knowledge and they had to learn as they went along. Yet by 1815 some 338 miles of the Potomac had been opened.

There were many other projects in the South. The James River Company was chartered to improve navigation on the James at the same time the Potomac Company was chartered. It too was financed by both state and private subscriptions, and in time became a dividend paying company and still was when the state took over in 1820.

The Great Dismal Swamp Company, in which Washington was a heavy stockholder and manager, had been started before the war. Its purpose was to drain the Swamp and produce rice and naval stores. After the war it began digging a canal to connect the Swamp with the Elizabeth River in North Carolina. After many years this too was completed and is still in operation.

In 1786 South Carolina chartered a company to dig a canal between the Cooper and Santee rivers. The canal was not completed until 1800, but it was in use until 1858. There were other schemes both there and in North Carolina. Some of them achieved a little success and others remained only ideas on paper.

In the North the chief concern was with roads and bridges during the 1780's: their passion for canals was to come later. The most famous bridge company was The Proprietors of the Charles River Bridge, incorporated by the Massachusetts legislature in March 1785. There was heated argument in both prose and poetry on the subject of the bridge: its location, the materials of which it should be built, and the like.[45] The bridge was completed by the summer of 1786 and was at once profitable and continued to be so until its monopoly was at last broken by the building of the Warren Bridge and by the decision of the United States Supreme Court in the "Charles River Bridge Case." This bridge was followed by many others all through the North and most of them made money for their backers in a rapidly growing society.[46]

The demand for improved transportation also resulted in better roads. Maryland, Virginia, and Pennsylvania all passed legislation to provide for roads to the westward although the great emphasis

[45] *Massachusetts Centinel*, Jan. to March 1785.
[46] Davis: *Essays*, II, chs. ii–iii.

was not to come until the next decade. Stagecoaches had been few and far between in the years before the war but by the end of the 1780's mail was carried in stagecoaches from New Hampshire to Georgia. New "flying machines" were advertised in the newspapers and soon a flying machine promised to take passengers the ninety miles between New York and Philadelphia in one day. When it did, it was agreed that it was a wonder of the age and that perhaps the ultimate in speed had at last been reached.

But not quite, for the whole country was excited about balloons. Man's ancient dream of flying through the air had at last been realized by a Frenchman. Descriptions of balloon ascensions in Europe appeared in American newspapers. Illustrated articles describing a "machine, proper to be navigated through the air" likewise appeared. By midsummer 1784 it was reported that nothing was important unless it had the name balloon attached to it. Ladies and gentlemen of fashion wore balloon ornaments and even a farmer who came to town with vegetables cried: "fine balloon string beans." As always, a decent amount of fun was poked at the new fad. It was reported from New York that "Air-balloon dress is so much the fashion in this city, and so generally fancied, that some ingenious sempstresses have it in contemplation to establish a balloon petticoat, so constructed, as that every person may go up in it with safety." [47]

Poets likewise had a go at the new craze. Partly in fun and partly in prophecy was a poem called "The Progress of Balloons." After an invocation to the muses the poet declared:

> Let the Gods of Olympus their revels prepare,
> By the aid of some pounds of inflammable air
> We'll visit them soon—and forsake this dull ball,
> With coat, shoes and stockings, fat carcase and all.

The balloon was a French invention which would give them world power.

> At sea let the British their neighbors defy—
> The French shall have frigates to traverse the sky—
>
> If the English should venture to sea with their fleet,
> A host of balloons in a trice they shall meet,
> The French from the zenith their wings shall display,
> And souse on these sea dogs and bear them away.

[47] *Pennsylvania Gazette*, 30 June, 21, 28 July, 8 Dec. 1784; *Massachusetts Centinel*, 12 May, 14 July 1784.

Surveyors drawing meridians and parallel lines should build balloons and survey with ease. Astronomers can now go by balloon,

> And floating above, on our ocean of air,
> Informs us, by letter, what people are there.

A survey of the planets can be made and we can know at last what goes on on Venus, Mars, and the others.

> But now to have done with our planets and moons
> Come, grant me a patent for making balloons,
> For I find that the time is approaching—the day
> When horses shall fail, and the horsemen decay.

Post riders shall leave their "dull poneys behind and travel, like ghosts, on the wings of the wind." And stage drivers whose gallopers take you through the dirt at ten miles an hour,

> When advanc'd to balloons shall so furiously drive,
> You'll hardly know whether you're dead or alive.
>
> The man who from Boston sets out with the sun,
> If he has a fair wind gets to New York at one.
> At Gunpowder-Ferry drink whiskey at three,
> And at six be at Edenton ready for tea.
>
> (The machine shall be order'd we hardly need say,
> To travel in darkness as well as by day)
> At Charleston by ten he for sleep shall prepare,
> And by twelve the next day be the devil knows where.

After a fling at the ladies who would go forty miles high for their afternoon's airing, the poet concluded on a practical note:

> Yet more with its fitness for commerce I'm struck,
> What loads of tobacco shall fly from Kentuck
> What packs of best beaver—bar iron and pig,
> What budgets of leather from Bonocco-cheague.
>
> If Britain should ever disturb us again,
> (As they threaten to do in the next George's reign)
> No doubt they will play us a set of new tunes,
> And pepper us well from their fighting balloons.
>
> To market the farmers shall shortly repair,
> With their hogs and potatoes, wholesail, thro' the air,

Skim over the water as light as a feather,
Themselves and their turkies conversing together.

Such wonders as these from balloons shall arise,
And the giants of old that assaulted the skies,
With their Ossa on Pelion shall freely confess
That all they attempted was nothing to this.[48]

At the same time people were excited about balloons, they were little concerned with the development of steamboats, except to oppose them. Two inventors, a Virginia tavern keeper, James Rumsey, and a Connecticut Yankee, John Fitch, were bitter rivals. Both worked by rule of thumb and trial and error in developing a steamboat that would move against current and wind. Rumsey first tried a boat that moved by sticks forced against the bottom of the stream. He showed this to Washington when the great man visited the innkeeper's place in 1784. Thereafter Rumsey had the support of most of his fellow Virginians. He soon turned to jet propulsion: a steam engine which would pump water out the back of the boat and thus push the boat forward. Jet propulsion had the support of men like Franklin, while the paddle wheel was frowned upon.

John Fitch, wild and sensitive to the point of hysteria, worked on various ideas and fought bitterly with both backers and enemies. The great men of Virginia and men like Franklin supported Rumsey, for although he was an ex-tavern keeper, he was handsome, he had the manners of a gentleman, and was politically sound. Fitch was ugly, ill-clad, and had no manners. He had deserted his wife. He was an anti-Federalist and an extreme Deist. Each man sought and got monopolies for operating steamboats in the waters of various states. Fitch finally got a company behind him and during August 1787 ran a boat up and down the river at Philadelphia where members of the Constitutional Convention saw it. Rumsey's boat did not run until December 1787 and then only twice. But he was made a member of the American Philosophical Society. He was sent to England to get support, while Fitch continued to battle against odds that only a man with almost maniacal convictions could surmount. He won out, at least to the point where he had a boat running regular trips on the Delaware River during 1790. Seventeen years before Robert

[48] *Massachusetts Centinel*, 15 Jan. 1785.

Fulton "invented" the steamboat that ran on the Hudson, Fitch's boat had run thousands of miles on the Delaware.

Fitch was convinced, though he found it difficult to convince anyone else, that the steamboat was the answer to the problem of travel on the Mississippi River. He got that conviction when he had been a surveyor in the West and had laid the groundwork for "John Fitch's Map." All his efforts came to nothing for himself. He died a suicide, poverty-stricken, and half insane, in a little Kentucky town. His rival, Rumsey, died in England, also without achieving any of the greatness or the profit that he had hoped for.[49]

In this survey of the varied activities of Americans in the first years of independence one can realize something of the enthusiasm with which the citizens of the new nation worked at altering the pattern of society they had inherited from colonial times. It is true that much of what they did had earlier roots, but their achievements are also the result of a new freedom of choice and of a delight in national independence. This enthusiasm bolstered native optimism and furnished the motive power for new deeds in years to come.

[49] See James Flexner: *Steamboats Come True* (New York, 1944), a delightful and scholarly book.

7
The New Nation in a World of Empires

FOR ALL the enthusiasm with which Americans worked at improving the new nation, they did not, and could not, forget that they were still as much a part of the world as they had been as colonists. They had freed themselves from the British Empire but they still had to live in a world dominated by empires. Laws of trade and navigation covered most of the world they knew with an intricate network of monopoly restrictions on both shipping and goods. The export of the produce of farm, forest, and sea, and the import of manufactured goods was a vital part of American life. Hence, the legal definition of the place of the new nation in relation to the old ones was of the utmost importance.

While Americans were a part of the British Empire its acts of trade and navigation had both hindered and helped them. Many now greeted freedom from restrictions with joy as did the *Massachusetts Centinel.* It said that Americans should be grateful "to the supreme ruler of the universe by whose beneficence our commerce is freed from those shackles it used to be cramped with, and bids fair to extend to every part of the globe, without passing through the medium of England, that rotten island, absorbed in debt, and crumbling fast to annihilation." [1]

More than delight in freedom from economic shackles was involved in such statements. A large segment of American society had learned to hate Britain. Before 1775 the propaganda of the revolutionary leaders had dinned the fear of British tyranny into Americans. During the war itself propaganda made much of British "atrocities." Some of it was true and some not, but American leaders spread such stories in the army and among the civilian

[1] 31 July 1784.

population in order to whip up and keep up popular enthusiasm. As we have seen, David Ramsay believed that the war could not have been won without the efforts of American propagandists. Once the war was over, the return of Loyalists, of British merchants and agents, the outflow of American money to Britain, and the commercial and agrarian depressions, all lent fervor to popular dislike of the British. Such antagonism became a part of American folklore. It was embedded in American minds and was maintained there for generations by popular histories, Fourth of July celebrations, and continued disputes with Great Britain.

But not all Americans felt this way even during the Revolution. There were many reluctant revolutionists who had not wanted to leave the British Empire, and even when forced to do so, retained a fondness for what had once been their country. The many Americans who had been Loyalists and who stayed in the United States during the war or who returned afterwards, also retained their affection for Great Britain despite the bad treatment many of them received at her hands. The sentimental attachment of many Americans to Great Britain was a continuous force in American politics for many years. On the whole these people were conservative in politics; they objected as much to the French Revolution as they did to the social implications of the American Revolution; they were powerful in the Federalist party.

In 1828 Charles Carroll of Carrollton, the last living signer of the Declaration of Independence, helped break ground for the new Baltimore and Ohio Railroad. The news got to Timothy Pickering in Massachusetts, who had imagined himself the last of his generation. At once he wrote to Carroll recalling the days of their youth. He bewailed the fact that Americans born since the Revolution looked upon Englishmen very much as they did upon men of other nations. "But I," he said, "was born and grew up at a period when they and we were brethren, descendants from one common stock, and fellow heirs to the same best inheritance—political and civil liberty. . . . When peace returned all enmity died within me; and I again held our former British brethren as friends. Independently of this natural sympathy, I feel as a friend to public liberty, a deep interest in the welfare of the British nation, as the great bulwark of the rights of man." He concluded by saying that he had always "reprobated the reading of the Declaration of Independence, on the 4th of July celebrations, otherwise than as a mere historical document: seeing its obvious tendency (and the real object of many) was to excite in the rising generations, the spirit of hostility towards the British nation, which the keen feelings and the policy of the statesmen of 1776, naturally led them to express; but which they pledged themselves to lay aside on the return of peace." [2]

Added to the sentimental ties of men like Pickering, were the very practical desires of American importing merchants. They had not liked the bonds of the Empire when a part of it, but they had enjoyed its privileges, and after the war was over many of them did not think they could survive without them. They had made money largely by trade within the British Empire and they wanted to continue to do so. No one at the time or since then has ever presented an adequate balance sheet of the advantages and disadvantages of membership in the Empire.[3]

The main reason is that various Americans and groups of Americans were affected differently by such membership. Tobacco planters were hard hit by the complicated regulations and charges which took so large a part of the final selling price of their crop. But American shipowners, whose chief business was the carrying trade, had every advantage as members of a world-wide society. Merchants whose main business was the importation of British goods found little to quarrel with while those who wanted to import non-British goods might deplore the laws of trade and navigation as an attack on American liberties and a justification for smuggling. American "manufacturers" were artisans who faced the competition of British goods, but the day of their political influence was not to come until after 1783. When it did, they demanded and got protective tariffs. The mass of farmers probably had little opinion one way or another on the British connection except when it served to bolster the political and economic position of the local American aristocracies, or when it tried to block western expansion. It is therefore difficult to say that there was any attitude or interest common to all Americans, either before or after the Revolution. It is this diversity of interest among Americans which helps to explain the actions of American govern-

[2] 17 June 1828, William Smith Mason Collection, no. 4588, YUL.

[3] See the discussion of Lawrence A. Harper: "Mercantilism and the American Revolution," *Canadian Historical Review*, XXIII (1942), 1–15.

ments during the 1780's. It was plain when proposals were made to regulate trade, to discriminate against foreign shipping, or to protect domestic manufactures, that there were many different notions in the land as to what was "good," and therefore, as to what economic policies should be adopted.

At the end of the American Revolution the ideal of free trade existed in England and America, but was practiced only in America, and there but briefly. Yet the American peace negotiators, all men from the leading commercial towns of the United States, had no notion of going it alone. They wanted both independence and all the commercial advantages they had had as dependent members of the British Empire. And for a time it seemed that they might stay within the protecting walls of the Acts of Trade and Navigation. In October 1782 John Jay and Richard Oswald included the idea of complete commercial reciprocity between the two nations in a preliminary draft of the treaty of peace.[4] This scheme had at least the advantage of being a policy at a time when the British government had none at all for its former colonies.

It was plain also that influential groups in England were willing to break down the Navigation Acts in favor of the United States. Lord Shelburne, influenced perhaps by sentiment, and certainly by the new and therefore radical doctrines of Adam Smith, was favorable to the idea. The English merchants whose chief business before the war had been the American trade, wanted to resume that trade with all its old freedom. They were loud and insistent in their demands. They were afraid that European competitors might steal from them the trade of what had been, and was for many years to be, England's greatest single market. The West India planters, a powerful pressure group, believed quite rightly that the very life of their islands depended on food, lumber, and other supplies from the former mainland colonies. They too wanted unhampered trade between the new United States and themselves.[5]

These groups were in a strategic position as the war came to an

[4] Wharton, V, 805–7.

[5] David S. Reid: "An Analysis of British Parliamentary Opinion on American Affairs at the Close of the War of Independence," *Journal of Modern History*, XVIII (1946), 202–21. He points out that the great merchants in the House of Commons did not support the merchants outside who wanted free trade.

end, for Lord Shelburne was prime minister during the negotiations that led to the drafting of the preliminary treaty. However, the startling idea of complete commercial reciprocity was dropped from the Jay-Oswald draft. All that remained was the statement in the preamble that in the future a treaty, based on grounds of "mutual advantage and convenience," should be made. Commerce, said the British, could not be included in the peace treaty because "some statutes were in the way which must be repealed before a treaty of that kind could be well formed, and that this was a matter to be considered in Parliament." [6]

Shelburne and his followers, however idealistic they might be, were not unaware of political realities. It would be difficult enough to get Parliament's approval of the preliminary articles without including in them the destruction of the Navigation Acts, which, despite Adam Smith, were still a sacred part of British economic thinking. Men like Adam Smith preached what few politicians could absorb, much less put into practice. "You, Dr. Smith, from your professor's chair," said Edmund Burke, "may send forth theories upon freedom of commerce as if you were lecturing upon pure mathematics; but legislators must proceed by slow degrees, impeded as they are in their course by the friction of interest and the friction of prejudice." [7] Parliament soon demonstrated Burke's realism. When it met it denounced both Shelburne and the preliminary treaty. Late in February 1783 Parliament voted to censure the terms of peace, and Shelburne resigned. For a time thereafter no administration was in control, for George III displayed an understandable and even laudable aversion to a ministry led by Lord North and Charles James Fox.

Meanwhile, English merchants clamored for resumption of trade and something needed to be done before the definitive treaty of peace was signed. Young William Pitt, chancellor of the exchequer, introduced a bill repealing all laws prohibiting trade with the United States and providing that American ships carrying American goods should be treated as if they were British ships, including the payment of the same duties. Goods exported to the

[6] Benjamin Franklin to Robert R. Livingston, 5 Dec. 1782, Wharton, VI, 112–3.

[7] Quoted in Gerald S. Graham: *Sea Power and British North America, 1783–1820, A Study in British Colonial Policy* (Harvard Historical Studies, XLVI, Cambridge, 1941), 19.

United States should have the same drawbacks, exemptions, and bounties as if exported to British colonies.[8]

The opposition tore the bill to bits. The Americans be damned; they would take the West India trade. They would compete with British shipping within the Empire and the great nursery of British seamen would be lost. Britain would decline in peace and be helpless in war. Said William Eden, "the bill would introduce a total revolution in our commercial system. . . ." The provision trade of the West Indies with Ireland would be ruined; England would lose the carrying trade between the West Indies and Europe, a trade in which 600 English ships were employed; English sugar refineries would be ruined. Above all, America might attract to itself English manufacturing tools and workers. Delay such a bill and give the Privy Council the right to regulate trade while negotiations for a commercial treaty with the United States were carried on.

Among others who attempted an answer was Edmund Burke. He said it was ridiculous to suppose that Britain would lose manufactures to the United States while the Americans had cheap land. Burke would treat Americans as fellow subjects, not as aliens, and he would improve the old commercial system rather than introduce a new one. Another speaker was for free trade between the United States and the West Indies. He assured the house that British merchants in general were anxious to have the bill passed despite the inconveniences.[9]

Such arguments convinced no one, and the bill was defeated. The Fox-North coalition took over. It repealed the Prohibitory Acts although men like Pitt argued that this would not restore trade, that it was unnecessary since the grant of independence achieved the same purpose.[10]

Next a bill was introduced to do away with manifests and other documents provided by royal officials. This was an obvious thing to do since royal officials were no longer in charge of American governments, but even this mild measure roused the ire of the

[8] A copy of the bill is in Bryan Edwards: *The History, Civil and Commercial, of the British Colonies in the West Indies* (2 vols., London, 1794), II, 401–4, n.

[9] T. C. Hansard: *The Parliamentary History of England from the Earliest Period to the Year 1803* (London, 1814), XXIII, 602–14, 644.

[10] House of Commons, *Journals*, XXXIX, 362–3, 365, 370, 384; Hansard, XXIII, 728.

ever-more rabid opponents of America. They predicted fraud and smuggling and said that the treaty negotiators should be left unconfused by parliamentary legislation. Repeal would open up the whole West India trade which should now belong exclusively to the remaining colonies. All this proved that the King in Council should have the power to regulate trade, and the bill was so amended.

Lord Sheffield moved into the fray and demanded rigorous treatment of the former colonials. Men like Fox, said Sheffield, would treat Americans like British subjects and they would never agree to a commercial treaty. Why not treat Americans like foreigners? The Navigation Acts must be kept unchanged. They had given Britain the carrying trade of the world and if their principle was understood and followed "the country might still be safe." The commercial treaty to be negotiated with America was the most important the country had ever known. It would decide whether or not England had been ruined by the independence of America. "The peace in comparison, was a trifling object. . . ."[11] Lord Sheffield plainly spoke the growing sense of the House. The bill was passed. It dropped the requirement of certification for American ships in the direct trade between Great Britain and the United States. It gave the Crown power to direct commerce with the United States in any manner it saw fit, "any law, usage or custom, to the contrary notwithstanding," until 20 December 1783.[12]

While Parliament was laying down policy, discussion of the definitive treaty of peace continued. David Hartley, another old friend of Franklin, replaced Richard Oswald as British negotiator. Hartley believed in complete commercial reciprocity but he had no power to make binding commitments.[13] The Americans at once proposed to add commercial reciprocity to the definitive treaty, but when Hartley asked his government for approval it was promptly refused.[14] Hartley then proposed other articles favorable to the Americans but once more his government turned

[11] House of Commons, *Journals*, XXXIX, 371, 377, 390, 392, 393, 394, 395, 410, 411, 414; Hansard, XXIII, 728–30, 762–5.

[12] Danby Pickering, ed.: *The Statutes at Large* [of Great Britain], XXXIV, 261–2.

[13] Herbert C. Bell: "British Commercial Policy in the West Indies, 1783–93," *English Historical Review*, XXXI (1916), 429–41.

[14] Wharton, VI, 396–7; Henry Laurens to Livingston, London, 17 June 1783, ibid., VI, 491–2.

him down.[15] Henry Laurens wrote from London to his colleagues in Paris that " 'Reciprocity,' since the 10th of April, has undergone a certain degree of refinement. The definition of that term appears now to be possession of advantages on one side and restrictions on the other. The Navigation Act is the vital of Great Britain, too delicate to bear a touch." [16] Remaining hopes were shattered by the issuance of the order in council of July 1783 which shut American shipowners out of the British West India carrying trade. The American commissioners, tired of dawdling with Hartley, and struck by the order in council, agreed among themselves to drop all commercial articles from the definitive treaty, something John Adams had wanted to do at least a month earlier.[17]

Whatever Fox's own wishes might be, the actions of Parliament and the acts of the Privy Council, for the time being at least, took care of the regulation of trade. So the preliminary treaty, minus all mention of commerce and its regulation, became the definitive treaty of peace. This document, signed on 3 September 1783, formally brought an end to the war for independence.[18]

Meanwhile the Privy Council used the powers granted it by Parliament. The draftsman of the various orders that came forth was William Knox, a man whose bitterness toward the United States knew no limit. His estate in Georgia had been confiscated during the Revolution. At the end of the war the Rockingham ministry abolished his job as undersecretary for the American Colonies. Above all, Knox believed in the Navigation Acts and in the subordination of colonies. His rule was that "it was better to have no colonies at all, than not to have them subservient to the maritime strength and commercial interest of Great Britain." [19]

[15] Hartley's proposed Article of Agreement and his comments on it are in ibid., VI, 442–4; Laurens to Livingston, London, 17 June 1783, ibid., VI, 492.

[16] To the Peace Commissioners, 17 June 1783, ibid., VI, 493. Laurens thought that the sudden arrival of ships and cargoes from America might have caused the change.

[17] Franklin, Jay, and Laurens to Robert R. Livingston, Paris, 27 July 1783, ibid., VI, 600; Adams to Livingston, 23 June, ibid., VI, 500.

[18] Franklin to Vergennes, 16 Aug. 1783, ibid., VI, 655; Adams, Franklin, and Jay to Hartley, 30 Aug. 1783, ibid., VI, 662–3, 673. Hartley stayed on in Paris hoping to write a commercial treaty long after the Americans had given up trying. Franklin to Benjamin Vaughan, 26 July 1784, Benjamin Vaughan Papers, CL. Lord Carmarthen ordered Hartley to stop; Hartley would not, so Carmarthen fired him outright. To Hartley, 17 Sept. 1784, David Hartley Papers, CL.

[19] Graham: *Sea Power and British North America*, 26.

Imagine, then, the horror of such a man for all the ideas implicit in the Pitt Bill, in reciprocity, and above all, in no punishment for a people so stupid as to wish to be outside the Empire.[20]

The first order on 14 May 1783 legalized the import of oil, unmanufactured goods, and other merchandise of the United States that had arrived in Great Britain since January. The same drawbacks were to be allowed on re-export of goods to the United States as on re-exports to the colonies.[21] On 6 June another order was issued allowing the importation of pitch, tar, turpentine, indigo, masts, yards, bowsprits, and tobacco. The British were anxious to retain their position as European distributors of American tobacco. The order therefore provided that tobacco could be imported and re-exported on terms far more favorable than had existed in colonial times.[22]

Then on 2 July came the order which was to cause the shipowners of America, and particularly those of New England, so much anguish for so many years: that dealing with the West India trade. It was passed by the Privy Council, wrote the delighted Lord Sheffield to William Knox, "exactly as you drew it." The country very nearly suffered great mischief but "our carrying trade, consequently the foundation of our navy, is now safe." [23] Four years later Knox claimed that he had carried the order through despite the opposition of Fox and Burke and thereby saved "the navigation and maritime importance of this country and strangled in the birth that of the United States. . . ." [24]

The order in council provided that certain American produce: pitch, tar, turpentine, hemp, flax, masts, yards, bowsprits, staves, heading boards, timber shingles, and all other kinds of lumber; horses, neat cattle, sheep, hogs, poultry, and all other kinds of livestock and live provisions; peas, beans, potatoes, wheat flour,

[20] Knox was asked to prepare drafts of acts regulating trade between the United States and the British West Indies and other matters relating to intercourse with America. But Knox noted that, since Parliament had empowered the King in Council to make such regulations, "there was no need for an act, and he therefore prepared orders in council instead." Captain Howard V. Knox Manuscripts, Historical Manuscripts Commission, *Reports on Manuscripts in Various Collections*, vol. VI (Dublin, 1909), Cd. 4382, in *Reports from Commissioners, Inspectors, and Others*, vol. 50, House of Commons, LX (1908), 190.

[21] *Acts of the Privy Council, Colonial Series*, V, 527–8.

[22] Ibid., V, 528–9.

[23] 3 July 1783, William Knox MSS., CL.

[24] Knox to Lord Walsingham, 20 Aug. 1787, Historical Manuscripts Commission, *Var. Colls.*, VI, 198–9.

bread, biscuit, rice, oats, barley, and all other kinds of grain could be shipped from the United States to the West Indies only in "British built ships owned by His Majesty's subjects and navigated according to law. . . ." Rum, sugar, molasses, coffee, "cocoa nutts," ginger, and pimento could be shipped from the West Indies to the United States as if they were British colonies.[25] American products that could not be sent to the West Indies were cured meats, fish, and dairy products, exports of great importance to the northern states.

These various orders and later ones dealing with administrative details were brought together in one general order 26 December 1783. This order provided, in addition, that all unmanufactured goods and merchandise produced in the United States, and whose importation was not prohibited by law (with the sole exception of whale oil), might be imported into any port in Great Britain in either British or American ships "upon the same terms as from a British colony. . . ." Furthermore, the same drawbacks, exemptions, and bounties were to be paid on goods exported from Great Britain to the United States as to the British colonies in America.[26] Therefore, so far as direct trade with England was concerned, the Americans now had the same privileges they had had as colonists.

The legal framework of American trade with Great Britain and her colonies was thus established by the end of 1783. The hope of the supporters of the system in Great Britain was that the remaining British colonies would take the place of the lost thirteen in supplying the British West Indies; that meanwhile British shipping would take the place of American in carrying American supplies to the islands. Above all they had saved, so they believed, the principle of the Navigation Acts. British shipping would, of course, continue to carry manufactured goods to the United States. Thus Britain would develop a happy and lucrative triangle trade: manufactured goods to the United States, their produce to the West Indies, and West Indian products to England.[27]

[25] *Acts of the Privy Council, Colonial Series*, V, 530.

[26] Ibid., V, 528–9. Parliament extended the power of the Privy Council year after year until 1788 when the whole system was embodied in a Parliamentary act. Pickering: *Statutes at Large*, XXXVI, 331–7.

[27] Gerald Graham's two books, *Sea Power and British North America* and *British Policy and Canada, 1774–1791: A Study in 18th Century Trade Policy* (New York, 1930), are the best accounts of this scheme of the British, and of its failure in the face of the economic facts of the time.

Hardest hit by the new rules were the New England shipowners and fishermen. Their screams of anguish have shrilled so loudly through the pages of history ever since, that it has not been recorded that the rest of the United States was little harmed by such rules, and that the country as a whole enjoyed the new freedom to trade and sell outside the British Empire. West India planters were even more bitter than American shipowners. One of them, Bryan Edwards, wrote a pamphlet and a history of the West Indies in a vain attempt to present the evidence.[28] West India assemblies and groups of planters appealed to Parliament for redress, and their efforts were applauded by sympathetic American newspapers.[29] By the time Parliament met in the spring of 1784 "petitions, complaints, and remonstrances, were poured in from almost every island in the West Indies." Some said they had but six weeks' provisions; all expected slave rebellions; prices had risen from fifty to a hundred per cent as soon as the order was made known.[30] Americans threatened retaliation. A press campaign in England demanded relaxation.

It was known that the cabinet was divided but such facts mattered not, for the defenders of ancient traditions had not confined their efforts to Parliament. In pamphlet and in newspaper, they appealed to the British public against any favor for the lost colonies, or any relaxation of the Navigation Acts. They insisted that there was nothing to fear except liberality. The leader in this campaign was the Earl of Sheffield, "the tribune of the shipbuilders and shipowners." [31] He was a landowner who got interested in matters of trade at the end of the war and went out to do battle against the new "economists" who were preaching the idea of freer, if not free, trade. In 1783 he published his *Observations on the Commerce of the American States*. It appealed to the

[28] *Massachusetts Centinel*, 12 June 1784, advertised the publication of Bryan Edwards: *Thoughts on the late proceedings of government, respecting the trade to the West India islands, with the United States of North America* and declared that it sold so fast in England that several editions had been printed in a short time.

[29] See Lowell J. Ragatz: *The Fall of the Planter Class in the British Caribbean, 1763–1833* (New York, 1928), 173; *Pennsylvania Gazette*, 10, 17, 24 Dec. 1783; 31 Aug., 14 Sept. 1785 for reports of activities in Antigua, Jamaica, and Barbadoes. The *South Carolina Gazette*, 6–9 Dec. 1783, prints in full resolutions of the people in Antigua against the order.

[30] Edwards: *History of the West Indies*, II, 405–6; Ragatz: *Fall of the Planter Class*, 186–7.

[31] Graham: *Sea Power and British North America*, 23.

old and tried and true as against the new and radical. It went through enough editions to indicate its popularity and great influence. The Revolution was no calamity, as so many Britishers had been thinking, for now Britain could regain the British West India carrying trade which had been lost to the Americans long before the war. Britain need not worry about losing the American market for British manufactures: the Americans had to have them and British shipowners would carry them there. The Americans would be helpless for years to come. The book was filled with facts and figures of trade in the past. Its tables and appendices proved conclusively, for those who wanted such proof, that Sheffield was right and that if anything, Britain was being much too easy on her former colonies.

When Pitt took over in December 1783, after the Fox-North coalition came to its timely end, he made no such rash moves as he had done when impelled by the joint pressure of principle and English merchants. Instead of introducing a bill, he handed the question of policy over to a committee of the Privy Council for investigation. This committee heard witnesses on all sides. The pleas of West India planters were discounted. Instead, the committee accepted the argument of one set of witnesses who argued that Canada and the Maritime provinces could take the place of the United States. And why should not the committee think thus when "glowing panoramas of waving wheat fields, multiplying flour and lumber mills, and busy harbors resounding to the blows of the shipbuilders' hammer were being painted with enthusiasm by responsible men of colonial experience." [32] Therefore let things stand as they are, was the policy recommended by the committee and adopted by Pitt.

That policy and reality did not coincide, all parties concerned soon learned. British North America could not supply the West Indies: in fact, most of the supplies that they did send they got from the United States. British North America actually needed and got American supplies in American ships. So did the West Indies. Smuggling was not a lost art for American ship captains. West Indian governors yielded more often to the pressure of local planters than to rules laid down by London. Thus, as we shall see later, trade went on in the old channels determined by want and need and was only irritated by the acts of legislators and tra-

[32] Ibid., 28–31.

ditionalists. The West Indian restrictions had far more usefulness for American politicians than they had serious effect on American shipowners—though the latter protested loud and long.

While English politicians were planning how to punish their former colonies, the rest of the world looked forward to a share of the trade which had so long been England's monopoly. France and Holland were the two chief competitors, although Sweden, Denmark, and many a lesser nation showed interest and took part. The English colonies had carried on trade with the French and Dutch islands in the West Indies long before the Revolution. French officials had tried to hold that trade for French merchants, but French West India planters had as great a need for American food and lumber as their English competitors. Furthermore, they had offered better terms since early in the eighteenth century, with the result that the British planters had lobbied the Molasses Act of 1733 through Parliament in an effort to force the Americans to trade with them alone.

By 1763 the French government had legalized the importation of American products and the exportation of molasses and rum. A few years later two ports were set aside to serve as depots for foreign merchandise: the Mole St. Nicholas in Santo Domingo and the careenage of St. Lucia. French merchants protested in vain. When the treaty of alliance and commerce was made in 1778, French policy was made directly favorable to the Americans. One article provided that the Americans should have one or more free ports in France itself to which they could bring and sell their produce. It was agreed that ports in the French West Indies should be kept open as they had been. Other articles of the treaty granted Americans most favored nation treatment. After the war this policy was extended even further. By an *arrêt* of 30 August 1784, seven ports were declared open and the French West Indies were opened to salt fish and other American products. French merchants wailed, and in 1785 managed to get a bounty placed on dried codfish carried to the French islands in French vessels. In 1787 the bounty was increased and a duty placed on foreign vessels carrying such fish, but it is doubtful that this had much effect, since the Americans were as adept in avoiding rules in the French islands as in the English.[33]

[33] For the details see Henri Sée: "Commerce between France and the United States, 1783–1784," AHR, XXXI (1925–6), 732–52; Edmond Buron: "Statistics

Every effort was made by the French government to build up trade between the United States and France itself. Consuls or vice-consuls were appointed for most of the states. They had orders to collect information and point out changes and additions that French manufacturers could make to suit the American market.[34] The ports of Dunkerque, L'Orient, Bayonne, and Marseilles were opened as free ports, as Macpherson, annalist of commerce, said, "to allure the envied trade of America to their own country." [35] The Isle of France and the Isle of Bourbon (Mauritius) were opened to Americans on the road to China so that they might buy provisions and sell their wares.[36]

Such privileges marked the interest of the French government in American trade. There were some slight changes and many false rumors, such as the one that all American vessels were excluded from the French trade early in 1784. When sifted, it was found that the exclusion applied only to Cap François and that it was the result of a glutted flour market there. All other ports were open, reported the *Pennsylvania Gazette*, and disposed to confer every favor on Americans.[37] An *arrêt* of 29 December 1787 allowed Americans to deposit their goods for six months in any French port. Import duties were levied on various American products, such as whale oil, grains, flour, hides, furs, potash, lumber, turpentine, and tar. American fish oil and salt fish were to pay no more than those of the Hanse towns and the most favored nations. To encourage the export trade to the United States, bounties were promised on such articles as firearms, hardware, jewelry, millinery, woolen and cotton goods. The protests of French merchants continued, and the next year fish and fish oils were exempted from the right of deposit. Such restrictions were relatively minor in determining the trade of the period, as we shall see, for the administration of the tobacco trade stood in the way of a free flow of

---

on Franco-American Trade, 1778–1806," *Journal of Economic and Business History*, IV (1931–2), 571–80; Frederick L. Nussbaum: "The French Colonial Arrêt of 1784," *The South Atlantic Quarterly*, XXVII (1928), 62–78.

[34] Edward Bancroft to William Frazer, Philadelphia, 28 May 1784, Bancroft: *Constitution*, I, 370. American newspapers reported with pride the appointment of French and other consuls.

[35] David Macpherson: *Annals of Commerce. . . .* (4 vols., London, 1805), IV, 56.

[36] *Pennsylvania Gazette*, 21 July 1784.

[37] 17 March 1784.

commerce. Even then the Americans were the great gainers in a trade increasingly to the disadvantage of the French.[38]

The Dutch, like the French and the English, had chartered monopoly companies for trade in the new world, but the Dutch discovered long before most that relative freedom of trade was not only idealistic but exceedingly profitable. Their West India islands were way stations in illegal trade during the Revolution. John Adams had long sought a treaty with the Dutch. Finally, in October 1782 the Dutch agreed to a treaty based upon the principles of the French commercial treaty of 1778.

As soon as the war was over Peter John Van Berckel, the first Dutch minister to the United States, reported that illegal trade was going on at a great rate between the Dutch West Indies and the United States, to the injury of the Dutch West India Company.[39] The Dutch government did nothing about it except to encourage loans to assist the American government and to smile on private credits to American merchants, and thus trade flourished in the years after the Revolution.

Sweden soon offered to make a treaty and, after short negotiations with Franklin, a treaty was signed 3 April 1783 by the Swedish ambassador in Paris. This treaty, like that with the Dutch, was based on the French treaty of 1778. As a result of the French, Dutch, and Swedish treaties, Congress sent instructions to Franklin, Adams, and Jefferson who at once opened negotiations with other nations. Two more treaties of amity and commerce were the result: one with Prussia, signed in September 1785 and one with Morocco, signed in January 1787.[40] Many other European states were interested. Some made inquiries, some sent envoys to the United States to investigate the possibilities of trade with them. Among these were Denmark, Saxony, Portugal, Naples, Venice, and Hamburg.[41]

[38] See Buron: "Statistics on Franco-American Trade, 1778–1806," JEBH, IV, 571–4. See also the table of imports and exports, 576–80.

[39] Van Berckel to the States General, Philadelphia, 6 April 1784, Bancroft: *Constitution*, I, 352.

[40] Samuel F. Bemis, ed.: *American Secretaries of State and their Diplomacy* (10 vols., New York, 1927–9), I, 205–7.

[41] Vernon G. Setser: *The Commercial Reciprocity Policy of the United States 1774–1829* (Philadelphia, 1937), 56–7. Some of Setser's generalizations about restrictions cannot be maintained in the face of the evidence on the actual extent of trade. See *post*, ch. ix.

The concessions made to the new nation were well-nigh revolutionary in terms of eighteenth century policy and practice, and they were the result of the hope of profit. They came for the most part as a result of pressure from merchants and were expressed in the main by legislative and executive acts.

The war left many other problems for diplomatic argument and none was sharper than those arising from the various treaties at the end of the war. In the Treaty of Peace with Great Britain, the United States agreed that "no lawful impediment" should be placed in the way of British creditors who sought to collect pre-war debts in America. It was also agreed that the persecution of Loyalists should be stopped and that Congress should recommend to the states the restoration of confiscated Loyalist property. The British agreed to surrender the military and trading posts they held along the Great Lakes frontier. Failure to carry out these agreements on both sides was a sore spot in Anglo-American relations.

Publication of the Treaty in the United States produced an immediate split in American state politics. Most of the conservative political leaders were willing and even anxious to have the Loyalists come back, or to remain if they had not left. Likewise they wanted the state courts opened to British creditors. They wanted an immediate re-establishment of trade and credit relations with Great Britain and the prompt collection of pre-war debts was felt to be basic in such matters. On the other hand, the radical revolutionary leaders and the people at large were violently opposed to the return of the Loyalists and to the return of, or compensation for, confiscated property. Yet despite popular opposition, state after state repealed the laws in conflict with the Treaty of Peace. By the end of 1787 it was reported in American newspapers that the last of the laws in conflict with the Treaty had been repealed and that Britain now would have to invent some other excuse for hanging on to the western posts.[42]

The British had promised to give up such posts as Oswego, Niagara, Detroit, and Michilimackinac "with all convenient speed." But at once powerful demands for the retention of the posts appeared. The Quebec fur traders appealed to the govern-

[42] *Massachusetts Centinel*, 22 Dec. 1787. State action on the provisions of the Treaty of Peace is discussed in ch. xiii, "The Aftermath of War."

ment to hang on for at least three years until they could sell their property and move out their goods.[43] Even more powerful was the fear of the Indians in the Northwest. The British had given the Indians a solemn promise not to desert them, but the Treaty gave the Old Northwest and tens of thousands of Indians to the United States. British commanders in the West, afraid of Indian war, wanted to hold the posts as a token of good will toward the Indians. The British therefore decided to hold the fur posts before there were any violations of the Treaty by the United States.[44]

British troops on American soil made many Americans, particularly westerners, more bitter than ever. The British forbade American ships on the Great Lakes, stationed a customs officer at Oswego, New York, and continued to dabble in Indian affairs far within the boundaries of the United States. Westerners had an unshakeable conviction that the British aided and abetted every Indian raid on advancing frontier settlements. Meanwhile, John Jay as secretary of foreign affairs, but ignorant of British reasons for retaining the posts, told the British privately that they were entirely justified in retaining them because of American violations of the Treaty. Jay was one of those righteous men in action who are so often wrong in fact.

Jay had become secretary of foreign affairs late in 1784. As a powerful personality with intense convictions, he soon acquired much power. He spoke on the floor of Congress, wrote reports on all sorts of subjects, and was ready to offer advice on all the problems facing Congress. His attitude toward the West, like that of many a fellow easterner, was no better shown than in his dealings with the Spanish.

The Spanish had been reluctant partners in the war. They had consistently demanded that the Americans give up any claim of right to use the Mississippi and even all claim to lands west of the Alleghenies. At the end of the war, Spain got Florida back from Great Britain. Meanwhile, the British and Americans had secretly agreed that if Spain did get Florida, the southern boundary of the

[43] Shelburne Papers, vol. 72, CL.

[44] Samuel F. Bemis: *Jay's Treaty, A Study in Commerce and Diplomacy* (New York, 1923), emphasizes the fur trade as the chief motive for retaining the posts. A. L. Burt: *The United States, Great Britain, and British North America* (New Haven, 1940), ch. vi, "The Retention of the Western Posts," presents the evidence for the Indian problem as a decisive factor.

United States should be the thirty-first parallel instead of a line a hundred miles to the north which had been the boundary during British possession. Spain refused to recognize the secret deal and she continued to hold Natchez on the Mississippi. She claimed sovereignty over the Indians, most of whom, like the Northwest Indians, preferred anyone to the oncoming Americans.

The Spanish were frightened of the Americans and their example, and they twisted and turned in an effort to check the western expansion of the United States. They intrigued with westerners and encouraged secession movements. They tried to fill the bottomless pockets of General James Wilkinson with gold. Meanwhile, in 1784 they closed the mouth of the Mississippi to American commerce, and the West exploded. When Washington returned from a trip to the West he reported that "the western settlers (I speak now from my own observation) stand as it were upon a pivot; the touch of a feather would turn them any way." [45]

The next move of the alarmed Spanish was to send Diego de Gardoqui to the United States. He was instructed to get the United States to give up their claim to the use of the Mississippi. The Spanish knew from experience during the war that many Americans were afraid of or disliked the growth of the West and were willing to stop it if they could. They knew that John Jay, Gouverneur Morris, and other leaders from the middle states had been willing to give Spain the whole of the trans-Allegheny region and to surrender any claim to the Mississippi. The desire of such men to limit American expansion was born of many things. Few American merchants had any vision of the great profit that was to be made in trade with the West: they faced eastward across the Atlantic. Land speculators with large eastern holdings believed that the opening of western lands would lower the price of eastern.[46] Conservative political leaders in the East feared the future power of a rapidly growing society in which they believed all men were crude and apt to be unpleasantly democratic. The West had nothing in common with the East, said Rufus King. Eventually the difference would result in separation. If the West had free use of the Mississippi he would look upon "every emi-

[45] To Gov. Benjamin Harrison, 10 Oct. 1784, *Writings*, XXVII, 475. Washington's letter was a long argument for the opening of better transportation between East and West.

[46] Timothy Pickering, 1 June 1785, Pickering Papers, MHS.

grant to that country from the Atlantic states as forever lost to the Confederacy." [47]

Gardoqui was sure he would have sympathetic listeners when he got to New York, and he had long since taken the measure of John Jay and his wife while Jay was in Spain. Jay, said Gardoqui, was "a very self-centered man" and his wife abetted him. Not only that, but "she likes to be catered to and even more to receive presents." She dominated her husband who loved her blindly, and her opinion always prevailed though he might at first disagree. From this, Gardoqui said that he inferred that "a little management in dealing with her and a few timely gifts will secure the friendship of both, because I have reason to believe that they proceed resolved to make a fortune." Gardoqui pointed out that Jay was not the only American who had such a weakness and therefore "a skillful hand which knows how to take advantage of favorable opportunities, and how to give dinners and above all to entertain with good wine, may profit without appearing to pursue them." [48]

Gardoqui was not merely justifying his large expense account, for he worked at the job. He did everything from getting Spanish jackasses for George Washington to squiring Mrs. Jay to one dance after another. "Notwithstanding my age," he reported, "I am acting the gallant and accompanying Madame to the official entertainments and dances, because she likes it and I will do everything which appeals to me for the King's best interest." [49] Gardoqui's success with the Jays was unquestioned, but the instructions of the two men blocked negotiation. Congress said Jay must not surrender the "right" while the Spanish government told Gardoqui he must not admit the "right" of the Americans to use the Mississippi. However, Gardoqui was authorized to make trade concessions if the Americans would give up their claim.

This was gilded bait which American merchants yearned to swallow, so Jay asked Congress to allow him to surrender any claim to use the river for twenty or thirty years. Congress, after a bitter debate, voted seven states to five, to change Jay's instruc-

[47] To Elbridge Gerry, 4 June 1786, Charles R. King, ed.: *The Life and Correspondence of Rufus King* (6 vols., New York, 1894–1900), I, 175–6.

[48] Samuel F. Bemis: *Pinckney's Treaty: A Study of America's Advantage from Europe's Distress 1783–1800* (Baltimore, 1926), 73.

[49] Ibid., 84.

tions. The five southern states, without a dissenting vote, opposed any change, and seven northern states voted for it.[50] The South and the West roared with anger. The Virginians led the fight. During the war they had opposed the sacrifice of the West to Spain as they now fought against its sacrifice to eastern merchants. James Madison, who agreed with the conservative politicians on so many things, was a sound Virginian on this issue. "The use of the Mississippi" he said, "is given by nature to our western country, and no power on earth can take it from them." [51] To Lafayette he wrote that if the United States agreed to the closure of the Mississippi "they would be guilty of treason against the very laws under which they obtained and hold their national existence." [52] The westerners were violent. They would seize New Orleans. They would join Spain or England. "To sell us and make us vassals to the merciless Spaniards is a grievance not to be borne," said one. "Should we tamely submit to such manacles we should be unworthy the name of Americans, and a scandal to the annals of its history." [53]

Popular opinion thus blasted Jay's plans. The West's well-founded suspicion of the East was fortified. As Kentuckians prepared to send delegates to the Virginia ratifying convention of 1788, men met and declared that the power to regulate trade in the new constitution would mean that "we lose the navigation of the Mississippi: population will cease, and our lands become of little value." [54] The Spanish relaxed their grip in 1788 when they allowed Americans to use the Mississippi on the payment of duties, but the diplomats continued to wrangle. Eventually a treaty was agreed upon in 1795.[55]

But the prime fact, as Jefferson believed and the Spanish realized, was the irresistible movement of Americans westward.

[50] 29–31 Aug. 1786, *Journals*, XXXI, 574–613.

[51] To James Monroe, 8 Jan. 1785, *Letters and Other Writings of James Madison* (4 vols., Philadelphia, 1867), I, 121.

[52] 20 March 1785, ibid., I, 137.

[53] Thomas Green to Georgia officials, 23 Dec. 1786, *Secret Journals of The Acts and Proceedings of Congress* (4 vols., Boston, 1821), IV, 315.

[54] Memorial to the Court of Fayette County on the proposed Federal Constitution, Draper MSS., 11J182, Wisconsin Historical Society.

[55] Arthur P. Whitaker: *The Spanish American Frontier 1783–1795* (Boston, 1927), is the best account of this and offers some contrasts with Bemis: *Pinckney's Treaty*.

Time and the growth of population were to take from Spain her vast dominions in western America. As Henry Adams said, "in the end, far more than half the territory of the United States was the spoil of Spanish empire, rarely acquired with perfect propriety. To sum up the story in a single word, Spain had immense influence over the United States; but it was the influence of the whale over its captors—the charm of a huge, helpless, and profitable victim." [56]

Abroad, John Adams was minister to Great Britain and Thomas Jefferson was minister to France. The British found it difficult to take the stiff Mr. Adams, but he kept digging away at the problems he faced. He and Jefferson were able to get the British merchants to agree to waive interest payments on debts during the war, a not inconsiderable victory. Adams did not get a commercial treaty but he was too realistic to expect one, however much his fellow countrymen might hope for it. Commercial policy had been set for years to come before he landed in London and was not to be altered except by war and slow changes in economic balances. "The truth is," he wrote Mercy Warren in 1807 as he commented on her history of the Revolution, "a great deal was done, and will appear to the world, if ever my letters to Congress and their instructions to me, together with Lord Carmarthen's letters to me, should be published." [57]

In France Jefferson was an ideal successor to Franklin. He too had difficulties, for the French government showed a persistent interest in the repayment of revolutionary loans. Here too Jefferson could do little, although the Dutch bankers made plain their faith in the new nation by offering to buy the entire debt of the United States to the French government. Jefferson worked hard to thwart Robert Morris's tobacco contract with the Farmers General, and while he could not get it cancelled, he helped block its renewal in 1787. His greatest triumph perhaps was his continuation of the tradition of the cultivated citizen of the world so well set by Franklin. With such men as Jefferson and John Adams, however different they might be, the new nation might well have been content and should have been proud.

[56] Henry Adams: *History of the United States of America During the Administration of Thomas Jefferson* (4 vols., New York, 1889–90), I, 340.

[57] 11 July 1807, "Correspondence Between John Adams and Mercy Warren," MHS *Collections*, 5th ser., IV, 323.

But whatever the failures and successes of diplomatic negotiations, the basic fact was that although the United States were independent, they were not excluded from trade in a world blanketed with laws of trade and navigation. It is true that the British attempted to punish Americans by trying to keep their shipowners out of the West India trade, but they allowed most of the usual American products to be taken there in British bottoms, or in American if emergencies arose, and it is astonishing how many emergencies there were. American ships could come to Britain on the same basis as they had when colonials, and on the payment of the same duties. Long before the war France had recognized the fact that English America carried on trade with her West Indies and after the war she opened even more ports to the United States and ports in France as well. The policy of the French government, whatever French merchants might think of it, was to strike yet another blow at English commerce and English power. The Dutch showed no concern over the new nation except to increase trade with it in every way. The rest of the nations interested sought earnestly, if with less effect, to share in the trade of England's onetime monopoly. The result was that, while the shipowners of the United States were somewhat hampered by the order keeping them out of the West India carrying trade, new channels were being opened.[58]

Since American merchants were men of various degrees of vision and ability, their actions and their explanations of what happened are varied indeed. Unfortunately for the good of the United States, the bulk of American trade resumed old channels as soon as the war was over. But the chief trouble was that more was bought than could be paid for. The boom was followed by a collapse in which English suppliers, American wholesalers and retailers, and American consumers all were hurt. Then came the inevitable shrieking and name-calling in which almost everything except human greed and stupidity were blamed for the depression. Retaliation against Great Britain was demanded and the demand was met by the state governments in an effective fashion, despite the clamors of merchants and politicians who wanted such power placed in the hands of the central government.

The account of American economy which follows is a necessary

[58] See *post*, ch. ix.

background for understanding the political and economic arguments of the 1780's. It is a further illustration, if one be needed, of the wide divergence that so often appears between economic facts and economic theories, especially when the theories are devised and used to achieve political ends.

PART THREE

The Pattern of American Economy

THE DETERMINING forces in the history of the United States after the Revolution were many: both personal and impersonal, idealistic and selfish. But the overshadowing fact lying back of political and personal forces was the stress and change in the pattern of economic relationships. The nature of the economy and its problems were disputed then, and have been ever since. The "economic interpretation" of the period long precedes the appearance of a noted book on that subject in the twentieth century. During the Confederation there was endless reiteration of the idea that a more powerful central government would solve the country's economic problems. During the struggle over the ratification of the Constitution of 1787, its supporters insisted with unvarying monotony that if the new constitution were not adopted, economic chaos would follow. Their opponents, on the other hand, insisted with equal monotony that the times were not difficult and that the argument of chaos to follow was political in purpose.

The population of the newborn nation was predominantly agrarian: more than ninety per cent of the people lived on farms and thereby made their living. The ultimate prosperity of America was in large measure the prosperity of its farmers, which was in turn dependent in great measure on the export of farm produce to Europe and the West Indies. Those farmers who did not produce for export were self-sufficing to a large extent, so that it mattered little whether ships left harbors but it was important what kind of taxes were laid. Their thinking was the unvoiced kind of those who are rooted in the soil and who work with their hands. Thus while they were "America" in terms of its population and its produce, their needs, wants, and problems seldom found their way into the documents from which history is written. However, they did influence elections to and the policies of legislatures. So powerfully did they make themselves felt during the Confederation that by 1786 seven of the thirteen states had once more adopted some form of paper money as a means of agrarian relief. It is significant that later historians have usually discussed such measures in terms of unsound finance, or even of morality, but almost never in terms of an attempt to solve the pressing problems of an agrarian society.

That history has been so written is partly because historians have had little sympathy with the problems of the agrarian majority and partly because their understanding has been clouded by the sources they have used. The sources were the product of a minority in society, as perhaps they always are. In this case the dominant note was sounded by American merchants and business men who lived mostly in the seaport towns. They exported the produce of farm and forest and in turn imported the necessaries and luxuries which were paid for by that produce. They were the middlemen who made fortunes and had influence in the American states out of all proportion to their numbers. Their power was born of place, position, and fortune. They were located at or near the seats of government and they were in direct contact with legislatures and government officers. They influenced and often dominated the local newspapers which voiced the ideas and interests of commerce and identified them with the good of the whole people, the state, and the nation. The published writings of the leaders of the period are almost without exception those of merchants, of their lawyers, or of politicians sympathetic with them. Thus it is that subsequent thinking about the period has been guided in one direction.

Often the interests of a minority group are identical with the public or the national "good," but this is not invariably so. The Confederation period was a time when great numbers of people either denied or did not believe that the "good of the whole," as defined by the merchant class, was an adequate definition. It is therefore necessary to examine carefully the respective parts played by the merchants and commerce, by the farmers, and by American governments during and after the Revolution, if one is to arrive at a somewhat balanced view of the history of the period.

8

War and Peace: Boom and Bust

THE ASSOCIATION at the beginning of the Revolution was a stunning but not fatal blow to American economy. Americans stopped importing British goods. Farm produce could not go to its normal markets along the coast, the West Indies, and Europe. Nearby armies were a temporary but often a dubious market. Merchants were hemmed in ports by British troops or ran the risk of losing their ships to the British navy if they ventured out of port. In many towns the pattern of economic relationships was upset by such events as the burning of Norfolk, the flight of Loyalist merchants from Boston, and the occupation of New York, Philadelphia, and Charleston by the British.

As the war went on the effects of its outbreak wore off except in the immediate presence of fighting. Commerce found its way back into many old channels, and found new ones, for Americans were at last free of the trammels of the English Navigation Acts. In both old and new channels American merchants found greater risks, but also greater profits than they had dreamed of before the war. By 1778 European luxury goods as well as necessities were advertised in American newspapers as they had been before 1776.[1]

The steady rhythm of farming was little interrupted except in the immediate presence of warring armies. Even this was no unmixed evil, for the British and the French armies traveled with cash in hand to pay for supplies. After 1776 New England farmers were untouched except by militia duty. The back country of the middle states continued to produce the breadstuffs for which it

[1] Edward Channing: *A History of the United States* (6 vols., New York, 1905–25), III, ch. xiii.

was famous. Virginia and the South were hard-hit during the winter of 1780–81 by the march and countermarch of Cornwallis, Greene, and lesser generals, but even there the "duration" was exceedingly short, except for fleeing politicians. There were rising prices and inflation until 1780. The demand for foodstuffs was great and from time to time there were serious shortages of food in the towns. The result was that many farmers made money as they never had before.

The ancient antagonism between town and country dwellers grew more bitter, but with a different twist, for now the townsmen believed themselves exploited by the farmers. Even if high prices benefited only the larger farmers who raised a surplus, it won for all farmers the enmity of town dwellers.[2] John Clarke said that the seaports were in a forlorn condition, subjected as they were to "the inhumanity (for it deserves no milder name) of our brethren in the country. . . . One more winter such as the one just past would finish us." [3] In Baltimore merchants bewailed the "small representation of the mercantile interest in the respective assemblies," and found unaccountable the "universally prevailing prejudice of planters and farmers against the trading interest." [4]

The prejudice against merchants as a class was based on the facts of wartime trade and speculation. No money that was made during the Revolution was made so openly and blatantly as that made by the merchants in war supplies, food, and clothing; in all of the necessities of war and peace as well as the luxuries of life. Men of all shades of political opinion united in condemning this, even when they disagreed as to the remedy. The ordinary consumer could see the issue as plainly as the statesman and acted more directly.

In the summer of 1777 Boston merchants had on hand large supplies of coffee and sugar. But they refused to sell, for they were waiting for prices to rise. The housewives of Boston, wanting both commodities, united and marched upon the store of one of the

[2] See Ralph V. Harlow: "Economic Conditions in Massachusetts During the American Revolution," CSM *Publications*, XX (1917–9), 163–90, where he emphasizes the prosperity of the farmers at least until 1780. James T. Adams: *New England in the Republic 1776–1850* (Boston, 1926), 55–7, insists that the average farmer was falling behind steadily in the period of rising prices.

[3] Harlow: CSM *Publications*, XX, 179–80.

[4] Samuel and Robert Purviance to Robert Morris, 8 Dec. 1778, Robert Morris Papers, LC.

leading engrossers. They demanded his goods and when he refused, they grabbed him and tossed him in a cart. From this ignominious position he surrendered his keys to the housewives, who entered his store and walked out with what they needed.[5]

In Philadelphia townspeople besieged the residence of James Wilson who was for the moment harboring some of the town's leading merchants, who were accused of shipping badly needed food supplies out of the city.[6] In 1779 the price of flour was said to be high because "those termed speculators are as thick and industrious as bees, and as active and wicked as the devil himself. . . ." [7]

It was plainly an age of profiteering and luxury for those in a position to take advantage of war's dislocations and opportunities. They were denounced by men as far apart politically as James Warren and George Washington. James Warren wrote to Sam Adams that "most people are engaged in getting and some in spending money as fast as they can." Shortly thereafter he declared that "folly and wickedness stalk abroad with the same shameless rapidity. . . ." His wife, Mercy, asked John Adams: "How much longer shall we be embarrassed and distressed by the selfish insidious arts of gamblers, courtiers, and stockjobbers among ourselves. . . ." [8] Washington declared that "speculation, peculation, engrossing, forestalling with all their concomitants, afford too many melancholy proofs of the decay of public virtue; and too glaring instances of its being the interest and desire of too many who would wish to be thought friends, to continue the war." [9]

Such complaints were not the talk of captious critics but of observers and participants in a war in which they were not profiting personally. The merchants made money and they admitted it. Carter Braxton of Virginia complained to a correspondent that "your high prices for goods tend to ruin our cause. Three hundred per cent on a West India invoice for dry goods is enough,

[5] Abigail Adams to John Adams, 30 July 1777, Charles Francis Adams, ed.: *Familiar Letters of John Adams and his Wife Abigail Adams, During the Revolution* (New York, 1876), 286–7.

[6] Brunhouse: *Counter-Revolution*, 75–76.

[7] Caesar Rodney to John Dickinson, 17 Oct. 1779, George H. Ryden, ed.: *Letters to and from Caesar Rodney, 1756–1784* (Philadelphia, 1933), 324.

[8] Letters of 25 Oct., 16 Dec. 1778, 29 July 1779, *Warren-Adams Letters*, II, 59, 82, 114.

[9] To James Warren, 31 March 1779, *Writings*, XIV, 312.

and is what I sold the *Hero's* for. Indeed many complaints were made against me even at that." He urged merchants to ask "moderate prices," else the vengeance of the people and the legislatures would be called down on their heads. "Let us be content to receive moderate rewards for our labors and recollect that the people who ultimately pay these prices are the poor soldiers and officers who are fighting for us and exposing their lives while we are trading and growing rich. . . ." [10] In North Carolina Richard Ellis modestly asked for a profit of one hundred per cent on a cargo of gunpowder and arms. But this was in 1776. By 1778 a cargo from France sold for seven and a half times its value.[11] In Boston Samuel Otis urged his brother not to be in a hurry to sell his winter goods for they were scarce and he might as well make one hundred per cent as five.[12]

Such things make "accountable" the antagonism of farmers, planters, and consumers toward the merchants of the United States. This antagonism expressed itself politically in most of the states, although perhaps nowhere more strongly than in Maryland in 1779, when the assembly resolved that henceforth no merchant could represent it in the Continental Congress. This action was the result of a charge that Samuel Chase, as a member of Congress, advised his partner in Maryland of an expected purchase of wheat by Congress so that the partner could corner the market. Alexander Hamilton wrote a scorching denunciation of Chase and all other speculators in four essays signed "Publius," and Charles Carroll of Carrollton, Chase's political enemy, engineered the action of the Maryland legislature.[13]

Despite such assaults on the merchant minority, the war still offered vast opportunities for gain. They complained at length about such things as paper money, yet they made money as it depreciated—that is, as prices rose. They bought goods and held them while prices went up. The proceeds of sales were hurriedly reinvested in new goods which were again held for lengthy periods. What merchants dreaded above all were price fixing and legal

[10] 1 Nov. 1777, *Magazine of History*, VIII (1908), 373.

[11] Charles Crittenden: *The Commerce of North Carolina, 1763–1789* (New Haven, 1936), 143.

[12] Samuel E. Morison: *The Life and Letters of Harrison Gray Otis, Federalist, 1765–1848* (2 vols., Boston, 1913), I, 22.

[13] Philip A. Crowl: *Maryland During and After the Revolution* (Baltimore, 1943), 96–100.

tender acts. These they fought with vigor and they contributed much to the destruction of efforts by Congress and state governments to fix the price of commodities.[14] Even men like Washington, who bemoaned speculation, opposed price fixing. He wanted speculators, forestallers, and extortioners punished and heavy taxes laid, but the remedy was "not to limit the prices of articles, for this I believe is inconsistent with the very nature of things, and impracticable in itself. . . ."[15]

No defense of eighteenth century "free enterprise" was more bland than that of Gouverneur Morris, one of its most able practitioners. At a time when inflation was rife, when things looked black for government and people alike, and when, if ever, the demand for price controls and the taxation of wealth was justified, Morris wrote a series of essays attacking any control or taxation of the well-to-do. His argument rose to supreme heights when he declared that a tax on money would be iniquitous and impolitic and would drive it from the country; that it could never be collected, for "money is of too subtle and spiritual a nature to be caught by the rude hand of the law." Such things as legal tender laws were simply fraudulent attempts to get something for nothing. Price fixing was equally bad. Monopoly would be a good thing for the community if it could be established, and profit making was a positive good.[16]

It is true that during the war some merchants lost property: those who became Loyalists, those who lost their interest in the fisheries, or those who suffered because of British occupation. But the change was one of personnel rather than of basic structure: individual merchants did disappear, but the merchant class was probably as numerous and certainly as wealthy at the end of the war as at its beginning, for new men took the place of old. Commerce during the war was risky but profitable, and the years after the war were to be ones of great opportunity for gain in fields far wider than most merchants conceived possible before 1776. Some old avenues, such as the West India trade, were closed or at least overgrown with legal tangles. But independence meant that American products could be carried any place in the world

[14] East: *Business Enterprise*, 215–6.
[15] To James Warren, 31 March 1779, *Writings*, XIV, 313.
[16] These essays, signed "An American," are summarized in Sparks: *Morris*, I, 218–22.

where there was a market. No American products were now enumerated for the British market alone.[17]

Much of the wealth was in the form of ships, wharves, stores, and goods, as had been the case before the war. But there was new wealth in the form of government debt, of private debts growing out of the war, of new hopes in new markets, and of the expansion of old ones. Vast new areas of land had fallen to state and central governments; shelves were stocked with goods; privateering and war profits had set new and more expensive standards of living; hard money, spent by British and French armies, was more widely spread throughout the country than ever before.[18] Americans were jubilant over their new position, but before they could realize its benefits, they had to pick the bitter fruits of independence as well as the sweet.

As the war came to an end, the ports of the United States were open to all the world, and Dutch, French, Danish, Swedish, and other Europeans set sail for them. English merchants were anxious to continue handling the greater share of American commerce. American merchants were anxious to resume old trade relations and to explore new ones.

Elkanah Watson of Philadelphia, in London even before the signing of the preliminary articles of peace, asked Lord Shelburne if he could purchase English vessels and goods, send them to Holland, and thence to America. The goods were liable to seizure if they came directly, for America and England were still at war; but if they came from a country allied with the United States, they would be safe on arrival in America. A little later he asked about the regulation of commerce between Britain and America, for a "great number of respectable American merchants in the different parts of Europe stand ready to grapple the first opening to revive and give energy to the springs of commerce in its old and natural channel. . . ." [19] The anxiety of British merchants to regain old trade appeared even earlier. A ship sent from Virginia to New York on an official mission in the summer of 1782 returned well stocked with British goods. There was no law against it, the purchasers were eager, and Edmund Randolph suggested

[17] Channing: *History*, III, ch. xiii; East: *Business Enterprise*, ch. x.

[18] Swan: *National Arithmetick*, 82, estimated that there was nearly three times as much gold and silver in the country in 1783 as in 1774.

[19] Letters of 5 Oct., 8 Dec. 1782, Shelburne Papers, vol. 87, CL.

that Congress reiterate its horror of British manufactures in order to put an end to such traffic.[20]

When hostilities ended, British vessels appeared everywhere. In Virginia they claimed to be in distress or claimed the right to trade because of the cessation of hostilities.[21] English merchants circularized former customers. Joseph Banfield of Falmouth, England offered his services to all his former correspondents. He expressed the hope that mutual understanding and confidence would "ever subsist between this nation and America, and that an uninterrupted commerce may cement the bonds, and unite us, in a lasting and firm friendship. . . ." [22] London merchants urged Parliament to restore American commerce to the position it had held when a part of the Empire: they asked for the equivalent of free trade with what was now, in law at least, a foreign country.[23]

Without waiting for legislatures to determine the channels of trade, merchants from all over Europe sent cargoes to the United States. English merchants or their agents appeared in most American towns with cargoes and plenty of credit. Some American merchants who had spent the war years in England, returned to America and sought to re-establish themselves. French merchants had great hopes of taking the place of the English in American trade. The rush to America was on in 1783. An index to its greatness is that "between May and December, 1783, twenty-eight French vessels, and almost the same number of English merchantmen brought cargoes, worth almost half a million dollars into Boston Harbor alone." [24]

These goods came to markets adequately if not oversupplied. Credit and easy terms were offered American merchants to induce them to buy. They bought, and they bought too much. In

[20] Edmund Randolph to James Madison, Richmond, 16 Aug. 1782, Madison Papers, LC.

[21] Edmund Randolph to James Madison, 9 May 1783, Madison Papers, LC.

[22] Sylvanus Bourne Papers, I, LC. See also the letter of Mrs. Mary Hayley to Christopher Champlin, 1 Feb. 1783, *Commerce of Rhode Island 1726–1800* (MHS *Collections*, LXIX–LXX, Boston, 1924–5), II, 170–1. Mrs. Hayley was a sister of John Wilkes and the widow of a merchant who had been in the American trade before the war. She came to America in 1784 where her arrival was reported widely in the newspapers.

[23] Edmund C. Burnett, ed.: "Observations of London Merchants on American Trade, 1783," AHR, XVIII (1912–3), 769–80.

[24] Samuel E. Morison: *The Maritime History of Massachusetts 1783–1860* (Boston, 1921), 35.

turn they sold to the people on credit and sold them too much. Mechanics were reported to be buying silk stockings and farmers' daughters buying silks. It is little wonder that rugged old Puritans thought the world was coming to no good end.[25] Newspapers everywhere carried merchants' advertisements. William Sitgreaves of Philadelphia announced in January 1783 that he had brought in from Holland and France fine and superfine broadcloths, low priced "ditto," plain and embossed serges, blankets and carpeting, hose of all kinds, velvet, sheeting, Irish, Laval, and Holland linens, Britannias, duck, drilling, bedticking, chintzes, calicoes, diapers, dimities, lawns, taffetas and other cloth in almost endless profusion. His list concluded with the statement that he had also brought in "a good Forte Piano." [26] Such accounts can be found in almost every other newspaper in the United States in the first happy days of the boom. But the boom could not and did not last long. The news of peace itself had an immediate effect on the market. In May 1783 the New York market was reported glutted, the prices low and expected to go lower, for even more cargoes were expected from Europe. Everyone was reported anxious to enter into trade, and this, too, it was predicted, would soon be overdone.[27] The same thing happened in Philadelphia where it was reported in May that seven more foreign vessels had just arrived and that "goods fall prodigiously." [28] Embarrassment for Americans was predicted, and even worse embarrassment for European merchants who were offering their goods on easy credit.[29] Dry goods in Boston went down and it was difficult to make profitable sales by August 1783.[30] By October 1783 the market in Boston was "miserable." Great quantities had come in, mostly in foreign bottoms. Only the losses European merchants were sure to suffer would teach them to allow Americans to import for themselves. The fine things imported had

[25] James Warren to John Adams, 24 June 1783, *Warren-Adams Letters*, II, 219.

[26] *Pennsylvania Gazette*, 8 Jan. 1783.

[27] William Paterson to his brother, 12 May 1783, William Paterson Papers (Bancroft Transcripts), NYPL.

[28] William Clajon to General Horatio Gates, Gates Papers, NYHS; Madison to Edmund Randolph, 13 May 1783, Burnett, VII, 164. Goods sold for even less than they cost in Europe, Clement Biddle wrote to Washington, 28 May 1783, Washington Papers, LC.

[29] James Warren to John Adams, 24 June 1783, *Warren-Adams Letters*, II, 218–9.

[30] Sears and Smith to Henry Knox, Boston, 13 Aug. 1783, Knox Papers, MHS.

destroyed all "ideas of frugality which necessity had before given, and drained us of our money." How money had been found to purchase all these things James Warren could not understand.[31]

The money left behind by the armies of France and Britain poured back to Europe. By November 1783 it was predicted that all the coin in America would soon be gone and that it would take at least three years of American exports to pay for all that had come in during the previous six months.[32]

The boom that started as a buying spree by war-prosperous Americans in the seaport towns continued as a credit-supported balloon and too few, indeed, realized that such beauteous moments in history have but one inevitable end. The collapse did not come suddenly in one great panic. Actually, from the end of the war on, it was plain that matters were getting worse in the seaport towns. By the spring of 1784 the glutted market, the scarcity of specie, and the overextension of credit all combined to produce a serious commercial depression, although imports continued to arrive during the spring of 1784. By then merchants and shopkeepers in Philadelphia were in difficulty, although they sought to conceal their difficulties by selling their goods at a loss.[33] In Charleston a merchant said that he had never seen money so scarce and that it was growing scarcer. He reminded his hapless correspondent that his note was due in September.[34] It was said that Boston merchants had stopped importing and were offering goods at little more than cost.[35] Ships sailing from Boston to England found it difficult to get cargoes. An English newspaper reported that two ships had arrived in London in ballast and carrying only specie, an export which could only aggravate the depression in America.[36]

The Americans were not the only people affected. The shrinkage of specie remittances and the light cargoes, particularly from ports like Boston, hit hard those British merchants who had overex-

[31] James Warren to John Adams, 27 Oct. 1783, *Warren-Adams Letters*, II, 232.

[32] Edward Bancroft to William Frazer, Philadelphia, 8 Nov. 1783, Bancroft: *Constitution*, I, 333.

[33] Charles Pettit to Joseph Reed, 18 April 1784, Joseph Reed Papers, NYHS.

[34] Nicholas Eveleigh to Jacob Reed, 21 April 1784, Emmet Coll., no. 1216, NYPL.

[35] William B. Weeden: *Economic and Social History of New England 1620–1789* (2 vols., Boston, 1891), II, 819.

[36] Justin Winsor, ed.: *The Memorial History of Boston, 1630–1880* (4 vols., Boston, 1880–1), IV, 199.

tended credit to American merchants. In August 1784, five great London merchant houses trading with America closed their doors, one with a loss of £140,000. Unlike the American merchants, they could not use American courts to collect bad debts.[37] Yet, as late as the fall of 1784, the English "American merchants" were reported in American newspapers to be in high spirits because of large remittances and large orders from America.[38]

By the summer of 1784, people were asking themselves what had happened, why it had happened, and what they could do about it. Like other men in other depressions from the beginning of time to the present day, few blamed either their own greed or stupidity. Some said that the government was to blame: it should keep out the British. But at once there was wrangling, for the merchants wanted to keep out only their British competitors, not British goods, while the "mechanicks"—the budding manufacturers—wanted to keep out British goods as well. Others blamed the women for all the extravagances, and this was a popular idea. In an article first printed in Boston, but picked up and printed with relish by New York and Philadelphia newspapers, it was announced that commerce had extended her blessings over us in a way unprecedented. Foreign productions were low-priced but they were superfluities and everyone possessed of republican principles should feel anxious at the vast quantity of specie leaving the continent daily to pay for these baubles. The "fair Americans" should exercise self-denial. They should "dispense with that ostentatious pageantry, now so much in vogue" since such things are calculated to give fashionable grace only to those in want of beauty, for,

> The beauteous female, unadorn'd and plain,
> Secure to please while youth confirms her reign,
> Slights every borrow'd charm that dress supplies,
> Nor shares with art the triumph of her eyes.

"The softer sex, did during the revolution, display virtues, honorary as they were useful: And shall it ever be said that meagre want, and cold hand poverty stalk'd through our country, occasioned by the inordinate desire of its inhabitants for foreign

[37] Ibid., IV, 200.
[38] *Pennsylvania Gazette*, 10 Nov. 1784.

gewgaws."[39] Such appeals might be comforting to masculine writers and readers but they did not solve any problems. The same was true of appeals to practice industry and frugality and to lessen imports until they balanced exports, which were so common in the papers and private correspondence.[40]

The placing of blame on British merchants and their agents was popular everywhere. James Warren, in Massachusetts, and many of his fellow citizens ran the full course of denunciation. So did people in Charleston, South Carolina. There, in June 1785, it was said that scarcity of cash was making the place dismal and that the old merchants were being ruined. No crops were had last year and very few were to be expected during 1785. "British merchants will be . . . the ruin of not only this state, but all America; for every dirty advantage they can take, they eagerly catch at." The people should rise and send such ministerial agents and factors from the land.[41]

Such evasions of the ultimate responsibility, which lay on individual Americans themselves, did not alter the course of the depression. Some men in 1785 believed that all was black. James Warren declared that in Massachusetts, manners, morals, commerce, and agriculture all would soon be at an end: "the same imbecility, the same servility and the same inattention still prevail and are likely to continue. Money is the only object attended to, and the only acquisition that commands respect."[42] Stephen Higginson moaned that Massachusetts trade had reached a low ebb by the summer of 1785 and he prophesied that it would go still lower.[43] In Philadelphia, Thomas FitzSimons was complaining of the good markets he had heard of in the Madeiras and of his inability to hire vessels to go there. Many different causes had

[39] *Massachusetts Centinel*, 12 June 1784; *Pennsylvania Gazette*, 30 June 1784. More than two years later the ladies of Hartford organized what they called an "Oeconomical Association." One hundred ladies of the "first families" agreed not to buy such items as gauze, ribbons, lace, beaver hats, etc; to dress plainly, giving due attention to local manufactures. The agreement was to last until 25 June 1787. *New Haven Gazette*, 16 Nov. 1786.

[40] *Pennsylvania Gazette*, 15 Sept. 1784; Mercy Warren to John Adams, 27 April 1785, *Warren-Adams Letters*, II, 252.

[41] Extract from a letter from Charleston, 4 June, *Pennsylvania Gazette*, 29 June 1785.

[42] To John Adams, 28 Jan. 1785, *Warren-Adams Letters*, II, 249.

[43] To John Adams, 8 Aug. 1785, J. Franklin Jameson, ed.: "Letters of Stephen Higginson, 1783–1804," AHA *Annual Report* (1896), I, 723.

served to check the enterprise "for which our merchants were so eminent. The price of our produce is so high and the choice of markets so few that exportation is very unprofitable."[44]

And, as always in such times of despair, the ever old and ever new cry of "return to the land" was set forth by sellers of real estate. A land office at Boston advertised a seventy-acre farm but ten miles from Boston, with a never-failing brook, excellent springs, fruitful orchards, hay, and corn. It declared: "At this dying time with trade who would not wish for rural independence, where life is innocent, sweet and long."[45]

As one goes farther, one begins to find that not all contemporary opinion agreed as to the nature of the country's ills. Furthermore, one finds that conditions varied from north to south and from east to west. John Adams, safe in England, received many a letter deploring the iniquities of his fellow men, their lust for riches, their loss of morals. He agreed that the times might be serious but he doubted that Americans were any different after the war than they had been before or during it. He declared that his countrymen had never been "Spartans in their contempt of wealth" and he hoped they never would be for it would render them "lazy drones."[46]

In Philadelphia, James Wilson, attorney for the Bank of North America, was busy defending it against the charge that it had caused the depression. He examined the commercial depression. The fact that he did so for a fee does not make his analysis any less valid. He said, "the disagreeable state of our commerce has been the effect of extravagant and injudicious importation. During the war, our ports were in a great measure blocked up. Imported articles were scarce and dear; and we felt the disadvantages of a stagnation in business. Extremes frequently introduce one another. When hostilities ceased, the floodgates of commerce were opened; and an inundation of foreign manufactures overflowed the United States: we seemed to have forgot, that to pay was as necessary in trade as to purchase; and we observed no proportion between our imports, and our produce and other natural means of remittance. What was the consequence? Those who made any payments made them chiefly in specie; and in that way diminished

[44] To James Searle, 4 April 1785, Emmet Coll., no. 9465, NYPL.
[45] *Massachusetts Centinel*, 10 Aug. 1785.
[46] To James Warren, 4 July 1786, *Warren-Adams Letters*, II, 277.

our circulation. Others made no remittances at all, and thereby injured our credit. This account of what happened between the European merchants and our importers, corresponds exactly with what happened between our importers and the retailers spread over the different parts of the United States. The retailers, if they paid at all, paid in specie: and thus every operation, foreign and domestick, had an injurious effect on our credit, our circulation, and our commerce." [47] Such analyses were not common in 1785, but they do put in better perspective the cries of men caught in a web spun of their own greed.

It seems plain that the commercial depression hit the New England states the hardest. Colonel Christian Febiger, a Danish soldier who stayed in America after the war to act as agent for merchants in the Baltic countries, traveled about looking for products that could be sold in Scandinavia and for markets for its goods. He left Philadelphia in the spring of 1785 and traveled northward. He wrote a Danish correspondent that he had found an amazing superfluity of English goods everywhere in New England. Philadelphia and New York had such goods too, but not as much as Connecticut, Rhode Island, and Massachusetts. He said the reason was obvious for "they have no back country to consume their goods, being bounded by Canada." [48]

The picture that has come down to us has been painted mostly in terms of the complaints from the town of Boston. But Boston was not typical of all the commercial towns of the United States, or even of New England. English writers made much point of this. As early as 1784 an English newspaper remarked that "Boston was once the most flourishing place in America, and employed near five hundred sail of shipping, besides coasting and fishing vessels, which were numerous to a degree. Besides the trade which subsisted within themselves, they were to America what Holland has been to Europe—the carriers for all the other colonies. At present their distillery is entirely at a stand; their peltry and fur trade, once so considerable, is entirely over; the fishery is exceedingly trifling. . . ." [49] Whatever the truth or lack of it in such a

[47] Randolph G. Adams, ed.: *Selected Political Essays of James Wilson* (New York, 1930), 145–6.

[48] To J. Sobotken, 15 June 1785, *Magazine of American History*, VIII (1882), 352. On the other hand the *Massachusetts Centinel* declared 17 Sept. 1785 that very few English goods were to be found in Boston.

[49] 9 March 1784, quoted, Winsor: *Memorial History of Boston*, IV, 199.

statement, the important fact is that New England had depended too much on her role as a carrier. This was of immense significance in the formation of New England opinion and particularly that of seacoast Massachusetts.[50]

The depression was by no means as serious farther to the south. New York, an occupied city for seven years, had been partly burned and had to start from the beginning when the war was over. Yet it made astonishing gains. Philadelphia business was hurt, but not many business men were ruined by extravagant importation. Indiscreet or unlucky ones went to the wall but many others continued to make substantial gains. In Charleston, times were bad but this was due as much to the chaos South Carolina found itself in at the end of the war as to "riotous" importations. Baltimore business men were alarmed during 1785 by "daily failures," [51] but the town was the boom town of the 1780's.

Rural America, particularly from New York to the south, was not so sharply affected by the war. Planters generally had entered the war burdened with debt to British merchants, but some of them had managed to pay off those debts, in form at least, during the war. They were now chary of great purchases from abroad although European agents, particularly the hated Scotch, flocked through the planting South searching for new customers and trying to collect pre-war debts. Tobacco planters were at last freed from the drain the Navigation Laws had imposed on the sale of tobacco. This was one product for which there was a ready market throughout Europe. At war's end there was for a time a good price for it everywhere. Wheat and corn crops, too, were good, and sold for high prices.[52]

Good prices for farm produce lasted at least until 1785 and even when they fell, they remained above pre-war levels.[53] But this fall in prices, coupled with heavy taxes and stringent debt

[50] Even in Massachusetts men like James Swan believed recovery was on the way by 1786. *National Arithmetick*, preface, vii.

[51] Richard Curson to General Horatio Gates, 14 July 1785, Gates Papers, NYHS.

[52] East: *Business Enterprise*, 140, 176, 244; Joseph Reed to Dennys DeBerdt, 8, 17, 30 Oct. 1784, Joseph Reed Papers, NYHS, in which, on his return from a trip to England, he comments on the crowded city of Philadelphia, its apparent prosperity, the high rents, the many vessels in the harbor, and the high price of country produce.

[53] Arthur H. Cole: *Wholesale Commodity Prices in the United States 1700–1861, Statistical Supplement* (Cambridge, Mass., 1938), 52–92.

collections, led to agrarian distress which resulted in strident demands for farm relief in most of the states. The farmers were not too much concerned with the plight of artisans and merchants, but they did want government credit. The merchants, as creditors and money lenders, were bitterly opposed to agrarian relief while demanding relief for themselves. The merchants wanted American ships favored over British, and they were successful in virtually every state. They did not want protective tariffs because they made their money importing manufactured goods. The artisans, whose manufactures had been boosted by the war, wanted protective tariffs adopted by the states, and they too were successful in those states where the artisans were an important part of the population. The artisans did not care whether American ships got special benefits or not.

It is a striking fact that most Americans in the eighteenth century agreed that government should intervene in economic life. They disagreed only as to the nature of the intervention and as to which groups were to benefit thereby. The history of the conflict among the various groups in American society in their demands for state aid lends richness and variety to the history of state politics during the 1780's.[54] Moreover it throws new light on the factors involved in the movement for a stronger central government, as do the following chapters on the roots of recovery.

[54] See chs. xiv, xvi.

9
The Roots of Recovery: Expansion of American Commerce

As one examines the evidence for the expansion of American commerce and business enterprise after the Revolution, the simple picture of economic depression as a cause of the movement for a stronger central government begins to disappear. Even a brief analysis of the complex interests and ideas at work in the United States demonstrates the inadequacy of such "an economic interpretation," although it is accepted without question by those writers who in the same breath denounce Charles A. Beard's *An Economic Interpretation of the Constitution of the United States.*

He who would examine economic life during the 1780's must content himself with only the most scattered figures. Statistics have about them an aura of immutable truth for men of the twentieth century. Men of the eighteenth century professed a belief in immutable laws, but they were "laws of nature." Twentieth century tables, graphs, and charts would be a meaningless jumble for them. Instead, they were concerned with the relations of man to man and of class to class in society, not with figures as we use them. They kept records, of course, but in a casual way that both shocks and intrigues. Many of their records have been lost; others are cryptic or, at best, the notations of a kind of bookkeeping which viewed life as a series of relationships rather than as a matter of the annual balancing of accounts.[1]

Toward the end of the eighteenth century men began to use

[1] See W. T. Baxter: *The House of Hancock* (Cambridge, 1945), ch. ii, "Trade without Money," for a charming account of the kind of "bookkeeping" that was a part of the eighteenth century business life.

statistics as political weapons. Lord Sheffield produced long tables to argue that England could ignore her former colonies and discriminate against them. Histories of commerce began to appear, replete with tables of imports and exports. Citizens of the new United States, who bought more than they sold immediately after the war, added up figures to prove a variety of things. The records that reflect the nature of American economy are scarce indeed. Here and there are materials on the tonnage of ships and on exports and imports that can be relied upon as indicating trends, but few indeed that can be accepted as having statistical finality.

After the Revolution Americans were free to trade with the world at large and they did so, although the largest part of their trade continued to be with the British Empire despite the hope of many Americans for economic disentanglement as well as political independence. The statistics relating to post-war trade vary with the source and often with the purpose of the compiler. In general, however, the facts indicate that American merchants and shipowners profited largely from the independence which had been thrust into their timid and reluctant hands.

In 1786 Jefferson prepared an estimate of American import and export trade, admitting that "calculations of this kind cannot pretend to accuracy, where inattention and fraud combine to suppress their objects." His "approximations" showed that the value of United States exports to Europe and the West Indies exceeded their imports from Europe, the West Indies, and Africa, by over a quarter of a million louis. It is important to remember that men at the time assumed that the United States had a favorable balance of trade with the world as a whole.[2]

Americans had always bought more from Great Britain than they sold to her and they had made up the difference in many ways: crops not grown in England, freights, ship sales, the West India trade, and shipments of specie gotten in that trade. In 1783, in the first days of the boom, America bought more than ever from England, despite plentiful stocks of goods and declining prices. Imports from England fell off sharply with the depression, so that the average imports for the decade of the 1780's were less than before the war. In 1791 the Privy Council made an investigation of British-American trade. It reported that the average annual value of the exports of British manufactures to the colonies

[2] Jefferson to Lafayette, 17 July 1786, *Writings* (Bergh ed.), V, 371–6.

in the six years ending in 1774 was £2,216,970. The average value for the six years ending in 1789 was £2,119,837. The annual decrease in the exports of manufactures since the war was thus nearly £100,000. The value of all other articles exported since the war had declined by a little over £300,000 a year, making the average decline in British exports to the United States nearly £400,000 a year.

While Americans were buying on the average of £400,000 a year less from Great Britain after the war, they were also exporting far less to her than before the war. In the six years ending in 1774, America had sent an average of £1,752,142 to Great Britain. In the six years to 1789 the average export to Great Britain was £908,636, an average annual decrease of £843,506. The Privy Council accounted for the great decrease in American exports to Great Britain almost entirely in terms of tobacco and rice. Before the war all tobacco had had to go to Great Britain and four fifths of it had been re-exported to other countries. The Council estimated that the average annual decrease in the value of tobacco shipped from the United States to Great Britain was £582,987 and that the decrease in the value of rice was £196,526.[3]

The generalized pattern presented by such figures does not reveal the ups and downs of year-to-year business. The big year of British exports to the United States was 1784 when goods valued at £3,679,467 were shipped. In 1785 the value of British exports dropped over a million pounds. It dropped another £700,-000 in 1786. In 1787 the value of exports began rising sharply. After a small drop in 1788, it started rising again. By 1790 it had almost reached the 1784 figure. In 1791 and 1792 exports to the United States jumped way beyond what they had been in 1784. The upturn in United States imports is thus evident by 1787. The presumption is that commerce had settled down to a more even course after the post-war boom and collapse. Its steady growth was not to be interrupted until war between France and England. This threw to American shipowners the golden gains

[3] *Report of a Committee of the Lords of the Privy Council on the Trade of Great Britain with the United States. January, 1791* (Washington, Department of State, 1888), 10–12. The report declared that while there had been a decrease of exports to the United States, the total exports to the United States and the remaining British possessions had increased, and that the increase had been that of British manufactures, while foreign merchandise exported through England had fallen off greatly.

falling to the lot of neutrals able to sell to all sides in war time.

American exports to Great Britain do not show ups and downs except in 1786: they show a steady increase. There were small shipments during the war, the first big increase coming in 1783. The value spurted upward sharply in 1784 and then increased until 1792. In that year exports dropped and they continued to do so until 1794 when they were lower than they had been at the end of the Revolution.[4]

The balance of trade against the United States was a continuation of the problem that had always faced the colonists. Sectional differences remained what they had been, too. The merchants of the northern United States imported far more from England than they exported to her. Before the war they had brought goods into Boston, New York, and Philadelphia and thence sold them to retailers and consumers, not only on the mainland, but in the West Indies as well. As carriers they had entered largely into the West India trade, from which they derived profit and cash in quantity with which to redress the unfavorable balances arising from their direct import-export relations with Great Britain.

After the war, as we have seen, American merchants and their ships retained their old privileges in English ports.[5] They did so by act of Parliament and order in council. In addition, they managed to evade whatever rules there were, both American and British. Ships carried double sets of manifests, one containing the real amount of tobacco on board, the other a much smaller quantity. American ships also carried double papers so that they could appear as British ships in British ports, and American ships in American ports, thus evading both British duties on American shipping, and American duties on British shipping. Usually this was achieved by partnerships between British and American merchants.[6] American merchants seldom, if ever, spoke of their legal

[4] The most convenient, though erratic and often unreliable, source for the figures given above is Timothy Pitkin: *Statistical View of the Commerce of the United States* (New Haven, 1835). His materials are taken mostly from Macpherson: *Annals of Commerce*, IV. Bemis: *Jay's Treaty*, 33–5 gives figures for the trade 1790–4.

[5] See *ante*, ch. vii.

[6] J. Franklin Jameson, ed.: "Letters of Phineas Bond, British Consul at Philadelphia, to the foreign office of Great Britain, 1787, 1788, 1789," AHA *Annual Report* (1896), I, 513–659. Such devices are described in detail on pages 524, 537, 591, and 603.

advantages or their illegal practices, for obvious reasons. Instead, they focused the fire of their wrath upon the one real restriction that Britain laid upon the trade of her former colonies: the order in council of July 1783 which required that all food and other supplies from the United States must go to the West Indies in British rather than American vessels. Thus, only American shipowners, not American goods, were shut out of the West Indies, although the anguish of the shipowner was made so much of that it seemed as if all trade with the West Indies had been made impossible by the malevolent British.

The West India trade before the war had been of crucial importance to Americans. The trade with the British islands was relatively less important than that with the foreign West Indies. As early as 1733 the West India planter lobby in Parliament forced through the Molasses Act in an effort to meet the competition of those islands. By 1750 the British islands were no longer able to supply the Empire's demand for sugar. During the Revolution they were hurt by short supplies from the United States and by the much higher prices they had to pay. After the French entered the war, their islands were a center of warfare. Once the war was over, hopes of recovery were shattered by British policy which meant even higher prices for the needed supplies from the United States at the same time that the price of West India produce declined. In fact, the only real beneficiaries of British policy seem to have been the Americans who carried on illegal trade. British policy did not win the carrying trade for British merchants and it helped to speed the destruction of the planter class in the islands. As both British and American sources testify, American shipowners had not lost the old art of smuggling. There is every indication that the British order in council remained for the most part ineffective and that trade with the West Indies went on after the war as it had done before.

Of such things policy-makers in London remained oblivious despite the fact that naval officers and governors on the spot furnished them with all the material needed to adapt policy to reality.[7] The overruling fact was that the Americans' desire to sell and the West Indians' need to buy meant trade between them, no matter what the rules might say.

[7] On the whole problem of the British West Indies and their relation to American trade, see Ragatz: *Fall of the Planter Class*, *passim.*

In the West Indies both planters and colonial governors connived with American shipowners. Governors declared "emergencies," sometimes because of need, but not invariably. Another device was to enter forbidden ports and declare that one's ship needed repairs. Easygoing customs officers could be induced to give permits to unload and sell the cargoes in order to pay for the "expense" of the "repairs." Dutch and French islands became way stations for indirect trade. American cargoes were landed there and then small boats carried the produce to the British islands. The British government passed laws declaring the indirect trade illegal, but loopholes for "emergencies" were left.[8]

A few British officials fought valiantly but hopelessly to enforce the letter of the law. If Horatio Nelson had not fought Trafalgar and loved Lady Hamilton, his place in history might have been recorded in nothing but a footnote about an obscure British naval officer whose best efforts in the West Indies were shattered by the ingenuity of the local planters and the interloping American ship captains. When he seized American vessels with British registers, local law officers refused help. When he persisted, American vessels turned up with Spanish registers, for by ancient ruling Spanish vessels could come from Spanish West India ports. No sooner did Nelson leave a port than American vessels dashed in and unloaded. The ultimate indignity came in 1785 when he seized four American vessels flying British flags at the island of Nevis. The "injured" ship captains and local merchants got the island officials to issue warrants for his arrest and claimed £4,000 damages. Feeling was such that Nelson was forced to stay on board his ship for two months to avoid conviction in the local courts.[9] In despair he reported home that the opposition of civil authorities in the West Indies had practically ended all efforts to stop the illegal trade.[10]

British restrictions were a failure. They irritated Americans and brought about effective discrimination against British ship-

[8] Pickering: *Statutes at Large*, XXXVI, 15–6, 331–2; Channing: *History*, III, 416–22.

[9] Ragatz: *Fall of the Planter Class*, 183–4.

[10] Sir Nicholas Nicolas, ed.: *The Dispatches and Letters of Vice-Admiral Lord Viscount Nelson* (7 vols., London, 1845–6), I, 171–86. The illicit trade was reported as a matter of course in American newspapers. See the *Pennsylvania Gazette*, 12 May 1784, 23 Aug., 1786; *Massachusetts Centinel*, 8 Dec. 1784; *South Carolina Gazette*, 25–7 May 1784.

ping by the American states. They made American supplies more expensive for West India customers. The hope that the remaining North American colonies would take the place of the United States was vain. Exports from Nova Scotia to the West Indies did increase, but most of the goods came from New England.[11] The West Indies had already begun their long decline, and stubborn adherence to the Navigation Acts helped shove them farther down the economic ladder.

Far more important to the merchants of the new nation than restrictions on the West India trade was the fact that the commerce of the United States was no longer limited to the British Empire. New opportunities everywhere in the world were open to Americans, who took advantage of them with such zest that what had been lost by separation from the Empire was more than replaced. The greatest gains were made in three directions: to France, Holland, and the Orient. Traffic in the goods of these lands was not unknown before the war, but the freedom to traffic was new. The French had high hopes of capturing a large share of English trade with America and the hopes were expressed with enthusiasm and many public acts.[12] The Dutch had equally high hopes but they said less than the French and worked harder at the actual business of shipping goods back and forth across the Atlantic. The Americans opened up the Orient for themselves.

French policy, as we have seen, was one of breaking down her exclusive empire in order to attract the trade of the United States. It was a policy begun even before the war, for the French, more rationally than the British, had realized that if Americans wanted to trade with the French islands, they would do so, no matter what the rules. The Americans must be given favors in the West Indies, wrote a French statesman in 1784, or "they would engage in an illicit commerce which our colonists themselves would invite." [13] French merchants protested to small purpose at the free ports of France and to the privileges in the West Indies granted to the Americans who, be it said, took them as a matter of course rather than of privilege.

However, it was the direct trade between France and the United

[11] Edwards: *History of the West Indies*, II, 423–4; Stephen Higginson to John Adams, July 1786, AHA *Annual Report* (1896), I, 737; Philadelphia *Freeman's Journal*, 4 Aug. 1784.

[12] See ch. vii.

[13] 15 Feb. 1784, Bancroft: *Constitution*, I, 341.

States that the French government and many Americans hoped to develop in order to reduce the British share of American commerce. Frenchmen who knew America well were appointed consuls. Francois Barbé-Marbois, who had fought in the Revolution, was one of these. Hector St. Jean de Crevecoeur was another. These men reported at length on American needs and appetites, but they also set forth the difficulties that stood in the way.

The fact was that many Americans preferred English manufactures and continued to buy them despite artisans and politicians who deplored continued economic dependence on Britain. English merchants provided credit and they knew the American market from long experience. French merchants often depended on ship captains to sell goods, and failed to establish American connections. However, they did supply a certain market. French brandies, silks, linens, gloves, and other luxury goods were cherished in America and bought in quantity, but this in no way interfered with the flow of goods between the United States and England. Thus French policy failed, but the United States gained greatly as a result of the exchange, for France bought far more from America than she sold to her.[14]

American profit in the trade with France began in the West Indies. It was estimated that in 1786 the French West Indies imported goods worth nearly 21,000,000 livres from foreign countries and exported to them over 14,000,000 livres. Of the imports, over 13,000,000 were from the United States, which took in turn 7,263,000 from the islands: a handsome balance in favor of the United States. American tonnage in the French West Indies trade at the same time was estimated at over 100,000.[15] The reasons for American dominance were plain. Americans could provide supplies far cheaper than any others, including the French. Boards

[14] See: "Commerce Between France and the United States, 1783–1784," AHR, XXXI, 732–7; and Buron: "Statistics on Franco-American Trade, 1778–1806," JEBH, IV, 580. On the appointment of consuls see Edward Bancroft to William Frazer, 28 May 1784, Bancroft: *Constitution*, I, 370. See also Washington's succinct analysis of the reasons for French failure and English victory in his letter to the Count de Moustier whose feelings had been hurt on his arrival in America. Washington assured the Count of American affection for the French but he pointed to easy British credits, which he deplored; to their possession of "magazines" in one place with all articles required; and to their knowledge of the precise goods wanted by Americans. 26 March 1788, *Writings*, XXIX, 446–9.

[15] Pitkin: *Statistical View*, 217–8.

from France cost four to five times as much as those from the United States. The same was true for hoops, planks, and other supplies.[16]

The direct trade with France itself shows an even greater balance in favor of the United States than that with her West Indies. During the nine years from 1775 through 1783 the French had naturally supplied far more to the United States than they got from her, although American exports picked up sharply beginning in 1781. The years of peace reversed the trend and placed France deeply in debt to the United States. It was estimated that the net balance in favor of the United States in 1792, at the end of eighteen years of trade, was 63,496,000 livres. Beginning in 1783 the United States never shipped less than 9,000,000 livres worth of goods to France, and never took as much as 2,000,000 livres per year from her.[17] This balance of well over a million dollars a year in the direct trade with France alone does much to explain the striking revival of American commerce after nine years of warfare.

This trade was not without difficulty, for monopoly raised its ubiquitous head in the person of Robert Morris and his tobacco contract with the powerful and corrupt French Farmers General. France was the greatest European market for American tobacco which came to her through England before the war. French policy makers pinned high hopes on the creation of a direct trade in American tobacco, but the Farmers General who controlled its importation insisted that the price of tobacco, a third higher than before the war, must be forced down. They bought only one shipload in 1782, whereupon the Americans sent tobacco to the Dutch who were anxious to act as European distributors. In 1783 only 3,000 hogsheads went to France. The Farmers General then made a contract with a Scotch firm in Virginia for 15,000 hogsheads at a price so low that no tobacco could be bought. After these preliminary skirmishes the Farmers General entered into an agreement with Robert Morris which had repercussions in both France and America. It was mutually profitable to the contracting parties but it hindered the growth of a healthy trade and produced political discontent in the United States. As minister to France, a major task of Thomas Jefferson was his effort to destroy the

16 Buron: "Statistics on Franco-American Trade, 1778–1806," JEBH, IV, 574.
17 Ibid., IV, 580.

monopoly contract which cut the price of tobacco produced by his fellow planters.

The contract called for the delivery of 20,000 hogsheads a year for 1785, 1786, and 1787, to be shipped in American vessels to certain French ports. These ports were *other* than the free ports for American trade established in 1784, and thus a blow was struck at free trade between France and America. The Farmers General agreed to pay thirty-six livres per hundred for the tobacco and they agreed to buy tobacco from no other Americans, either directly or indirectly. In addition, they advanced 1,000,000 livres to Morris to be used in manipulating the market in America. Hence, any American who wanted to sell tobacco in France must first sell to Robert Morris, and at his price. And those prices were catastrophically low. The French consul in New York reported that the price agreed on was equal to only twenty-four shillings of Virginia money at a time when tobacco in Virginia was selling at forty shillings a hundred. Morris thus was able to force the price down from forty to a little over twenty-two shillings a hundred. He had an enormous advantage with the cash advanced him by the Farmers General, but he also manipulated the discount rates of the Bank of North America to force down prices while he was buying up tobacco, a practice he started in 1784.[18]

Angry protests arose from Maryland and Virginia. Jefferson in France worked with Lafayette and other Frenchmen, including merchants interested in the American trade, to have the monopoly cancelled. The Farmers General were too powerful to defeat directly, but they were forced to make concessions. Much American tobacco had been brought to the French free ports in the hope that it could be marketed and the Farmers General agreed to take it, although secretly they told their agents to ignore the orders. The best that Jefferson and his group could do was to get an agreement that the monopoly would not be renewed after 1787. He was able also to get a consolidation of all the other privileges that had been granted piecemeal to Americans, first in the form of a letter, and then later in the form of an *Arrêt du Conseil.* However, no real headway could be made against the Farmers General. Only the overwhelming power of the French Revolution was able to destroy their corrupting strangle hold on French

[18] Morris to Tench Tilghman, 10 April 1784, Robert Morris Papers, NYPL.

economy. And as for Robert Morris, his own greed for land speculation lost for him whatever profits he made from the deal.[19]

Despite the obstacles, American tobacco was the largest single export to France during the 1780's. It amounted to seventy per cent during 1787, the peak year. American grain and flour were another twenty-five per cent, although when the French Revolution began they jumped to more than half of American exports. Jefferson worked hard to increase French consumption of American rice. Such products were largely from the middle and southern states but Jefferson worked also to find a better market for New England's whale oil and in a measure succeeded, for the French took almost as much whale oil in terms of value as they did rice. Such various products accounted for the bulk of American exports. The remainder was a miscellaneous lot of plank, indigo, naval stores, and the like.

The biggest single import from France was brandy, which accounted for thirty per cent of the value. Wine and vinegar ranked second, with twelve per cent. Linen, cloth, hemp, and silk were smaller but important items. The balance consisted of luxury items like hats, perfumes, gloves, glassware, and parasols.[20] But even for luxuries, Americans often turned to England. Jefferson himself apologized to Lafayette for buying harness there. English harness was "plated" and the French made none. "It is not from a love of the English but a love of myself that I sometimes find myself obliged to buy their manufactures." [21]

Another large part of the trade that had been Britain's went to the Dutch who were supplied with money, ships, and a vast knowledge of trade, both direct and devious. During his early contacts with them John Adams declared they were a nation of idolators. They lent money and hired transports to the English, sold goods to Americans, and naval stores to France and Spain. In short, they get "money out of all nations, but go to war with none. . . . Such a nation of idolators at the shrine of Mammon

19 The above account is based in part on Frederick L. Nussbaum: "American Tobacco and French Politics, 1783–1789," PSQ, XL (1925), 497–516. See also the *New Haven Gazette*, 17 Aug. 1786, for a lengthy account of the contract. Gray: *Agriculture*, II, 604, doubts that Morris made much from the contract.

20 Buron: "Statistics on Franco-American Trade, 1778–1806," JEBH, IV, 576–8.

21 Paris, 3 Nov. 1786, Gilbert Chinard, ed.: *The Letters of Lafayette and Jefferson* (Baltimore, 1929), 108.

never existed, I believe, before. The English are as great idolators but they have more gods than one." [22] Eventually the Dutch were forced into the war and they came out of it with an interest in American trade, whetted by the fact that their West India Islands had been profitable way stations in wartime trade.

Americans were interested in trade with the Dutch too. The firm of John de Neufville and Sons of Amsterdam had American contacts. Before the war was over, letters ordering goods came to them from merchants in Boston, Providence, Newburyport, and Philadelphia. In the fall of 1782 de Neufville refused to ship goods except in armed vessels, but the news of the preliminary articles of peace changed reluctance to calm assurance. The house wrote to a concern in Petersburg, Virginia. They had a particular interest, they said, because of "our great consumption of tobacco and our exports to Germany, the best market for that article." They pointed out that much of the tobacco shipped to other European ports was reshipped to Amsterdam and they pointed to the profits of a direct trade between Virginia and Amsterdam. To Christopher and Charles Marshall of Philadelphia they wrote that England used to carry many articles from Holland and Germany to America. These could now be shipped directly and more cheaply from Amsterdam, which would, in addition, make possible the highest prices for American produce. De Neufville looked forward to an increase of trade with "our sister states." [23]

In the first flush days after the war English mercantile houses overextended credit and in 1785 and 1786 many of them went bankrupt. English exports fell off sharply but the Dutch exports to and imports from the United States increased steadily. The Dutch had vast wealth but they used it cautiously. Dutch bankers started loaning money to the United States government in 1782. In 1786 they showed enough confidence in the United States to offer to buy its debt to the French government. By 1788 the Dutch were speculating in American debt certificates and the "credit of the American government was better in Holland than that of any other government." [24]

[22] To James Warren, 9 Dec. 1780, *Warren-Adams Letters*, II, 154.

[23] John de Neufville & Sons, Letter Book, 1780–1785, LC. See particularly the letters to the Robert Donald Company, Petersburg, Va., 15 Feb. 1783, and to the Marshalls, 4 March 1783.

[24] Albert L. Kohlmeier: "The Commerce Between the United States and the Netherlands, 1783–1789," Indiana University *Studies in American History*, XII,

Dutch mercantile houses established branches or had representatives in America, particularly in New York, Pennsylvania, and Maryland, where they did their largest business. State tonnage duties favored the Dutch as opposed to the British, although such duties were higher on Dutch ships than on American. Duties were not a handicap, however, for Dutch skill at smuggling could not be outmatched even by New Englanders. Even more simple was the device of branch houses in American cities. A ship leaving Holland might be Dutch but when it arrived in Philadelphia it belonged to the Philadelphia branch. The process was reversed on the return voyage. In the case of the house of Willinks, bankers of Amsterdam, John Adams decided that they should have the privileges of American citizens since they had loaned the American government money.[25] It worked both ways, however. Peter John Van Berckel, Dutch envoy to the United States, found soon after his arrival that traders brought not only rum and molasses from the Dutch West Indies, but forbidden products as well. Whole shiploads of coffee, sugar, indigo, and cotton were brought to Philadelphia, New York, and Baltimore in American ships and with such boldness that the coffee and cotton bales still bore the marks of the Dutch plantations from whence they were taken.[26]

The extent of the trade with the middle states was indicated by the newspaper advertising. In Philadelphia and Maryland newspapers, half or more of the advertisements offered Dutch, German, and even Russian goods for sale. Such items as Russia duck, Haarlem tape, Brabant sheeting, Flanders bedticking, Silesian linen, German steel, Delft ware, and Rhenish wine were to be found in the cities of the middle states, while New England continued to list goods that were largely English in origin.[27]

American exports to Holland grew steadily and increased at a far greater rate than the exports to England. In 1785 sixty-five ships entered Rotterdam and Amsterdam with American cargoes worth nearly a million dollars. One third of the value was in tobacco; another third rice, and the remaining third naval stores,

nos. 66–8 (Bloomington, 1926), 10; Thomas Jefferson to John Jay, 26 Sept., 12 Nov. 1786, *The Diplomatic Correspondence of the United States 1783–1789* (7 vols., Washington, 1833–4), III, 140, 175.

[25] Kohlmeier, XII, 14–6.

[26] To the States General, 6 April 1784, Bancroft: *Constitution*, I, 352.

[27] Kohlmeier, XII, 17–23 with detailed references to contemporary newspapers.

hides, wood, and the like. By 1788 exports to Holland were estimated to be worth more than $4,000,000.[28]

No matter how important the new trade with France and Holland might be, it could not equal the interest, the glamor, and the hope of profit that the beginnings of trade with the Orient excited in Americans. Americans soon were everywhere in the Orient, but Canton, the world's great tea market, was the center toward which most men turned. The Revolution was hardly over before Robert Morris, whose hand was everywhere and in everything, had plans under way to send a ship to China. Careful preparations were made for the voyage. Official recognition from the United States was needed. Gouverneur Morris, co-worker with Robert Morris, wrote Charles Thomson, secretary of Congress, asking for letters worded in "ample terms." Captain Greene was a naval officer of the United States, and this deserved "peculiar" notice. The "design" itself deserved some countenance since it would help open up direct trade and thus prevent European powers from draining the United States of specie in exchange for the superfluities of the East.[29] Congress responded with a letter of introduction addressed to the "most serene, serene, most puissant, puissant, high, illustrious, noble, honorable, venerable, wise, and prudent Emperors, Kings, Republics, Princes, Dukes, Earls, Barons, Lords, Burgomasters, Councillors, as also judges, officers, justiciaries and regents" of all places where Captain John Greene might visit. The letter certified him as a citizen of the United States and his vessel as the property of American citizens.[30]

While these preparations were under way, a doughty captain from Hingham, Massachusetts, set forth in a fifty-five-ton sloop loaded with ginseng. He got only as far as the Cape of Good Hope where he met British East India traders. They sensed the danger of American competition and bought out the captain's cargo for twice its weight in Hyson tea and sent him happily back to New England.[31]

[28] Ibid., XII, 25–6. In 1785 America sent England goods valued at $4,333,000. By 1788 the value of goods sent to England had risen to over $5,000,000, a substantial increase but insignificant compared with the increase of exports to Holland. Kohlmeier has elaborate tables and calculations to demonstrate that Dutch-American commerce was far greater than ordinarily supposed. pp. 44–7.

[29] Philadelphia, 30 Dec. 1783, Charles Thomson Papers, LC.

[30] 30 Jan. 1784, *Journals*, XXVI, 58–9.

[31] Morison: *Maritime History of Massachusetts*, 44.

The *Empress of China* was not so waylaid. With John Greene as captain and with Major Samuel Shaw, aide to General Henry Knox during the Revolution, as agent for the owners of the vessel, she sailed from New York, 22 February 1784. She was loaded with ginseng which optimistic Chinese believed would restore virility to the aged, and with many another product, to a total value of $120,000. They made the island of Java early in July and Canton on 30 August. There they stayed until the end of December when they set out on their return voyage, arriving in New York, 11 May 1785.[32] The *Massachusetts Centinel* announced the return of the *Empress* and declared that "this passage is one of the greatest nautical prodigies we ever recollect hearing. . . ." [33]

The voyage was a great feat and news of it and the rumored profits excited interest everywhere. In December 1785 the sloop *Experiment* set out for China. The *Pennsylvania Gazette* in reporting the departure urged the greater cultivation of ginseng and proposed that its export to any country except China be forbidden. In this way the export of specie could be stopped and all the profits kept at home.[34] The problem of providing something that could be traded in China led to a report that some New York "gentry" were in "speculation deep indeed" in old continental money in the hope of sending it there.[35]

The *Empress of China* reloaded and started back. The *Hope* soon followed her. On her, rather than on the *Empress*, was Samuel Shaw, who had fought bitterly with Captain Greene on the first voyage.[36] Shaw now had an appointment from Congress as consul to China. Thomas Randall, who had been his assistant on the first voyage, went with him as vice-consul.[37] In China Shaw and Randall acted both as consuls and as private merchants. Shaw sent back long reports to Congress on the nature of the China trade and on its advantages for Americans. Congress itself barely toyed

[32] Excerpts from Shaw's Journal are printed in the *Pennsylvania Gazette*, 18 May 1785. Shaw's account of the voyage is also contained in a letter to John Jay, 19 May 1785, *Diplomatic Correspondence 1783–1789*, VII, 429–35.

[33] 18 May 1785.

[34] 4 Jan. 1786.

[35] *Massachusetts Centinel*, 11 Feb. 1786.

[36] See Knox Papers, MHS, 1785 and 1786.

[37] *Massachusetts Centinel*, 8 Feb. 1786; John Jay recommended the appointment of consuls in a letter to Congress, 20 Jan. 1786, and informed Shaw of his appointment on 30 Jan. 1786. *Diplomatic Correspondence 1783–1789*, VII, 439–40.

with a suggestion that trade with the Orient be a public matter. A Mr. Wingrove arrived from England late in 1785 with the proposal that an American establishment be set up, but Congress decided that the trade would be more prosperous "if left unfettered in the hands of private adventurers, than if regulated by any system of a national complexion." [38]

While New Yorkers and Philadelphians were planning their ventures, New Englanders were equally busy. In 1784 Christopher Champlin of Rhode Island arranged with his nephew, William Green of London, to send out the latter's ship, the *Hydra*, to India and China, there to sell the cargo and to bring back Indian goods to America. Champlin agreed to call the ship his own in case of emergency, got a pass from Congress, and eventually Rhode Island citizenship for his nephew.[39] In the same year Connecticut merchants asked the state legislature to help them in a China venture but got no help.[40]

Men of Salem, Massachusetts had their eyes on India and China the year the war was over. In 1784 Elias Hasket Derby of Salem sent his ship *Grand Turk* to the Cape of Good Hope. She returned to Salem early in August 1785. In December she set forth for the Isle of France. Her cargo was sold there and another cargo was carried on to China, the first New England ship to get there. When she got back to Salem, Derby was reported to have made a fabulous profit.[41] Profits were in many cases as fabulous as the rumors. Muslins and calicoes from Calcutta "customarily" netted one hundred per cent. Benjamin Silsbee sold glass tumblers costing less than a thousand dollars for $12,000 in the Isle of France.[42]

The chief problem of the trade was providing something valued by the Chinese. Ginseng was worth a fortune but even it, or perhaps the illusions of aged Chinese, had limits. The men of Boston and Salem were finally convinced by John Ledyard that he had the answer. This New England romantic had been with Cook on his third voyage and his account of it was published at Hartford in 1783. The Chinese had paid unbelievable prices for the furs that Cook's men had picked up on the coast of the Pacific Northwest. The answer was primer-simple. Send out ships with goods to

[38] Rufus King to John Adams, 3 Feb. 1786, King: *Life*, I, 155.
[39] *Commerce of Rhode Island*, II, 201–4, 206–7, 216–8.
[40] Weeden: *Economic and Social History of New England*, II, 820–1.
[41] James D. Phillips: *Salem and the Indies* (Boston, 1947), ch. v.
[42] Weeden: *Economic and Social History of New England*, II, 825–6.

trade to the Indians for sea otter skins; take the skins to China and grow rich. Six Boston business men put up the money. Two vessels, the *Columbia* and the *Lady Washington*, were fitted out under Captain John Kendrick and Captain Robert Gray. They left Boston in September 1787, and eleven months later met at Nootka Sound on Vancouver Island. There they spent the winter of 1788–9 making scrap iron into "chisels," which for the moment were prime currency in trading for otter skins. In July 1789, Gray took command of the *Columbia* and set out for China. There, sea otter skins were traded for tea, and so on around the world sailed the *Columbia* to Boston—the first American vessel to girdle the globe.[43]

Other captains soon followed in the wake of the *Columbia* with cargoes to the Indians of the Pacific Northwest, and with furs from there to China. The profits were great as long as the otter were plentiful and the Indians could be kept ignorant and their fickle tastes easily satisfied.[44]

Upon this trade in old iron, blankets, trinkets, furs, fine silks, fragile china, tea, and many a necessity and exotic, some fortunes were founded and others were enlarged. It was a difficult trade, for the Chinese were difficult, and their guile was as great as that of the notoriously guileful sea captains of New England. European traders did not like the brash Americans and they found them serious competitors. Furthermore, the Americans imported far more than they could use, but they did not store goods to molder away. They found their way by devious means to Europe and to England itself. All the efforts of British consuls in America could not check the flow of traffic, which by all the laws of trade and navigation was illegal. Phineas Bond, British vice-consul in Philadelphia, reported home that tea was to be shipped to the West Indies covered with Indian corn and he predicted that the traffic would no doubt "through some other

[43] Foster R. Dulles: *The Old China Trade* (Boston, 1930), ch. iv, "The Northwest Coast," is a popular account. Tyler Dennet: *Americans in Eastern Asia* (New York, 1922), chs. i–iii has valuable material.

[44] Pitkin: *Statistical View*, 249–50; Dulles: *Old China Trade*, 210. The total figures of trade with the Orient are impossible to arrive at but the estimates of tea imports alone are an index to this new trade which suffused the commercial skies with golden light. In 1784–5 nearly 900,000 pounds of tea were brought in. There was a sharp drop in 1785–6, than a jump to 1,181,860 pounds in 1786–7, a drop again in 1787–8, with a sharp rise to 1,188,800 in 1788–9.

medium of deception be extended to Britain and Ireland. . . ." Moreover, he declared that European agents and factors in the United States were helping Americans in this trade by supplying them with goods on credit, hoping to get their money back after the goods had gotten to Europe, by whatever devious means.[45] Stephen Higginson remarked in 1789 that imports from the Isle of France had been re-exported to Europe and the West Indies "with advantage" but he made no comment as to how such products were packaged.[46] Meanwhile Bond urged that the attention of revenue officers ought "not to be confined to the mere exterior of casks and packages, but to a strict examination of their contents." [47]

With the rest of the world, the Americans carried on a lesser trade, some of it legal and some of it not. Sweden had been the first of the Baltic countries to offer a treaty.[48] Americans found their way into the Baltic soon after the war was over and ex-army officers like Christian Febiger stayed in America to act as agents for Scandinavian mercantile houses.[49] American vessels turned up on the west coast of Africa in sight of British forts but out of range of gunfire, and there carried on the slave trade.[50] The town officials of a starving village in the Azores sent an address to the inhabitants of America asking for Indian corn, flour, and other provisions.[51] Portugal was a market for American fish and flour, but this trade and that to the Mediterranean was subject to attack by the Barbary corsairs who were bloodthirsty but always willing to make deals and concessions for cash in hand.

The British government, despite its pride and its powerful navy, paid tribute to these pirates and in turn issued passes to British ships. This made it possible for them to sail in and out of the Mediterranean with only minor difficulties. The Americans had

[45] To Lord Carmarthen, 2 July, 20 Nov. 1787, AHA *Annual Report* (1896), I, 541, 554.

[46] To John Adams, 17 Jan. 1789, ibid., I, 762.

[47] To Lord Carmarthen, 2 Dec. 1788, ibid., I, 590.

[48] John Adams to James Warren, Paris, 15 Dec. 1782, *Warren-Adams Letters*, II, 187. One trading company of Hamburg offered its services and its goods in an address to the governor, council, and assembly of New Jersey in a letter dated 20 Dec. 1782, *Pennsylvania Gazette*, 26 Nov. 1783.

[49] On the trade with northern Europe see *Commerce of Rhode Island*, II, 249–50, 257–60; Phillips: *Salem and the Indies*, ch. iv.

[50] *Pennsylvania Gazette*, 14 July 1784.

[51] Ibid., 26 Oct. 1785.

had such privileges as colonials and they had developed a fine market for fish, wheat, flour, and even West India produce in ports like Barcelona and Leghorn. In return they got salt and other produce. It was a trade, said Stephen Higginson, "as profitable to us as any part of our European trade." [52] The market remained after the war and Americans sought to supply it, only to find themselves subject to capture and imprisonment.

American statesmen differed as to what should be done. John Adams, with an eye on every possible market for New England fish, suggested the payment of tribute as the British were doing: borrow two or three hundred thousand guineas at six per cent and pay an interest bill of perhaps 18,000 guineas a year. The United States was losing a million sterling a year because of the pirates. Give Congress the power to levy duties to pay the interest. Adams snorted that he had "never heard or read of sluggards who saw so many fantastical lions in the way, as our people appear to have seen since the peace." [53] Thomas Jefferson scoffed at bribery; go to war with the pirates; we ought to build up a navy if we mean to carry on commerce. "We cannot begin in a better cause nor against a weaker foe." [54] John Jay was reported as wanting to arm privateers but Congress was timid, for how could the United States subdue the pirates if so many powerful nations in Europe were not able to do so? [55] Britishers like Lord Sheffield were delighted with the horrid prospects facing American commerce in the Mediterranean.

While men in high places debated policy, merchants actually found out how trade could be carried on. The British government provided passes for its ships. Nothing was simpler than to forge a British pass. "The mischief is become more alarming, as the fraud is become more general," reported Phineas Bond. Most American vessels sailing to the Mediterranean carried forged passes so far as he could learn.[56] Bond was merely documenting the failure of Sir John Temple, British consul general at New York, to stop the practice the previous year. Temple had complained to John Jay of the "atrocious forgery of national documents" and Jay had deplored such practices with high moral fervor. Jay wondered if

[52] To John Adams, 8 Aug. 1785, AHA *Annual Report* (1896), I, 723–4.
[53] To James Warren, London, 4 July 1786, *Warren-Adams Letters*, II, 276.
[54] To General Horatio Gates, Paris, 13 Dec. 1784, Emmet Coll., Misc., NYPL.
[55] Otto to Vergennes, 8 Oct. 1785, Bancroft: *Constitution*, I, 460.
[56] To Lord Carmarthen, 21 Feb. 1787, AHA *Annual Report* (1896), I, 523.

proof could be found; Temple said it could. Thus ran the course of diplomacy.[57] Meanwhile such passes were openly sold at Philadelphia and Temple himself bought one for twelve guineas and sent it back to England, calling the attention of the Lords of the Admiralty to the clever forgery of their signatures.[58] By 1786 American newspapers reported that "English newsmakers" were no longer saying much of the Algerines. There were difficulties, but most of the stories were said to be fabricated by the English and "calculated to operate upon the credulous and uninformed of this country, who think nothing safe, except in British bottoms." [59] Eventually in 1787 a treaty was made with Morocco at a cost of only $30,000 in presents. This success was partly due to the King of Spain who thus hoped to strengthen his demand for a treaty closing the mouth of the Mississippi.[60] But Algiers, Tunis, and Tripoli refused to concede anything to the United States until the presidency of Thomas Jefferson. He sent naval squadrons to war on Tripoli and by 1805 had the Barbary States very willing to leave the United States alone.

Only one conclusion can be drawn regarding the paths of commerce in the eighteenth century. Governments marked them out by law but provided only the weakest means of enforcement. Merchants and shipowners followed the paths if they seemed profitable. If not, and if greater profits could be found elsewhere, the laws be damned. So Americans, as well as English, Dutch, and other traders, evaded laws, perjured testimony, forged documents, and made money. Only here and there did the idea of free trade raise its head. It was partly an ideal, and partly a recognition of the fact that commerce would go wherever its practitioners willed it, governments, laws, and high heaven itself to the contrary. Robert Morris, one of the eighteenth century's most able merchants, sang the credo of the merchant when he declared: "A merchant, as such, can be attached particularly to no country. His mere place of residence is, as merchant, perfectly accidental. . . ." [61]

The world-wide ventures of American merchants take on par-

[57] *Diplomatic Correspondence 1783–1789*, VI, 25–32.

[58] Channing: *History*, III, 420.

[59] *Pennsylvania Gazette*, 22 Feb., 17 May 1786.

[60] Bemis: *American Secretaries of State*, I, 267–8; *Massachusetts Centinel*, 11 Aug. 1787.

[61] To Clark, 30 May 1782, Wharton, V, 449.

ticular meaning when one turns from the general picture of ocean-borne commerce to the particular history of the seaport towns. Such facts as have come down to us are a further demonstration of the proposition that independence was a boon to American commerce despite the inevitable dislocations caused by severance from the British Empire. Those dislocations produced bitter complaints in the newspapers and led to extravagant charges against both state and central governments, but in no case do the records of imports and exports and ship tonnages bear out the cries of havoc.

Most New England seaports, except Newport, had not been hurt by British attacks or occupation after 1776. New England fisheries were well-nigh ruined and normal trade routes were closed, but privateering and indirect trade in war supplies soon provided profitable, if temporary, substitutes. Many wealthy Boston merchants turned Loyalist but their places were taken by merchants from smaller seaport towns and these new men made up in enthusiasm and enterprise what they lacked in prestige and standing as it had been known in 1776. Merchants moved into Boston from Salem, Marblehead, Gloucester, and other towns and soon made themselves felt.

These men demanded laws favoring their ships as opposed to those owned by British subjects. They sought everywhere for trade opportunities. As a group, perhaps, they were less inhibited by old traditions than the pre-war aristocracy. If they were less so, it was an advantage in making the transition to commerce in the new nation.

Wherever statistics have come down to us they show the same trend: rapid increase of shipping after the war. Thus 42,506 tons cleared Boston in 1772,[62] and over 55,000 cleared the same port in 1788.[63] Salem exported an average of 24,000 quintals of fish annually in the ten years before 1775 and from 1788–90 the annual average was 75,000.[64] Only for New Haven is there a continuous

[62] Virginia D. Harrington: *The New York Merchant on the Eve of the American Revolution* (New York, 1935), appendix G.

[63] Account of the Exports and Clearances of the Port of Boston for the Years 1787 and 1788, Mass. Misc., MSS. Div., LC. The document gives no statement as to the tonnage entering the port.

[64] The figures for the pre-war period are from Pitkin: *Statistical View*, 84. Those for 1788–90 are from Records of the Bureau of Customs, District of Salem, Abstracts of Exports, NA. Pitkin's figures are highly untrustworthy.

record for the Revolutionary era. That shows that about 3,100 tons a year cleared the port in the 1760's while over 5,800 tons a year cleared from 1785 to 1789.[65]

New York was an occupied city from the summer of 1776 until the late autumn of 1783. About a third of the city had been burned and the bulk of the shipping had been burned or moved elsewhere. During 1770–2 an average of 26,000 tons cleared the port each year.[66] James Madison declared in 1789 that 55,000 tons of shipping were owned by New York alone and that an additional 30,000 tons of foreign-owned ships used the port during the same year.[67] Thus New York had made a remarkable recovery in a few short years and was well on the way to becoming America's greatest seaport.

Philadelphia was the metropolis of the United States although New York was rapidly moving to the fore. An average of about 45,000 tons of shipping a year cleared the port from 1770–2.[68] In 1789 Madison estimated the tonnage of Pennsylvania to be about 72,000. Of this amount about 44,000 tons were Pennsylvanian and 28,000 tons were foreign ships.[69]

The circumstances of southern trade were in contrast with those of the North. Before the war, Virginia, Maryland, and the two Carolinas exported and imported more than half of the goods going in and out of the thirteen colonies. Furthermore, a much greater proportion of their exports and imports were directly to

---

He says, for example, that Salem exported only 16,000 quintals a year from 1786–90, 59,000 a year less than shown by the customs records. Further materials on Salem trade are given by James D. Phillips: "Salem Ocean Borne Commerce . . . 1783–1789," Essex Institute *Historical Collections*, LXXV (1939), 135–58, 249–74, 358–81; ibid., LXXVI (1940), 68–88.

[65] Records of the Bureau of Customs, District of New Haven, NA. The records show also that most of the ships were owned in New Haven, that the bulk of the trade was with the West Indies, and that most of the ships were built during the 1780's.

[66] Harrington: *New York Merchant*, appendix G.

[67] 5 May 1789, *Annals of the Congress of the United States* (Washington, 1834), I, 258–9. Samuel D. McCoy: "The Port of New York (1783–1789): Lost Island of Sailing Ships," *New York History*, XVII (1936), 379–90, says that the tonnage of New York was over 100,000 by 1789. "It is a tribute to an amazing activity, a feat without parallel. New York's merchants and shipmasters had returned from exile to find their city's wharves stripped bare of ships; and in six short years they had, by superhuman effort, acquired at least a thousand vessels."

[68] Harrington: *New York Merchant*, appendix G.

[69] *Annals of Congress*, I, 258–9. Such figures, of course, do not show all of Philadelphia's commerce, for, as we have seen, the illegal trade was important.

and from Great Britain than were those of the northern colonies. The southern colonies were therefore much less dependent on a complicated series of trade relationships. The problem of balancing trade accounts was not so great as in the North and often did not exist. The southerners welcomed competition among the carriers of their produce. With the exception of Charleston, there were no ports as crucial in southern economy as were Boston and New York in the North. Southern produce did not for the most part compete with British produce, and furthermore, it had a ready if often low-priced market everywhere. All these factors continued to be of importance during the Revolution, and they help to explain the conflicts over commercial policy between northern shipowners and southern planters after 1783 and the rapid recovery of the South from the effects of the war.

Charleston had been the third port of the colonies in terms of tonnage. In the five years, 1768–72, an average of 31,000 tons a year cleared the port. In 1780 it was captured by the British and both it and much of the low country were occupied until the end of 1782. Property was damaged, crops were lost, slaves were stolen, and commerce was virtually destroyed. No other major seaport, except perhaps New York, suffered so much as a result of the war. Despite this, Charleston, like New York, recovered rapidly, as the tonnage leaving the port shows. Between November 1783 and November 1784, 50,961 tons of shipping cleared outwards.[70] Since there was no sharp reduction of price levels after the war, as compared with price levels before it, and since South Carolina tonnage soon doubled, one may conclude that the commerce of South Carolina was well on the way to recovery before the end of the 1780's.

North Carolina, which before the war was so often bracketed commercially with its southern neighbor, made even more remarkable gains as a result of the war itself and of the post-war expansion of her agriculture, merchants, and markets. During the first part of the war, many North Carolina merchants made fantastic profits in the importation of war supplies and consumers' goods, but the last years of the war, when seacoast North Carolina was the scene of war, resulted in ruination of much of that com-

[70] The tonnages for 1768–72 are given in Harrington: *New York Merchant*, appendix G, and for 1783–7 in Madison Papers, VIII, f. 46, LC. The accounts in the Madison Papers give quantities of exports and the number and types of ships.

merce. Yet within a few short years North Carolina commerce rose to heights undreamed of before 1776. By 1788 over 47,000 tons of shipping cleared her ports, a more than one hundred per cent increase over 1769. There were sharp changes in the direction of commerce as well. Before the war a third had gone to Britain, a third to the West Indies, and a third into the coastwise trade. By 1788 only a tenth went to Britain, nearly a half went to the West Indies, and about two fifths to the other American states. The growth of the West India trade is a further demonstration of the fact that British restraints had little practical effect. The clearances for the British islands were fifty per cent greater, while the clearances to French, Dutch, and Danish islands were two thousand per cent greater than before the war.

Thus North Carolina, like South Carolina, recovered rapidly from the effects of the war and pushed out into new lines of endeavor untrammeled by British regulations. It is true that the channels of trade remained more or less the same, but the emphases were different. British merchants lost the hold they had had. Their place was taken by local merchants and those of Baltimore and Philadelphia. The merchants of New England, while still important, no longer played the part they had before the war.[71]

The commerce of Virginia and Maryland went in and out through many individual plantations and small ports, as well as through towns like Baltimore and Philadelphia. The statistics that remain are for the trade of these states as a whole. In the year 1769, 52,000 tons of shipping cleared from Virginia and nearly 31,000 tons from Maryland.

The rapid expansion of tobacco production beyond pre-war levels, new levels of grain production, and the development of exports such as lumber, are evidence of the rapid growth of southern economy after the war. That growth expressed itself in the tonnages clearing from Virginia and Maryland ports. During the year October 1789 through September 1790, 93,925 tons of shipping cleared the ports of Virginia in overseas trade. During the same period 72,096 tons cleared from Maryland ports. Thus Maryland and Virginia clearances had doubled since 1769.[72]

[71] Crittenden: *Commerce of North Carolina*, ch. x, "Peace and Prosperity, 1783–1789."

[72] Gray: *Agriculture*, II, 601–6; Augustus Low: Virginia in the Critical Period, 1783–1789 (Ph.D. Thesis, University of Iowa, 1941), 79–83.

Such figures, though open to question, point in only one direction: the rapid recovery of American commerce after the American Revolution. Freedom from the shackles of the British Empire, the help of the navigation acts of the states, and of those of the national government after 1789, and the enterprise of American merchants, all played a part in the burgeoning trade of the new nation.

There is nothing in the knowable facts to support the ancient myth of idle ships, stagnant commerce, and bankrupt merchants in the new nation. As long ago as 1912, Edward Channing demonstrated with adequate evidence that despite the commercial depression, American commerce expanded rapidly after 1783, and that by 1790 the United States had far outstripped the colonies of a few short years before.[73] The evidence of the growth in the amount of commodities exported, and of the tonnage of American ships, shows that not only did Americans regain much of their old commerce, but that they had increased it over the dreams of merchants in 1775. Their ships were larger and more numerous; their cargoes were greater in quantity and variety; the whole world was now a market and source of supply. Of course the bulk of their trade continued to be with England, but that was as both English and Americans wanted it and as economic facts dictated it must be.

[73] *History*, III, ch. xiii.

10

The Roots of Recovery: Growth of Business Enterprise

As AMERICANS reopened old trade routes and found new ones after the Revolution, they also developed new opportunities within the United States. They turned to manufacturing as they had never done before, and they began founding banks that were to be relatively permanent. There had been repeated demands for the development of manufacturing during the colonial period. Colonial legislatures from time to time had aided local manufactures by gifts of land and freedom from taxation. But manufacturing developed slowly, for it was an agricultural society in which labor was high, land was cheap, and ordinarily goods could be brought from England more cheaply than they could be made in the colonies. When successful colonial manufactures did develop, such as beaver hats, finished iron, and woolens, Britain attempted to check them. Some times, as in the case of naval stores, she gave bounties for the development of colonial products needed in England. But in general, the manufactures of the colonies were local in importance and domestic in character: boots, shoes, cloth, nails, and the like, and they were produced in homes and small shops.

The Revolution freed American artisans in many ways. It did away with British restrictions; the war itself acted as a protective tariff; the need for army clothing aided cloth manufactures; the need for powder and guns focused attention of American governments and artisans on that business and helped to expand the development of iron manufactures. The release from old restraints and opportunities born of war turned more and more men to manufacturing. Such a man was Benjamin Gale who declared that he had always been anxious to promote manufactures, and that since the break with Great Britain he was convinced that the only way to win real independence was to develop them. He and his two sons-in-law had erected a furnace for casting hollow ware. They contracted with the United States for sixty tons of shot and shell and were now running the second blast. During the summer of 1780 he erected a pottery factory and hoped to get someone from France who could help him produce "French Delph ware." [1] Barnabas Deane, Jeremiah Wadsworth, and General Nathanael Greene organized a company which dealt in many kinds of business, including the manufacture of rum, salt, and the operation of gristmills.[2]

New industries did not collapse with the end of the war. The flood of imported manufactured goods after the war was slowed up when merchant credit ran short. Thus the commercial panic was probably a boon for local industries.[3] By the time commercial recovery was at hand, the artisan manufacturers in New England and Pennsylvania had gotten protective tariffs which helped them meet the competition of foreign manufactures.[4]

Contemporary sources illustrate the success of the new nation in widening its economic base. In January 1783, John Biddis of Philadelphia was offering white lead "allowed by the best judges in this city to be equal in quality to any imported from Europe." In addition, he offered colors ground in oil, paint brushes, and other necessities for painters.[5] By the end of 1785 Stephen Higginson reported that "to increase our manufactures has become the rage of the day." The farmers were busy making nails during the winter. Boots, shoes, wool cards, coarse woolens, and iron were also produced in Massachusetts and already "very considerable quantities of some of these articles" were being exported to the southern states. But as a merchant, he could not but view with alarm too great an attention to manufactures, for to attempt to produce all a country might need within itself "would be in effect

[1] Benjamin Gale to B. F. Killingsworth, 5 Nov. 1780, Bache Coll., APS.

[2] Weeden: *Economic and Social History of New England*, II, 796; Greene Papers, CL.

[3] Victor S. Clark: *History of Manufactures in the United States* (3 vols., New York, 1929), I, 229.

[4] See *post*, ch. xiv.

[5] *Pennsylvania Gazette*, 15 Jan. 1783.

to attempt the destruction of all commerce. . . ." [6] The fears he thus expressed were a reality, not for his, but for a future generation of New England merchants. Such fears could not dampen the new interest in national self-sufficiency. The *Massachusetts Centinel* reported that a factory in New Hampshire was making buttons, thread, and cloth. It declared that the benefits for the United States in the encouragement of local manufactures was obvious and that no one with "one spark of patriotism" should withhold it.[7] In New Haven, Connecticut, a local paper declared "with pleasure and a degree of blameless pride" that over 160,000 silkworms had been raised in New Haven during the season. This was in response to reports in Pennsylvania papers of a family which owned 2,000 silkworms.[8] Such reports are more proof of American persistence than anything else, for Americans had been trying to raise silkworms since early in the seventeenth century. Far more important was the manufacture of nails and this, too, the papers reported with pride. The *Pennsylvania Gazette* and the *New Haven Gazette* within a few days of one another printed an identical report from Providence, Rhode Island. The report declared that "the establishing of manufactories in our young country is a matter of the greatest consequence. . . ." In the east parish of the town of Bridgewater, there was made one morning before nine o'clock, when the workmen usually went to breakfast, "61,500 good tenpenny nails—may success attend industry!" [9] Later in the same year it was stated that the manufacture of nails in Pennsylvania alone would save the country £100,000 sterling annually.[10] The *Pennsylvania Gazette* reported that wool was in greater demand than "was ever known" and that all kinds of woolen and linen manufacturing were going on with great spirit.[11]

The actual production of nails, woolen goods, spinning wheel irons, and the like was more than matched by all sorts of schemes that for the moment did not pan out. During 1784 Samuel Wetherill set forth in Pennsylvania newspapers a prospectus for the creation of a cotton manufacturing establishment. Wetherill had interviewed one Roger Fursdon, who had previously ad-

[6] To John Adams, 30 Dec. 1785, AHA *Annual Report* (1896), I, 730–1.
[7] 4 Jan. 1786.
[8] *New Haven Gazette*, 13 July 1786.
[9] *Pennsylvania Gazette*, 22 Feb. 1786; *New Haven Gazette*, 16 Feb. 1786.
[10] Ibid., 19 Oct. 1786.
[11] 23 May 1787.

vertised for capital. Fursdon can do what he claims, said Wetherill. All that is needed is yarn. Then, if investors can be found, a building fifty by one hundred feet and five stories high will be built on a constant stream of water. It will house 16,000 spindles. The whole can be built for about £9,000 if they begin with one third of the spindles. To this should be added £11,000 to carry on the business. To run such a plant would take ten men—overseers, mechanics, and clerks, whose wages would average twelve shillings a day apiece. For labor they would need 83 women whose wages would average 3s. 6d. per day, and 134 children from eight to ten years of age whose wages would average 2s. 6d. per day. With such a labor force they could spin a thousand pounds of yarn a day. The "neat profit" could be estimated at £162 14s. 6d. per day or £48,000 a year.[12]

James Wilson, who had come from Scotland and who was to become a justice of the United States Supreme Court, and who died as such while fleeing from sheriffs who wanted to jail him for debts, was equally optimistic during the 1780's. To prospective Dutch investors he described the rolling and slitting mills which he said he and his brother-in-law, Mark Burd, were building on the Delaware near Philadelphia. The names of Robert Morris and Peter John Van Berckel, minister from the States-General of the United Netherlands, were given as references. Wilson claimed that he and his brother-in-law had large fortunes [in land] but that money could not be borrowed in America at the moment. As security he asserted that he had real estate worth 750,000 florins on which he wished to borrow but 500,000 florins.[13]

The interest, the schemes, the hope of the future, and aid by state governments after the Revolution, combined to bring about a rapid expansion of American manufacturing. Within ten years after the Revolution, Brandywine Creek had about sixty mills along the seven or eight miles of its course through Delaware. Household production of cloth was such that the state of New Jersey had forty-one fulling-mills at a time when there were no manufactories of cloth in the state. A few years after the Revolution a shop in Philadelphia sold fifteen hundred sets of spinning wheel irons in a single year.[14] Manufacturing spread rapidly to the

[12] *Pennsylvania Gazette*, 14 Jan. 1784.

[13] Draft letter, 6 Jan. 1785, James Wilson Papers, PHS.

[14] Jameson: *American Revolution Considered as a Social Movement*, 60–1.

frontier. By 1790 the people of Kentucky were producing a greater variety of things than the people of New York had done in 1765. By 1790 American paper mills, developed to supply the rapid increase of newspapers and magazines, were supplying most of the American market. Glass making was firmly established as an American industry. In fact, so substantial was the general increase that Pennsylvania alone was reported to be taking the place of Great Britain in supplying the need for manufactured goods in the southern states.[15]

Tench Coxe of Philadelphia summarized the growth of American manufactures in a speech to a group of men who met in Philadelphia in August 1787. The group had met for the purpose of forming a society for the encouragement of manufactures and the "useful arts." Coxe declared that despite the disadvantages "it must afford the most comfortable reflection to every patriotic mind, to observe their progress in the United States, and particularly in Pennsylvania." For a long time the forefathers' needs were supplied by the work of European hands. "How great—how happy is the change! The list of articles we now make ourselves, if particularly enumerated, would fatigue the ear, and waste your valuable time. Permit me, however, to mention them under their general heads: meal of all kinds, ships and boats, malt liquors, distilled spirits, potash, gun-powder, cordage, loaf-sugar, pasteboard, cards and paper of every kind, books in various languages, snuff, tobacco, starch, cannon, muskets, anchors, nails, and very many other articles of iron, bricks, tiles, potters ware, millstones, and other stone work, cabinet work, trunks and windsor chairs, carriages and harness of all kinds, corn-fans, ploughs and many other implements of husbandry, saddlery and whips, shoes and boots, leather of various kinds, hosiery, hats and gloves, wearing apparel, coarse linens and woolens, and some cotton goods, linseed and fish oil, wares of gold, silver, tin, pewter, lead, brass and copper, clocks and watches, wool and cotton cards, printing types, glass and stoneware, candles, soap, and several other valuable articles, with which the memory cannot furnish us at once." [16]

[15] Clark: *History of Manufactures*, I, 230. See Weeden: *Economic and Social History of New England*, II, *passim*, for the many developments in New England. Lawrence C. Wroth: *The Colonial Printer* (Portland, Me., 1938), 151–2, says there were 195 paper mills in the United States by 1810.

[16] Tench Coxe: *A View of the United States of America* (Philadelphia, 1794), 45–6.

American manufactures had no more able propagandist than Tench Coxe, but there were many others. Matthew Carey, editor of the *American Museum*, printed article after article, some of which he wrote himself, urging Americans to manufacture. Old mercantilist doctrines were set forth with new fervor. National self-sufficiency was of the highest importance. We could never be truly independent unless we were economically independent.[17] If we purchased foreign manufactures and did not produce at home, money would continue to be drained from the country. Not only would the development of manufactures produce a home market for farm produce and thus help the farmers, it would eventually provide goods for export.[18] It was nonsense to fear that the development of manufactures would draw workers away from the farms. The women, children, and the idle of the cities would work in the factories. Above all, factories were the solution of the old problem of the industrious poor.[19] Furthermore, the development of manufactures was one way of attracting desirable European immigrants. We were already attracting them, said Coxe, for we offer them "substantial freedom, liberal wages, and cheap and excellent living. . . ." America should likewise concern itself with labor-saving machinery. The cost of manual labor is no argument against such machines, for they yield the greatest profit in countries where wages are the highest. "The first judicious European capitalists, who shall take good situations in the United States, and establish manufactories, by labor-saving machines, must rapidly and certainly make fortunes." [20]

To fortify such arguments, manufacturing societies were organized much along the line of the scientific societies and often with the same members. They supported the idea of protective tariffs; they investigated European inventions; they encouraged American inventors; they promised prizes for new ideas. The most important society was the Pennsylvania Society for the Encouragement of Manufactures and Useful Arts which was organized during the summer of 1787. The moving spirit behind it was Tench Coxe. Thomas Mifflin was elected president, with such men as David Rittenhouse and Samuel Clymer as vice-presidents.

[17] William Barton: "Essay on the promotion of American Manufactures," *American Museum*, II, 257–61.

[18] *American Museum*, I, 116–9; Coxe, 53.

[19] *American Museum*, I, 19; Coxe, 55.

[20] Ibid., 98–9, 165–6, 443.

Membership was open to all citizens of the United States willing to pay the fee of ten shillings a year. In addition the society set up a Committee on Manufactures to be chosen by subscribers to a manufacturing fund. The shareholders were to own grounds, buildings, and any other property.

The Committee decided to promote cotton manufacturing. Two machines for carding and spinning cotton were ordered from England. The *American Museum* recorded the arrival of the machines and pointed out that five lads of fifteen and a girl of twelve could tend the machines and card and spin 12,000 pounds of cotton a year.[21] By 1788 a factory was in operation. By the end of that year more than 11,000 yards of cotton and linen had been woven.[22] The next year the Pennsylvania legislature subscribed £1,000 to expand the factory, which ran until it was destroyed by fire in 1790.[23] Meanwhile the society offered prizes for improvements in textile machinery and for the production of hemp, cotton, flax, candles, pot and pearl ashes, and other produce of Pennsylvania.[24]

Similar societies were established in Boston, New York, and Baltimore in 1788, and in other cities in the following years. Ordinarily these societies did not manufacture. They were concerned with the promotion of the idea of American manufactures, the awarding of prizes for good examples of American production, and assistance to artisans with particular skills and ideas.[25] The Rumsean Society of Philadelphia, for instance, was created for the particular purpose of assisting James Rumsey in developing his steamboat.[26]

These societies had in them few, if any, of the artisans and mechanics who were the real "manufacturers" of the 1780's. This was still the age when things were made by hand in small shops and homes by multitudes of artisans who were for the most part self-employed, with only a few apprentices at most. They began informal meetings shortly after the war was over. During July 1783, a group of "mechanics" met at the state house in Philadelphia and petitioned the legislature for protection from foreign

[21] III, 286.

[22] John L. Bishop: *A History of American Manufactures from 1608 to 1860* (3 vols., Philadelphia, 1868), I, 407–8.

[23] Scharf and Westcott: *Philadelphia*, I, 461.

[24] *American Museum*, II, 507–9.

[25] Davis: *Essays*, II, 258.

[26] Bates: *Scientific Societies*, 26.

imports.[27] The next year the manufacturers of Boston petitioned the general court for similar aid.[28] During the spring of 1785 they met again and created an organization to exercise more direct pressure on the legislature and to get in touch with similar groups in other states.[29] Twenty-six trades were represented and they agreed to call themselves The Association of the Tradesmen and Manufacturers of the Town of Boston.

During the same year a similar group met in New York and organized the General Committee of Mechanics. The trades represented give a picture of the character of American "manufactures" during the Confederation. The society contained potters, carpenters, tobacconists, butchers, masons, tallow chandlers, sailmakers, coach makers, stay makers, coopers, blacksmiths, stonecutters, silversmiths, rope makers, tailors, blockmakers, tanners, pewterers, plumbers, comb makers, bookbinders, ship joiners, brewers, skinners, saddlers, bolters, ship carpenters, hairdressers, and bakers. This organization was interested in protecting their products, but went beyond this. They created a formal organization known as the General Society of Mechanics and Tradesmen of the City of New York. Fees were levied, and the fund thus created was to be used for loans, primarily to members of the society, and for relief of members and of the aged and unfortunate. Eventually it merged with the Manufacturers Society of New York in the fight for protection.[30]

The society went into politics when it applied for a charter of incorporation and was turned down by the council of revision after the legislature passed the bill. The mechanics denounced the lawyers and merchants of the city. They declared that "the great, the mighty and powerful ones, are constantly classified together; for what purpose? to prey upon the weak, the poor, the helpless, . . . are there no men worthy of our confidence but merchants and lawyers? The last are of all men in society the most to be guarded against." In the next election they nominated a variety of mechanics for the legislature. They elected only a

27 Scharf and Westcott: *Philadelphia*, I, 427–8.

28 Winsor: *Memorial History of Boston*, IV, 74–5.

29 *Massachusetts Centinel*, 20, 27 April, 25 May 1785.

30 Thomas Earle and Charles T. Congdon, eds.: *Annals of the General Society of Mechanics and Tradesmen of the City of New York from 1785 to 1880* (New York, 1882), 7–14.

shoemaker and a smith from their number, but in addition several men friendly to them were elected. Not until 1792, however, did they get the charter they asked for.[31]

The Philadelphia mechanics were extremely active, as were those in Baltimore, Charleston, and Providence, although their organizations were not so formal as those of Boston and New York.

As we shall see, they and the other supporters of American manufactures were outstandingly successful in getting state legislatures to adopt protective tariff legislation and in time many of them were converted to the support of the Constitution of 1787 by the promise that it would mean even further protection for American artisans.[32]

While both farmers and artisans were achieving the results described by Tench Coxe, other Americans, far fewer in numbers but not less in influence, were engaged in the founding of banks. Throughout the eighteenth century Americans had experimented with banks. They knew of the Bank of England and of land bank schemes in Europe. As colonists, they had had land and silver banks. The land bank idea was an effort to create a workable form of credit for an agrarian society, something that was not finally achieved until the creation of the Federal Farm Land Banks in the twentieth century. Such schemes were fought bitterly by the merchant-creditors of the eighteenth century who usually were able to defeat them. The merchants wanted a bank operated by and useful to merchants, and they first achieved such a bank with the formation of the Bank of North America in 1781. They had been slow to subscribe during the dark days of the war, although some of them were aware of great profits that might be made. One such man was William Duer who subscribed for stock and who offered to explain "the advantages to the proprietors, in order that private interest may unite with public zeal in promoting the plan." [33] Morris, despite his persuasions, was unable to start the bank until Congress got a shipment of specie

[31] Spaulding: *New York in the Critical Period*, 107–8; Earle and Congdon, 14.

[32] See *post*, ch. xiv.

[33] William Duer to Robert Morris, 11 July 1781, Robert Morris Papers, LC. The early organization of the Bank of North America and its relations with the government are discussed in chapter iii.

borrowed in France. Morris, in charge of congressional finances, used some of this cash to buy stock in the bank which then got under way during 1781. The final history of the Bank of North America is still to be written, but certain facts are clear. The bank loaned money to the United States, whose funds had made the bank possible. It loaned to or withheld loans from private individuals.

The bank made money. Within a year Joseph Nourse reported: "the bank daily accumulates wealth." [34] Shortly after the official news of peace the directors announced a dividend of six and one-half per cent for the six months since 1 January 1783 and stated: "the printers on the Continent are requested to give this advertisement a place in their papers." [35] During the next six months the dividends rose to eight per cent, making a total of fourteen and a half per cent on the capital stock for the year 1783.[36]

The growing wealth and power of the bank created fear and jealousy among those not so fortunate as to be among its members or friends. Jonathan Mifflin wrote the secretary of Congress that the "merchantile part of the city is greatly agitated, many of the merchants begin to look at Mr. Morris with jealous eyes, and conceive that a connection of the financier, the president of the bank, and the receiver of continental taxes have a flow of money at their command which may be employed to the great prejudice of all; but the total destruction of those, who having but small capitals, depend on the public opinion of their integrity. . . ." Morris's followers planned to ask the assembly for acts of bankruptcy similar to those of England. If such laws were passed, Mifflin declared, "every house in the city must lay at the mercy of the Financier and his party; who from their uncontrollable power in the present bank may blast the credit of whom they please, by refusing to discount their notes. . . ." This fear produced "an alliance composed of every political complexion who have published their proposals for forming the Bank of Pennsylvania. . . ." The proposed bank had the support of small business men. Mifflin said that it was by "the contention of the greater bodies such little fellows as myself may stand some chance of

[34] To General Horatio Gates, 9 March 1782, Gates Papers, NYHS.
[35] *Pennsylvania Gazette*, 9 July 1783.
[36] Ibid., 7 Jan. 1784.

swimming, but should the current of the former prevail we might be overwhelmed by the torrent." [37]

The newspapers took up the battle. "Liberty" charged that the only objection of the stockholders of the old bank to a new bank was that they wanted to keep a sole monopoly of the banking business. But, "Liberty" asked, how could a farmer or a tradesman borrow money from it when the Bank of North America had raised the rate to sixteen per cent and then as high as ninety-six per cent a year? What was needed was competition among banks to lower rates of interest.[38] The bank met the challenge of a new bank by offering 1,000 new shares of bank stock at $500 a share.[39] In a short time it lowered the price to $400 and increased the number of new shares to 4,000. Thomas Willing, Thomas FitzSimons, James Wilson, and Gouverneur Morris explained to the public that the bank was actuated by a belief that the interests of both Pennsylvania and the United States were concerned and that it might be fatal to the commerce of the United States if a new bank were started. A single enlarged bank could be of far more service to the people, commerce, and the governments.[40]

The admission of new members killed the plan for an opposition bank, although some of the original members of the bank disliked the new company and withdrew from it.[41] The bank had other internal dissensions too. Jeremiah Wadsworth of Connecticut, the largest single stockholder, came to a meeting of the bank and denounced the directors for engaging in alarming practices such as loaning nearly $100,000 to James Wilson. Wilson told in detail of his "schemes and disappointments" and the president of the bank made "some wise speeches and wiser remarks" but Wadsworth said that he had come "to do business and not to altercate" so he did not pay too much attention.[42]

Meanwhile, opposition to the bank was growing and finding expression in a demand for the revocation of its charter by the

[37] To Charles Thomson, 23 Jan. 1784, Charles Thomson Misc., LC. The proposal for the establishment of a Bank of Pennsylvania is in the *Pennsylvania Gazette*, 21 Jan. 1784.

[38] Philadelphia *Freeman's Journal*, 10 March 1784.

[39] *Pennsylvania Gazette*, 14 Jan. 1784.

[40] Ibid., 3 March 1784.

[41] Franklin to George Whatley, 18 May 1787, *Works* (Bigelow ed.), IX, 388.

[42] Jeremiah Wadsworth to Alexander Hamilton, Philadelphia, 9 Jan. 1785, Hamilton Papers, LC.

state of Pennsylvania. The bank defended itself in the newspapers. It was not to blame for the scarcity of money. Rhetorically, it asked whether or not it was "the nest-egg of public and private credit?" Had it not lured merchants with "immense capitals" to settle among us? Had it not forced merchant houses in sister states to establish branches in Philadelphia for the convenience of transacting business? Had it not raised Philadelphia to pre-eminence above all the cities of the United States? Did not the bank feed, clothe, and in part pay the army and thus force the British to withdraw their troops and acknowledge our independence? [43]

The answer of the opposition in effect was a loud "no." Whatever the bank's version of its services to American economy, the fact was that it was also a weapon of the Republican party in Pennsylvania which was striving to undo the democratic Constitution of 1776. Its opponents knew it and in 1785 the Pennsylvania legislature, again in the hands of the Constitutionalists, revoked the charter. At the same time the legislature set up a state loan office to issue paper money on landed security.[44] The bank had appealed to the rights of corporations in fighting repeal, and had denied that even the body which created it could annihilate it "on motives of mere caprice, personal considerations or partial policy." [45] In asking for a new charter, the bank emphasized its economic services both past and present. In defending the bank in 1785, James Wilson denied that it had caused the commercial depression. He argued most ably that it was due to natural causes. But by 1786 the bank's defenders were declaring that commerce had decayed and houses were unbuilt because the bank had lost its charter. "Restore the charter of the bank and industry and trade will be invigorated, and bread will be given to thousands." [46]

Thomas Paine wrote a forthright essay, once more defending the interests of Robert Morris and his group as he had defended their land speculations in his pamphlet, *Public Good*.[47]

[43] *Pennsylvania Gazette*, 4 Aug. 1784.

[44] Brunhouse: *Counter-Revolution*, 173–5; Davis: *Essays*, II, 36–43.

[45] Protest of Thomas Willing to the Speaker of the Pennsylvania Assembly, *Pennsylvania Gazette*, 5 Oct. 1785.

[46] Ibid., 29 March 1786. See also issues of 15, 22 March, 5 April.

[47] Thomas Paine to [David C.] Claypoole, Emmet Coll., no. 2936, NYPL; *Pennsylvania Gazette*, 21 Dec. 1785; "Dissertations on Government; The Affairs of the Bank; and Paper Money," Moncure D. Conway, ed.: *The Writings of Thomas Paine* (4 vols., New York, 1894–6), II, 132–87.

The endless reiteration of its case doubtless had its effect, but of more importance was the recapture of the legislature by the Republicans in the spring of 1787. They at once pushed through a re-charter bill and staved off most of the efforts to democratize the bank's procedures.[48] Meanwhile the bank had continued to operate and to declare dividends, although there was confusion among the stockholders and smaller dividends as a result of the increase in the shares of stock.[49]

Despite its political difficulties in Pennsylvania the bank was looked upon as an example and as an ideal by capitalists in other states. Thomas Willing, its president, was asked for advice by a group of Boston merchants led by William Phillips, Thomas Russell, Stephen Higginson, and others. To them he replied "with the greatest diffidence, but with the utmost cheerfulness. . . ." He assured them that he was not jealous of their scheme but on the contrary was anxious to help. "I am too much a citizen of the world, to wish to confine this very useful science of business to any particular spot or set of men." When the Bank of North America was first opened, the business was a novelty. "It was a pathless wilderness, ground, but little known to this side of the Atlantic." There was no book of interior arrangements or rules observed in Europe. "Accident alone threw in our way, even the form, of an English bank bill. All was to us a mystery. . . ." So the men of Philadelphia adopted the only safe method to avoid confusion. "Educated as merchants we resolved to pursue the road we were best acquainted with—we established our books on a simple mercantile plan. . . ." As a result they had been able to carry on so far without "a material loss." The transactions of the past six months in cash paid and received, amounted to nearly twenty-six and a half million dollars. Willing went on to give details of how the bank kept its books, took precautions to prevent the counterfeiting of its notes, and the like. He concluded by saying: "in short, our science of business has been greater than our most sanguine expectation ever had formed. . . ." There were some details "grafted on experience, which render it more easy and certain" which he felt could better be told to a mutual friend than included in a letter. He hoped that the Boston men would not think him "too minute—the world is apt to sup-

[48] *Pennsylvania Gazette*, 21 March 1787; Brunhouse: *Counter-Revolution*, 195–7.
[49] Franklin to Whatley, 18 May 1787, *Works* (Bigelow ed.), IX, 388.

pose a greater mystery in this sort of business than there really is. Perhaps it is right they should do so, and wonder on—but you may proceed without fear. . . ." [50]

With such advice and with whatever private information they had by word of mouth, the merchants of Boston organized the Bank of Massachusetts.[51] Like the Bank of North America, it too was the subject of attack and was charged with sending specie out of the country. One critic queried "whether if the bank continues there will remain a SINGLE DOLLAR in this Commonwealth." [52] But such criticisms seemed not to affect the tight little oligarchy which ran the bank. No man in it had the flamboyant ambitions and imperial visions of a Robert Morris to embroil it, as an organization, in the politics of its state.

There was talk of banks for Baltimore and Charleston,[53] but the only other bank founded during the Confederation was the Bank of New York. In this business Alexander Hamilton played a large part. He had written much advice on the subject of banking to Morris before the creation of the Bank of North America. Early in 1784 a group led by Chancellor Robert R. Livingston petitioned the legislature for the establishment of a bank, one third of the shares to be paid in cash, and the remainder to be secured by mortgages on New York and New Jersey lands. Hamilton was galvanized into action by the proposal. His brother-in-law, John B. Church, and Jeremiah Wadsworth also had a scheme on foot for the establishment of a bank. Hamilton decided for their sake and "for the sake of the commercial interests of the state, to start an opposition. . . ." He pointed out to the "most intelligent merchants" the absurdity and inconvenience of the land bank. The result was a plan for a money bank. Its merchant backers applied to the legislature for a charter and asked that a land bank be denied exclusive privileges. The opposition was too strong and the Bank of New York could not get a charter. Chancellor Livingston had convinced "the country members" that "the land bank was the true philosopher's stone that was to turn

[50] Thomas Willing to William Phillips et al, Philadelphia, 6 Jan. 1784, N.S.B. Gras: *The Massachusetts First National Bank of Boston, 1784–1934* (Cambridge, Mass., 1937), 209–12.

[51] Ibid., *passim; Massachusetts Centinel*, 27 March 1784.

[52] Ibid., 30 April 1785.

[53] *South Carolina Gazette*, 14–7 Feb. 1784; *Pennsylvania Gazette*, 17 March 1784.

all their rocks and trees into gold. . . ." Nevertheless, the merchants went ahead with their plans and the bank opened for business in June 1784. Like the banks in Boston and Philadelphia it was subject to criticism, but it survived and during the 1790's even became intimate with the government of the state of New York. To this day it is engaged in business.[54]

Most of the men who founded banks, planned factories, and sought out new markets in the far reaches of the world had not visualized the future in 1775. At that time they had clung to membership in the British Empire because they feared that independence would mean social and political revolution in a new nation. Once that independence was gained, they were faced with the potentiality of the thing they had feared in 1775. They worked hard to achieve a government which would protect property, guarantee stability of contracts, restrict credit for debtors, and at the same time provide credit for enterpreneurs. They achieved the kind of government they wanted, but meanwhile they seized upon the economic opportunities which were quite literally global in scope, now that they were free of the British Empire. They were men whose vision and optimism were limited only by the facts of life in a pre-industrial society. Because it was such a society they lacked capital, transportation facilities, and a labor supply in a nation in which most men wanted to be and could be farmers. They were men with a Midas touch for whom the object of desire was too often just beyond their reach. In their striving for what they well knew was the golden future of the new nation, they often overreached themselves and ended in crisis, disaster, and bankruptcy. The capital they gained from the new government after 1789 was so much greater than they had ever used, that they speculated madly and without enough experience. Hence men like Robert Morris, William Duer, and James Wilson went down in one crash after another during the 1790's. If they had had the experience and the means of a later generation of tycoons, they might have enjoyed the riches they so well realized could be gained in the new nation.

[54] Hamilton to John B. Church, 10 March 1784, *Works* (Lodge ed.), IX, 396–8; Davis: *Essays*, II, 44–6.

II

The Farmer in the New Nation

THE EXPANSION of American commerce in the years after the American Revolution was based for the most part on an increase in the output of American farms. The surplus crops of the American farmer had been in the past, and were to be for many years to come, a dominating fact in American economic life. The export of farm produce provided the interest and payments on the foreign capital borrowed to build up much of American industry, and the steamboats, canals, and railroads that eventually made possible explosive expansion across a continent. Yet during the Confederation, as before and after, there was the paradox of an expanding agriculture coupled with the often desperate plight of the farmer as an individual.

During these years the American people increased and spread fanwise northward, westward, and southward so rapidly that by 1790 much that had been wilderness in 1776 was as "civilized" as the seaboard settlements. This growth and movement was largely that of farmers whose life, beyond mere subsistence, depended on the export of their crops to foreign markets. During the war itself, some farmers made money and some did not. Wartime inflation raised the price of what they had to buy, as well as of what they had to sell. Many ran into debt for new lands or remained in debt acquired before the war. Perhaps as important as any other factor in the creation of debt was the movement onto new lands which were seldom if ever free except for those who "squatted" until men with legal title arrived to sell to or evict the original settlers.

Deflation began before the war was over. The mercantile and creditor forces regained control of most of the states and the central government by 1780–1 and reshaped government policies. The paper currency used to finance and win the war was given a final blow. By the end of 1781 it was no longer in use, and most of the country was on what amounted to a "gold standard." Most of the "hard" money was in the hands of the merchants who were creditors of both the governments and of individual citizens. Not only did the creditor groups possess considerable amounts of specie, but they insisted that debts to them be paid in specie; that all obligations must be met at face value, not market value.

Conditions varied from the North to the South at the end of the war, not only in terms of weather and crops, but in terms of state government policies with regard to the collection of private debts and public taxes. On the whole, the southern farmers were far better off than those of the North. By 1784 James Madison was reporting that "this country [Virginia] has indirectly tasted some of the fruits of independence." The price of the last crop of tobacco on the James River was from thirty-six to forty-two shillings a hundred and "has brought more specie into the country than it ever before contained at one time." [1] This was the region that had been raided by Cornwallis and Arnold, who had destroyed tobacco, warehouses, and houses, and had carried off slaves. Virginia lost perhaps 30,000 slaves to the British and they were not returned after the war. Other southern states suffered as well. South Carolina lost perhaps 25,000 slaves, and likewise had property destroyed.[2]

But such losses of property were of small importance compared with the vast gain of the South as farmers from the North and from Europe flooded the back country, planted crops, and sent the surplus to be shipped abroad. The tobacco trade revived rapidly, although the tidewater did little more than hold its own. Tobacco growing was spreading into new areas: Kentucky, Tennessee, and the back country of South Carolina and Georgia. By 1792 American tobacco exports were thirty-six per cent greater than in 1770. Furthermore, the average price for tobacco in the decade after the Revolution was higher than in the decade before.[3]

[1] To Jefferson, 20 Aug. 1784, Gaillard Hunt, ed.: *The Writings of James Madison* (9 vols., New York, 1900–10), II, 66.

[2] Gray: *Agriculture*, II, 595–6. Gray says that some of the loss of slaves was due to pestilence.

[3] Ibid., II, 602, 605–6; Low: Virginia in the Critical Period, 83.

In South Carolina the growing of indigo revived rapidly and by 1792 more indigo, in terms of both quantity and value, was being shipped abroad than before the war. However, this was a temporary advantage, for the British government developed indigo in the British East Indies by the middle 1790's.[4]

The decline of indigo was more than compensated for by the rapid growth of cotton planting. Cotton had been raised for local use all the way from Virginia to Florida before the Revolution, and a cotton gin was in common use long before Eli Whitney made his improvements in 1793. A sudden expansion of the demand for cotton came from England during the decade of the 1770's as a result of changes in machinery. During the 1780's, Americans were much concerned with this growing market. In 1786 a proposal was made in Virginia for a tax on tobacco in order to provide an export bounty on cotton. Farmers everywhere experimented with cotton growing with remarkable results. By 1793 back-country South Carolina and Georgia were raising between two and three million pounds a year for domestic use. Charleston exported less than 10,000 pounds in 1790, but by 1801 her exports had risen to 8,300,000 pounds.[5]

Of equal importance was the rapidly increasing production of grain which went hand in hand with the growth of the small farmer population of the southern back country and with the shift from tobacco to cereals in the tidewater, a shift which had begun years before the Revolution. The war itself had put more emphasis on food production. After the war the islands in the West Indies continued to need American food, and when France and England went to war in 1793, the demand for American supplies was greater than ever. Even during the 1780's peak prices were higher than before the Revolution. Corn was double the price it sold for in 1774 and 1775, and wheat brought six shillings a bushel, two shillings more than before the war. By 1800 wheat was selling for twice what it sold for in 1786, while the price of tobacco remained the same.

The South made astonishing progress as a grain-producing area. The Middle Colonies had been the "bread colonies" before the Revolution, but after it, the southern states became the "bread states" for a time. In 1792 the South produced over sixty per cent

[4] Gray: *Agriculture*, II, 610–1.
[5] Ibid., II, 678–81.

of the corn, sixty-three per cent of the wheat, and thirty-eight per cent of the flour exported from the United States. Flour mills were to be found in the southern back country. Alexandria, Virginia, became one of the world's great grain ports.[6]

The growing European market for American grains was a new factor in American economy. From almost the beginning of settlement the northern colonies had been plagued by the fact that their grain crops and other farm produce competed with those of Great Britain. They faced a problem which the southern colonies with their staple crops of tobacco, rice, and indigo did not have to face until overproduction and debt drove them into crops that meant self-sufficiency, if nothing more, for the plantation system. But the new and growing post-war market made it possible for the northern states to expand their exports. The growth of northern agricultural exports was by no means as rapid as that of the South but it was substantial enough. In 1770 the northern colonies exported 851,240 bushels of wheat and 45,868 tons of bread and flour. The average exports of the northern states for the five years 1790–4 was 1,028,792 bushels of wheat, 71,257 tons of flour, and 80,413 barrels of bread. The export of Indian corn in 1770 was 578,349 bushels; the average for 1790–4 was 1,697,364 bushels.[7]

The broad canvas that can be painted with such statistics obscures detail. Agriculture grew, but what happened to the farmer? Cash came in quick return for tobacco, but not all tobacco farmers shared alike. The old bogy of overproduction shadowed the land. The old plantations in the tidewater still had a burden of pre-war debts. Exhaustion of the soil forced constant movement to new land. Some planters were able to move, sometimes in the wake of, but often in advance of the small farmers. Others were left behind, shifting their crops so that travelers remarked on the endless fields of Indian corn where once there had been only tobacco.[8] But most tidewater planters were doomed to distress, if not bankruptcy. The farmer beginning with new soil and producing for the rising wheat market had every advantage over the man tied to a tobacco economy. But whether raising old crops or new, every farmer was faced with the age-old problem of getting his crops to

[6] Ibid., II, 606–9; Low: Virginia in the Critical Period, 84–5.

[7] Percy W. Bidwell and John I. Falconer: *History of Agriculture in the Northern United States 1620–1860* (Washington, 1925), 137.

[8] Low: Virginia in the Critical Period, 75–6.

market, the need of a medium of exchange, and the means for the payment of private debts and taxes. Here the policies adopted by the southern states, dominated as they were by farmers both big and little, were far more suited to the needs of the times than those of the northern states where the merchants had a larger share of power.[9]

Yet the planters were still tied to merchants as they had always been. British merchants and their agents reappeared to collect pre-war debts. Great Britain, anxious to remain the middleman between American planters and European consumers, gave American ships carrying American tobacco all the privileges they had had as colonists. American merchants too rushed in to get a larger share than they had had before the war. In 1782 Philadelphia merchants moved into the tidewater with ready cash, awaiting the formal declaration of peace.[10] Then came Robert Morris and his tobacco contract with the French Farmers General. The result was a sharp drop in prices as Morris used his power to restrict credit and wielded his monopoly with the greatest single purchaser of American tobacco. More and more it seemed to Virginia planters that they had merely gotten new chains in place of old, but they now came from Philadelphia and Baltimore instead of from London and Glasgow. In 1787 it was reported that tobacco was worth a hundred per cent more in Philadelphia than it was in Virginia.[11]

When one turns from the South to New England, one finds a sharp contrast. During the war, people in towns like Boston complained bitterly of the greed of the farmers and of the money they made in their dealings with city folk. Doubtless many farmers did make money, especially when armies were near by, but this did not affect most of the farmers of New England, many of whom served from time to time in the state militias and in the continental army. Most New England farmers were subsistence farmers who traded their small surpluses to local storekeepers for sugar, salt, tea, rum, and other domestic necessities. Clear evidence of a subsistence rural economy is the fact that the seaport

[9] See chs. xv–xvi.

[10] [Edmund Randolph] to James Madison, 7 Sept. 1782, Madison Papers, LC.

[11] Phineas Bond to Lord Carmarthen, 17 May 1787, AHA *Annual Report* (1896), I, 535. Bond said the difference was due in part to the illicit trade with England.

towns of New England depended on the middle and southern colonies for their bread and flour. Boston established a public granary as early as 1728 and a committee of town fathers bought and sold grain for over a half century. Not until 1784 did the town give over to private business the job of bringing in its grain supply.[12]

The merchants' day books that have come down to us show that even during the Revolution the average farmer did not live on the luxurious scale charged by town dwellers. Only now and then did the hundreds of rural customers of merchants in towns like Worcester buy a few yards of calico or other imported cloth. Most of the time they bought only the staples they could not produce at home.

Not only was rural New England a poor area, there was actual decline of wealth during the revolutionary era. In many a town in rural Massachusetts, wealth in the form of houses, livestock, and cultivated land disappeared as compared with pre-revolutionary days. Tilled land became pasture, pasture became bush.[13] In 1785 a young English traveler visited a tenant farmer in Rhode Island who was supporting a family of eleven people on seventy-six acres of land. The land was good and the tenant industrious: he had to be. The young traveler concluded that "the peasants in general here are miserably poor and in debt." [14]

Despite such poverty among many farmers, there were signs of overall improvement for agriculture. The crops in 1784 were reported the best in years and it was thought that this would "make cash plentier among the farmers, than by their complaints they seem to indicate." [15] By 1785 there was a big increase in exports of butter and cheese.[16]

Yet individual New England farmers, especially those in the back country, were growing more and more desperate. The financial and tax policies of the New England states, and particularly

[12] Bidwell and Falconer: *Agriculture*, 142.

[13] See for example the valuation tables for 1781 and 1786, for the town of Mendon in John G. Metcalf: *Annals of the Town of Mendon from 1659 to 1880* (Providence, 1880), 405, 430.

[14] Hadfield: *An Englishman in America*, 219.

[15] *Massachusetts Centinel*, 8 Dec. 1784.

[16] Stephen Higginson to John Adams, 30 Dec. 1785, AHA *Annual Report* (1896), I, 731.

those of Massachusetts, were such as to make it almost impossible for the poorer farmer to survive as a property owner, and were soon to drive him to open revolt.[17]

The farmers in the middle states with better lands and better transportation shared in the growth of exports of grain and meats. Furthermore, governments were favorable to them, particularly in New York, where George Clinton as governor led the small farmers year after year in the adoption of tax laws that helped the farmer and brought anguished howls from the merchants.

The basic problem of the small farmer everywhere was stated by James Swan of Massachusetts in 1786. He had been a member of the legislature. He was keenly aware of how legislation could affect the economic well-being of various groups in society. In his *National Arithmetick* he pointed out that "when a farmer brings his produce to market, he is obliged to take up with the buyer's offer, and is forced, not infrequently, to take merchandise in exchange, which is totally insufficient to discharge his taxes. There is no family that does not want some money for some purposes, and the little which the farmer carries home from market, must be applied to other uses, besides paying off the [tax] collector's bills. The consequence is, distraint is made upon his stock or real estate." [18]

Thus when heavy taxes payable in specie were levied, many a farmer who saw little hard money from one year to the next, was subject to court action, the loss of property, and even a debtor's prison, not only for his taxes but for private debts as well. It is little wonder that he demanded stay laws, the privilege of paying taxes in kind, and the issuance of paper money. To him no talk was more idle than that about the sacred obligations of the state to public creditors; for him it was a mask of greed and a cloak for the legal confiscation of property. He was bitterly attacked for his demands. He was damned by lawyers, creditors, and all the "best people."

Yet at the same time that such people refused to recognize the needs of the small farmer, they were showing a remarkable interest in the improvement of agriculture. They were closely in touch with and influenced by scientific developments in Europe. This was shown in their organization of "scientific societies." They were

[17] See ch. xv.
[18] P. 25.

also keenly aware of the agricultural revolution in Europe; of new theories of crop rotation, livestock breeding and care, and of the development of new farm machinery. Such Americans and their European friends bewailed the failure of the American farmer to keep up with such developments.[19] The American Academy of Arts and Sciences and the American Philosophical Society took up agricultural improvement with enthusiasm. The American Academy in stating its aims declared that "agriculture stands in great need of attention. As the solid prosperity of the country will much depend upon the cultivation of our lands, too much regard can not be paid to this subject." Hence it determined to investigate soils, manures, blights, destructive insects. All these problems provided room for experiment, and it was hoped that this "will engage the minds of the curious and inquisitive, and meet with encouragement from gentlemen of property." [20]

The Academy appointed a committee to promote agriculture. It offered cash premiums for good manures, for experiments in crop rotation, for methods of preserving pork and beef to be shipped to the tropics, and the like.[21] It made investigations of many kinds, and published papers in American newspapers and magazines on the raising of silkworms, hemp, tobacco, maize, carrots, and experiments with manures.[22]

The American Philosophical Society likewise encouraged agricultural experimentation and published the results. It took over a silk society and for a time manufactured silk with the aid of a grant from the Pennsylvania legislature.[23] But its interests in the economic field were even broader. It was interested in mineral deposits. It encouraged the development of transportation by aiding James Rumsey with his steamboat schemes.[24]

The interest of the "scientific" societies in agriculture was only a part of their program, and it was not long before societies whose only interest was agricultural improvement began to appear. There had been some examples of these earlier in the eighteenth

[19] *Massachusetts Centinel*, 6 April, 30 July 1785.

[20] *Memoirs of the American Academy of Arts and Sciences* (Boston, 1785), I, x.

[21] *American Museum*, II, 355–6.

[22] Ibid., I–III contains many of these papers as do the *Massachusetts Centinel* and the *Pennsylvania Gazette*.

[23] *Early Proceedings . . . 1744 to 1838* (Philadelphia, 1884), 108, 112–3, 115, 116–7.

[24] Ibid., 133, 135, 159–60; *Massachusetts Centinel*, 12 May 1787.

century, but they appear in numbers and with a far greater range of interest and membership in the 1780's. The creation of such societies was urged even by Tench Coxe, whose main interest was in the promotion of manufactures.[25] The first of these societies to be formed was in Philadelphia. In the spring of 1785 a "number of gentlemen" met and organized a "Society of Agriculture, for promoting improvements in the husbandry of America, similar to what have advanced that of Europe to a degree that ought to excite our apprehensions, and inspire every American with the most spirited endeavors to keep pace with the Europeans, and even excel them in this grand basis of the wealth, strength and happiness of nations!" [26] This was the Philadelphia Society for Promoting Agriculture which soon presented its program to the public. It promised to concern itself only with agriculture and rural affairs for the purpose of increasing the yield of land in the American states. Its members were to be both resident and honorary. The honorary members were to be made up of those elected, and also of all members of agricultural societies in the other states and in the world. It announced that it would give prizes for written accounts of "actual experiments and improvements." [27] It proposed to give prizes and medals for the best crops of hemp and flax, and for farmyard experiments in the raising of, and improvement of livestock. A prize of a hundred dollars was offered for the best experiment in crop rotation.[28] The society was active; it met often and it awarded prizes. It investigated the Hessian fly which did so much damage to wheat crops. It published papers on the Hessian fly, crop rotation, and even on the bad effects of the use of liquor by farmers. One man assured the society that his farm was run without liquor with great success. Much concern was shown over machinery. A drill plow was imported from England. When Judge Bordley of Maryland, one of the charter members, gave it a model threshing machine, the *American Museum* remarked that "machines appear to be objects of immense consequence to this country," and went on to say that it was the duty of every American at home and abroad to "keep a

[25] Coxe, 34–5; Rodney H. True: "The Early Development of Agricultural Societies in the United States," AHA *Annual Report* (1920), 295–306.

[26] *Pennsylvania Gazette*, 9 March 1785.

[27] Ibid., 6 April 1785.

[28] Ibid., 27 April 1785; *American Museum*, III, 173–9.

vigilant eye upon everything of that kind which comes in his way. We may invent, and we may borrow of Europe her inventions. Possessed of soil without end, everything that saves the labor of hands, is a gain of peculiar value to us." [29]

In this society, as in others, there were very few "dirt farmers." Perhaps the outstanding "farmer" was Judge John Beale Bordley of Maryland. Other members were men like Benjamin Franklin and Timothy Pickering. The latter was the very active secretary of the society. Honorary members were selected in each of the states and included General Benjamin Lincoln, General Nathanael Greene, Jeremiah Wadsworth, James Bowdoin, and of course, George Washington, who was an honorary member of almost every society organized in the period, and who in this instance was better qualified than almost any other person in it for membership. The society offered its awards and prizes to all the citizens of the United States, and it tried to keep in touch with other societies in the United States and Europe.

The South Carolina Society for the Promotion of Agriculture was founded in 1784. It was made up of wealthy planters. It too elected honorary members, with Washington as honorary president and Jefferson as honorary vice-president.[30] The dues were high and the proceeds were used to provide prizes. It offered rewards for better methods of combating insect pests, and others for the production of a great variety of crops. In common with many other groups and with state governments, it was interested in the securing of merino sheep to improve the quality of wool, and it offered a prize for the person who would bring the first full-blooded merino sheep into the state.[31]

There was no society in New York during the 1780's although there had been a society in the 1760's which offered premiums for reports of practical work done on agricultural problems.[32] Washington was constantly engaged in agricultural experimentation

[29] Ibid., I, 456–9; II, 296–300; III, 491.

[30] True: AHA *Annual Report* (1920), 296; William Drayton to Washington, 23 Nov. 1785, Washington Papers, LC.

[31] Arthur H. Cole: *The American Wool Manufacture* (2 vols., Cambridge, Mass., 1926), I, 73.

[32] True: AHA *Annual Report* (1920), 296; *Pennsylvania Gazette*, 5 Oct. 1785, citing a complaint from New York that neither the legislature "nor any select body of men" in the state had turned their attention "to so useful an institution."

and was in correspondence with Arthur Young in England. He was a member of other agricultural societies and he could not understand why Virginians did not organize them.[33]

These societies, made up as they were largely of city dwellers, most of whom were politically antagonistic to the mass of small farmers, probably had very little direct influence upon them. The follies of the people who refused to pay attention to better methods of cultivation were denounced in city newspapers.[34] Nevertheless, these societies stimulated thinking about improved methods of farming and had some effect in persuading state legislatures to offer bounties for crops thought useful to the country. However, this did little to solve the problems of the small farmer who was such a large part of the population of the new nation. When he demanded aid for the specific problems that beset him, he got far more denunciation than help, a fact which lent irony as well as bitterness to the struggle for power in the states.[35]

[33] To Alexander Spotswood, 13 Feb. 1788, *Writings*, XXIX, 417.

[34] *Pennsylvania Gazette*, 1 June 1785.

[35] See chapters xv and xvi for the impact of state financial policy on agriculture and the farmers' demands for relief.

12
The Conflict of Opinion

Americans during the 1780's held a remarkable variety of opinions about the economic life of the times. Various groups had various notions as to what had happened, why it had happened, what should be done and who should do it. American merchants were faced with competition from British ships, American artisans by imports of British manufactured goods. Farmers and debtors were caught by the scarcity of money. Over them all hung the pall of post-war depression. Some blamed the governments, some blamed themselves, and almost everyone blamed the British.

The question of what the state and central governments should do, and which governments should do it, was the subject of endless debate. The merchants demanded navigation acts and they wanted Congress to have the power to pass them, but lacking that, they appealed to the state governments for immediate aid. The artisans were not interested in navigation acts. They wanted protective tariffs and got them from the states. Farmers and debtors wanted paper money that could be used to pay taxes and debts, and laws that would delay or ease legal proceedings for debt collection. They too appealed to the states for aid.[1]

Under the Articles of Confederation the states alone had the power to legislate on economic matters; yet throughout, one body of opinion insisted that the central government alone should have such power. This was the conviction of those who wanted a stronger central government and who looked with disfavor on any success of the states in the new nation. These nationalists swore that economic recovery was impossible without centralized con-

[1] See chs. xiv, xvi.

trol, and that chaos would be the only result of state legislation. This was essentially a partisan argument, yet it has been accepted by most writers since the 1780's as a valid interpretation. Several things stand in the way of its validity. First of all is the fact that such arguments were used in an effort to strengthen the central government *before* the post-war depression began. Secondly is the fact that recovery was well on the way before any centralized control had been achieved. This took away much of the point and some of the fervor of the argument, for even the nationalists agreed that such recovery had come before they achieved their ideal. Thirdly, was the fact that the nationalists had consciously used the argument as a political weapon. They were charged with it publicly in the newspapers and they admitted it privately to one another.

Despite the pessimism of particular groups during the 1780's, there was a body of opinion, widely held, that the economic gains of the Revolution far outweighed its losses. This optimism, which was so clear in other fields, was at least as great a force in economic thinking as the gloomy forebodings that are to be found. While artisans and merchants were bemoaning their fate and demanding government aid for the solution of their problems, other Americans were exhorting their fellow men to be frugal, bold, and industrious. They pointed to the basically sound condition of the American land and its people, and to the bright future ahead of them. While some croaked endlessly about the lack of cash, others insisted that the very scarcity would teach Americans self-denial and bring them to their senses.[2] Even in gloomy Massachusetts "Honestus" wrote to the *Salem Gazette* that all was not lost: "Our national debt is small, our resources almost untouched, and our means of discharging it, if wisely improved, nearly inexhaustible; foreign conveniences and luxuries are at a lower rate in this country than in any other, and of course can bear a tax. The sales of vacant lands, the property of the continent or state, should not be strained for the highest price, but be immediately sold for the most they would readily bring." [3] Americans had been acting like children whose money burned in their pockets. Failure of American remittances to Europe would stop American credit there, and

[2] *Massachusetts Centinel,* 24 March 1784, 5 Jan., 3 Aug. 1785; *Pennsylvania Gazette,* 10 Aug. 1785.

[3] Quoted in the *Pennsylvania Gazette,* 22 June 1785.

then Americans would have to go to work. That would be the only way to be a happy people. Nature has furnished Americans with rich soil. If it is cultivated it will pay for all the luxuries the people could want.[4]

Such exhortations to frugality, honesty, and hard work, and the insistence on the basic soundness of the American states and their economy are as common in the newspapers as are gloomy predictions of chaos to come. And it was true that Americans were being forced to live within their national income, whether they liked it or not. Furthermore, it was more and more apparent that times were getting better, at least for the merchants.

Much time and ink have been spent in trying to decide *just when* economic recovery began in the United States. Various standards have been used, such as price levels, trade statistics, and the like. Such data are incomplete and inconclusive and can be used in many ways.[5] The same is true of contemporary opinion, which must be judged in terms of its political purpose as well as of its economic meaning. Even in 1785 complaints of stagnation can be matched with statements of the essential soundness of things. By the end of that year comments on specific economic conditions take a new turn. Stephen Higginson of Massachusetts had complained in detail of the difficulties facing Massachusetts merchants, but in writing to John Adams late in 1785 he said that he had a different tale to tell. Things had at last changed for the better. The coastwise trade with Pennsylvania, Virginia, and Carolina during 1785 had resulted in more exports to those states than imports from them. "The consequence has been highly beneficial to us, by saving the money which we used to send to those states, and extending the culture or manufacture of those articles which they take from us." Those who had imported largely from the British had incurred debts they never could pay. Such people were in distress and this would spread to others in business with them. While this might be painful, it would in the end be good for it would revive habits of industry and teach people that to be easy and independent in circumstance, they must "confine our expenses within reasonable bounds." The cod fishery, he reported,

[4] Ibid., 10 Aug. 1785.

[5] For example see the discussion of price levels in Anne Bezanson, Robert D. Gray, and Miriam Hussey: *Wholesale Prices in Philadelphia, 1784–1861* (Philadelphia, 1936), 103–4, in which they criticize Channing's analysis of recovery from the post-war depression.

had greatly increased during the year and the prices had been high. The whale fishery had declined, but a bounty by the state government had probably saved it. The manufacture of pot and pearl ashes had revived after being suspended during the war. Other manufactures were developing. The export of country produce had greatly increased and Higginson expected it to supplant the Irish in West India and other markets.[6] Higginson was not the only man in Massachusetts who thought this way. John Adams wrote back to Rufus King: "Your picture of the prosperity of our country, its agriculture, and fisheries is a charming one." [7] Even in an unimportant town like Plymouth recovery was under way. The cod fisheries had been the town's main business but they were destroyed by the war: "the very arms of support lopped off," and the people reduced to indolence and poverty. Yet by 1785 the town was reviving. For two seasons the fisheries had been equal to the "most sanguine expectations" and the promise for the future was that the town would "in process of time emerge from its present reduced state to its former standard of wealth and prosperity." [8] James Swan, a former member of the Massachusetts legislature, insisted that Massachusetts was on the way to recovery, but he urged a governmental policy more favorable to agriculture, which he believed should be the basis of Massachusetts economy.[9]

Opinions such as these from Massachusetts late in 1785 and in 1786 are more than matched there and elsewhere in 1786. No one in America was more optimistic than Benjamin Franklin. He returned to Philadelphia in September 1785, after nine years abroad. Cannon were fired, bells were rung, and he was escorted to his house with cheers of welcome.[10] He soon appeared at a meeting of the Fire Company, which he had helped found in 1736. He explained his long absence, apologized because his bucket was in such bad condition, but promised to have it in good order before the next meeting.[11] On his eighty-first birthday in January 1786, the printers of the city gave him a party at the Bunch of

[6] Stephen Higginson to John Adams, 30 Dec. 1785, AHA *Annual Report* (1896), I, 728–33.

[7] John Adams to Rufus King, London, 22 Jan. 1786, King: *Life*, I, 150.

[8] Dr. Thacher's Description of Plymouth, 1785, Misc. MSS., 1784–6, MHS.

[9] *National Arithmetick*, preface vii, 43–8.

[10] *Pennsylvania Gazette*, 21 Sept. 1785.

[11] Ibid., 5 Oct. 1785.

Grapes Tavern. They drank thirteen toasts beginning with one to "that venerable printer, philosopher and statesman, Dr. Franklin" and drank on through the liberty of the press, the United States, the state of Pennsylvania, Washington and the late army, Thomas Paine, and lastly to "the printers throughout the world." [12]

As he surveyed his native land, it was therefore natural for him to view it with a mellow eye, but also with a degree of objectivity that was his lot more than that of most men. He wrote many letters to friends in Europe in which he said this new experiment in self-government would not fail. The "lying English newspapers" came in for his particular scorn. The stories of American distresses, discontents, and confusions "exist only in the wishes of our enemies. America never was in higher prosperity, her produce abundant and bearing a good price, her working people all employed and well paid, and all property in lands and houses of more than treble the value it bore before the war; and, our commerce being no longer the monopoly of British merchants, we are furnished with all the foreign commodities we need, at much more reasonable rates than heretofore. So that we have no doubt of being able to discharge more speedily the debt incurred by the war, than at first was apprehended." [13] Franklin wrote to English friends in the same fashion. English newspapers were lying to please "honest John Bull" but actually prices were high. He cited the fact that wheat in November 1786 was selling for eight shillings sixpence per bushel. He pointed to the astonishing increase in the number of buildings in Philadelphia, the rising price of new lands, and the expansion to the westward as further evidence of the happy state of the new nation. "In short," he said, "all among us may be happy, who have happy dispositions; such being necessary to happiness even in paradise." [14] He looked on Shays's Rebellion as of minor importance and in no way affecting the steady growth of America. Paper money did not excite him: he thought it useful. He told Lafayette not to worry about what former enemies might think: let them think us weak and friendless so that "they may then not be jealous of our growing

[12] Ibid., 25 Jan. 1786.

[13] To M. Le Veillard, 6 March 1786, *Works* (Bigelow ed.), IX, 300–1. John Jay writing to Lord Lansdowne, 16 April 1786, made similar charges against English papers. *Correspondence*, III, 188–90.

[14] To William Hunter, 24 Nov. 1786, *Works* (Bigelow ed.), IX, 348.

strength, which, since the peace, does really make rapid progress. . . ."[15]

Franklin was always optimistic, but George Washington can never be accused of being misty-eyed about the nature of the times in which he lived. Yet Washington agreed with Franklin before Shays's Rebellion frightened him out of retirement and into politics. He wrote that despite the refusal to grant Congress power over trade, "our internal governments are daily acquiring strength. The laws have their fullest energy; justice is well administered; robbery, violence or murder is not heard of from New Hampshire to Georgia. The people at large (as far as I can learn) are more industrious than they were before the war. Economy begins, partly from necessity and partly from choice and habit, to prevail. The seeds of population are scattered over an immense tract of western country. In the old states, which were the theatres of hostility, it is wonderful to see how soon the ravages of war are repaired. Houses are rebuilt, fields enclosed, stocks of cattle which were destroyed are replaced, and many a desolated territory assumes again the cheerful appearance of cultivation. In many places the vestiges of conflagration and ruin are hardly to be traced. The arts of peace, such as clearing rivers, building bridges, and establishing conveniences for traveling &c. are assiduously promoted. In short, the foundation of a great empire is laid, and I please myself with a persuasion, that providence will not leave its work imperfect." Like Franklin, he knew that the picture of the United States in Europe was quite different, and like him he blamed it on British newspapers.[16] Washington, on his farm in Virginia, said that he was remote from the main stream. However, Mount Vernon was a way station for travelers, both American and foreign, so that he must have been in touch with much that went on in America.

Charles Thomson, secretary to the Congress since 1774, was at the very center of things at the capital in New York. Like Washington and Franklin, he scoffed at the pictures of American distress to be found in European newspapers. He told Jefferson that he would "venture to assert there is not upon the face of the

[15] 17 April 1787, ibid., IX, 375. See also his letter of 15 April 1787 to the Duke de la Rochefoucauld, ibid., IX, 368–71.

[16] To Chevalier de la Luzerne, Mount Vernon, 1 Aug. 1786, *Writings*, XXVIII, 499–501.

earth a body of people more happy or rising into consequence with more rapid strides than the inhabitants of the United States of America. Population is increasing, new houses building, new lands clearing, new settlements forming, and new manufactures establishing with a rapidity beyond conception, and what is more, the people are well clad, well fed and well housed." Not that everyone was contented, for the merchants and farmers were complaining of dullness, the landlords that rents were falling, the extravagant because they were compelled to pay their debts, and so on.[17]

Robert R. Livingston of New York, cool toward independence in 1776 and supporter of the Convention of 1787, was another man who pictured the prosperity of his country in 1787. New York's population had increased by 40,000 in the past twelve years despite the war. Few traces of war itself were left. Houses were building, lands were clearing, and the "best criterion of the state of trade is that the commodities and labors of the country still bear a better price than they did before the war. . . ." The next year he fought valiantly to get the Constitution ratified in New York but while some of his fellow "Federalists" painted the picture black for political purposes, he decried the idle talk of American weakness and distress with which British and some American newspapers had been filled. He agreed that the governments had been weak but that the people had been "easy and happy." [18]

In 1788 Washington, like Livingston, could relax as he looked forward to the inauguration of the new government. He knew, and Livingston did too, that the relationship between the demand for the new government and the basic economy was tenuous at best. One more state needed to ratify, said Washington, "and then, I expect, that many blessings will be attributed to our new government, which are now taking their rise from that industry and frugality into the practice of which the people have been forced from necessity. I really believe, that there never was so much labor and economy to be found before in the country as at the present moment. If they persist in the habits they are ac-

[17] To Jefferson, 6 April 1786, Charles Thomson Papers, NYHS *Collections* (1878), 205–6.

[18] To Lafayette, 24 April 1787, 17 Sept. 1788, Robert R. Livingston Papers (Bancroft Transcripts), NYPL.

quiring, the good effects will soon be distinguishable. When the people shall find themselves secure under an energetic government, when foreign nations shall be disposed to give us equal advantages in commerce from dread of retaliation, when the burdens of war shall be in a manner done away by the sale of western lands, when the seeds of happiness which are sown here shall begin to expand themselves, and when everyone (under his own vine and fig-tree) shall begin to taste the fruits of freedom, then all these blessings (for all these blessings will come) will be referred to the fostering influence of the new government. Whereas many causes will have conspired to produce them." [19]

The skeptical may say that such private correspondence was of little value in shaping public opinion, even granting that such gentlemen were accurate reporters. The answer is that Americans who could read newspapers could find, side by side with wails about hard times, optimistic accounts of economic conditions. "A. B." wrote to the *Pennsylvania Gazette* in May 1786 concerning the complaints about hard times in the newspapers. He said there was a foundation for such stories since in every country there were some people who had no profitable trade, and who had little money because they had nothing to give in exchange for it. "It is always in the power of a small number to make a great clamor." "A. B." therefore demanded a cool view of things. First of all, "the great business of the continent is agriculture." There are a hundred farmers for every merchant or artisan. The crops have been good, and despite the quantity produced in 1785 "never was the farmer better paid for the part he can spare to commerce, as the published price currents abundantly testify." The farmers' lands are rising in value with the increase of population, and he gives good wages to all those who work for him. All who are acquainted with the old world will agree that in no part of it are "the laboring poor so generally well fed, well clothed, well lodged, and well paid, as in the United States of America." When one turns from the farms to the cities, there is the same prosperity: "we find that, since the Revolution, the owners of houses and lots of ground have had their interest vastly augmented in value; rents have risen to an astonishing height, and thence encouragement to increase building, which gives employment to an abun-

[19] Washington to Lafayette, Mount Vernon, 19 June 1788, *Writings*, XXIX, 525–6.

dance of workmen, as does also the increased luxury and splendor of living of the inhabitants thus made richer. These workmen all demand and obtain much higher wages than any other part of the world would afford them, and are paid in ready money." Such people should not complain of hard times, and they are a large part of the city inhabitants.

"A. B." concluded his analysis of American economy by saying that "whoever has traveled through the various parts of Europe, and observed how small is the proportion of people in affluence or easy circumstances there, compared with those in poverty and misery; the few rich and haughty landlords, the multitude of poor, abject, rack-rented, tithe-paying tenants, and half paid and half starved ragged laborers; and views here the happy mediocrity that so generally prevails throughout these states, where the cultivator works for himself, and supports his family in decent plenty, will, methinks, see abundant reason to bless divine providence for the evident and great difference in our favor, and be convinced that no nation known to us enjoys a greater share of human felicity." [20]

In September 1786 the *Gazette* reiterated the idea that the condition of the United States was basically sound. It said flatly that the "impious clamors" were "the result of that busy and restless spirit, to the malignant influence of which every free country is exposed, and which unprincipled men are ever exciting." The country has had and still has troubles, but these are largely the result of the war. "Our situation is neither so bad as artful designing men have represented. . . . Any different system must expose us to the wiles of bad men, who constantly avail themselves of the real or imaginary troubles of the people, to excite their passions and raise themselves to places of honor in their country, at the expense of truth and the weal of the state." [21]

The *Massachusetts Centinel*, like the *Pennsylvania Gazette*, was solidly behind the movement for a new constitution, but it too did not consistently picture hard times. It declared that "the complaints of the decay of *trade* are without foundation. It should rather be said there is a decay of *traders*. A few merchants are

[20] *Pennsylvania Gazette*, 17 May 1786.

[21] Ibid., 6 Sept. 1786. Compare this with a similar analysis by William Otto, the French consul in New York, in reporting to his government on political life in the United States, and particularly on the motives of the backers of the Annapolis Convention. Bancroft: *Constitution*, II, 399–401.

sufficient to import and sell all the goods America requires. Let those of them who complain of hard times betake themselves to the cultivation of the earth, or to the establishment of some useful manufacture. Until ninety-nine out of an hundred of the citizens of America are farmers, artificers or manufacturers, we can never be rich or happy." [22]

A few days later it reprinted an article from a Rhode Island newspaper. This was an attack on the "writers of paragraphs and publications" throughout the United States who have filled the newspapers with "paragraphs pregnant with the most pernicious consequences to this country, tending to impress the people and the world at large with ideas of evils arising from their republican forms of government, which in fact do not exist at all, or spring from other sources." The paper charged that "restless men" who promote popular dissension to make themselves important are responsible for such tales. Newspapers should consider themselves guardians of the public honor and exclude from papers articles tending to bring their country into disrepute. An intelligent foreigner coming to America and knowing nothing except what he could find in the newspapers "would conceive us to be a poor, miserable, distracted people, distressed and suffering almost for the necessaries of life—without order or government—in anarchy and confusion." But if he were to go to public meetings such as balls, commencements, or celebrations of independence, he would see people brilliantly clad in American manufactures. He would be unable to understand that he was among the same people about whom he had been reading in the newspapers. If he were to see the profusion of imports of foreign articles such as tea, coffee, sugar, and chocolate and other luxuries, he would have to decide that he was in a country much more rich and fertile than any in the old world. He would have to conclude that their troubles came not from their forms of government "which in general are the best on earth" but to their folly and extravagance and the use of "foreign gewgaws" and other goods which they should manufacture themselves.[23]

In October 1787 the *Massachusetts Centinel* declared that "it is a fact as true as consolatory, that the internal resources of America

[22] 11 Aug. 1787.
[23] *Massachusetts Centinel*, 22 Aug. 1787.

never were in so flourishing a state as at present. The wounds of the war are in a great degree healed; the stock on our farms, which had been lessened by it, is replaced. . . ." More land is now tilled than ever before and the crops are good so that, despite grumbling, Americans can pay their debts if they will. During the same year, conditions in the back-country counties of Pennsylvania were reported good. "The earth though charged with few of the luxuries of life, teems with all necessaries: the houses though small, are commodious, though artless are neat; and so, in other respects, though little is done for ostentation, everything seems calculated for comfort." [24]

Contemporary opinion in America plainly does not support the picture of unmitigated gloom so often set forth by the writers of history who follow in one another's footsteps with more faith than research. When both "founding fathers" and the newspapers say that recovery from the effects of war has been miraculous, that the stories of hard times are at best dubious, and that the strident emphasis on them was born of the political designs of ambitious men, it is plain that politics as well as economics were involved in contemporary "thought" on economic matters.

This is made clear in the letters of nationalist leaders. While popular opinion was damning the British for closing the West Indies to American ships, Gouverneur Morris was greeting that action joyfully, for that "conduct will itself give Congress a power, they might not otherwise be possessed of." The "eastern" and "southern" states might now be convinced that it is necessary to give "proper force" to the "federal government." Morris of course did not believe in retaliation, and said so. The British would lose because of higher costs in British ships.[25] A few months later he wrote, "Do not ask the British to take off their foolish restrictions. Let them alone, and they will be obliged to do it of themselves. While the present regulation exists, it does us more political good, than it can possibly do commercial mischief." [26]

Joseph Reed, newly arrived in London, assured John Adams that the American Union had been strengthened, and gave credit in part to British restrictions which he said had "substituted a

[24] *Pennsylvania Packet*, 17 May 1787.
[25] To John Jay, 24 Sept. 1783, Sparks: *Morris*, I, 259.
[26] To John Jay, 10 Jan. 1784, ibid., I, 266–7.

new bond of Union to that which peace and a cessation of the influence of common danger had in some measure dissolved." [27] John Jay agreed. European restrictions would be a blessing if they tended "to raise a national spirit in our country." [28] When Jay returned to the United States he became secretary of foreign affairs and continued to work for a stronger central government. From his new vantage point he reported that the merchants felt the restraints on trade, and looked to Congress for relief. "Good will come out of evil; these discontents nourish federal ideas." The decline of trade meant that the farmers would suffer and therefore the "yeomen will be as desirous of increasing the powers of Congress as our merchants now are. All foreign restrictions, exclusions, and unneighborly ordinances will tend to press us together, and strengthen our bands of union." [29]

Rufus King put the matter more specifically. He said that the danger from the Barbary pirates was real, "but for mercantile purposes is magnified." He went on to say that if this "well-founded uneasiness" were attended to by "wise and moderate men" in the several states, "it may be improved to purposes most beneficial, to our national government, as well as to our national commerce. . . ." But too much precipitancy might injure us.[30]

The steady recovery from the effects of post-war deflation did much to nullify the argument for centralized power, and its supporters realized it. Stephen Higginson of Massachusetts was not a nationalist of the Robert Morris variety, but as a merchant he wanted Congress to have power over trade. He recognized the opposition of the southern states to any centralized control. He concluded finally that "perhaps nothing less than an apprehension of common danger will induce the states, to attend less to their separate and more to the general interest in such cases; but, however plain it may appear to the real politician, it is not easy in the moment of peace to impress upon the public mind, an apprehension of danger from such interested principles. . . ." He accompanied his thoughts with a description of economic recovery which he recognized as beginning by the end of 1785.[31]

[27] 30 Jan. 1784, Joseph Reed Papers, NYHS. See also Adams to Reed, The Hague, 11 Feb. 1784, Joseph Reed Papers, NYHS.

[28] To Charles Thomson, Paris, 7 April 1784, Charles Thomson Papers, LC.

[29] To the Marquis de Lafayette, 15 July 1785, *Correspondence*, III, 160–1.

[30] To Elbridge Gerry, 1 May 1785, King: *Life*, I, 93.

[31] To John Adams, 30 Dec. 1785, AHA *Annual Report* (1896), I, 729.

It was natural that the demand for a strong central government which long antedated the post-war depression should not end with the recognition of recovery. It is difficult if not impossible to arrive at any final truth, for the evidence can be interpreted many ways. It is clear, however, that in every state a multitude of issues divided the citizens into many groups. The less democratic refused to see any good in the political changes that had come as a result of the Revolution. The more democratic refused to see any good in proposals for adding power to the central government, however logical and obvious they might be. The conflict over economic problems, and their remedies, was only one part of the total argument over the nature and function of governments and the relationship of the states to the central government. This is set forth in the following account of the struggle for power in the states.

PART FOUR

The Struggle for Power in the States

THE DISLOCATIONS and shifts in emphasis in American economy after the winning of independence meant inevitably a struggle for the control of state governments, for they alone, under the Articles of Confederation, had the power to pass laws affecting the individual citizens of the United States. American merchants, farmers, and artisan manufacturers all had needs, both fancied and real, and they appealed to the state governments to satisfy them. The merchants wanted legislation favoring their ships as opposed to foreign ships. As creditors of individuals, they demanded stringent debt collection by the state courts. As creditors of governments, they demanded payment of interest and capital. The interests of the artisans were opposed to those of the shipowners who imported foreign manufactures. The artisans wanted protective tariffs to keep those goods out of the country. The farmers, however much they might differ in the amount they produced and the saleability of their crops, had common problems all the way from New Hampshire to Georgia. They needed some form of money with which to pay private debts and public taxes. As they moved away from the coast their need for better roads and bridges grew ever more urgent. The problem of land titles faced all of them, for more often than not the speculator arrived in advance of the actual settler. On the cutting edge of the frontier the problem of defence against the Indians was a reality that only the people along the coast could view with objectivity.

None of these problems was new, for all of them had existed long before the Revolution. The new fact was that for the first time in over a century and a half the local governments could do as they pleased without the restraining hand of external and superior authority. The "will" of the state legislatures, whether it expressed the wishes of the agrarian majority, or that of the artisan or merchant minorities, was final and complete. Since elections were annual and the political resources of the various groups were ample, what was "final and complete" could be changed once every twelve months. It is for this reason that the struggles for power in the American states are an illuminating commentary on the workings of democracy. As often as not, democracy was a potentiality rather than an actuality, but it was no less real, whether as fact or threat, for those who disliked it. During the Confederation political lines formed and changed on various issues, but always there emerged from the welter of complexities the broad outline of social cleavage. There was clear demonstration of this in the issues rising as an immediate aftermath of war. The soldiers returning from the army had claims on governments for which they demanded satisfaction. The ex-officers, organized as the Society of Cincinnati, were a pressure group at which many Americans looked with dubious eye. The desire of many Americans who had been Loyalists either to stay in America, or return there if they had fled, stirred angry passions in most of the states. The Treaty of Peace aroused alarm for it pointed to, if it did not settle, the problem of the pre-war debts owing to British creditors. Of basic importance were the ancient problems of finance—the incidence of taxation, the question of paper money, and the method for payment of private and public debts. Such problems were old but were now debated with new freshness, for the war itself had created public debts greater than Americans had ever dreamed of, and the method of their payment would affect the distribution of wealth and political power. Arising from such controversies, and affected by the defeats and victories in state politics, was the continuous debate within the states as to their relation to the central government and the measure of power to be allotted to or withheld from it.

Therefore the struggle for power in the states, given vitality and urgency by the fact of annual elections and the political supremacy of those elected, had a significance equalled only by the internal struggle for power preceding the outbreak of the Revolution.

13

The Aftermath of War: The Veterans, the Loyalists, and the Pre-war Debts

AMERICANS, PARTLY as a result of their English heritage, and partly as a result of their experience with British troops after 1763, had a healthy dislike of anything smacking of the professional military man. Revolutionary constitutions one after another forbade standing armies in peace time. The effort to create a permanent military force at the end of the Revolution was turned down. But many Americans who served during the Revolution as officers developed a keen desire to continue a military career. From almost the beginning of the war they demanded half pay for life, as was the custom in European armies. Eventually they "struck" and forced an unwilling promise of half pay from Congress. At the end of the war the promise of half pay for life was "commuted" to full pay for five years. There was violent opposition, especially in New England. Pamphlets were written denouncing the officers. In Connecticut a state-wide convention was held to protest commutation. The lower house of the legislature likewise protested. It was said that the officers were "mercenary," that the scheme was the beginning of a dangerous aristocracy, and that Congress had attacked state sovereignty.

The founding of the Society of Cincinnati as the war ended was only further proof to many Americans that military men must be feared and controlled by civil power. The Society of Cincinnati was a stench in the nostrils of good democrats because its membership was hereditary. The scheme was worked out by General Henry Knox and his friends at the same time that they were dabbling with the idea of a military revolution at Newburgh in the spring of 1783. The purpose behind the organization was partly political and partly social. Many officers felt that they must unite in order to be effective in their appeals to Congress and the states. In addition, friendships which many officers hoped to perpetuate had been formed during the war.

The Society was created in May 1783 with Washington as president and Knox as secretary. As news of it spread abroad it was denounced in press, private letter, and pamphlet. Not only was there popular opposition, but men in high places, like Jefferson, John Adams, Sam Adams, and John Jay thought it a threat to new-won liberties. Judge Aedanus Burke of South Carolina led off in 1783 with a pamphlet whose title itself was an indictment: *Considerations on the Society or Order of Cincinnati: Lately Instituted by the Major-Generals, Brigadier-Generals, and other Officers of the American Army. Proving that it Creates a Race of Hereditary Patricians, or Nobility. Interspersed with Remarks on its Consequences to the Freedom and Happiness of the Republic. Blow Ye the Trumpet in Zion.* The judge, an Irishman who had once studied theology in France, declared that the order was planted "in a fiery hot ambition, and thirst for power; and its branches will end in tyranny." If not checked, the country would be divided into two classes, the patricians and the rabble. Enemies at once charged that the judge had written the pamphlet because he had not served in the army long enough to become a member. The man who said that was a liar, replied the judge: he had been opposed to the order even before he had been turned down for membership.[1] The pamphlet did have influence. Even in New England, where opposition to all things military was so strong, James Warren said the people had not realized the danger of the "Cincinnati Club" until "roused and alarmed" by Judge Burke. The objection to commutation of half pay was subsiding when the pamphlet got to New England but after that town meetings and county conventions met and denounced the Cincinnati.[2]

Samuel Osgood declared his fear of the Cincinnati and their demands on government. Their threats were only implied, but he was convinced that if Congress did not pay them, the purpose of

[1] *South Carolina Gazette*, 13–15 May 1784.

[2] James Warren to John Adams, 26 Feb. 1784, *Warren-Adams Letters*, II, 237; Wallace E. Davies: "The Society of the Cincinnati in New England 1783–1800," *William and Mary Quarterly*, 3rd ser., V (1948), 3–25.

the order would be "to connect throughout the continent a large and important body of men to watch over the doings of the Congress or of the state legislatures. . . ." Three or four of them were already in Congress. Their eyes were on the public treasury and once funds were established, they, the "aristocracy," and all the "unprincipled and subtle intriguers of America" would overmatch "the honest and independent." [3] In Massachusetts, John Morgan, a "one-armed soldier" produced and offered for sale "The Wonder of Wonders, or the strange Appearance of a Devil and Ghost to Capt. —— ——, One of the new-fangled American Nobility or Order of Cincinnati." The advertisement for this pamphlet concluded with a verse which declared

Though still the prime, infernal prince of hell,
Against Columbia's rights shall urge rebel:
Yet white clad ghosts shall in their country's cause,
Shake that vile heart that dare infringe her laws.[4]

In Connecticut "People" declared that "the names of departed heroes are disturbed, the feelings of the people are agitated, the convulsion extends to the basis of our constitution; such avarice, such encroachment, such plundering of honor is too egregious to be borne." [5]

The popular clamor was so great that legislature after legislature denounced the Society. In Massachusetts a committee of both houses declared that the Society was "unjustifiable, and if not properly discountenanced, may be dangerous to the peace, liberty and safety of the United States in general, and this commonwealth in particular." [6] In North Carolina a bill was introduced in the legislature to prevent any member of the Society from ever having a seat in either house.[7] There was talk of disfranchisement of all members in Rhode Island.[8]

[3] To Stephen Higginson, 2 Feb. 1784, Burnett, VII, 434–5.

[4] *Massachusetts Centinel*, 3 April 1784.

[5] Boston, *The Independent Chronicle and the Universal Advertiser*, 1 April 1784.

[6] *Massachusetts Centinel*, 27 March 1784.

[7] Walter Clark, ed.: *The State Records of North Carolina* (vols. XI–XXVI of *Colonial and State Records of North Carolina*, Winston and Goldsboro, 1895–1905), XIX, 743.

[8] Edgar E. Hume: "Early Opposition to the Cincinnati," *Americana*, XXX (1936), 613–14. Hume's article is a useful compilation with many references to sources of contemporary opinion.

When the Society met in its first convention in May 1784 it discussed its reputation. Washington pointed to the "violent and formidable" opposition and called on the delegates to report on sentiments in their home states. As a result of their discussions they adopted an altered and amended "institution." The hereditary character of the Society was abolished and the funds of the state societies were to be put in the keeping of the state legislatures.[9] The changes were publicized in a circular letter signed by Washington. The circular defended the purity of the Society's principles. It admitted that it had been proposed to use "collective influence in support of that government, and confirmation of that union, the establishment of which had engaged so considerable a part of our lives," but since this was deemed improper, the Society would not think of opposing their fellow citizens.[10] The changes were made largely at Washington's insistence. He believed sincerely that if they had not been made, the country would have been in an uproar.[11]

The clamor did die down. The Society seemed to lose its character as an organized pressure group, but more than one citizen kept a wary eye upon its members. In New York it was respectable enough to be allowed to congratulate the president of Congress during the Fourth of July celebration in 1786; yet Rufus King declared that he was witness to the "degradation of Government in seeing them received. . . ." [12] In 1787 John Quincy Adams said that the Society was daily acquiring strength and "will infallibly become a body dangerous, if not fatal to the Constitution." [13] James Warren wailed that the people had already forgotten the Society's efforts to introduce "distinctions," and now its members were creeping into public office and the legislature.[14]

The Society was plainly not on the popular side of any controversy in the states. In Massachusetts it declared Luke and Elijah Day unworthy of membership for siding with Daniel Shays.[15] In the Constitutional Convention of 1787, twenty-seven of the

[9] Ibid., XXX, 616–18. The changes were never ratified by all the state societies, and eventually the original "institution" was retained.

[10] *Massachusetts Centinel*, 2 June 1784.

[11] To Arthur St. Clair, 31 Aug. 1785, *Writings*, XXVIII, 240.

[12] To Elbridge Gerry, 4 July 1786, King: *Life*, I, 186.

[13] To John Adams, 30 June 1787, Worthington C. Ford, ed.: *Writings of John Quincy Adams* (7 vols., New York, 1913–7), I, 33.

[14] To John Adams, 18 May 1787, *Warren-Adams Letters*, II, 291–92.

[15] *Massachusetts Centinel*, 11 July 1787.

members were of the order and only four of them refused to approve of the Convention's work.[16] It was probably more the community of interest among former comrades in the army than the organization, as such, which influenced its members. Yet Benjamin Rush, who was in hearty sympathy with the purposes of the majority in the Convention, believed that the Cincinnati as a group would be willing to use force, if necessary, to achieve the adoption of the Constitution when it appeared.[17] Not all Americans regarded the new government as either wise or efficient, but the Cincinnati did not need to act as a group in its behalf. Very rapidly it disappeared from sight as a political group, although as a social organization it still exists.

The struggle over the Society of the Cincinnati was evidence of a basic political division in the Patriot forces. Of far greater political and economic significance was the question of what to do with those Americans who in spirit or in action had been loyal to Great Britain during the war. Perhaps a third of the Americans had been "loyal" in one way or another. Some fled to Great Britain. Others remained behind British lines. But some of them either fought valiantly, as in the southern back country, or remained neutral as best they could. But now that the war was over they wanted to return to their old homes, or to stay in America after the British army left. Meanwhile during the war all the states had passed legislation aimed at the Loyalists. Every state adopted a "test" law whereby men were required to forswear allegiance to George III and declare their loyalty to the state. Virtually all of the states passed further laws limiting freedom of speech for Loyalists. Five of the states directly disfranchised them. Nine states passed laws exiling them. Every state passed laws confiscating Loyalist property or taxing their estates heavily.[18]

As the war drew to an end the Loyalists appealed loudly for redress of grievances. The result was the inclusion of two articles in the Treaty of Peace relating to the problem of the Loyalists. Article Five declared that Congress should recommend to the

[16] Edgar E. Hume: "The Role of the Society of the Cincinnati in the Birth of the Constitution of the United States," *Pennsylvania History*, V (1938), 105–6.

[17] To Richard Price, 2 June 1787, "Richard Price Letters," MHS *Proceedings*, 2nd ser., XVII (1903), 367–8.

[18] These laws are summarized in Claude H. Van Tyne: *The Loyalists in the American Revolution* (New York, 1902), appendices B and C.

state legislatures the restitution of the property of actual British subjects and of those people in territory occupied by the British, if they had not borne arms against the United States. All other persons were to have liberty to return for twelve months to seek recovery of property that had been confiscated. The states were to be further advised to revise their laws in conformity with justice and equality and a spirit of conciliation. Article Six provided that there be no further confiscation of property; that there be no further prosecution of persons for their part in the war; and that all those in confinement at the time of ratification of the Treaty be released.

Many Loyalists expressed the desire to return to their former homes even before the appearance of the Treaty of Peace. Many of them had kept up their friendships with fellow Americans who had fought for independence. As the war came to an end they sought the aid of these friends. In March 1783 Charles Inglis wrote from New York City to James Duane and asked for an interview. He said that independence would soon be a fact and that he hoped that all the passions of the war would be ended. He declared that he had not knowingly injured any individual; that his part in the war had been the result of "principle and conscience"; that he believed he was promoting the welfare of America; but that now he must acquiesce in the decisions of providence since the "views of divine providence respecting this country were different. . . ." [19]

Another Anglican who wanted to return was the Reverend Jacob Duché, who had prayed so eloquently at the First Continental Congress that even the Quakers had wept. He wanted to return to his "native city." He declared that he knew nothing of politics and that he had avoided them in England where he had a position as chaplain and secretary to a charitable female institution. He would willingly give up his salary of £300 a year to get back to Philadelphia where his successor had signed an agreement to give up the job if Duché ever returned.[20]

From New York, Peter Van Schaack reported to his Patriot

[19] 28 March 1783, Duane Papers, NYHS. Inglis eventually left New York and became the first bishop of Nova Scotia.

[20] To Benjamin Franklin, Lambeth, 28 Jan. 1783, Bache Coll., APS, and to George Washington, 2 April 1785, Washington Papers, LC.

friend Theodore Sedgwick that he was "among the great number of Loyalists who wishes to stay. . . ." He declared that all the passions of war should be forgotten and that the new treaty should be sacred; by it persons and property should be secure. It would be bad for the country if men of property were forced to leave because they had been Loyalists.[21]

The Loyalists who appealed to Americans did not appeal in vain. Their Patriot friends for the most part held identical political and social ideas, although they had disagreed on the question of independence. The conservative wing of the Patriot party was a minority and as such it wanted all the help it could get in the fight against what it believed to be democracy. When Samuel Ogden went to New York as the British were evacuating, he wrote back to General Henry Knox that he was taking leave of some of the "dearest connections" who were sailing to England, perhaps forever. Two of his friends were staying on in their houses while hundreds were sailing. He was afraid the two ladies might be "exposed to insults from the vulgar" and he begged Knox to see to their protection when the American army moved in.[22]

Alexander Hamilton declared that actions of the state of New York were frightening men into leaving. "We have already lost too large a number of valuable citizens." [23] Timothy Pickering maintained that he was sorry to see the violent feeling against the Loyalists. He believed that if some who had remained in the country could be exchanged for some of those who had fled, the country would be the better for it.[24]

The Loyalists thus had strong and influential friends among the conservative members of the Patriot party. But the people and some of their leaders hated the "Tories" with a violence born of civil strife and economic and social distinctions. The Tories must not be allowed to return to enjoy the independence which they had fought to avoid. The spirit of the people was high on the arrival of the news of peace, reported William Paterson from New Jersey. They were determined to prevent the "refugees" from re-

[21] 10 April 1783, Sedgwick Papers, MHS.

[22] 11 Nov. 1783, Knox Papers, MHS.

[23] To James Duane, 5 Aug. 1783, Duane Papers, NYHS.

[24] To Mrs. Mehitible Higginson, Newburgh, 15 June 1783, Pickering Papers, MHS.

turning to live among them. Thousands were leaving New York for Nova Scotia: "Speed to them all." [25] From Philadelphia it was reported that associations were forming everywhere to keep the Loyalists from returning to Pennsylvania and the other northern states.[26]

The political division between the radical and the conservative wings of the revolutionary party was apparent in every state and the issue was handled not in terms of justice, though the word was much used, but in terms of whichever group was in power and could thus work its will. In 1778 the New Hampshire legislature prepared a list of Loyalists and declared that if they left the United States they could not return without a special act of the legislature. Acts were passed confiscating their property. But once the war was over the opposition to the Loyalists was ineffective and in 1786 all barriers to their return were removed.[27] The inhabitants of Rhode Island, perhaps because they had so many other things to wrangle about, did very little about the Loyalists except to pass general confiscation acts and an act forbidding the return of certain merchants to the state.[28]

In Connecticut about 2,000 out of a total of 25,000 adult males in 1775 were Loyalist. They were for the most part wealthy men who feared the results of civil war. Many of them fled to the British army for safety, while others went to England. About half of them stayed in the state. The state legislature was more kindly than most, with the result that the Loyalists had little to fear. The legislature was dominated by conservative men whose political and social ideas were much nearer those of the Loyalists than those of the radical revolutionists. When the war was over these men wanted reconciliation with, not punishment for, their social equals who had taken the other side on the issue of independence. Even before the war was over they permitted Richard Smith, a Loyalist merchant who had been exiled from Massachusetts, to bring his goods and settle in Connecticut. The action of the legislature was denounced by various towns in the state, and protests

[25] William Paterson to his brother, 12 May 1783, William Paterson Papers (Bancroft Transcripts), NYPL.

[26] John Armstrong to General Gates, 9 June 1783, Emmet Coll., no. 815, NYPL.

[27] *Laws of New Hampshire* (10 vols., Manchester, Bristol, Concord, 1904–22), IV, 177–80, 456–9; V, 195–6.

[28] *Rhode Island Acts and Resolves* (July 1780), 19–20.

came from Massachusetts and Rhode Island. This wrangle went on for months.

Meantime various town meetings opposed the return of the Loyalists. Writers in the newspapers charged that they did not belong in a democracy. Despite such arguments the conservative element repealed most of the laws relating to Loyalists before the end of 1783.[29] The opposition to their return had come from the rural areas, whereas the merchant attitude was best expressed by the action of a New Haven town meeting in March 1784. A committee report declared that by the federal constitution each state was "sovereign and independent" as to its internal policies. Every town in Connecticut had a right to admit or reject inhabitants for there was no state law on the subject. Justice should be done as provided by the peace treaty and recommended by Congress. Furthermore, New Haven was well situated for commerce and the return of the Loyalists would bring wealth back to the town. The town meeting agreed to the report and to its publication in the newspapers.[30]

The Loyalists had a more difficult time of it in Massachusetts. On 17 April 1783 the Boston town meeting passed resolutions protesting against the return of the Loyalists. The Committee of Correspondence sent the word out to other Massachusetts towns. Before long, replies came back to Boston in support of its opposition.[31] In the spring of 1784 the legislature repealed previous acts against the Loyalists, but passed a new one declaring that those who had borne arms against the United States, or who had been specifically named as traitors, could not come back. Other Loyalists could return only if they got a license from the governor, which must be renewed at each session of the General Court unless a special naturalization act was passed in favor of the individual involved.[32] The day this law was passed the *Massachusetts Centinel* discussed both sides of the argument. Some people were against their return "from political principles." Others were strong for

[29] Oscar Zeichner: "The Rehabilitation of Loyalists in Connecticut," *New England Quarterly*, XI (1938), 308–30. In 1787 the legislature passed an act repealing all laws repugnant to the Treaty of Peace at the request of Congress. However, the legislation of 1783 really ended the issue so far as Connecticut was concerned.

[30] *Connecticut Journal*, 10 March 1784.

[31] Boston Committee of Correspondence Papers, NYPL.

[32] 24 March 1784, *Acts and Resolves of Massachusetts, 1782–83* (Boston, 1890), 661–4.

their return "as the wealth they will bring will more than counterbalance the detriment they can possibly be of." Time only can tell, said the paper, but since the citizens of one state can settle in any other, it will frustrate those who are opposed to their return and produce animosities. "Though monarchial government is never to be wished, the above shows the weakness of democracy." [33]

Despite all opposition, Loyalist Americans returned to their old homes. The bitterness against them was expressed repeatedly in the newspapers. No writer was more violent than one who called himself "Observer." These people, he said, "conceived no enormities too flagitious, nor cruelties too brutal, when their countrymen were the objects: that they exhibited a conduct at which the savages with whom they associated, would shudder, and the most depraved imagination view with horror. . . ." Even now when the war is over they try to "sap the foundation of our great superstructure of Independence." Do not permit them to stay after the time allowed them by the treaty. "Shall intemperance, with her sickly train; and riot and debauchery, with their contagious attendants, be introduced with impunity, by these miscreants, and shall they be permitted to intoxicate our youth with the candied pill?" Throw out these people who hanker for "the leeks and onions of Britain"; demand redress of the fathers of the people and "extirpate the leeches." [34] Despite such attacks the legislature in the fall session of 1785 finally repealed all laws against the Loyalists.[35] This action was greeted with the comment that interest as well as honor was involved, for the laws keeping out the Loyalists had excluded much wealth from Massachusetts, and furthermore, they had created rivals in "our most lucrative trade," that with the West Indies.[36]

The controversy in the New England states was mildness itself compared with the struggle that raged in New York where perhaps half the population had been Loyalist in 1776. Most of the merchants who belonged to the Chamber of Commerce were Loyalist, but so were many tenant farmers up country. Ten years before the Declaration of Independence a rebellion of tenant farmers had been suppressed by violence, and John Morin Scott,

[33] 24 March 1784.

[34] *Massachusetts Centinel*, 9 Feb. 1785. See also the issue of 26 March which attacks the Tories who are bringing in British goods for sale.

[35] Ibid., 19, 26 Nov., 3, 21 Dec. 1785.

[36] *Pennsylvania Gazette*, 25 Jan. 1786.

one of the revolutionary leaders in the city of New York, had sat on the court which condemned their leaders to death. The tenant farmers of New York, like the back-country men of North Carolina, had an understandable aversion to supporting leaders in the fight against Britain who at the same time seemed equally willing to fight men who demanded a measure of justice at home.

New York had suppressed Loyalists with vigor throughout the war and had confiscated many large estates. As the war came to an end, Patriots began moving back into New York City before the British troops left. A Loyalist reported in April 1783 that "the town now swarms with Americans, whose insolence is scarce to be borne." [37] Men who felt this way about "Americans" had friends among the Patriots who sympathized with Loyalists' dislike for the rabble. One such man was Alexander Hamilton who deplored the fact that men with money, although merchants of "second class" and of no political consequence, might carry away eight or ten thousand guineas each. "Our state will feel for twenty years at least the effects of the popular frenzy." [38] Robert R. Livingston, safe in his manor, sniffed about the "restless mechanics" in New York City who wanted to "ingross all to themselves, without any regard to treaties or the virtue of brotherly affection. . . ." [39]

The feelings of the aristocratic members of the Patriot group were plainly not those of the people. In community after community all over the state, public meetings were held and resolutions were passed insisting that those who had joined the British should not be allowed to return, or if they had returned, that they be forced to leave in short order. From everywhere in the state came demands that the "Tories" be expelled or disfranchised. The legislature which met in the spring of 1784 reflected the popular clamor. In May it disfranchised all who had been British officials, who had helped the British in any way during the war, who had left the state, or who had actually joined the British. It was a sweeping law, for it disqualified two thirds of the inhabitants of

[37] I.N.P. Stokes, ed.: *The Iconography of Manhattan Island* . . . (6 vols., New York, 1915–28), V, 1159.

[38] To Robert R. Livingston, New York, 13 Aug. 1783, Robert R. Livingston Papers (Bancroft Transcripts), vol. 167, NYPL. See also W. S. Smith to George Washington, New York, 26 Aug. 1783, Washington Papers, LC. Smith asserts that Carleton was not evacuating New York because of the need for protecting the "refugees."

[39] To James Duane, 22 March 1784, Duane Papers, NYHS.

the city and county of New York and of the counties of Richmond and Kings, with a lesser number in other areas.[40]

A source of immediate conflict was a Trespass Act which allowed people who had fled from the British to recover damages from those who had used their property during British occupation. The most famous case brought under this act was by a widow, Elizabeth Rutgers, who had owned a brewery before the war. During the war Joshua Waddington, an American representative of a British brewing business, used the brewery under authority of the British army. The widow brought suit for damages in February 1784. She was assisted by a battery of lawyers including the attorney general of the state. Alexander Hamilton defended Waddington. He argued that under international law the property was at the disposal of the captors and that amnesty had been guaranteed by the Treaty of Peace. Like many another lawyer with Loyalist clients, Hamilton argued that the Treaty was superior to state law. The plaintiff's lawyers argued the opposite of these points in the case which was heard by the mayor's court in New York City, with Mayor James Duane presiding. Duane straddled the issue by "interpreting" the law of the legislature "reasonably." The widow could collect while Waddington operated the brewery under commission of the commissary general, but not from 1780 until the end of the war while he operated it under an order from the British commander in chief, for the latter was acting under the law of nations governing belligerents.[41] The assembly was so indignant that it censured Duane and even muttered about removing him from office.

After 1784 there was no anti-Loyalist legislation and the bitter spirit began to ebb, but it was impossible for the friends of the Loyalists to have legislation against them repealed until 1788 when all laws inconsistent with the peace treaty were abolished by one act of the legislature.[42]

Pennsylvania, like New York, had a large number of Loyalists who remained in the state, and in addition, a large population of Quakers and Mennonites who had objected to the war on religious grounds. To combat disloyalty and indifference, the supporters of

[40] Oscar Zeichner: "The Loyalist Problem in New York after the Revolution," *New York History*, XXI (1940), 284–302.

[41] Edward P. Alexander: *A Revolutionary Conservative, James Duane of New York* (New York, 1938), 161–4.

[42] Zeichner: *New York History*, XXI, 297–302.

the Revolution passed various laws known as "Test Acts." That of June 1777 was characteristic. It required that all the white male inhabitants must take an oath renouncing fidelity to George III, pledging allegiance to Pennsylvania, and agreeing to expose conspiracies. If they refused to take the oath, they could not hold office, vote, serve on juries, buy, sell, or transfer real estate, or sue for the collection of debts. Thousands of Pennsylvania residents refused to take the oath and were thereby deprived of citizenship.[43]

When the war was over large numbers of Loyalists remained in the state and others returned. Opposition soon showed itself in mass meetings where resolutions were passed denouncing all those who had not supported the war for independence. A meeting at Germantown appointed a committee to instruct assemblymen to oppose the return of the "enemy"; to voice the displeasure of the town to anyone harboring such people; and to investigate strangers who might be Loyalist refugees from other states.[44] A meeting in Philadelphia pointed to the many resolutions passed in other states and declared that Pennsylvania should not become "a receptacle for the outcasts of America." It declared that anyone who had left the country, or who had been banished, or legally attainted, should not return to the state. It was their duty as citizens and individuals to expel all those who had returned. The restoration of estates forfeited by law was incompatible with the peace, dignity, and safety of the state. Instructions should be given to members of the assembly to work for the passage of a law "on these important subjects." [45] These and other resolutions indicate a large block of opinion at the end of the war, but they had little effect. The assembly was at the time in the control of the Republicans who not only refused to consider such legislation, but who worked to achieve repeal of the test laws which they said disfranchised half the population.

The Republicans could not repeal the test laws in 1784 despite all their efforts, and they lost the election to the Constitutionalists in the fall. Not until 1786 were the test laws revised so that the bulk of the adult males could vote, and finally in March 1787, the last of such laws were repealed. They were replaced by the simple

[43] Brunhouse: *Counter-Revolution*, 40–1.
[44] *Pennsylvania Gazette*, 18 June 1783.
[45] Ibid., 18 June 1783.

requirement of a declaration of allegiance to the state before one could vote and hold office.[46]

Meanwhile prominent Loyalists in sympathy with the Republicans stayed on in Pennsylvania. Edward Shippen, father-in-law of Benedict Arnold, became chief justice in 1799. Robert Proud, teacher and historian of the state, lived there until 1813. Benjamin Chew, who had been chief justice, returned to the state after a temporary exile and became president of the High Court of Errors and Appeals in 1790. Governor John Penn returned, and died in Bucks County in 1795. The Reverend Jacob Duché returned in 1790. Joseph Galloway wanted to come back in 1790 but eventually his lawyer withdrew the request and Galloway died an exile.[47]

Throughout the South the most important Loyalists were merchants, most of whom were immigrants from England and Scotland. There were merchant Loyalists in the North, particularly in Massachusetts and New York, but these were for the most part native Americans. Where there were native American merchants in the South, as in Baltimore and Charleston, they tended to be Patriots. The appeals to the British commissioners investigating Loyalist claims after the war show this very well. Of the ninety-three claimants from Virginia, fifty were merchants. Of the ninety-three, only thirteen were natives of the state. Sixty-four of them were natives of the British Isles, only fifteen of whom came to Virginia before 1760.[48] Of 101 North Carolina Loyalists of whom there is record, forty-eight were merchants. Only ten of the 101 were natives of the colony. Sixty-eight of them were natives of the British Isles, only thirteen of whom came to the colony before 1760.[49] In South Carolina the bulk of the wealthy Loyalists were likewise recent immigrants from the British Isles who were interested in commerce.[50] Most of the native South Carolina merchants were Patriots. The southern planters, as a group, were Patriots although there were exceptions like William Byrd III in Virginia.

[46] Brunhouse: *Counter-Revolution*, 154–5, 179–81, 197.

[47] Wilbur H. Siebert: *The Loyalists of Pennsylvania* (Columbus, Ohio, 1920), 86–7.

[48] Isaac S. Harrell: *Loyalism in Virginia* (Philadelphia, 1926), 62–63.

[49] Isaac S. Harrell: "North Carolina Loyalists," *North Carolina Historical Review*, III (1926), 580.

[50] Charles G. Singer: *South Carolina in the Confederation* (Philadelphia, 1941), 102.

But some of the most violent Loyalists in the South were the back-countrymen of the Carolinas, who stayed to carry on a vicious civil war with their Patriot neighbors. Some of them were the newly arrived Highland Scotch. Others were Scotch-Irish and German pioneers. The loyalism of many of these people was the direct outcome of the suppression of the Regulator Movement only five years before. They had been defeated in open battle in 1771 and many of them had been condemned to death by the very men who were the leaders of the opposition to Great Britain. They looked upon the Patriot leaders as natural enemies and automatically took the side of Great Britain. In fact, as in the case of the tenant farmers who rebelled in New York, they got more sympathy from the British government than they did from the American political leaders.[51]

In South Carolina there was little punitive action against the Loyalists until after the British capture of Charleston in the fall of 1780. The British army promptly did more to convert leading South Carolinians to patriotism than all the exhortations of the revolutionary leaders. David Ramsay predicted accurately that the invasion would "leave the people of Carolina most excellent Rupublican materials." [52] Patriot leaders were sent on prison ships to St. Augustine, their lands were confiscated and their slaves taken. As a result, when the South Carolina assembly met at Jacksonborough in January 1782, Governor John Rutledge issued what was in effect an invitation to punish Loyalists and to confiscate their estates. The response was a series of acts banishing some people, confiscating the estates of others, and fining still others ten or twelve per cent of their total estates in return for pardons.

The British, who were still in control of Charleston, threatened to seize still more slaves to compensate Loyalists if the acts of confiscation were carried out. Those affected by the laws were a source of potential trouble. The governor was so alarmed that he begged Congress to allow General Nathanael Greene and the continental troops to remain in the state to prevent anarchy.

Actually there was no anarchy and when the legislature met again it behaved mildly. British merchants had appealed to the

[51] Robert O. DeMond: *The Loyalists in North Carolina During the Revolution* (Durham, N. C., 1940), 34–52.

[52] To [Gen. Benjamin Lincoln], 13 Aug. 1781, Emmet Coll., no. 1260, NYPL.

governor to be allowed to stay on to wind up their affairs after the British army left. The governor said they could stay for six months, but that they could not sue a citizen without asking permission of the legislature. Early in 1783 the legislature agreed that the British merchants could stay on until June 1784 and that they could buy and sell goods. The legislature was lenient to those whose estates had been confiscated and who had been banished. Numerous estates were exempted from confiscation and many people, including merchants, were readmitted to citizenship.

But when the news of the provisions of the Treaty of Peace reached the state, a reaction against mildness set in. In August 1783 General Greene reported "several little mobs and riots lately in this town owing to the indiscretion of some of the British merchants and to the violence of temper of some of the Whig interest." [53] A popular riot took place in Charleston during which confiscated goods were burned. Leading citizens of the town held more dignified mass meetings in which the legislature was urged to banish Loyalists and to grant no favors to British citizens other than those provided for by the Treaty.

The fact that excited citizens of all ranks in South Carolina, as in Maryland and Virginia, was the treaty provision recommending the payment of pre-war debts to British creditors. Many Charleston merchants owed such debts, and strict payments would result in bankruptcy. In addition, the British merchants who had come in with the British army in 1780 and who had stayed on after it left, were soon creditors of the planters whom the war left impoverished. They provided slaves and supplies and charged interest as high as fifty per cent.

As a result the merchant and planter debtors of the tidewater united with the back-country representatives in thwarting Article Four of the Treaty. Yet at the same time the tidewater group sought to repeal the legislation providing for banishment of and confiscation of the property of those Americans who had been Loyalists. Here the sharpest kind of division flared up among the populace of Charleston. They attacked John Miller, a British citizen and editor of the *South Carolina Gazette and General Advertiser*, who supported the return of Loyalists. He was denounced as the "Very Lick-Arse of power." [54] An organized campaign got

[53] To Washington, 8 Aug. 1783, Washington Papers, LC.
[54] *South Carolina Gazette*, 2 Aug. 1783.

under way to cancel all subscriptions to his paper and to withhold all advertising from it.[55] A Marine Anti-Britannic Society was organized with James Fallon as secretary. At its meetings the members drank anti-British toasts and demanded the restoration of "our chamber of commerce. . . ." [56] During the spring of 1784 handbills were posted listing the names of people who should be forced to leave the state despite the fact that the governor and legislature had permitted them to stay.

The continued threat of mob action united the conservative forces. Judge Burke denounced those who opposed the Loyalists and urged decency and brotherly love.[57] When the handbills were posted ordering thirteen people to leave the state, Governor Guerard offered a thousand dollar reward for information concerning those "thus impiously daring to insult the sovereignty, dignity, laws, and peace of the state, by issuing and ordering to be posted up the said most flagitious mandate." [58]

Some newspaper writers assured people that there was really law and order in Charleston; that an "Association of the Good Citizens" was organizing to put it out of the power of a "Bacchanalian Society" to disturb the peace in the future. The actions of the Anti-Britannic Society, "overcareful reformers and self-created censors," were a disgrace to republicanism and were helpful only to men of "aristocratical principles"—to those interested in a return to monarchy.[59]

The forces of law and order soon won out over the populace. During 1784 many estates were restored to former Loyalists and many more were given back their citizenship. By the end of 1786 most of the confiscated estates had been returned or some form of compensation had been given, although the confiscation laws were not repealed. However, the legislation preventing the collection of debts and delaying the payment of interest was still effective, for on this issue debtor planters and farmers remained united, not only against British but against American creditors as well.[60]

[55] *The Gazette of the State of South Carolina*, 8 April 1784.

[56] *South Carolina Gazette*, 16–8 Dec. 1783.

[57] Charge to the Grand Jury, District of 96, 26 Nov. 1783, ibid., 16–8 Dec. 1783.

[58] Ibid., 27–9 April 1784.

[59] Ibid., 27–9 April, 11–3 May 1784.

[60] The above account is based in part on Singer: *South Carolina in the Confederation*, ch. v, "The Treatment of Loyalists," and Robert W. Barnwell:

In Maryland and Virginia the question of the return of the Loyalists was tied up with the problem of pre-war debts as in no other states. The planters of Maryland owed more than a half million pounds sterling to British merchants and their factors at the beginning of the war, while the Virginia planters owed over £2,300,000.[61] During the war both states passed laws allowing their citizens to pay state and continental currency into the state treasuries in return for certificates stating that their debts to British creditors had been paid. Not only was this procedure extraordinary, since the actual creditors were not consulted, it also involved payment at a rate far below the real value of the debts. Technically, Maryland citizens were thus able to pay off £144,574 and Virginians £273,554 of the face value of their debts. In sterling terms the Maryland payments came to £86,744 and the Virginia ones to £12,035.[62] Some of these debts were owed directly to Glasgow, London, Liverpool, and Bristol merchants, others to their agents and to independent British and Scottish merchants who had been located in the seaport towns of the colonies.

During the war these factors and independent merchants were driven out and their property confiscated. But even before the war was over they began returning to their former homes and demanding payment of old debts. They found that Maryland had passed a law prohibiting the use of the courts to collect pre-war debts. This law was due to expire on 1 January 1784. The return of one determined Loyalist merchant after another created a popular demand for further legislative protection. All the legislature would do was to allow the judges of the state to disqualify attorneys who were Loyalists or British sympathizers. The law expired in 1786 and nothing further was done by the legislature. The house was willing, but the senate refused. The conservative senate was made up of men for the most part sympathetic to the idea of rigid debt collection, or friendly to the returning merchants who had played so important a role in Maryland before the war. The conclusion of the dispute was the passage of a law in 1786

"The Migration of Loyalists from South Carolina," South Carolina Historical Association *Proceedings* (1937), 34–42.

[61] Bemis: *Jay's Treaty*, 103, cites a list of debts submitted by British merchants in 1791. The total amount claimed came to £4,930,656. This included fourteen years of interest.

[62] Harrell: *Loyalism in Virginia*, 26–8; *Journals*, XXXI, 796; Crowl: *Maryland*, 65.

declaring the Treaty of Peace to be the supreme law of the state.

The populace, local lawyers, and even county judges objected bitterly to the collection of debts. Even where they agreed to the payment of principal, they refused to pay interest for the war period. There was at least one popular riot and there were threats to assassinate debt collectors, threats which the collectors, at least, took at face value.[63]

The situation in Virginia was far different. There the debts were greater, the legislature more subject to popular influence, and a great popular leader, Patrick Henry, fought the collection of debts. The popular question in Virginia was said by George Mason to be: "If we are now to pay the debts due the British merchants, what have we been fighting for all this while."[64]

As in Maryland, merchants or their agents began returning to the state before the war was over. Popular demand produced a law in May 1782 declaring that no debt due a British merchant could be recovered in a court of the state. If a Virginia citizen had bought the debt, he must prove that he had gotten it before May 1777, the time when British merchants had been ordered to leave the state. But the law did not prevent the return of the merchants, nor stop them from taking an oath of allegiance to the state, achieving citizenship, and thus being in a position to use the courts. The legislature met this problem by forbidding British merchants to enter the state and providing punishment for any magistrate who gave such merchants the oath of allegiance.

All this took place before the news of the preliminary treaty in the spring of 1783; when it came new outbreaks occurred at once. Some demanded the exclusion of all Loyalists. Others insisted that debts be not collected. Meetings were held and petitions were sent to the legislature demanding protection. But in Virginia, as in other states, there was support for the return of Loyalists and for the collection of debts. Some Virginians had bought up merchant claims against other Virginians. Those who were alarmed by popular rumblings and the general distaste for the payment of taxes and debts wanted the courts to function in

[63] Ibid., ch. ii, "The Collection of Pre-War British Debts."

[64] George Mason to Patrick Henry, 6 May 1783, William W. Henry: *Patrick Henry Life, Correspondence and Speeches* (3 vols., New York, 1891), II, 187. Mason himself was sharply opposed to any legislation interfering with the peace treaty. To [Col. William Cabell], 6 May 1783, Emmet Coll., no. 9540, NYPL.

orderly fashion against all debtors and for all creditors, whatever the accidents of political allegiance in wartime.

Governor Harrison issued a confused proclamation in July 1783 forbidding the return of all those who had left the state in 1777. But many had already returned, and their friends in Virginia were alarmed. The governor was said to have adopted "the spirit of the resolutions of the committees to the northward, who act as if the treaty were within their power to repeal." [65] Violence broke out in Norfolk, which Randolph said seemed doomed to perpetual dissension: smallpox before the war, and now the Loyalists, for the people of Norfolk were trying and expelling people.[66]

The Loyalists and their friends demanded citizenship and denounced the governor, who in turn declared that such people wanted the yoke of slavery more than they wanted American independence. The whole issue of citizenship was put before the legislature which declared that those who had borne arms against the United States could not come to Virginia, but that all others might do so, although they could not vote or hold office. At the same time all laws prohibiting intercourse with British subjects were repealed.[67] The law was ignored in many communities where citizens met and ordered merchants to leave. The British and Scottish merchants, for the most part, had not taken any active part against the United States and therefore could and did return, and they did try to collect debts. Men such as George Mason and James Madison urged that all laws at variance with the Treaty be repealed, while others such as Patrick Henry insisted that the stay laws be kept, although he did not object to the return of former Loyalists. The result was a series of deadlocks. By the fall of 1785 the Virginia assembly was told that it alone of all the states was failing to carry out the Treaty of Peace. Still the majority of the assembly would not act.

Meanwhile Jefferson and John Adams carried on negotiations with British merchants for some practical means of paying prewar debts. Both men insisted that interest should not be collected

[65] [Edmund Randolph] to James Madison, 12, 18 July, 23 Aug. 1783, Madison Papers, LC.

[66] To Madison, 13 Sept. 1783, Madison Papers, LC.

[67] Harrell: *Loyalism in Virginia*, 136–40; William W. Hening, ed.: *The Statutes at Large . . .* [of Virginia] (13 vols., Richmond, 1819–23), XI, 324–5. This law was not changed until the fall of 1786 when a new act combined various acts relating to immigration and citizenship.

for the seven years of war, and ultimately forced the British merchants to agree both to the surrender of interest and to payment of the debts in five annual installments.[68] The agreement was forwarded to John Jay, secretary for foreign affairs, who in turn laid the whole question before Congress. Congress declared that the states did not have the right to pass acts "interpreting, explaining or construing a national treaty" which by ratification became a part of the "law of the land and are not only independent of the will and power of such legislatures but also binding and obligatory on them." [69] This was followed by a letter to the states asking them to repeal laws in conflict with the Treaty.[70]

All of the states that had not yet done so responded by passing such legislation. There was bitter last-ditch opposition in Virginia. Edmund Randolph said that not even the resurrection of the prophets would convince those in debt to Great Britain that Congress should have more power.[71] In the final debate in the legislature Patrick Henry was as bitterly opposed to such a law as he was to the whole idea in the Virginia ratifying convention the next summer. One unfriendly spectator reported that his anxiety could not be concealed and that it was such that it made him sweat at every pore and appear to great disadvantage.[72]

At last, in December 1787, the Virginia legislature passed a law repealing all laws in the way of the recovery of the debts. But the opponents of the measure proceeded to annul its practical effectiveness by adding a provision suspending the law until the British should surrender the military posts in the Northwest and return or pay for the slaves they had taken during the war.[73] Not until the Constitution of 1787 was adopted, the national courts established, and the Virginia supreme court overruled by the new Supreme Court of the United States, were the British merchants to have the victory in Virginia that had come to them in other states before the end of the Confederation.

[68] Harrell: *Loyalism in Virginia*, 148–50.
[69] 21 March 1786, *Journals*, XXXII, 124–5.
[70] 13 April, ibid., XXXII, 176–84.
[71] To James Madison, 11 April 1787, Madison Papers, LC.
[72] Archibald Stuart to James Madison, 2 Dec. 1787, Madison Papers, LC.
[73] Hening, XII, 528.

14

The Demand for Government Aid: The Merchants and the Artisans

By winning their independence, Americans freed themselves from the British laws which had furnished the framework of colonial economy. Many of them believed that they might shape their future destiny by passing laws affecting the economic life of the new nation. But others believed that economic life should develop naturally. Many a colonial had anticipated Adam Smith's ideas and his *Wealth of Nations* soon made its way to the United States where it was bought and read and where parts of it were printed in newspapers.[1] People who accepted its views believed that governments should not meddle with economic life and particularly with trade. They could accept the statement in the *Pennsylvania Gazette* in 1784 that government should do no more than protect trade. "Most of the statutes or acts, edicts, arrets and placarts of parliaments, princes and states, for regulating, directing or restraining of trade, have, we think, been either political blunders, or jobs obtained by artful men for private advantage, under pretence of public good." [2] Such ideas were common enough to convince some Europeans that Americans were determined to break down the whole European system of trade and navigation acts. David Hartley, who had engaged in long and fruitless negotiations for a commercial treaty with John Adams and Franklin, was convinced that this was so. He

[1] *New Haven Gazette*, 13, 20, 27 July, 2 Nov. 1786; General Knox to Rivington, 10 Aug. 1783, Knox Papers, MHS, thanking Rivington for a copy which he had long wanted.

[2] 17 Nov. 1784. The remarks were thought to be those of Franklin.

declared that it was the great object of the Americans "as the first fruits of their independence, to destroy all those commercial restraints which were formerly imposed upon them by European authority, by introducing general and unlimited freedom in every branch of intercourse." To him, the request of Congress for power to regulate trade in order to force reciprocity from nations like Great Britain, was conclusive proof of the ideas he had gotten from talks with Adams and Franklin.[3]

But the future was to be shaped by economic realities. The British were to become free traders, not because of Adam Smith, but because of changes in British economy. And the Americans discarded almost at once the notion of government abstention from economic affairs. They were faced with the economic problems left by the war and with various groups clamoring for government aid: the manufacturers, the merchants, the farmers, the public creditors. Ever since the founding of the colonies, Americans had been accustomed to government intervention in economic matters. Colonial governments had given lands, tax exemptions, and monopolies to various forms of economic enterprise thought desirable or necessary. During the Revolution the manufacture of salt, arms, and clothing was encouraged by bounties and tax concessions. Exports and imports were likewise regulated by state laws.

Therefore, at the end of the war when prices fell, British goods poured in, specie poured out, and when heavy taxes were levied, it was natural for Americans to demand government aid. But here agreement ended and argument began. Should government promote one form of economic life as opposed to another? Should agriculture, commerce, or manufacturing be the chief concern of Americans? If they had power to shape destiny, what form should it take?

In New Hampshire John Sullivan urged the "Freemen of New Hampshire" to manufacture their own militia uniforms. He scorned the notion that it was better to buy foreign manufactures simply because they were cheaper and people could save money. If the whole community did this, manufactures would stop, idleness set in, and all cash be drawn off to pay for foreign labor and materials. A balance of trade against a nation would eventually leave debtors at the mercy of the rich, lower the value of all

[3] To Lord Carmarthen, 9 Jan. 1785, David Hartley Papers, V, CL.

property, and finally double the quantity of goods that must be produced to pay for importations.[4] Some men, like James Swan in Massachusetts—although he believed that agriculture should be the basis of the state—wanted a government policy that would produce a balanced economy. He wanted tariffs and bounties to protect farmers and to encourage certain needed crops. He would likewise give state bounties for useful domestic manufactures. There should be heavy import duties on luxury goods. There should be high taxes on useless workers such as domestic servants and high license fees on such idlers as musicians, orators, painters, opera singers, and actors.[5]

During 1786 the Connecticut legislature discussed the question of what the state should do: should it promote commerce, agriculture, or industry, or all three? One delegate insisted that the encouragement of manufactures was essential to the political security of the state. Aid for shipowners resulted only in the importation of "superfluities." Therefore there should be duties on imports, particularly on nails, enough of which could be produced by the idle boys in any one of the five cities of the state to supply twice the number needed. Colonel Wadsworth replied that the manufacture of nails was so profitable that it needed no premium. Commerce and agriculture should be encouraged instead. He declared that the farmer was "perhaps the most useful and valuable man in society. . . ." What Connecticut needed to do was to encourage the export of valuable articles for which cash was paid. Money came from the West Indies for horses, cattle, provisions, and lumber, and from France and Spain for fish and whale oil. France wanted more whale oil than could be supplied, and it could be sold in London for a profit, even after the payment of heavy duties. Therefore, he argued, lay no burdens on either agriculture or navigation: "Let us not lay burdens on any order of men; let us make no distinctions; they are impolitic; they are destructive." [6]

Similar debates took place in other legislatures and were carried on by newspaper writers. The situation of America was never more favorable for the growth of wealth, independence,

[4] *New Hampshire Gazette*, 18 Feb. 1785.

[5] *National Arithmetick*, 21–2.

[6] Proceedings of the General Assembly, 12–3 Oct. 1786, *New Haven Gazette*, 19 Oct. 1786.

and happiness, declared a writer in August 1787. She needed only to adopt the proper means. "These means are, agriculture and manufactures. She has no business with commerce, until she derives it from the products of the earth, or from her own arts." [7]

The attack on merchants and commerce had other supporters. The idea that the prosperity of the country depended on commerce was denied flatly. Trade had resulted in a scarcity of money. It would be no advantage if we had the mines of Mexico; look at Spain with all her mines. She is weak, while England with her industry is strong. Too much money produces idleness and luxury and this is what happened during the Revolution. Fortunes were made in trade and speculation. It was not a mere matter of paper money either. There was plenty of specie in the country at the end of the war, but the people who had it went into trade and brought in useless goods. If such money had gone into manufactures, America would have had every advantage. Instead, both the money and the produce are gone. National power and wealth do not primarily "consist in or depend on trade," but in manufacturing.[8]

In South Carolina it was said that the "planter and the mechanic form, in every state, the broad foundation of the community; the visibility of their property, and the permanency of their situations" make them the "constant and firm pillars of the constitution." Merchants are among the first of the subordinate classes in the community, but they should not be allowed to say who shall carry on trade. Only the people at large can do this: one should avoid the "griping hand of a monopolizer at home. . . ." [9]

There were those, of course, who doubted the wisdom of manufacturing for Americans. The importing merchants saw the threat to their business. Thomas Jefferson saw the growth of a working class, dependent on employers, as a threat to the kind of agrarian democracy he believed in. But in general there was widespread support for American manufactures, and it was given driving power by the continuation of strong anti-British feeling among the mass of the population. The demand for the encouragement of American artisans had fact and logic as well as feeling on its

[7] *Massachusetts Centinel*, 11 Aug. 1787.
[8] "Observator," *New Haven Gazette*, 16, 23 Nov. 1786.
[9] "A Patriot," *South Carolina Gazette*, 19 July 1783.

side. Household manufacturing had long been a basic part of American economic life. Great strides forward were made during the Revolution, and once the war was over the influx of British goods gave more point than ever to the demand for government aid.

The states responded to the demand. In 1788 North Carolina exempted all lands devoted to iron manufactures from taxation for ten years. In the same year Connecticut freed all iron manufactories, except slitting mills, from taxation. New Hampshire similarly exempted oil mills, rod and nail works, and sailcloth factories.[10] Loans were made to industry. In 1786 Pennsylvania lent a man £300 without interest for five years to assist him in making steel. In the same year Massachusetts lent £200 to Robert and Alexander Burr to help them finish models of new machinery for carding, roping, and spinning wool and cotton. In 1788 Pennsylvania paid John Hague £100 for bringing "a useful machine for carding cotton" into the state.[11]

Pennsylvania perhaps did more than any other state. In 1788 it passed an elaborate law to "encourage and protect the manufactures of this state." The law was necessary, it said, to prevent "ill designing persons" from exporting tools and machines used in manufactures and to prevent them from "seducing" artificers and manufacturers "to leave this country." Various fines and penalties were provided. However, the law was not to prevent the export of wool and cotton cards or any other tools and implements that were or might be manufactured for sale and export from Pennsylvania or the United States.[12]

During the next year the state passed a law to assist cotton manufacture. It pointed to the "patriotic citizens" of the state who had subscribed to a fund to establish a cotton factory, but it declared that the funds subscribed were inadequate for the plan "which it is the interest of this state to promote." Therefore the treasurer was authorized to buy 100 shares and £1,000 were allocated for the purpose.[13]

Some states granted lands to assist industry. North Carolina

[10] Clark: *History of Manufactures*, I, 45–6; *Laws of New Hampshire*, V, 163–4.

[11] Clark: *History of Manufactures*, I, 43.

[12] 29 March 1788, James T. Mitchell and Henry Flanders, eds.: *The Statutes at Large of Pennsylvania from 1682–1801* (16 vols., Harrisburg, 1896–1911), XIII, 58-62.

[13] 26 March 1789, ibid., XIII, 239–40.

offered 5,000 acres of land in 1788 to anyone setting up a successful iron works. In 1789 Massachusetts gave state lands valued at £500 to the incorporators of the Beverly Cotton Factory.[14]

Several states encouraged the development of raw materials used in manufactures. As early as 1778 New Jersey gave bounties for wool, flax, and hemp raised and sold within the state.[15] This was a war measure, but New York in 1785 granted a bounty of eight shillings a hundredweight on all hemp raised in the state and provided funds for it by levying tariff duties on foreign hemp and cordage.[16] In 1787 Connecticut allowed tax listers to deduct forty shillings per acre from the listings of individuals for each acre of hemp sowed by them.[17]

Such laws show the widespread interest in developing manufactures, but their significance is small when compared with the protective tariff legislation of the states. The passage of such legislation involved sharp battles with the American importers. The merchants wanted navigation laws favoring their ships over foreign competitors, but they wanted to continue the importation of manufactured goods without restraint. They did not want tariff duties which would cut those imports down. The issue was sharply drawn in the states where manufactures had developed most rapidly: Rhode Island, Massachusetts, and Pennsylvania.

The commercial crisis at the end of the war gave the merchants an immediate advantage in the argument. They could and did argue that the British were to blame for what happened. Therefore the thing to do was to keep out British merchants and their ships. The British order in council of July 1783 was used to justify demands for such legislation. Since attacking the hated British was a popular pastime, there was general support for some form of retaliation.

At once this involved another question: should Congress have the power to regulate trade, levy tariffs, and the like, or should that power remain with the states? Before the Revolution many Americans had denied such powers to Parliament and the American states had refused to give Congress that power in the Articles

[14] Clark: *History of Manufactures*, I, 40.

[15] 14 April 1778, Peter Wilson, ed.: *Acts of the Council and General Assembly of the State of New Jersey* (Trenton, 1784), 42.

[16] *Laws of the State of New York* (Albany, 1886), II, 120.

[17] Charles J. Hoadly and Leonard W. Labaree, eds.: *The Public Records of the State of Connecticut* (Hartford, 1894–), VI, 291–2.

of Confederation. Once the war was over many Americans, however much they might dislike the British and groan at the "British caused" depression, were very dubious about granting Congress power over trade. The merchants, of course, believed in centralized regulation. Joseph Galloway had argued for it in the First Continental Congress and he was supported by merchants who became Patriots as well as by those who became Loyalists. In 1777 Benjamin Harrison of Virginia, partner of Robert Morris, wondered if the Confederation could not be so interpreted as to give Congress the power by implication, even if it did not do so directly.[18]

No amount of "interpretation," however adept, could change the Confederation. Yet when the war was over, the rush of foreign ships to American ports and the commercial crisis that followed reinforced the demand for congressional power. Meanwhile the actual power to regulate trade and discriminate against foreign ships lay with the states, which, as a committee of Congress said tactfully in 1783, "being sovereign and independent possess the power of acting as may to them seem best. . . ." [19]

Although merchants as a group did not like state regulation, some of them accepted it in practice because they wanted immediate results. Charles Pettit of Philadelphia circularized the merchants of the United States early in 1784 urging them to support a grant of power to Congress, but at the same time he engaged in what he called "delicate work" to get the Pennsylvania legislature to pass legislation wanted by merchants.[20] Other merchants predicted that such "particular" legislation would result in confusion.[21] They were afraid that popular dislike of the British would result in extreme measures. They were afraid that it would lead the states to exclude British goods as well as British shipowners. Merchants like Robert Morris "and the most sensible men" wanted a duty on British ships entering and leaving the United

[18] Benjamin Harrison to Robert Morris, 18 Dec. 1777, *Confidential Correspondence of Robert Morris* (Stan. V. Henkels, Catalogue no. 1183), 15.

[19] *Journals*, XXV, 663. See ch. xx for an account of the effort to give Congress power over trade.

[20] Charles Pettit to Joseph Reed, Philadelphia, 13 Feb. 1784, Joseph Reed Papers, NYHS. In May 1785 a committee of Philadelphia merchants wrote to Boston merchants agreeing on the necessity of centralized regulation but stating that as a last resort the states should use their own powers. Emmet Coll., no. 9328, NYPL.

[21] John Langdon to Tench Tilghman & Co., 13 April 1784, Bancroft: *Constitution*, I, 355.

States. Otherwise they wished to continue trade with Britain as usual. Furthermore they wanted Congress, not the states,[22] to have the power, for they wanted "uniform" regulation. Merchants in one state were afraid they would lose business if their own state acted and its neighbors did not.

The fears of the merchants had real foundation, for the artisans and the "mechanicks," who as manufacturers were quite literally makers of things by hand, were an increasingly vocal and important part of American society. The products of their skill ranged all the way from nails, shoes, and spinning wheel irons to the lovely silver of Paul Revere. The war had increased the market and the output of American artisans and, now that it was over, they resented the British goods dumped wholesale on the American market by British and American merchants. The manufacturers' concept of the "public good" was quite different from that of the importers and the issue between them was sharply drawn in such cities as Philadelphia and Boston.

The demand for protection was set forth in the newspapers. The importation of foreign luxuries was damned for draining cash from the country and fathering extortion and corruption in the land. "Censor" in the *Massachusetts Centinel* declared that even the farmers, who of all the community might be imagined to be the least corrupt, were now asking three times what produce was worth and considered it no offence against the Supreme Being. The rich were extorting high rents. He who rented a house became the landlord's slave. The legislature should lay an ax to the root of extortion, fix prices and rents and thus destroy the vice of luxury so inconsistent with republican government. An end should be put to speculation in the necessaries of life, of "grinding the faces of the poor and laborious, as if there was no God who regards or takes cognizance of the actions of mankind." [23]

Others were specific. The way to stop the outflow of specie and the growth of luxury was to have the legislature pass excise duties on foreign manufactures and thus stop their consumption.[24] Stop trade with Britain and develop trade with France, or Americans will be on "the direct road to a national bankruptcy," said still another.[25]

[22] Edward Bancroft to William Frazer, 8 Nov. 1783, ibid., I, 332.
[23] *Massachusetts Centinel,* 1 Feb., 4 June, 3, 20 Aug. 1785.
[24] "An American," ibid., 22 Dec. 1784.
[25] Ibid., 12 March 1785.

One impetus to passage of protective tariffs came from the "Master Cordwainers" of Philadelphia who held a meeting on 10 March 1785. They discussed the bad results of importing European goods, and particularly those goods which could be manufactured as well in America. They decided that it was their duty, so far as they could do it, to stop the importation of boots and shoes. They agreed that they would neither buy nor sell, nor even mend, imported shoes and they got the support of the journeyman cordwainers for their program.[26]

This action of the Philadelphia shoemakers was greeted as a "noble example" by the artisans of Boston who urged the "mechanicks" of the town to follow the Philadelphia example and to elect members of the legislature who would promote manufactures. Some citizens of Boston were alarmed but they were told that the action of the "mechanicks" of the town was not due to a spirit of turbulence but to "the effect of those feelings natural to persons out of employ, who have wives and children asking for bread." [27]

Increasingly violent attacks were made on British merchants and their American abettors. "Thousands" urged: "Ye miscreants depart! and, tremble ye double-faced Americans" for justice will be done, but not by the legislature which is in the hands of those hired to support the British and the returned Loyalists. One writer presented a "Translation of the Indian Message" in which he proclaimed that the "Indians" were as ready to act as they had been when they drove out the tea merchants. Another urged that the "Rubicon" be crossed, that the locusts be exterminated, and that the ghosts of "Warren and Montgomery" be allowed to retire.[28]

The images were gloriously mixed but the lesson was plain to the merchants. They got busy and held a meeting of their own in which they set forth their point of view and outlined a program of action. The problem, said they, was the "alarming state of our trade and navigation." They agreed that the presence of British merchants, factors, and agents in the town of Boston, with their ample supply of goods, was apt to give these British a monopoly which would be "to the prejudice of the interest of this country." The merchants decided to ask merchants in other Massachusetts

[26] *Pennsylvania Gazette*, 23 March 1785.
[27] *Massachusetts Centinel*, 2, 9 April 1785.
[28] Ibid., 9 April 1785.

towns and in other states to urge their legislatures to grant Congress the power over trade for which it had asked in April 1784. Meanwhile they agreed to refuse to have commercial dealings of any kind with British agents, except those approved of by the selectmen of the town. They agreed not to rent or sell any warehouse, shop, or house to British agents and to refuse to employ truckers and carters who worked for them. A committee was appointed to visit all those who had already rented any property to British agents. As a feeble sop to the mechanics, they promised lamely to promote the manufactures and produce of the United States, so far as it lay in their power.[29]

The mechanics were aroused. A correspondent of the *Centinel* said that, whether British factors or American merchants imported hats, gloves, or shoes, the effect was to kill the business of the local artisan. The mechanics now called a meeting of their own while defenders of the merchants pleaded with them not to be violent.[30] Outside the state it was said that the Patriots had been urged to throw out the British agents "though *timid Whigs* and *cringing panders* may cry no *mobs* and *riots*. . . ." [31]

Others blamed the women who, it was said, were willing to sacrifice the community to satisfy their desire for fancy dress. These women ignored the resolutions passed by the men and therefore foreign agents dared to open their stores. "Brutus" insisted that the names of all those who fatten on "the blood of their country" should be published for all to read and condemn.[32]

When the "manufacturers" met they declared that it made no difference whether "our *own merchants*, or *foreign agents*" brought in goods that could be manufactured as well in America: the result was ruin. They voted to petition the General Court for a protective tariff on a list of articles made in Massachusetts. They agreed to watch for violations of any laws passed and to boycott all foreign agents until the legislature could act. To the merchants and traders, who had said they would do all they could to encourage manufactures, the "manufacturers" voted their appreciation, and coupled it with a promise to keep the prices of

[29] Ibid., 20 April 1785, reporting the meeting 10 April. See also Joseph Russell to Jeremy Belknap, Boston, 2 May 1785, "Belknap Papers," MHS *Collections*, 6th ser., IV, 295–6.

[30] *Massachusetts Centinel*, 13, 20 April 1785.

[31] *Pennsylvania Gazette*, 4 May 1785.

[32] *Massachusetts Centinel*, 30 April 1785.

their manufactured articles at a moderate level. They specifically protested against exporting cash since it tended to impoverish the people and to make it difficult to carry on business and pay taxes.[33]

A few days later another meeting was held at which twenty branches of manufacturing were represented. It denounced European importation whether by foreigners or American merchants. A letter from John Hancock was read. He had lately resigned the governorship, although not his grasp on local politics. He was now caught between his public role as a friend of the people and his private interests as a merchant. Hancock found the letter of the mechanics "interesting" and the times "critical." He urged them to look to the United States Congress for relief but promised to use his influence with the General Court. A committee reported a letter to manufacturers in Massachusetts urging them to join in a petition to the General Court asking for a protective tariff on all articles usually manufactured in the state. Furthermore, the tradesmen and manufacturers should see to it that "proper" members were elected to the General Court.[34]

The result of public discussion and political pressure was the introduction of a bill in the legislature. It went through the house, but was blocked in the senate. Some argued that Congress should have the power to regulate trade but this argument was denounced as hypocritical. "How artful is the conduct of certain men among us? One time we hear of the necessity of investing Congress with certain powers to regulate the commercial system of the whole union, and without such power nothing can be effected; at another time a 'Jonathan of the valley' or some other of the junto, are exclaiming against any power being given in Congress. . . . These are the arts of our enemies! Enemies they are, however they may start at the appellation!" [35]

The result of the conflict was the passage of two laws: a navigation law for the merchants and a protective tariff for the artisans. The navigation act provided that after 1 August, the goods of Massachusetts and the other states could not be exported in any kind of vessel belonging wholly or partly to subjects of Great Britain. A duty of five shillings per ton was levied on all foreign

[33] Ibid., 27 April 1785, reporting a meeting of 25 April.
[34] Ibid., 7 May 1785, reporting a meeting of 5 May.
[35] "Thousands," ibid., 2 July 1785.

vessels. Goods imported in such vessels were to pay double the duties paid on goods imported in ships belonging to American citizens. The act was to last until the United States was given power to enact laws regulating commerce.[36]

This was followed a few days later by the passage of an act the preamble of which declared that it was "highly necessary for the welfare and happiness of all states, and more especially such as are republican, to encourage agriculture, the improvements of raw materials and manufactures, a spirit of industry, frugality and economy, and at the same time to discourage luxury and extravagance of every kind . . ." The act raised import duties to a higher level than in previous acts in 1783 and 1784. The duties on specified articles made up a list long enough to include almost every conceivable form of manufactured product.[37] In addition, excise taxes were imposed on a variety of luxury goods.

Once the laws had been passed, Governor Bowdoin sent a circular letter to the governors of the other states. He said that the Massachusetts navigation law was a temporary expedient by which one state was attempting to defeat the ruinous effects of British commercial policy. The British, he said, counted on the jealousies of the states to prevent them from giving Congress the power to regulate trade. Until Congress got such power, Bowdoin asked the other states to join Massachusetts in similar acts to defeat the designs of foreigners, but also to avoid having one state suffer a loss of trade because of its zeal for the common safety. The governor seemed unaware of what other states had done to encourage American shipping, and he did not mention the fact that Massachusetts had adopted a tariff to protect its manufactures.[38]

The states varied in their response. The governor of Delaware did not reply for nearly nine months. He then said that his assembly had vested Congress with the power to regulate trade and that this was the best way to counteract British schemes.[39] The

[36] 23 June 1785, Massachusetts *Acts and Resolves, 1784–85*, 439–43. The governor was given the right to suspend the prohibition of exports in British vessels if the British allowed open trade.

[37] 2 July 1785, ibid., 453–7.

[38] James Bowdoin to Gov. Nicholas Van Dyke, 28 July 1785, Nicholas Van Dyke Papers, LC.

[39] Gov. Nicholas Van Dyke to Gov. Bowdoin, 15 March 1786, Emmet Coll., Misc., NYPL.

governor of South Carolina was enthusiastic. He agreed that Congress should have the power to regulate trade but said that meanwhile the states must do so.[40]

While Massachusetts citizens were angrily debating policy, Rhode Island quietly adopted an act to encourage the manufactures of Rhode Island, and of the other states as well. Foreign scythes and hoes were taxed twenty per cent of their value. A variety of tools used by shoemakers, tanners, farmers, and carpenters was taxed ten per cent. Ready-made garments, canes, watches, toys, and the like were taxed twenty-five per cent. A great variety of other items such as axes, hats, pewter, boots, shoes, and saddles; cordage, candles, manufactured tobacco, and carriages, were taxed at rates running from five to twenty per cent. Such duties were in addition to those which had been levied previously for the purpose of raising revenue.[41]

New Hampshire had levied impost duties on manufactured articles in 1784. In 1785, like Massachusetts, she forbade the export of American goods in ships belonging wholly or partly to British subjects. In 1786 she added the idea of protection to her impost duties.[42]

Equally significant was the discussion of a protective tariff in Pennsylvania. Philadelphia, the largest city in the United States, teemed with artisans and manufacturers. As early as June 1783 "A Friend to Mechanics" declared in "A Hint to the Mechanics and Manufacturers of the City and Liberties of Philadelphia" that it was "an essential part of the duty of a wise legislature" to encourage manufactures. The war itself had served as an encouragement. During the war the manufacturers enabled the farmer to feed the soldier, and the soldier to meet the enemy in the field. Therefore such people should not be forgotten when the war was over. Manufacturers would be out of work if certain articles were imported. These were bar iron, slit and rolled iron, steel, nails, saws, anchors and ship work, wire, wool cards, axes, spades, shovels, scythes, sickles, copper and tin ware, gold and silversmith's work, hats, iron casting, tanned leather, boots and shoes, writing paper, cordage, candles, soap. He concluded his

[40] Gov. Moultrie to Gov. James Bowdoin, 20 Sept. 1785, Bancroft: *Constitution*, I, 458–9; *Pennsylvania Gazette*, 22 Feb. 1786.

[41] Rhode Island *Acts and Resolves* (June 1785), 18–9.

[42] 17 April 1784, *Laws of New Hampshire*, IV, 562–3; 23 June 1785, V, 78–81; 4 March 1786, V, 146–8.

list: "&c. &c. &c." [43] The next thing to do was to present a "decent remonstrance" to the next session of the legislature for a redress of grievances.

As we have seen, it was the refusal of the Philadelphia shoemakers to handle foreign shoes that gave the impetus to the action of their fellow artisans in Boston. During the same year, 1785, the Pennsylvania manufacturers grew ever more insistent, but, as in Boston, they were opposed by the merchants who were willing to concede no more than a tariff for revenue. A Philadelphia meeting declared in favor of manufacturing but insisted that Congress be given the power over trade, for the union might be dissolved if the various states regulated trade for themselves.[44]

A protective tariff bill had been introduced in the legislature as early as March 1785. It got nowhere at first. The *Pennsylvania Gazette* urged the artisans to send in essays, letters, and paragraphs so that the assembly might be educated. It was well known, said the *Gazette*, that three-fourths of the assembly were farmers or country gentlemen who knew nothing of the principles of trade or commerce.[45]

The rural element, which was so large a part of the Constitutionalist party in Pennsylvania, acted on the eve of the elections in the fall of 1785. They might be indifferent to commerce and manufactures, but they could not ignore the votes of the Philadelphia artisans. The legislature passed a tariff law which imposed a long series of duties on specified manufactured articles. It also placed a duty of seven shillings six pence for every ton, "carpenters measure," for each and every voyage of foreign ships, except the ships of those countries having treaties with Congress. This was in complete contrast with the unreasonable provisions of the Massachusetts navigation act of the same year.[46]

In Massachusetts the struggle between the importing merchants and the artisans continued. The merchants did not like the tariff. The artisans were distrustful of the merchants. Stephen Higgin-

[43] *Pennsylvania Gazette*, 25 June 1783.

[44] Ibid., 22 June 1785.

[45] Ibid., 27 July 1785; Brunhouse: *Counter-Revolution*, 173.

[46] *Pennsylvania Gazette*, 5 Oct. 1785; Pennsylvania *Statutes at Large*, XII, 99–104. This law, with various subsequent amendments, remained the policy of Pennsylvania until the adoption of the Constitution of 1787. Various groups appealed for changes and special privileges and many of them got them. Brunhouse: *Counter-Revolution*, 181–2.

son said that such legislation was experimental and of doubtful value.[47] Samuel Shaw swore that the laws made it impossible to do business in Boston after they were in operation a week. Above all, he was sure that Massachusetts commerce would be ruined unless the other states passed similar legislation.[48]

The artisans predicted many happy effects from the new laws, but at the same time one of their spokesmen pointed out that the interests which had delayed the bill in the senate to the very last day were still active. ". . . these *snakes in the grass*—ADDRESSORS, BRITISH AGENTS, &c." did not dare declare themselves publicly, but wrapped up their false conclusions in the dark and were secretly instilling their poison artfully and subtly.[49]

Therefore the Boston artisans kept up their organization. They continued to hold meetings and to write to fellow artisans in other American towns. They kept watch on local merchants suspected of evading the laws.[50] To the "Tradesmen and Manufacturers" of Philadelphia, Baltimore, Charleston, and other towns, they wrote letters telling of their success in getting a protective tariff. They agreed that legislation by one state was not enough however, and they recommended the formation of similar associations in other American towns and states. These should make it their business to promote manufactures, to correspond with similar associations elsewhere, and to urge state legislatures to pass tariff laws. Then, above all, if an association could be formed among such state associations, they could exchange the manufactures and produce of all the states, and this would be a bond to union.[51]

In October, at a meeting at the Green Dragon Tavern, the Association of Tradesmen and Manufacturers declared that all persons who tried to weaken or counteract the law were "ENEMIES TO THE MANUFACTURING INTEREST OF THIS STATE." They voted to

[47] Stephen Higginson to John Adams, 8 Aug. 1785, AHA *Annual Report* (1896), I, 723.

[48] Major Samuel Shaw to Henry Knox, 8 Aug. 1785, Knox Papers, XVIII, 67, MHS.

[49] "Brutus," *Massachusetts Centinel*, 9 July 1785.

[50] Captain Hector McNeil to Samuel Adams [Aug. 1785], Emmet Coll., NYPL.

[51] Copy of letter "To the Tradesmen and Manufacturers of Philadelphia," Boston, 20 Aug. 1785, *Pennsylvania Gazette*, 14 Sept. 1785. The mechanics and tradesmen of Baltimore held meetings and sent the Boston request to other towns in Maryland. They organized an association like that in Boston and appointed a committee of correspondence. Ibid., 5 Oct. 1785; *Massachusetts Centinel*, 26 Oct. 1785.

assist those appointed by the selectmen to watch for breaches of the act. Their fervor was kept up by reiterated demands of the merchants for congressional control and attacks on the "novel" laws of the states.[52]

The fact was that the navigation act of June 1785 had been too sweeping: it discriminated against all foreign ships, whereas most of the states encouraged their own, French, Dutch, and other shipping at the expense of the British. Furthermore there was the treaty with France. French merchants objected to the Massachusetts and New Hampshire navigation acts in a statement to Congress. The French insisted that the acts were unfair because they restricted French vessels to certain ports, whereas all the French ports, in addition to free ports, were open to American vessels. They insisted that the tonnage duty was inconsistent with the Treaty of 1778. John Jay, secretary of foreign affairs, agreed that French objections were valid and used the occasion to reiterate the need of Congressional control of trade.[53] The conflict with the treaty with France and the obvious unworkability of too drastic a law brought an alteration of the navigation act late in 1785. The extra tonnage duties and double duties on goods brought in in foreign vessels were removed, but the restrictions on British vessels were retained. Other states were notified of the step and the hope was once more expressed that they would join Massachusetts, New Hampshire, and Rhode Island in similar measures. Then in July 1786 Massachusetts suspended her navigation act entirely until her sister states would cooperate with her.[54]

At the same time Massachusetts gave further help to her artisans. The impost of 1783, with all the subsequent additions to it, was continued for another three years. Then in November 1786 higher duties than in the act of 1785 were levied on a great variety of imported manufactured goods.[55]

Massachusetts was now aligned solidly with Pennsylvania in the protection of growing manufactures. Shipowners might not

[52] Ibid., 5, 8 Oct. 1785.

[53] *Journals*, XXIX, 817–20.

[54] 29 Nov. 1785, Massachusetts *Acts and Resolves* (1784–5), 489; 5 July 1786, ibid. (1786–7), 36; Gov. James Bowdoin to Gov. Matthew Griswold of Connecticut, 7 Dec. 1785, Massachusetts Misc., 1779–1864, MSS Div., LC.

[55] 8 July, 17 Nov. 1786, Massachusetts *Acts and Resolves* (1786–7), 67–68, 117–30.

be happy, but the artisans were. Practically all of the states encouraged local manufactures as well, if not directly, as did Rhode Island, Massachusetts, Pennsylvania, and New York, then indirectly through impost duties whose purpose was revenue. Virginia collected large revenues from imposts; and the movement for a protective tariff had its supporters. Madison reported in 1787 that the Virginia house was willing to impose "enormous duties" partly for revenue and partly to "force" manufactures.[56]

Even in the states where manufacturing was not important and the ownership of ships of small concern, American products were encouraged and American shipping was given the advantage over European. When Massachusetts gave up her navigation act in July 1786, Governor Bowdoin declared that she had done so because other states would not cooperate and had used the law in an abortive attempt to injure her.[57] This assertion was based either on ignorance of, or unwillingness to face, the knowable facts. By 1786 virtually all of the states had passed legislation favoring American ships, much of it before Massachusetts acted, and most of that legislation, unlike hers, was continued until the United States took over such powers in 1789.

The immediate impetus to such action was the British order in council of July 1783. Maryland was the first to respond. In the November session of 1783 her legislature laid a five shilling tax on every ton of British shipping and a two per cent ad valorem duty on British goods brought in in British ships, over and above the duties paid by the citizens of Maryland and of the other United States.[58]

In 1784 Pennsylvania levied a duty of seven pence per ton in addition to other tonnage duties on all ships owned wholly or partly by people not citizens of the United States.[59] The next year, as a part of her protective tariff law, Pennsylvania added a tonnage duty of seven shillings six pence per ton—carpenter's measure—for every voyage on all shipping of foreign nations not hav-

[56] Madison to Edmund Pendleton, Richmond, 9 Jan. 1787, *Writings* (Hunt ed.), II, 306.

[57] To Gov. Van Dyke, 10 July 1786, Nicholas Van Dyke Papers, LC.

[58] A. C. Hanson, ed.: *Laws of Maryland* (Annapolis, 1787), ch. xxix. In addition, the law authorized the Maryland delegates in Congress to agree to an amendment to the Confederation giving Congress the power to prohibit the import and export of foreign goods in other than American vessels. See *post*, ch. xx.

[59] Pennsylvania *Statutes at Large*, XI, 329.

ing commercial treaties with the United States.[60] The next year it was decided that such duties were too high unless neighboring states were to pass similar duties, so they were repealed. The legislature, however, agreed that it was "reasonable" for the ships of nations having no commercial treaties with the United States to pay more than ships of the United States and of nations having commercial treaties. Therefore, such ships were required to pay an additional duty of two shillings six pence per ton.[61]

New York acted even more sweepingly. In November 1784 she provided that various liquors which were taxed two pence a gallon when imported in American ships should pay four pence a gallon if imported in British ships. The next year all foreign ships, except British, were put on the same footing as American ships. All goods subject to import duties had to pay double duties if imported in ships owned wholly or in part by British citizens.[62] In early 1785 Rhode Island added a seven and a half per cent impost to the regular two and a half per cent impost on all foreign goods, if imported in British ships. In the fall of that year, following the lead of Massachusetts, she prohibited British ships from carrying American goods out of Rhode Island harbors and denied entry to British ships coming from a British colony, province, or plantation. Like Massachusetts, she soon suspended this drastic action but continued to levy high duties on goods brought in in British ships.[63]

In the South, Virginia and North Carolina adopted legislation like that of Maryland in 1783. In October 1785 Virginia provided that vessels owned wholly or partly by British subjects should pay a duty of five shillings a ton in addition to the tonnage duties paid by all vessels. A year later this was revised to provide a duty of two shillings per ton on all American vessels, three shillings a ton for all vessels of nations having commercial treaties with the United States, and a duty of six shillings per ton on the vessels owned wholly or in part by the subjects of all other nations. To

[60] 20 Sept. 1785, ibid., XII, 103.

[61] 8 April 1786, ibid., XII, 233–5. Foreign-owned vessels built in Pennsylvania after 15 April 1783 were exempted.

[62] *Laws of New York* (1886 ed.), II, 11–2, 65–6. Foreign goods brought in from Rhode Island, Connecticut, New Jersey, and Pennsylvania were to pay the same duties as when imported in British vessels, unless it could be proved that they had not been brought into those states in British vessels.

[63] Rhode Island *Acts and Resolves* (May 1785), 29; (Oct. 1785), 29–30.

these tonnage duties was added the provision that goods imported in vessels of nations without commercial treaties should pay a duty of two per cent ad valorem beyond the duties regularly levied.[64] In 1784 North Carolina levied a series of duties on all foreign merchandise brought into the state. In 1785 she added twenty per cent to such duties if goods were imported in vessels owned wholly or in part by citizens of nations having no commercial treaty with the United States. She also continued the duty of five shillings per ton on all vessels belonging to people of such nations.[65] South Carolina passed various acts for both revenue and protection. In 1783 she levied various specific duties on enumerated articles and a duty of two and a half per cent on all other foreign goods.[66] Even Georgia with its small commerce required foreign goods to pay duties, although it reduced the amount if imported in American vessels.[67]

The trade and navigation acts passed by the states were strikingly effective and are a partial explanation of the rapid growth of American commerce after the Revolution. No men understood this better than the British shipowners. As early as March 1787 they complained to the Privy Council that state legislation was giving American ships an advantage in the trade between the two nations.[68] Despite such advantages American shipowners were not satisfied. Yet tonnage duties on foreign ships after 1789 were lower than state duties had been. However, they were uniform and the tariff duties of the national government were lower than those of the manufacturing states during the Confederation. This made the importation of British goods easier than it had been, a fact recognized by British merchants. When the Privy Council asked British merchants what effect the legislation of the new national government would have on British trade, virtually every British merchant replied that the new legislation was more favorable to them than the state legislation had been.[69]

Government intervention during the Confederation was thus

[64] Hening, XII, 32, 289–90.

[65] North Carolina *State Records*, XXIV, 549–53, 718–20.

[66] Thomas Cooper, ed.: *The Statutes at Large of South Carolina* (Columbia, 1838), IV, 578, 581.

[67] Allan D. Candler, ed.: *The Colonial Records of the State of Georgia* (26 vols., Atlanta, 1904–16), XIX, pt. 2, 499–502, 514–5.

[68] Memorial of the Committee of Merchants Trading to North America, 30 March 1787, cited in Setser: *Commercial Reciprocity*, 65, n. 40.

[69] *Report of the Privy Council, 1791*, 29, 37, 44–45.

effective for both artisans and merchants though neither group was satisfied with what it got and misliked the gains of its opponents. On the whole, victory lay with the artisans during the Confederation and with the importing merchants after 1789. But not for long. After the War of 1812 American manufacturers once more got tariffs raised to the level they had been in the manufacturing states during the Confederation, and the American merchant was soon to lose the dominating position he had held in American society for so many years.

15

The States, the Taxpayers, and the Debtors

THE MOST complex problem facing Americans after the Revolution was that of public and private finance. The Revolution resulted in a staggering burden of public debt as compared with colonial wars, which had been financed in part by cash grants from the British government. Furthermore, few Americans in 1775 envisaged the quantity of paper money that would be issued, or the way prices would rise. Laws passed to fix prices, and to make paper money legal tender in the payment of private debts and public taxes, all failed to stop the inflation that accompanied vast issues of paper money and wartime speculation and profiteering.

Despite exhortations by Congress and legislation by the states, inflation went on at so rapid a rate that in March 1780 Congress recommended that the states abolish old paper money as legal tender. At the same time Congress proposed a "new emission" of ten millions in paper to be backed by the states, but most of them refused to accept it. By the end of the war most of the states had declared that paper money was no longer legal tender in payment of private debts, and most of them refused to receive it for taxes.[1] While the states endeavored to meet expenses by specie

[1] State action can be traced in: Rhode Island *Acts and Resolves* (Nov. 1780), 20–4; *Laws of Maryland* (Hanson ed.), June 1780 session, ch. xxviii; Oct. 1780 session, ch. v; Hening, X, 412–3; *Acts of New Jersey* (Wilson ed.), 197–8, 204–5; Pennsylvania *Statutes at Large*, X, 337–44; *Laws of New York* (1886 ed.), I, 392; *Laws of New Hampshire*, IV, 411; Massachusetts *Acts and Resolves* (1780–1), 488–90, 709–11; South Carolina *Statutes at Large* (Cooper ed.), IV, 508–9; North Carolina *State Records*, XXIV, 485–8.

taxes and other means, they set about cancelling old continental and state money by heavy taxes levied for that purpose alone, or by converting old state money into an interest-bearing debt at a depreciated value.

Thus paper money, one of the most important means of financing the war, was largely repudiated. It was a method ancient at the time, and is still honored in practice. It relieved the central and state governments of a burden they could never have carried. But at the same time it was an act of deflation, for while the paper money was not worth much, it was the only medium of exchange for the average citizen.

The war brought great amounts of specie into the country. It might have served as an adequate money supply if widely distributed and if it had remained in the country. But merchants, anxious to resume commercial relations with Great Britain, exported the specie to pay for pre-war debts and post-war imports. The result was that within a year or two after the war, in a period of growing economic depression, there was a dearth of both paper money and hard money in the United States. The debtors and taxpayers were trapped. Everywhere during the 1780's they faced the problem of paying in hard money when none was to be had; and when they demanded paper money, the creditors rose in violent opposition.

At the end of the war state debts consisted largely of money owing to farmers and merchants for supplies, the remnants of depreciated currencies, and sums due to soldiers for back payments or inadequate pay. The total amount of the state debts may never be known with accuracy, for records were badly kept or are missing. The debt of Massachusetts was £1,468,554 in 1785;[2] Rhode Island's was nearly a half million dollars in 1783; New Hampshire's equaled that figure in 1784; while Connecticut had a debt of over three and three-quarter million dollars in 1783.[3] Pennsylvania contracted a debt of £4,641,535 during and after the war.[4] New York had a state debt of approximately

[2] Speech of Governor Bowdoin to the General Court, 20 Oct. 1785, Massachusetts *Acts and Resolves* (1784–5), 729.

[3] B. U. Ratchford: *American State Debts* (Durham, N. C., 1941), 45.

[4] John Nicholson to the Inhabitants of York County, *Pennsylvania Gazette*, 21 Feb. 1787.

£1,000,000 in 1790.[5] In 1784, the total debt of Virginia was estimated at £4,251,283.[6]

Whether these state debts should be paid off at the nominal figure or their current market value was a burning question during the 1780's. The payment of interest on the state debts, much less the principal, involved a burden of taxation undreamed of by Americans before the war. One estimate is that fifty to ninety per cent of state expenditures went for this purpose. The interest on the South Carolina state debt in 1786 was £83,184 out of a total expenditure of £103,526.[7] The interest alone on the Massachusetts state debt in 1785 was £88,112.[8] In 1784 a legislative committee estimated that Virginia's annual payments on interest and principal of the Revolutionary debt was £207,700 out of a total expenditure of £256,293.[9]

The new state governments were slow to levy heavy taxes on a people unaccustomed to paying them, and often without the means of doing so. The states did not begin taxing until 1777–8, and then only at low rates. Poll and general property taxes, and liquor, excise, and import duties were the main sources of tax revenue. For a time the sales of confiscated Loyalist estates added to the income of many states. After the war an important source of new revenue was the import duties levied by many states.

The income of state governments is a partial index to economic conditions. All too few figures are available, but these show that many of the states were working their way out of the financial difficulties resulting from the war. In New York imposts accounted for much of the state's income. From 21 September 1784 to 31 December 1785 it collected £184,486 from all sources, and of that amount over £90,000 came from the office of the customs collector in New York City. During 1786 the state's income was

[5] Thomas C. Cochran: *New York in the Confederation* (Philadelphia, 1932), 191. More than half of this consisted of national debt assumed by the state.

[6] 28 Dec. 1784, *Journal of the House of Delegates of the Commonwealth of Virginia* (Richmond, 1828), 88–90. By 1790 Virginia had reduced the debt to a little over a million pounds. Ibid., 28 Dec. 1790, 123.

[7] South Carolina *Statutes at Large* (Cooper ed.), IV, 739. The interest dropped to £64,000 in 1787. Ibid., V, 36.

[8] Gov. Bowdoin to the General Court, 20 Oct. 1785, Massachusetts *Acts and Resolves* (1784–5), 729.

[9] 28 Dec. 1784, Virginia House of Delegates *Journal*, 89–90. The committee reported that if further provisions were made for pensions, interest on loan office debt, and the like, the total expense to the state would be £435,118.

estimated at £249,038. That year the customs receipts dropped to about £33,000, the bulk of the "income" being a £200,000 issue of paper money in that year. Early in 1787 the state had a balance of £46,173 in the treasury. During 1787 the customs collections rose to over £48,000, and a special tax of the previous year brought in nearly £40,000. A balance of over £11,000 was left in the treasury at the end of the year.[10]

Virginia was even more successful in collecting revenue. In 1785–6 she took in £348,805. Over £40,000 was in tonnage and customs taxes, £27,637 in tobacco taxes, £128,985 in land and property taxes, and £127,000 in certificate taxes. In 1786–7 her tax collections grew to over £400,000. In 1787–8 the collections dropped to £305,000, as a result of the reduction in war certificate taxes, most of which had been taken in and destroyed by the state, and by the lowering of other taxes so bitterly opposed by the farmers. Not only did the state pay off a large part of its vast war debt, but the surplus in the treasury increased steadily. It was £25,905 in 1785–6 and climbed as high as £122,342 in 1787–8.[11]

If the incidence of taxation after the war had been just, complaints of its hardships and attacks on speculators in the public debt might have been less violent. One example of unfairness was taxation of land by the acre, regardless of value. In Virginia a tax of a shilling per one hundred acres was levied. Rich land paid no more than the poorest. In North Carolina land was taxed five shillings per hundred acres, although the land varied in value as much as in Virginia. There was sharp protest in both states. Back-country representatives in the legislature voiced the demands of their constituents. The result was that in 1782 Virginia divided the state into four "natural" regions for taxing lands.[12] In 1786 North Carolina was divided into three regions for the purpose of laying a graduated land tax.[13] South Carolina undertook a similar

[10] Cochran: *New York in the Confederation*, 188. New York had a good record of taxes collected during the war. Between 1778 and 1781 a total of over £2,-500,000 was paid into the treasury. Hamilton Papers, III, LC.

[11] W. F. Dodd: "The Effect of the Adoption of the Constitution upon the Finances of Virginia," *Virginia Magazine of History and Biography*, X (1903), 366, 369, n.

[12] Oct. 1782, Hening, XI, 140–2. Like acreage was taxed ten shillings in the tidewater, seven shillings six pence in the Piedmont, five shillings six pence in the valley, and three shillings beyond the Alleghenies.

[13] North Carolina *State Records*, XXIV, 802–3.

reform in 1784 when the back-country representatives secured the taxation of all land according to value.[14] In 1785 Georgia adopted an elaborate law valuing various kinds of land for purposes of taxation.[15]

In the North, taxation of real and personal property according to value was far more widespread than in the South. But the wealthy, particularly in Massachusetts, managed to shift much of the burden because the legislature raised a large part of state revenues from poll taxes.[16] The poll tax was opposed by poorer citizens, but only Virginia responded by abandoning it for a time.[17]

The inequalities of the tax structure, the heavy taxes levied to pay interest and principal on the war debt, and the difficulty of finding means to pay taxes, all led to sharp conflict. This became bitter as the debt accumulated in the hands of speculators. In Virginia soldiers who had been given military certificates were reported to be selling them for only a small part of their face value, even before the end of the war. An indignant officer reported that a soldier sold a £48 certificate for £4 and predicted that the soldiers would be ruined unless steps were taken to prevent "such base advantages." [18] In Massachusetts in 1782 many ex-soldiers were said to have sold their securities to sharpers for almost nothing, and it was predicted that the soldiers would turn to mob violence unless paid or allowed to use their certificates to pay taxes.[19]

The policies of the states varied as they undertook the payment of their debts. Despite the charge that the bulk of the state debts had passed into the hands of a few at enormous discounts, many of the state governments proposed to pay those debts at face

[14] 26 March 1784, South Carolina *Statutes at Large* (Cooper ed.), IV, 627–8.

[15] Georgia *Colonial Records*, XIX, pt. 2, 398–416.

[16] Harold H. Burbank: The General Property Tax in Massachusetts, 1775–1792, With Some Consideration of Colonial and Provincial Legislation and Practices (Ph. D. Thesis, Harvard University, 1915, [microfilm copy, WHS]), pt. 1, ch. ii, iii; pt. 2, ch. i.

[17] 1 Jan. 1788, Hening, XII, 431.

[18] William P. Palmer, H. W. Flournoy, eds.: *Calendar of Virginia State Papers* (11 vols., Richmond, 1875–93), III, 87; East: *Business Enterprise*, 270–2 for examples in other states.

[19] Joseph Hawley to Ephraim Wright, 16 April 178[2], AHR, XXXVI (1930–1), 776–8.

value. The over-burdened taxpayers demanded that debts be paid at their market value. The residents of James City, Virginia, for instance, petitioned the legislature in 1786 that military certificates be redeemed at their depreciated value.[20] Virginia made a determined and successful effort to pay its war debt. Its paper money was called in at one thousand to one, its current market value, and thus that "debt" was wiped out. The next biggest item was the vast number of military certificates issued to pay for supplies and to make up to Virginia soldiers their losses resulting from depreciation during the war. An unknown amount of such certificates was issued before 1782, and between 1782 and 1786 nearly a million pounds more. These certificates were paid off in two ways. Beginning in 1782 holders were allowed to exchange them for western lands, and in addition Virginia soon provided that taxes were payable in military certificates,[21] and even made it compulsory for some levies. The result of this form of taxation was that the state levied £625,000 in such taxes between 1783 and 1787, and thereby drastically reduced the largest remaining debt of the state.[22]

Massachusetts handled her war debt far differently than Virginia. Virginia called in its paper money at one thousand for one, and redeemed much of its certificate debt by laying heavy taxes payable in those certificates. Except for the soldier debt in Virginia, which received more favorable treatment, there was little opportunity for profitable speculation. Massachusetts had a paper debt of about £11,000,000 in 1780, most of which was due to be paid by 1785. In the spring of 1780 the provincial congress postponed specie payment on all state debts until 1788, but as soon as the legislature met under the new constitution of 1780, it repealed this moratorium as a great injustice to the creditors of the government. It provided for liquidation of the debt by a scale of depreciation that was a gift to speculators. Instead of exchanging old notes for new at the current market value, the legislature declared that they should be taken in at the market value at the time of issue. The new notes were known as "Consolidated Notes" and the process of exchange was virtually complete by the end of

[20] 3 Nov. 1786, Virginia House of Delegates *Journal*, 21.
[21] Hening, XI, 22, 93–5.
[22] 2 Dec. 1786, Virginia House of Delegates *Journal*, 83; 106–07.

1784. The remainder of the state debt consisted of "army notes" which were given to former soldiers to make up for the depreciated money with which they had been paid during the war. The total funded debt was about £1,600,000. If Massachusetts had funded her debt as Virginia did, it would have been about £627,000, a manageable sum.

As it was, the amount of this debt was at least double its actual market value at the time of consolidation. It was, of course, greeted as a "sound money" policy by the happy owners of the debt, but it placed a burden of taxes on the people that they could not pay—a burden which was probably greater than that borne by the taxpayers of any other state. Massachusetts levied enormous taxes and made earnest attempts to collect them in specie. Between 1780 and 1786 direct taxes amounting to nearly £1,900,000 were levied. About a third of this amount was for payment of requisitions from Congress, nearly £400,000 was for interest on the state debt, and the balance for payments on principal and for government expenses. Taxes thus averaged more than three pounds a year for each of the 90,000 adult males in the state. Even propertyless males were expected to pay more than one pound a year through the poll tax.[23]

In Massachusetts, as elsewhere, there were angry attacks on the speculators who had bought up the debt for only a small part of its face value, and there were demands that the debt be scaled down to its actual value. Thus it was argued, not only would justice be done, but the tax load could be reduced so that the citizens could pay it without bankruptcy.[24]

Such demands were ignored, for the mercantile-creditor group had a firm grip on the government of the state. They owned most of the debt. They levied heavy taxes and shifted the burden onto the farmers who were least able to pay it. It is estimated that at least a third of an average farmer's income went in taxes after 1780. From thirty-three to forty per cent of the taxes levied were poll taxes, which bore most heavily on the poor, and particularly on the farmers on barren land in the western part of the state. Furthermore the laws demanded that most of the taxes be paid in

[23] Whitney K. Bates: The State Finances of Massachusetts, 1780–1789 (M. A. Thesis, University of Wisconsin, 1948), is the only clear statement I have seen of the relationship between state financial policy in Massachusetts and the debtors and taxpayers.

[24] *Massachusetts Centinel*, 8, 11, 15, 18, 22 Feb., 1, 4 March 1786.

specie, although a temporary "tender" law passed in 1782 allowed payment in kind for a few months.

The problem of tax collection is illuminated by the troubles of Constable Hoskins of Taunton. He seized a yoke of oxen for arrears in taxes, but when he offered them for sale "a few of the rabble" appeared and threatened to knock down anyone who bid. The constable then adjourned the sale to a later day. Once more the "rabble" appeared after mustering help from nearby towns. They swore that no more animals should be seized for taxes, they damned "all authority," and one Nathan Button swore that he hoped the British standard would be raised on Taunton Green. The local gentry gathered to bid and to "defend ourselves" and after considerable scuffling, the cattle were "struck off to one of our party." [25]

In addition, the courts functioned as the agents of the creditor interests demanding the payment of private debts. People lost both real and personal property and were jailed for unpaid balances. Often men were jailed for the pettiest debts, and sometimes for large ones. In Plymouth a local diarist reported: "At one o'clock came through the streets two officers and J. T. Esqr., with a rabble round them; they were carrying Mr. T. to jail upon execution for £225; he was in his slippers, wading through mud and wet; they stopped at the tavern, and the people were enraged at the officer; the gentlemen undertook to be answerable for Mr. T., to deliver the body or the money or sufficient security by Saturday night. . . ." [26]

There were rumbles of anger at the injustice of what was essentially the confiscation of property by legal process even before the war was over. Massachusetts farmers began holding county conventions in 1782. Hampshire County had seven of them in 1782 and 1783. The more conservative members wanted to send dutiful petitions to the legislature, while the more radical wanted to take violent action and prevent the courts from sitting.[27]

The state government did nothing to alleviate distress as the war came to an end. The courts continued to be filled with debt cases. In Worcester County in 1784 there were over 2,000 suits for

[25] Seth Padelford to Robert Treat Paine, 23 July 1782, Paine Papers, MHS.

[26] 1 April 1785, Fitch E. Oliver, ed.: *The Diary of William Pynchon of Salem* (Boston and New York, 1890), 209–10.

[27] Harlow: CSM *Publications*, XX, 185–8.

recovery of debts; in 1785 in the same county, ninety-four of the 104 people sent to jail were sent there for debts they could not pay.[28]

As the tension increased and the state government did nothing, an outpouring of people began that was eventually to carry New England institutions and town names all the way from Portland and Salem, New England, to Portland and Salem, Oregon. By 1784 cash was so scarce and the "rage for emigration" was so great that lands could not be sold for anything near their value.[29] In 1785 it was reported that "in almost all parts of the country, the people experience a scarcity of cash unknown in any former period. The goals being crowded with debtors, who find it impossible to raise money to pay their debts."[30] Despite unrest and obvious distress, the state government did nothing until open rebellion broke out in the western counties in the fall of 1786. In November of that year taxes assessed before 1784 were made payable in such articles as beef, pork, flax, leather, iron, whale oil, and the like. Another act the same month suspended the specie collection of private debts for eight months and allowed personal or real estate to be used to pay debts. Both acts appear to be the result of the outbreak of Shays's Rebellion rather than of any change of heart on the part of the creditor group in the legislature.[31]

When the latter act came up for extension the creditors continued to oppose it as unjust, impolitic, and unconstitutional. The proponents of the bill argued the scarcity of money and the low price at which property was sold to pay debts before the passage of the bill. The majority of the newly elected legislature was behind them and by successive acts extended the bill until June of 1788.[32]

The hard-pressed taxpayer was to be found in other states, but not all of them treated their citizens so harshly as Massachusetts. In 1785 when Massachusetts levied its heaviest tax of

[28] Walter A. Dyer: "Embattled Farmers," NEQ, IV (1931), 463.

[29] Theodore Sedgwick to Philip Van Rensselaer, Emmet Coll., no. 542, NYPL.

[30] *Massachusetts Centinel*, 14 May.

[31] 8, 15 Nov. 1786, Massachusetts *Acts and Resolves* (1786–87), 90–7, 113–6. A new legislature elected in the spring of 1787 levied no direct tax in that year, and taxes were much lighter in the years following. Bates: Massachusetts Finances, 128–32 and appendix iii.

[32] *Massachusetts Centinel*, 7, 10 Nov. 1787. The act was extended 30 June and 15 Nov. of 1787 and 26 March 1788, Massachusetts *Acts and Resolves* (1786–87), 560, 576–7, 622–3.

the period—about a pound per poll—the other New England states levied taxes only a fourth as large. Throughout the period, the latter shaped tax laws more nearly to economic realities.

The payment of private debts was a burden equally great. Men who could pay both debts and taxes at once were few and far between. Here, too, the other New England states were more liberal than Massachusetts. New Hampshire passed a tender law which ran from 1785 to 1789. Rhode Island had first a tender law and then paper money which could be loaned to the debtor. Connecticut refused to pass either tender or paper money laws, but the legislature relieved the pressure on individuals and on towns by abating taxes as the need arose and by increasing the time during which individuals might pay their debts and taxes.[33]

In the South, the Virginia legislature faced the same problem of reluctant and often impoverished taxpayers, particularly in the western part of the state. Virginia law allowed foreclosures when taxes were not paid, but often county sheriffs could not enforce the law. One sheriff reported that when he did seize property, men came at night and carried off the horses and slaves. Some taxpayers simply refused to pay taxes until their tobacco was sold, and threatened to shoot the sheriff if he seized their property.[34] Still other sheriffs could not find the taxpayers, much less their property. Sheriffs' reports repeatedly included after the names of taxpayers such laconic remarks as "backwoods," "not found," "no effects," "over Allegheny," "run away," "gone to Georgia," "gone to Kentucky," and "moved to Carolina." Petitions from county after county declared that lack of specie, high prices, and even such factors as the weather and poor roads made it impossible to pay taxes.[35] The sheriffs themselves listed scarcity of money, the poverty of the people, the low price of tobacco, and the fact that people did not want to pay taxes, as the most important reasons for difficulties in collections.[36]

The sharpest complaints came from the western counties where

[33] A careful comparison of the policies of the New England states is Richard D. Herschcopf: The New England Farmer and Politics, 1785–1787 (M. A. Thesis, University of Wisconsin, 1947). On Connecticut see Connecticut *State Records*, VI, *passim.*

[34] Sheriff Thomas Johnson to the Governor, 19 Jan. 1786, *Calendar of Virginia State Papers*, IV, 82.

[35] Low: Virginia in the Critical Period, 116, 118–19.

[36] *Calendar of Virginia State Papers*, IV, 9–10, 77–78, 185, 377–78 for examples.

much wheat and hemp, and relatively little tobacco, was grown. The Virginia legislature acted realistically, for however conservative many of its members might be, most of them were farmers and were far more sympathetic with farmers' problems than a legislature like that of Massachusetts. The Virginia legislature allowed westerners to pay taxes in hemp and flour, but it went even farther, for it suspended or lowered taxes when the protests became too great. In May 1784 all tax collections were suspended for six months.[37] In October of the same year another act relieved the people of half of the revenue taxes for the year 1785. The reason given in the law was that the taxes could not be collected "without great distress of the citizens of this commonwealth." [38] Taxes were reduced one third in 1788 because of nonpayment, and were cut one fourth for 1789.[39]

Thus Virginia shaped tax policy with an eye to the capacities of the taxpayers, and yet at the same time it managed to collect handsome revenues and to pay off a large part of the state debt. Furthermore, the opponents of paper money were able in this way to prevent its issuance although as late as the spring of 1787 the governor said "that paper money is hastening into popularity with great strides." [40]

[37] Hening, XI, 368.
[38] Ibid., XI, 540–3.
[39] Ibid., XII, 707–8; ibid., XIII, 29.
[40] Edmund Randolph to [Edward Carrington], 11 April 1787, Emmet Coll., no. 9375, NYPL.

16

The Debtors, the Creditors, and State Aid: The Paper Money Movement

THE PAPER money that was "hastening into popularity" in Virginia was one of the hottest issues in state politics during the Confederation. By 1786 clamorous public creditors and harassed taxpayers and debtors had forced seven of the states to adopt some form of paper money. The success of this movement in a majority of the states, and the threat of it in the others, created as much fear among conservative men of property as any other thing that happened during the Confederation. It was to this paper money movement that Edmund Randolph made particular reference in his opening speech in the Convention of 1787 when he spoke of the danger of democracy and the feebleness of the state senates as a check against it. The Constitution, when finished, included among the restraints on the states a clause forbidding the states to "coin money; emit bills of credit; make anything but gold and silver coin a tender in payment of debts. . . ."

After the Convention, Madison explained to Jefferson that some negative on state laws was necessary to secure the rights of individuals, for "the mutability of the laws of the states is found to be a serious evil. . . ." He went on to say that "the evils issuing from these sources contributed more to the uneasiness which produced the convention . . . than those which accrued to our national character and interest from the inadequacy of the Confederation. . . ." Finally, he declared that he did not feel that there were adequate "restraints against paper emissions, and violations of contracts" in the Constitution.[1]

[1] 24 Oct. 1787, *Writings* (Hunt ed.), V, 27–8.

The interests of the men who wrote the Constitution of 1787 were opposed to those of the debtors and ordinary taxpayers whose problems were at least as great as those of the artisans and the merchants. There had been more than enough "money" of various sorts during the war, but within a year after it there was a desperate scarcity. Wartime paper money was wiped out by 1783. The large amounts of specie on hand soon went overseas to pay for pre-war debts and post-war imports. The notes issued by the new banks circulated mostly among merchants. The various forms of public debt were more widely scattered, but they were being taxed out of existence or concentrated in the hands of speculators.

Thus the farmers, who made up the vast majority of the population, and who were the principal taxpayers and debtors, had little with which to pay the demands of state governments and private creditors. The farmer might raise ever larger crops, but he got little actual money in what was of necessity a barter system of exchange. Yet most of the states and the creditors demanded specie in payment. The private creditors kept up an unceasing clamor against "leniency," against any interference with the "sacred obligation of contracts."

The answer to the problem of the taxpayer and debtor was an answer with which most Americans were familiar, however much they might differ as to its merits. The taxpayers and debtors demanded government aid, as did the merchants and artisans. In some states, as we have seen, taxes were rebated or lowered when protests were loud or arrears in collections were large enough to demonstrate to even the most conservative legislator that the taxes levied could not be collected. Some states also passed laws providing for taxation more nearly in relation to ability to pay. But such measures did not meet the needs and desires of an agrarian majority in most of the states. Hence there was a continuous, growing clamor for paper money which could be used to pay taxes and private debts, and which could be used by the state governments to pay interest and principal on their own debts, and thus lower taxes.

This demand was continuous from the end of the war. In general it came from the rural sections, but there were startling exceptions. Most of the farmers who wanted paper money were small farmers, but in Maryland planter speculators who had bought more land than they could pay for were also behind the movement.[2] Most merchants opposed paper money, but in South Carolina the American merchants supported it and maintained it at par value.[3] Politicians like Patrick Henry, sensing the popular demand, supported it as a matter of course. But in general the split was between the debtor and the creditor in all the states.

The newspaper argument for and against paper money was endless. Those for it wrote of the lack of currency of any kind, of the sale of lands and goods for far less than their real value, and of the impoverishment of the people. The argument of "Crisis" in New Hampshire is typical of those who wanted paper money. He said he was glad "so great a man" as President Sullivan had admitted the existence of public distress. There were those who said that conditions were "ideal." Some said there was as much specie in the country as ever, that imports were cheap, that tradesmen charged too much for labor and lived too high, that there were enough state notes, final settlement certificates, and the like, to provide a currency; that the distresses of the people were imaginary and arose from faction, discontent, and the debtors. People who argued thus were the real oppressors, said "Crisis." They wanted to keep the poor as tenants, "reduce" the farmer, and lower the price of produce. What if imports were low priced, only those with specie could buy. The existing "facilities" were no good because they were not legal tender. This was just as well, for the various forms of debt were all in the hands of rich speculators who had bought them up at a seventy-five per cent discount. The need was for paper money "or even leather buttons, when stamped with authority and funded with realities, will answer for internal commerce as well as silver and gold." Several states have adopted it, bringing harmony, plenty, happiness. Let us do the same,[4] wrote "Crisis."

The other side of the case was presented by "Primitive Whig" in New Jersey. American character is declining, he said. Those who grumble and do not want to pay taxes are the laborer who works perhaps two days a week, gets twice what he earns, and spends the rest of his time in taverns; the London trader who makes more in two years than in ten years of honest work; and

[2] Crowl: *Maryland*, ch. iv.

[3] *New Haven Gazette*, 27 July 1786; *Pennsylvania Packet*, 17 Aug. 1786.

[4] "Crisis," *New Hampshire Gazette*, 20 July 1786.

the farmer who sends his daughters to a French dancing master when they ought to be home at the spinning wheel and clad in homespun. Only idle spendthrifts want paper money. They are the "dissipating drones of the community, who have felt the sweets, during the legal tender of depreciated paper, of living upon the sweat of their neighbor's brows; by those same drones, who, instead of repenting in sackcloth and ashes, for their late circumvention of their creditors, want to repeat the risk of being condemned for their meditated fraud. . . ." Where is the man of property or the man out of debt who is for paper money? It will be said that they are self-interested because they are creditors. This is true, but there is a great difference. "The interest of the creditor coincides with that of the community. Not so the interest of the debtor. The former desires no more than his own. The latter wants to pocket the property of another." One wants to restore the national credit by opposing fraudulent paper money, the other prolongs the disease. What has the legislature to do with farmers who have borrowed money to buy land and are now losing it? Such debtors are the objects of private compassion "but they are not the subjects of public legislation." The legislature did not involve them and is under no obligation to extricate them. It is better to leave a few individuals to the mercy of their creditors than to "set all property afloat. . . ."[5]

In the end, of course, the outcome depended on control of state legislatures rather than on argument. Pennsylvania was the first state to adopt paper money, and it did so as the Constitutionalists returned to power in 1785. But even in Pennsylvania, where party lines were usually so clearly drawn, there was confusion. The demand for paper money came partly from creditors of the state and of the United States, who wanted interest payments on their holdings. A group of Philadelphia creditors had organized and were sending repeated appeals to the legislature. They declared that not only did merchants who had invested in public funds need aid, but so did many widows, orphans, and aged whose livelihood depended on interest on their certificates.[6]

The Philadelphia merchants were split by the idea. Many of

[5] "Primitive Whig," nos. I, II, III, IV, *New Jersey Gazette*, reprinted in the *Pennsylvania Gazette*, 18, 25 Jan., 1, 8 Feb. 1786. "Primitive Whig" was Governor Livingston of New Jersey.

[6] Philadelphia *Freeman's Journal,* 21 July, 1 Dec. 1784.

them, particularly the followers of Robert Morris and the Bank of North America, did not want paper money. But other merchants, and particularly the heavy speculators in state and national debt, wanted interest paid on their holdings. Such men found allies among western leaders whose constituents were laden with taxes they could not pay. The result was a coalition between Philadelphia speculators and western politicians which proposed that the state issue paper money which could be used to pay the interest on the debt and could be loaned on farm mortgages. Since Pennsylvanians owned about a third of the national debt, payment of interest on it meant one of three things: an enormous new tax load, a loan, or an issue of paper money. The Bank of North America tried to block paper money by offering the state £300,000 but the westerners and the Philadelphia enemies of the bank refused to take the loan. Instead, they proposed to destroy the bank and its control of the credit of Pennsylvania and to put the state in its place as the source of money and credit.

The legislature issued £150,000 in bills of credit. Two-thirds of it was to pay interest on state and national debt owned by Pennsylvanians; the other third was set aside to be loaned on farm mortgages. These bills could be used to buy land from the state, to pay debts due the state, to pay arrears in taxes, and to pay customs and import duties. However, the creditor interests won a partial victory, for the money could not be used to pay private debts.[7]

Despite predictions of calamity, the money did not depreciate at first although its enemies were accused of trying to force it down by every means in their power.[8] By the summer of 1786 it was reported that the money had depreciated only seven and a half per cent despite "wicked and wanton attempts" of its enemies.[9] In 1787 the state decided to loan no more on real estate and began to destroy the money as it came in on payments. By the end of 1787, £40,000 had been destroyed. By 1789 the money no longer circulated and by 1793 less than £10,000 was left.[10]

[7] Pennsylvania *Statutes at Large*, XI, 454–86; *Pennsylvania Packet*, 24 Feb., 1, 8, 18 March 1785. The struggle over the assumption of interest payments on the national debt is discussed in ch. xix.

[8] *Pennsylvania Packet*, 28 June, 22 July 1785.

[9] Boston *American Herald*, 26 June 1786.

[10] *Report of the Register-General of the State of the Finances of Pennsylvania for the Year 1792*, appendix to *Journal*, Penn. House of Representatives, 1792–3 session.

The drive for paper money in Pennsylvania, which produced an unnatural alliance of western farmers and public creditors, had no precise counterpart in any other state. Yet there were alliances equally strange. An example is to be found in South Carolina which also issued paper money in 1785. The planters had lost thousands of slaves during the war. British merchants who stayed when the British army left provided the new slaves and the necessary credit with which to buy them. The result was an enormous load of debt acquired by planters within a matter of months. What happened was explained by the diarist Timothy Ford. He said: "A number of British merchants found means to remain in the country and foreseeing the great demand there would be for slaves and being the only persons possessed of capital they early imported vast cargoes from Africa. The planters impelled by their necessities to procure slaves eagerly grasped at the first opportunities that offered; and unable to pay down the cash, supplied themselves on credit, at whatever rate the British merchants were pleased to fix; and they failed not to take advantage of their necessities and advanced upon them from 50 to 75 per cent." [11] The British merchants were thus a large creditor element in South Carolina, but there were also American merchants to whom the planters owed money, and who in turn owed money to British merchants. As creditors, the American merchants were opposed to paper money, but as debtors of local British merchants they could see its uses.

When the legislature met in 1785 the governor told it that something must be done for the debtors. If not, all their property would go to "aliens" at far less than its real value. The governor proposed the issuance of £400,000 in paper money, and the fight was on.[12] Opponents soon realized that they could not block an issue so they fought to make it as small as possible and to prevent it from being made legal tender in payment of private debts. The result was a compromise that provided for an issue of £100,000 to be loaned out on land mortgages. This money could then be used for payments of all debts, duties, and taxes due the

[11] "Diary of Timothy Ford," *South Carolina Historical and Genealogical Magazine*, XIII (1912), 193.

[12] *Pennsylvania Packet*, 3 Nov. 1785; Singer: *South Carolina in the Confederation*, 20–2.

state after 1 May 1786.[13] The state in turn was to use the money to pay interest on the state debt.

Unlike merchants in most states, the Charleston merchants supported the paper money, for they could buy with it but they did not have to accept it on old debts. The planters objected at first because it did not solve the problem of their old debts. The result was that the money began to depreciate. Thereupon the merchants agreed to take the money only at par value and to refuse to buy from anyone who did not. A "Hint Club" was organized to "hurl down vengeance" on all speculators and depreciators. Eventually the planters agreed to support the money, eighty-three of them around Charleston alone signing a document to that effect.

This, along with the extraordinary boom in South Carolina exports that was apparent by 1786, made the paper money of South Carolina one of the success stories of its kind. By 1789 the bills were being used in preference to specie. The state treasury was still accepting the notes in 1815. David Ramsay reported that the state had made a profit of $300,000 on them by 1808.[14]

In North Carolina there was a clear-cut fight between debtor farmers and planters on one hand, and the merchants and a few wealthy planters on the other. The result was a sweeping victory for the debtors in the passage of a bill issuing £100,000 of paper money. The stated purpose of the bill was to help the state pay its share of the United States foreign debt, to pay part of the interest and principal owing to North Carolina soldiers and officers of the Continental Army, to redeem the interest certificates issued by continental loan officers in the state, and to provide money so that men could pay their debts. The money was legal tender in all cases. Thirty-six thousand pounds was set aside to buy tobacco. This tobacco was to be shipped abroad and the hard money received was to be turned over to Congress to help pay the foreign debt. The balance was used to pay off

[13] 12 Oct. 1785, South Carolina *Statutes at Large* (Cooper ed.), IV, 712–6. The money could be loaned on deposits of silver and gold plate as well as on land. Interest was seven per cent and the principal had to be paid within five years.

[14] Ramsay: *History of South Carolina*, II, 185. Newspapers in every state followed the South Carolina experiment with close attention. The *Pennsylvania Packet*, the *New Haven Gazette*, the Boston *American Herald*, and others reported events in detail.

one-fourth of what the ex-soldiers had coming. A tax law was attached to pay off the paper money but the payments under it could be in various other forms of paper, as well as the money itself, so it was no burden to the taxpayers.[15]

Confusion reigned, and corruption entered in at once. State agents offered twice the market price for tobacco, which made it impossible for private merchants to buy. Merchants refused to take paper money in payment for goods. The state tried to sell the tobacco but could not. The board of treasury in New York, anxious for money, urged Robert Morris to buy the tobacco but he offered only half of what the state had paid for it. The state by now had more than a million pounds of tobacco. Would-be buyers swore that a third of it was spoiled. Eventually Governor Caswell was forced to sell, the tobacco bringing about one half of what it had cost in paper money. The loss was not great for the paper had depreciated meanwhile. Purchasers paid the money into the treasury of the United States, and North Carolina was eventually credited with a little over $60,000. The money had not cost the state anything but the printing bill, the planters had gotten help in paying their debts, the United States got cash, and the tobacco commissioners were charged with corruption.

Meanwhile prominent men were appointed to liquidate the soldiers' accounts and to pay them their portion of paper money. Soon it was rumored that certificates were being forged, given in blank, and given to men who had performed no military service. The result was a series of trials and fines and imprisonment for some of the men who had defrauded the soldiers and the state. The North Carolina merchants who had opposed the issue from the start likewise helped to ruin the paper money and the combination of corruption, opposition, and depreciation gave the state's currency almost as bad a reputation as that of Rhode Island. Before the end of the 1780's North Carolina began calling in and destroying its paper money.[16]

The history of paper money in New York is in sharp contrast to that of North Carolina. Demand for it came from the farming counties and opposition came from New York City and nearby

[15] James Iredell and Francois X. Martin, eds.: *The Public Acts of the General Assembly of North Carolina* (2 vols., Newbern, 1804), I, 393–5.

[16] The materials for this story are scattered through the *State Records* for the years 1785–9.

districts. The assembly passed two paper money bills in 1784 and a third in 1785, but all were killed by the senate. By 1786 the paper money party in the assembly was stronger than ever and the senate had new and more sympathetic members.

The argument in the newspapers repeated what was being said in other states. The New York Chamber of Commerce denounced paper money in no uncertain terms and demanded that if it were issued, despite all the warnings, it should not be legal tender.[17] Thomas Paine's essay: his "Dissertations on Government; the Affairs of the Bank; and Paper Money" was published widely in the newspapers and in pamphlet form.[18] Money was money and paper was paper, he said. Gold and silver were emissions of nature and paper was an emission of art. The value of gold and silver was changeless. Issue paper money and the whole system of safety would be overturned and property set afloat. It would turn the people into stockjobbers and prevent the importation of gold and silver. Hobnails and wampum were worth more than paper money. Tender laws destroyed morality and any member of the legislature who proposed such a law should be punished by death. Paper money was like drinking: it relieved for a moment and then left the body worse than it found it. Paine proposed that the state borrow bank notes from the bank, the bank in turn being required to exchange its notes for hard money at stated intervals.

Such arguments, however soothing to the opponents of paper money, did not convince those who wanted it and who were not impressed by the argument that debtors would cheat creditors. It was not unknown that those who talked most loudly about the dangers of depreciation had bought up depreciated certificates from soldiers and hoped to be paid in full, or to use them to buy lands.[19]

In the spring of 1786 the assembly passed still another paper money bill and at last the senate was forced to agree. The bill provided for £200,000 in paper. Of that amount £150,000 was set aside to be loaned on real estate. The other £50,000 was to be used to pay one fifth of the interest due on the state and national debt owned by the citizens of New York. This money could be

[17] Spaulding: *New York in The Critical Period*, 144–50.
[18] Reprinted in Paine: *Writings* (Conway ed.), II, 133–87.
[19] East: *Business Enterprise*, 225.

used to pay taxes and import duties and it was declared to be legal tender if a creditor sued for the collection of debts.[20]

This issue did not have any of the dire results predicted for it. It did not depreciate, for the creditors knew they must take it if they tried to collect debts in the courts. The Bank of New York accepted the money. Even Hamilton agreed that the money was successful.[21] The public creditors got their holdings consolidated and part of their interest paid. With the new certificates they could buy confiscated estates and state lands. The debtor farmers were not helped much except when they were sued, but the payment of taxes was made easier, although the arrears were large for years thereafter. Thus, like Pennsylvania and South Carolina, New York adopted a workable, and on the whole, conservative scheme to solve the money problems that faced it.

The unhappiest opponents were stubborn tutors at Columbia College who refused to take the money except at a discount. They argued that they had been promised their pay in gold and silver, and furthermore, they had to pay cash for the books they imported. At once they were attacked as "college coxcombs." They were told that the paper was as good as specie in the stores and that it even circulated in neighboring states at par, and that only book importers supported them.[22]

Three more states issued paper money during 1786. New Jersey farmers had heavy debts and were hit by falling prices in 1785 as were farmers in other states. Governor Livingston, who wrote lively tracts against paper money, vetoed the first attempt to issue it in 1785, but he soon changed his mind. In May 1786, the state issued £100,000 to be loaned on real estate mortgages at six per cent interest. The money was made legal tender in payment of all public and private debts. Furthermore, £30,000 of "revenue money" which had been issued in 1781 was also declared legal tender in all payments.

At first the money was well received in the state. But New York and Philadelphia merchants, with whom New Jersey citizens had

[20] 18 April 1786, *Laws of New York* (1886 ed.), II, 253–72. Double security was required for money loaned on land and triple security if loaned on houses. Five per cent interest was charged; one tenth of the principal was due in 1791 and one tenth each year thereafter until the debt was paid.

[21] *Works* (Lodge ed.), II, 37, 41–42. See also *Pennsylvania Packet*, 31 Jan., 23 June 1787.

[22] New York *Daily Advertiser*, 29, 31 May; 3, 5 June 1788.

to deal whether they liked it or not, would not take the money at par. They started by discounting it at least fifteen per cent. The result was inevitable: by 1789 the money was no longer a circulating medium although it was still used to pay taxes. Furthermore, the money continued to exist, for as late as 1800 the state agreed to exchange specie for the money of 1786.[23]

In Georgia the back-country members of the legislature, supported by the governor and council, agreed to issue £50,000 to finance a possible war against the Creek Indians and to pay arrears due Georgia's soldiers of the Revolution. Actually only £30,000 was ever issued since the war did not materialize. The money was made legal tender in all cases. A large tract of land, still in the possession of the Indians, was pledged to pay off the issue within four years. This, said a letter from Savannah, was selling the bearskin before catching the bear.[24]

The money began to depreciate almost at once. Citizens around Savannah, both merchants and mechanics, were accused of refusing to take it. Merchants agreed to support it, but little was done and by 1787 it had fallen to four to one. It ceased to be legal tender in 1790, but some of it was in existence as late as 1830.[25]

Of the seven states that issued paper money, Rhode Island has received the most attention and has been the butt of the most violent attacks, both at the time and in histories since then. Rhode Island's reputation for unorthodoxy had been founded by Roger Williams and her citizens maintained it with fervor during the Confederation. During the war it had been occupied for a time by the British. Newport had been ruined as a commercial city. Providence and its merchants, however, made money during the war and for a time dominated the politics of the state. Meanwhile, farmers demanded relief. In March 1786 a paper money bill was defeated but personal and certain articles of real property were made legal tender if the creditor sued his debtor.[26]

This did not satisfy the paper money party and in the April

[23] McCormick: New Jersey in the Confederation, ch. viii, "Money the Familiar Remedy."

[24] *Pennsylvania Packet*, 9 Oct. 1786.

[25] Amanda Johnson: *Georgia as Colony and State* (Atlanta, 1938), 174; *Pennsylvania Packet*, 9 Oct., 22 Dec. 1786.

[26] Frank G. Bates: *Rhode Island and the Formation of the Union* (New York, 1898), 121; *Pennsylvania Packet*, 1 May 1786.

elections forty-five new men out of a total of seventy were sent to the assembly.[27] As soon as the legislature met, a motion for paper money was introduced. The usual heated debate followed, with all the usual arguments on both sides.[28] Despite the violent opposition led by the delegates from Providence, the legislature passed a bill issuing £100,000. The money was divided among the towns according to the most recent tax levies. Every freeholder could borrow an equal share. Loans were repayable within fourteen years. Interest was four per cent for the first seven years, but there was no interest at all for the last seven. The money so issued was declared legal tender in payment of taxes and private debts.

Creditors were swatted with brutal directness. If any creditor refused to accept the paper, his debtor might deposit the money with one of the judges of a county court. The judge was then to inform the creditor that he could collect from the court. If he did not, the judge was to advertise that the debt had been paid. If the creditor did not appear within three months, the money was to be taken by the state.[29] An enormous uproar followed in Rhode Island, while newspapers outside the state pictured the iniquities of the Rhode Island legislature in glaring colors. Rhode Island merchants refused to accept the bills and many closed their stores in a "strike" against them. Riots broke out as citizens tried to force the merchants to sell for paper. Around Providence farmers refused to sell produce. Similar boycotts were proposed in other towns. The legislature passed an act declaring that anyone refusing to take the money at face value would be fined £100 for a first offense and would have to pay a similar fine and lose his rights as a citizen for the second. A special session of the legislature in August 1786 provided further penalties and stipulated in addition that the money could be used to pay continental requisitions. However, Congress condemned the money and refused to take it. Meanwhile, harried creditors all over Rhode Island fled from their debtors, some even leaving the state. Attempts were made to pay debts outside the state in such towns as Boston, and even Rhode Island merchants took advantage of the law to pay debts they owed.

[27] Bates: *Rhode Island*, 123.
[28] Boston *American Herald*, 15 May 1786.
[29] Rhode Island, *Acts and Resolves* (May 1786), 13–7.

The crisis came in December before the supreme court of the state. John Weeden, a butcher of Newport, had refused to take the paper at par value from John Trevett. The butcher was defended by two conservative leaders, General James M. Varnum and Henry Marchant. They insisted that the forcing act had expired, that the butcher should be tried before a special court rather than the supreme court, and that furthermore, it was unconstitutional to try a man without a jury as the "forcing" act had provided.

Four of the five judges voted to dismiss the complaint on the ground that they had no jurisdiction. However, they gave it as their opinion that the law was unconstitutional. This action was greeted with joy by the merchants, who once more opened their shops. But the legislature again met in special session and called the judges before it. Two of them stayed away but the other three appeared and explained that the case did not belong in the supreme court. The legislature then dismissed them. Nevertheless it still proposed to force the use of paper money, even to the extent of requiring every citizen to take a "test" oath to support it and providing that no one could hold office unless he did take it. The test bill was finally voted down and in December the forcing acts were repealed. After this the money depreciated rapidly because the merchants refused to accept it on any except their own terms. The legal tender clause was finally repealed in the fall of 1789.

The Rhode Island debtors won a complete victory in passing legislation, but they were defeated by the economic power of the merchants. Many debtors doubtless paid their debts and they had been helped to pay taxes. Outside the state, Rhode Island was pointed to as the most horrible example of untrammeled democracy in action. The fact that the majority of the states that issued paper money had done so successfully was lost sight of in the uproar over Rhode Island.[30]

In the remaining six states the demand for paper money was blocked by head-on collisions, as in Massachusetts, or by yielding to pressure in other ways, as in Virginia and Connecticut.

Certain conclusions are evident for the seven states where paper money was issued. First of all, it was far more than a paper

[30] Bates: *Rhode Island,* 123–48. Virtually every newspaper in the United States carried accounts of the events in Rhode Island.

money issue: in five states—Pennsylvania, New York, New Jersey, South Carolina, and Rhode Island—it was a means of state loans on farm mortgage security. Not until a century and a quarter later were the needs of the farmers to be fully recognized and their demands met by the establishment of the Federal farm loan banks, which served one of the main purposes of the "paper money" laws of the 1780's. Still another purpose was served. In Pennsylvania, New York, North Carolina, Rhode Island, and New Jersey the money issues were used to fund state debts and in Pennsylvania, New York, and New Jersey they were used to fund the national debt.

Another issue involved in the 1780's was to plague American politics for generations. Should governments or private banks provide the money and the credit of the United States? During the 1780's a majority of the citizens believed that governments, not private banks, should be the source of money and credit at reasonable rates of interest.

The struggle over paper money was a clear demonstration of the political power of agrarian majorities when aroused. Its issuance in some measure served to relieve the plight of the debtor farmers and the taxpayers who were hard hit by the lack of money and by the enormous burden of post-war taxes levied to pay off the relatively small number of public creditors. At the same time, the struggle illustrated the direct economic power of the creditor and mercantile elements of the new nation. Where they were willing to support paper money, whatever their motives, as in Pennsylvania, New York, and South Carolina, it worked well, relieved distress, and in some cases made handsome profits for the state. In North Carolina, New Jersey, and Rhode Island, the opposition of the merchants did much to defeat the effectiveness of the paper money issues.

Nevertheless, the success of the debtor-taxpayer in seven of the states, qualified though it was, added mightily to the fears of those who disliked the workings of what they called democracy. Above all, as Madison said, it was this "mutability" of state laws which did more to contribute to the "uneasiness" which produced the Convention of 1787 than almost any other fact during the 1780's.

17
The States and Their Neighbors

THE STORY of major emotional and economic crises in the states, such as the return of the Loyalists and the campaign for paper money, does not end the account of political strife. Personalities in politics continued to play an enormous role. John Hancock, George Clinton, and Patrick Henry wielded much power in their states, partly as a result of their personal qualities. In the annual elections of every state there were controversies that can be described in many ways: struggles between ins and outs, democratic and anti-democratic forces, farmers and merchants, debtors and creditors, easterners and westerners, speculators and taxpayers, townspeople and countrymen, religious and irreligious. Lines formed and re-formed with changing issues and the passage of time. Certain issues, however, had a broader significance, as we have seen in the accounts of economic policies to be adopted by state governments. Of equal importance were the problems arising from the rapid expansion of the states and from the relations of the states with one another.

The rapid expansion outward to the frontiers had long been a source of conflict in colonial society. During the Confederation that conflict took two forms. Men in older settled areas of the frontier demanded that state capitals be moved away from the coast, while continued expansion resulted in a demand for the creation of new states within the boundaries of old ones.

The back-country citizens in virtually all the states east of the Alleghenies had long wanted the seats of government located nearer themselves, and this demand increased as the center of population shifted westward from the seacoast. It was a long and expensive journey for back-country representatives to get to legislative meetings, with the result that all too often the back country was not fully represented, even by the inadequate number of men assigned to it. They believed that moving the capitals westward would help to remedy this problem, and even more important, that they could free state governments from domination by the coastal aristocracy.

The attempt was successful throughout the South. The South Carolina Constitution of 1778 kept power in the hands of the tidewater although the center of population was far to the west. The westerners demanded that the capital be moved out of Charleston. By 1786 it was agreed to build an entirely new capital and the site of present day Columbia was chosen and lots were sold, including some under water. In 1789 the state officials moved to the new town. The low country men were unhappy about it and managed to have some offices established both at Charleston and Columbia. Although the tidewater was forced to yield on the capital, it kept the far more essential thing, political control of the state.[1]

North Carolina had no permanent capital until shortly before the war, when it was located at New Bern. During the war the legislature met when and where it could. There were long arguments about permanent location, but almost none of them involved returning to the tidewater. The conflict was chiefly among ambitious land speculators promoting rival locations in the back country. No less than seven sites were proposed in the ratifying convention of 1788 but not until 1792 did the legislature agree on a hill in Wake County, the present city of Raleigh, as the location of the capital.[2]

In Georgia, as in North Carolina, the legislature met on the run, if at all, during the war and the British government occupied the old capital of Savannah part of the time. The first legislature after the war met in Savannah, but the back country disapproved so the session soon adjourned to meet at Augusta. It returned to Savannah the next year but agreed that all the state officials should spend three months of every summer in Augusta to take care of back-country business. Then in 1786 the legislature moved

[1] Nevins: *American States*, 202, 404.

[2] Crittenden: *Commerce of North Carolina*, 167.

back to Augusta despite bitter objections from the tidewater, and in the end Augusta became the permanent capital.[3]

In Virginia, Jefferson proposed to move the capital from Williamsburg to Richmond in 1776, but the legislature refused. The proposal succeeded in 1779, the argument again being that Richmond would be safer from British attack. The tidewater continued to hope the move was temporary but failed to make Williamsburg the capital again once the war was over.[4]

In the North attempts to move capitals away from the seacoast were less successful. One of the grievances of many inland towns in Massachusetts was the meeting of the legislature in Boston, but all protests and proposals failed; the government was too firmly in the grip of coastal Massachusetts. The westerners of New Hampshire were more successful. They turned down three constitutions which favored the region around Portsmouth before accepting a fourth; they constantly demanded a capital near the center of the state and some counties made their point clear by joining Vermont for a time. The legislature met at Concord for the first time in 1782 and eventually the capital was located there.[5]

After the revolutionary government was driven from New York City in 1776 it had no permanent capital for twenty-one years. The small farmer element did not want either New York or Albany, but eventually agreed to the latter as the lesser of two evils.[6]

The capital fight in Pennsylvania was a straight party battle. In 1783 the Constitutionalists tried to move the capital out of Philadelphia and each year thereafter the question was agitated with one town after another as the favorite spot. In 1785 John Harris, the founder of Harrisburg, offered land to the state in return for making his town the county seat of Dauphin County. The capital was moved to Lancaster in 1798, and finally to Harrisburg in 1812.[7]

[3] Nevins: *American States*, 418.

[4] Ibid., 327, 339.

[5] Richard F. Upton: *Revolutionary New Hampshire* (Hanover, 1936), 180–84, 188, 245.

[6] E. Wilder Spaulding: *His Excellency George Clinton, Critic of the Constitution* (New York, 1938), 220; Spaulding: *New York in the Critical Period*, 95, 113.

[7] Brunhouse: *Counter-Revolution*, 114–5, 149, 197.

Each of these struggles to move the capitals reflects both the desire of the inhabitants of the old settled portions of the West to escape from tidewater influence and the interests of land speculators. Far more important was the demand for statehood on the new frontiers after 1783. There were repeated threats of secession from old states, one of which was carried out, and demands that new states be carved from old ones. Here too the democratic factor was involved, but so was the land speculator and to such a degree that the picture of simple western democrats fighting for self-government is smudged over with the image of the unscrupulous exploiter both in the West itself and in the East. West of the Alleghenies three main areas were involved: the Pittsburgh region, Kentucky, and Tennessee. To the east, the Connecticut settlers of the Wyoming Valley in Pennsylvania fought violently to create a new state, and in far-off Maine there was a polite statehood movement which died quietly.

No one knew where the boundary ran between Virginia and Pennsylvania west of the Alleghenies, but everyone knew that the whole region was covered with the overlapping land claims of Virginia and Pennsylvania land companies and individuals, as well as the rival claims of the states themselves. There was open conflict as early as 1774 between adherents of the two states. In 1776 some of the settlers petitioned Congress for help, declaring that they would not be enslaved and robbed by land speculators. They said that, as first occupants, they were entitled to their land by the laws of nature and of nations. They asked to be admitted to the union as the state of Westsylvania, but Congress did nothing nor had it the power to do anything. Again in 1780 several hundred settlers appealed to Congress for the creation of a new state in Kentucky and Illinois.

By this time both squatters and absentee speculators had counterclaims that made cloudy titles even more cloudy. Virginia responded by dividing Kentucky into three counties, but still, no one knew whether the upper part of the region was in Virginia or Pennsylvania. Virginia supporters along the Monongahela fortified themselves by getting titles from Virginia courts and running off all rivals by force. Their leader, Dorsey Pentecost, was the head of Virginia militia in the West. He had "money and smiles" and made all the "weakheaded magistrates" and "little pettifogging lawyers" in the region agree that all claims should be settled in Virginia courts. His loyalty to Virginia was temporary, but it helped him clear his own claims to large tracts of land: he was on the Virginia land office books for fifty-five grants of 1,000 acres each.[8]

Pennsylvania supporters in the area were in a bad way and finally in 1781 Pennsylvania set up Washington County and tried to complete the Mason-Dixon line beyond the mountains. But when boundary commissioners arrived in the West, the settlers told them that there was going to be a new state and then ran them out. Dorsey Pentecost, who had led the Virginia militia, now appeared as a member of the Pennsylvania executive council, but urged the people not to pay Pennsylvania taxes. Late in 1782 the Pennsylvania legislature ended the statehood movement in its part of the Ohio country by declaring that any effort to erect a new state was high treason punishable by death.

Meanwhile settlers farther down the Ohio were demanding statehood. They said in 1781 that the Virginia land law of 1779 allowed speculators to grab so much land that it prevented immigration, and that Virginia should give the actual settlers either more power or complete independence. The next year they carried their complaint to Congress which was already on edge as a result of the fight of the land companies against the Virginia cession of 1780.[9]

The leader of the early statehood movement in Kentucky was Arthur Campbell who was a county lieutenant and justice of the peace. Campbell had sat in the Virginia convention of 1776 and perhaps had imbibed something of the more democratic part of the revolutionary spirit. Now he was a land speculator and leader actually living in the West. As such, he was opposed equally to the Pennsylvania land speculators, organized as the Indiana Company, and to the speculators of eastern Virginia. He wanted to create a new state south of the Ohio to include both Kentucky and Tennessee. He believed that the West should be divided into

[8] Gray: *Agriculture*, II, 624.

[9] Various phases of this development are discussed in Frederick J. Turner: "Western Statemaking in the Revolutionary Era," AHR, I (1895), 70–87 and 251–69, in which the democratic side is emphasized; Thomas P. Abernethy: *Western Lands and the American Revolution* (New York, 1937), which emphasizes the role of the land speculator; Boyd Crumrine, ed.: *History of Washington County, Pennsylvania . . .* (Philadelphia, 1882); and in John M. Brown, *The Political Beginnings of Kentucky* (Filson Club Publications, no. 6, Louisville, 1889).

"free communities" united with the older states, but retaining their sovereignty and control of internal affairs. He refused to believe that the United States would have to be either a "consolidated empire" or broken up into separate groups.[10]

Meanwhile North Carolina land speculators led by William Blount, Richard Caswell, and others, gobbled up millions of acres of western North Carolina after the passage of the North Carolina land act of 1783. Then in 1784 the legislature ceded western North Carolina to Congress. The act required that all speculative claims in the region be validated. The speculators were aided in the passage of the act by the conservative element in eastern North Carolina. They looked on the westerners as "nuisances" and were willing to dump all responsibility for them on Congress. There was an immediate reaction in both the East and West. In August 1784 delegates from western militia companies met in a convention led by a henchman of Arthur Campbell. This convention voted unanimously for a new state which would include the Kentucky settlements to the north. In addition, it called a convention to meet in December to frame a constitution for the proposed new State of Franklin.

Congress, in the Ordinance of 1784, provided that new states might be begun by the people concerned. Western North Carolinians and the Arthur Campbell group in Kentucky were willing statemakers. They disliked eastern control and wanted to govern themselves, and dispose of the land as they saw fit. Meanwhile the radical element in eastern North Carolina got control of the legislature, revoked the cession to Congress, and divided the Tennessee country into four counties. This left the inhabitants of the would-be State of Franklin in a dubious position. When their convention met in December the majority renewed their declaration of independence, adopted the North Carolina constitution as a temporary one, and went ahead with the creation of a new state. By this time unanimity had disappeared. A vociferous minority now wanted to stay within the state of North Carolina.

In the spring of 1785 when the Franklin legislature met, it validated all land grants made by North Carolina, an action demonstrating that the speculators were now a powerful element in the new state. When a convention met in December 1785 to adopt a permanent constitution, the lines were clearly drawn

[10] To James Madison, 28 Oct. 1785, Madison Papers, LC.

between the western settlers and the speculators. The Arthur Campbell group proposed a democratic constitution. John Sevier, as governor of Franklin, but also as a representative and agent of the speculators, tried to keep his popular support while he protected the speculators' claims. He came out for adoption of the North Carolina constitution. While it might be democratic compared with some of the other state constitutions, it was thoroughly conservative compared with the constitution proposed by the followers of Arthur Campbell. That provided for a one house legislature, manhood suffrage, voting by ballot, and referendum of all laws to the people before final passage. The governor, council, and county officials were all elected by the people. A university was to be established before 1787 and taxes were set aside for its support.[11] Sevier and the eastern speculators behind him were afraid of what might happen if such a document were adopted. Their strength was such that they were able to defeat it and retain the North Carolina constitution.

For the rest of its brief history, Franklin was run by the land speculators who had staked out much of the state before it was created. While Sevier was governor of the "rebel" state, he was, unknown to the people of Franklin, actually working closely with Richard Caswell, Governor of North Carolina. Meanwhile, North Carolina held elections in the Franklin counties and in 1787 she appointed sheriffs. The result was violent argument and then fighting in Franklin. John Tipton led the forces wanting to return to North Carolina rule. John Sevier as governor led the forces of the independent state, but at the same time he too wanted to rejoin North Carolina.

The delicate maneuverings necessary were complicated by the fact that most of the followers, as well as the political enemies of Sevier, did not know what was going on. Tipton seized some of Sevier's property to pay North Carolina taxes. Sevier met the challenge by beseiging Tipton's house. By now Sevier's term as governor was over, the Franklin assembly no longer met, and original Franklinites were being elected to the North Carolina legislature. Sevier started an Indian war in which he treacherously murdered friendly Indians. He was arrested on the orders of the new Governor of North Carolina, Samuel Johnston, but he escaped and was pardoned in a general pardon act of the legislature.

[11] *The American Historical Magazine*, I (1893), 53–63.

In 1789 he was sent to the North Carolina senate by the voters of Greene County, still deluded by his words and unknowing of his deeds except as an Indian fighter, upon which he based his appeal for frontier support.

The story of Franklin is not a pretty one. The ordinary settlers who believed in the fine words of political leaders were doomed to disappointment. Perhaps a few saw the whole fight as a struggle between two groups of land speculators. The North Carolina group had captured the movement for independence started by the westerners led by Arthur Campbell. Sevier as their agent protected his claims and those of his friends, and eventually maneuvered Franklin back into North Carolina. The Franklin movement was not, except in an oddly loose sense, the "cry of the West for freedom." [12]

In Kentucky, Arthur Campbell and his followers were urging statehood as they were in Tennessee, but there too they lost control of the movement to the more recently arrived land speculators. By the end of 1784, William Fleming, leader of the large speculator element, was in control. He and his fellow speculators wanted no disturbance of their land claims arising from the Virginia land act of 1779. Two conventions were held in 1785. The second one asked for peaceful separation from Virginia. The big speculators in Kentucky were in close touch with powerful men in the Virginia legislature who helped out by removing Arthur Campbell as head of the western militia, and by having the legislature declare that anyone who tried to create an independent state was guilty of high treason. The Virginia legislature, however, passed an enabling act providing statehood for Kentucky under Virginia direction. Not unnaturally the act also guaranteed all Virginia land grants in the region.

Kentuckians were badly split. Some were afraid of the Indians. Daniel Boone hoped that "petisioning" for a new state would not prevent help. He said that the demand for a state was "intirely against the voce of the peeple at Large. A few individuals who Exspect to be States men have put this afoot." [13] James Wilkinson was double-dealing with the Spanish and

[12] Thomas P. Abernethy: *From Frontier to Plantation in Tennessee* (Chapel Hill, 1932), chs. iv–v, has a realistic account of the role of the land speculator and the State of Franklin. See also Samuel C. Williams: *History of the Lost State of Franklin* (Johnson City, Tenn., 1924).

[13] To —— ——, 16 Aug. 1785, Emmet Coll., no. 6277, NYPL.

promising to give the West to Spain. John Jay's dealings with Gardoqui, in which he agreed to close the Mississippi to western trade for twenty-five years in exchange for privileges in Spanish ports for eastern merchants, enraged the West. It convinced some that Kentucky must be completely independent. One man declared the proposal was unjust and despotic and that if it took place, people in the West would feel themselves "cleared from all Federal obligations" and at full liberty to make alliances wherever they found them.[14]

The one solid and increasingly powerful group in Kentucky were the large speculators who were coming in constantly from the East. They dominated the fourth Kentucky convention in 1787 and decided to ask Congress for admission as a state. The Virginia legislature aided by sending John Brown of Kentucky as delegate to Congress. There the Kentucky petition got caught in a web of jealousy: the "eastern" states were opposed to any more new states in the South.[15] Furthermore, a new national government would soon be in operation. At this point John Brown declared for independence, but the speculators in Kentucky were moving bodily into the Federalist party and were willing to wait for the security they would have as a state under the new constitution.[16] In Kentucky, as in Tennessee, western democracy was thus thwarted by powerful speculators who claimed vast areas and who got control of new state movements in the West in order to maintain those claims against the majority of the ordinary settlers, many of whom were squatters.

By all odds the most serious and violent statehood movement came within the recognized bounds of Pennsylvania. In the fall of 1782 a federal court decided that Pennsylvania had jurisdiction over Wyoming Valley, but declared that the Connecticut settlers in it should be confirmed in the possession of the lands on which they had settled.[17] The Pennsylvania legislature ignored the recommendation and sent militia to drive off the Connecticut settlers. Members of the legislature were not without claims in

[14] John Campbell to James Madison, Pittsburgh, 21 Feb. 1787, and George Muter to Madison, 20 Feb. 1787, Madison Papers, LC. See *ante*, ch. vii.

[15] John Brown to James Madison, 12 May 1788, Burnett, VIII, 733.

[16] Abernethy: *Western Lands*, 346–52.

[17] Before the Revolution the Susquehanna Company of Connecticut claimed that the Wyoming Valley of Pennsylvania was within Connecticut's charter limits and had settled Connecticut people there.

the region themselves. The result was civil war, for the Susquehanna Company supported its colonists. A company of "half share" men was organized under the leadership of John Franklin, a rough and tough frontiersman. These men agreed to live in the valley for three years under orders of the company representatives. In return they were to get a half share of a township. Franklin did more than fight the "Pennamites." He proposed that a new state, Westmoreland, be created to include the Susquehanna Valley not only in upper Pennsylvania, but in New York as well. Oliver Wolcott of Connecticut drafted a constitution for them. Ethan Allen and his Green Mountain boys came down to help out.

Meanwhile, unknown to the settlers in the valley, the governments of Pennsylvania and Connecticut made a deal. Connecticut agreed to withdraw its support of the people of the valley, and in return kept the "Western Reserve" when she made a cession of all her claims to Congress in 1786. Pennsylvania promptly set up Luzerne County and sent out Timothy Pickering, a New Englander who had been foot-loose since the war, as justice of the peace and register of deeds.[18] His New England origin did not serve the purpose hoped for by the Pennsylvania government: he was beaten and generally mishandled. Pennsylvania finally confirmed the claims of the settlers who had come before the decision of 1782. Eventually Franklin was seized and tried, although meanwhile he had been elected to the Pennsylvania legislature.[19]

The various statehood movements were natural in a rapidly growing country, and the story was to be repeated many times as Americans marched westward to the Pacific. Usually the same elements were involved: early settlers who wanted to run their own affairs; speculators who sought and often gained control of the local governments. Often the conflict led to violence, and always it alarmed the more sedate people to the eastward. Thus John Franklin was called the "western Shays" who had "uniformly labored to involve the country in a civil war." He was

[18] Pickering to the President of the Council of Pennsylvania, 25 Sept. 1786, Pickering Papers, MHS.

[19] Julian Boyd: "Attempts to Form New States in New York and Pennsylvania, 1786–1796," New York State Historical Association, *Quarterly Journal*, XII (1931) in New York State Historical Association *Proceedings*, XXIX (1931), 258–63.

not satisfied to be elected to the assembly. " 'Better to reign in hell, than serve in heaven,' has ever been a favorite sentiment with the demons of sedition." [20] Even so mild a movement as the proposed separation of the "three eastern counties" of Massachusetts excited hysterical comment. Such a move was "pregnant with alarming evils. . . ." European "friends" might annex us. But the evil did not end there, for such movements might infuse "a spirit of novelty and revolution in the interior part of several of our large states—which by being refused admittance into the Confederation, may bring on civil dudgeon. . . ." [21]

Before 1776 those afraid of independence predicted that there would be civil war between state and state, that large states would swallow up their neighbors, and claimed that only British power prevented such catastrophes. Their fears had some basis, for Pennsylvania and Virginia were fighting over the Pittsburgh region and Connecticut claimed that the Wyoming Valley of Pennsylvania was within Connecticut's charter rights, while Vermont was a bone of contention between New York and New Hampshire. Yet all these problems were settled during the years that followed. The Articles of Confederation provided a method for arbitrating such disputes. In 1782 the dispute between Pennsylvania and Connecticut was settled according to this method, although the actual settlers, as we have seen, were made unhappy for some time to come. Pennsylvania and Virginia finally agreed to run the Mason-Dixon line westward although the people were dissatisfied. Vermont settlers solved the dispute between New York and New Hampshire by setting up an independent state which eventually was admitted to the union.

Another argument of the opponents of independence was that a centralized government must regulate the trade of the colonies. Merchants, as a rule, supported this idea throughout the war and continued to demand it afterward. The difficulties in the way of American commerce were used as an argument for a stronger centralized government. No idea is more firmly planted in American history than the idea that one of the most difficult problems during the Confederation was that of barriers to trade between state and state. There had been such barriers in colonial times;

[20] *Pennsylvania Packet,* 8, 11 Oct. 1787.
[21] *Massachusetts Centinel,* 18 Jan. 1786.

Maryland, New Jersey, and Connecticut were the colonies that did most to build them. They exported most of their produce directly, but they imported through such ports as Philadelphia and New York. Such colonies struggled in vain to escape the economic magnetism of growing urban neighbors which could offer easier credit and better handling of goods.

As early as 1696 William Penn, as a proprietor of East Jersey, protested against customs collections in New York on goods coming to his province, and like other men nearly a century later, he too proposed a "national union." Both New Jersey and Connecticut levied higher duties on goods brought in from neighboring colonies in an effort to build up local commerce, but with total lack of success.[22]

After the Revolution, Connecticut and New Jersey continued the effort to attract merchants to their ports. In 1783 the New Jersey legislature declared its ports open and free to all merchants. New Jersey merchants were not satisfied with this. They demanded import duties on foreign goods brought in by way of other states, but each new legislature refused until June 1787 when a tax was levied on imported articles, except on those which were the growth or manufacture of the United States. The popular protest was immediate and violent; in October 1787 the legislature suspended the law. The legislature, dominated by farmers, knew that New Jersey could not develop an independent overseas commerce and realized also that such a tariff would function as a tax on consumers for the benefit of ambitious local merchants.

New Jersey also tried to build up its trade by establishing Perth Amboy and Burlington as free ports, but nothing was achieved. New merchants did not come in from outside the state, trade did not increase as a result of the laws, and those merchants who owned real estate in the free ports did not realize their desire for a land boom which had been one of the reasons behind the demand for such legislation.

The irritation that sprang up between New York and New Jersey was the result of New Jersey's refusal to discriminate against British goods and ships as virtually all of the other states were doing. In 1785 New York taxed British goods coming in across its borders unless the owners could prove that the goods were imported in ships belonging to citizens of the United States.

[22] Clark: *History of Manufactures*, I, 59.

Then in 1787 New York provided that foreign goods brought in from Connecticut and New Jersey must pay entrance and clearance fees four times higher than American goods. New Jersey responded by taxing the Sandy Hook lighthouse £30 a month.[23] This is the teapot tempest which is so often cited as an example of interstate trade barriers during the Confederation. Actually the New York law was of little economic importance since few foreign goods were re-exported from New Jersey or Connecticut.

Connecticut, like New Jersey, tried to attract merchants by offering concessions if they would settle in New Haven or New London. But Connecticut went farther, for she taxed foreign goods coming into Connecticut from the other United States in an effort to build up her own direct trade. The laws apparently had little effect, for few outside merchants seem to have been drawn to Connecticut. Connecticut trade did grow rapidly, but aside from the West India trade, the growth was largely in the shipping between Connecticut and New York which continued to be the chief source of supplies and the chief market for Connecticut produce, a fact made plain by the port records of New Haven.[24]

No matter how the citizens of New Jersey and Connecticut might feel about New York, they were tied to her then and forever after by her economic power. The arguments of their politicians that they had to pay tribute to her had only a partial foundation. In 1784 and again in 1787 the New York Legislature provided that goods brought in for re-export, if kept in original packages, should be free of duties.[25]

There is thus little factual basis for the ancient tale repeated so faithfully by writers who follow in one another's footsteps without examining the evidence. The supporters of centralized power used the few discriminatory laws as an argument for a new government, but they ignored other laws which disproved their case, and so partisan argument in time became "history." The adoption of the Constitution of 1787 made no change in the economic rela-

[23] McCormick: New Jersey in the Confederation, 131–46.

[24] Connecticut *State Records*, V, 325–6, 432–3; VI, 15–6. Like the other states, however, Connecticut exempted goods produced or manufactured in the United States from import duties.

[25] 22 March 1784, *Laws of New York* (1886 ed.), I, 603; 18 Nov. 1784, II, 14; 11 April 1787, II, 513. Pennsylvania passed similar legislation. Pennsylvania *Statutes at Large*, XI, 8–11, 188–91.

tions between New York and her neighbors except that duties were thereafter collected by the national government.[26] The idea that is plain if one looks at the trade laws of the states is the idea of reciprocity between state and state. The general rule was that all American goods were exempted from state imposts. American ships paid no higher tonnage duties in the ports of a state than did the shipowners of that state. Trade "barriers," contrary to the tradition, were the exception rather than the rule. In fact, there were no trade barriers at all during the Confederation as compared with interstate barriers which have grown up in the twentieth century.

The action of New York was characteristic. In March 1784 she exempted all United States products and manufactured goods from tariff duties and continued to do so in subsequent acts.[27] In 1784 New Hampshire passed an impost law in which she exempted hemp, salt, and "such articles as are the manufacture and growth of the United States of America" from the duties imposed.[28] In August 1783, South Carolina passed an impost law. As a result, duties were collected on American goods brought into the state. In the spring of 1784 the legislature passed a new law to prevent this. In addition, it ordered that all money collected from Americans should be repaid. The legislature declared that it was "injurious to the harmony which should ever subsist between these federal states, to impose any duties on the commodities of the respective states . . ." [29]

When Rhode Island passed the first of the protective tariffs adopted by the American states, it provided for duties only on

[26] McCormick: New Jersey in the Confederation, 336–8. One basic reason for New Jersey's support of a new government was that her citizens held a large amount of the national debt upon which the state had assumed interest payments. The New Jersey taxpayers were anxious to unload a burden which could not be carried by import duties on a nonexistent foreign trade.

[27] *Laws of New York* (1886 ed.), I, 599; II, 12, 511. In November 1784 New York required cordage from the other United States to pay duties, but this was dropped from subsequent acts. The only account of trade legislation by the states of any merit is Albert A. Giesecke: *American Commercial Legislation before 1789* (Philadelphia, 1910), ch. vi. By way of contrast see Spaulding: *New York in the Critical Period* which contains a chapter on the state impost which has no reference to the actual laws passed except for an act in 1787 providing entrance and clearance fees on coastwise vessels.

[28] 17 April 1784, *Laws of New Hampshire*, IV, 563.

[29] 26 March 1784, South Carolina *Statutes at Large* (Cooper ed.), IV, 647–8; *South Carolina Gazette*, 4–6 May 1784.

foreign articles and declared that the purpose of the act was to encourage manufacturing, not only in Rhode Island, but in the other United States as well.[30]

When Pennsylvania passed its first protective tariff in 1785 it did not make specific exemption of manufactures from the other states, but here and there the act makes it plain that foreign goods are meant and exceptions are made for such products as rum, if distilled in the United States or brought in in American ships.[31] Actually Pennsylvania had nothing to fear from other American manufactures since the state was rapidly becoming the supplier of many of the other states.

Massachusetts, in its protective tariff in 1785, levied duties only on goods "not made or manufactured in any of the United States." Furthermore, it soon provided, "in order to introduce a free trade with the interior parts of our neighboring states," that all goods exported by land should be as free of duty as if exported by water.[32] Connecticut, which was anxious to develop its fisheries and protect its nail industry, passed duties for that purpose, but exempted nails made "in these United States" and all fish caught by the citizens of Connecticut and the United States.[33] Georgia, though its trade was small, exempted all goods grown or manufactured in the United States from payment of duties and sharply reduced the duties on all foreign goods if brought in in American vessels.[34]

Virginia moved more slowly than the other states. In October 1786 an impost act exempted goods imported in American ships, if the goods were proved to be the growth, produce, or manufacture of the state from whence imported. A year later the law was brought into line with that of other states. All goods, wares, and merchandise, grown, produced, or manufactured in the United

[30] Rhode Island *Acts and Resolves* (June 1785), 18–9.

[31] 20 Sept. 1785, Pennsylvania *Statutes at Large*, XII, 99–104. An impost law in 1782 exempted certain war supplies and all "goods, wares and merchandise of the growth product or manufacture of the United States of America or any of them."

[32] 2 July 1785, Massachusetts *Acts and Resolves* (1784–5), 453–7; 8 July 1786, ibid. (1786–7), 67–8. The latter action was to reciprocate an act of New Hampshire exempting foreign goods owned by the citizens of Massachusetts from the New Hampshire duties. 23 June 1785, *Laws of New Hampshire*, V, 85; *Massachusetts Centinel*, 16 July 1785.

[33] Connecticut *State Records*, VI, 161, 292.

[34] Georgia *Colonial Records*, XIX, pt. 2, 501–2, 514–5.

States were exempted from all duties or imposts when imported in American vessels. The sole exception was "distilled spirits" gotten from materials not grown or manufactured in the United States.[35]

Thus the picture by the end of 1787 is not the conventional one of interstate trade barriers, but a novel one of reciprocity between state and state. American goods were free of duties, and foreign goods arriving in American ships were charged lower duties in most of the states than when brought in in foreign ships, and particularly, in the ships of non-treaty countries.[36]

Cooperation between the states extended to other matters than trade. Ancient disputes about boundaries and navigation rights were discussed and settled rapidly. Independence had created problems which the states were anxious and willing to settle. The usual procedure was for the states concerned to appoint commissioners, and, once these had agreed, for the legislatures to adopt the agreement, a process still followed as problems arise among American states.

New Jersey and Pennsylvania soon provided for the regulation of the Delaware River. Three commissioners from each state agreed in April 1783 that the river was to be a common highway except that each legislature reserved the right to guard the fisheries annexed to its respective shores. It was agreed that the states should have concurrent jurisdiction on the water. The state concerned was to have exclusive jurisdiction over ships in its harbors. They agreed that the islands in the river should be a part of the state to which they were nearest. The legislatures of the two states ratified the agreements and, so far as they could do so, solved the problems involved.[37]

Virginia and Maryland were concerned with the joint use of the Potomac and with opening it for navigation in order to tap

[35] Hening, XII, 304–5, 416.

[36] While this was happening, Madison, who wanted regulation of trade by Congress, wrote to Jefferson in France that separate regulations were likely to set the states "by the ears." He cited the Connecticut and New Jersey free ports as an example because they irritated New York. Actually, of course, such free ports benefited New York since it made it easier to carry goods from New York to New Jersey and Connecticut. See also Robert G. Albion: "New York Port in the New Republic, 1783–1793," *New York History*, XXI (1940), 400–1, where he reiterates Madison's errors.

[37] *Pennsylvania Gazette*, 15 Oct. 1783; *Acts of New Jersey* (Wilson ed.), 323–5; Pennsylvania *Statutes at Large*, XI, 151–4.

the commerce of the growing West, where they had vast land claims. In May 1785 a "numerous assembly of the first people" of both states met and organized a company with Washington as president. It was agreed to start work at once. It was said that "the vast consequence that must derive to the middle states . . . cannot be elucidated but by time, the discoverer of all great events." [38] Meanwhile commissioners of the two states made a compact for the use of the river and of Chesapeake Bay. It was agreed that all waters in Virginia were to be a free and common highway with reciprocal free use of harbors. Small vessels owned by citizens of either state and carrying their produce were to be free of all port duties. When merchant vessels entered both states, tonnage duties were to be divided between them. Trials for piracy and other crimes on the waters were agreed upon. The two states agreed to share equally the costs of aids to navigation on the Potomac; on Chesapeake Bay, Virginia agreed to pay five parts to Maryland's three.[39]

Pennsylvania supported Maryland and Virginia in their desire to improve a route to the Ohio River. Since it was necessary that a road from the head of navigation on the Potomac go through Pennsylvania, the legislature authorized the two states to build the road. It likewise authorized Pennsylvania county courts to provide for a road eighty feet wide, since ordinarily they could not authorize a road wider than fifty feet. This road was to be deemed a highway of the State of Pennsylvania, to be built and kept in repair by Virginia and Maryland, and to be free to the inhabitants of all three states. If the other two states neglected to keep the road in repair, Pennsylvania would take over and charge equal tolls to the citizens of all three states.[40]

Boundary disputes were likewise settled. Massachusetts and New York claimed the same area of land. Congress provided for a federal court to settle the case, but the judges refused to serve. Meanwhile the lands were being settled, so the two states appointed commissioners who were given final authority to settle the dispute, and by the end of 1786 they had done so.[41]

The story of interstate relations during the Confederation is

[38] *Pennsylvania Gazette*, 1 June 1785.
[39] Oct. session 1785, Hening, XII, 50–5.
[40] 15 March 1787, Pennsylvania *Statutes at Large*, XII, 409–12.
[41] King: *Life*, I, 139–40.

therefore not so much one of great difficulties, as a story of sincere and successful attempts at the solution of interstate problems. Of course many things remained to be solved. A minor issue was the dispute over the location of the national capital. A forewarning of the future was to be found as early as 1783 when the governor of South Carolina denounced the governor of Massachusetts for interfering with the return of Negroes belonging to the citizens of South Carolina. The Massachusetts courts had freed Negroes held for return, and Governor Hancock's legal advisers told him that no law or ordinance had been infringed and declared that there was no attack on the freedom, dignity, and independence of South Carolina. Furthermore they declared "that this has an connection with or relation to Puritanism, we believe is above your Excellency's comprehension, as it certainly is above ours." [42]

Far more important than any petty antagonisms that existed during the Confederation was the emergence of groups of Americans whose interests transcended state boundaries and who sought to break down the political and psychological barriers that existed between state and state. One such group was the Society of Cincinnati which was a bond of political as well as social significance for ex-army officers, many of whom were permanently uprooted by their service in the army. The rising manufacturers were another group who wrote to one another urging joint action in their campaign for protective tariffs. Opposed to them, yet also interested in transcending states lines, were the importing merchants who organized chambers of commerce and demanded national rather than state regulation of trade. There were obvious advantages for them in a uniformity of rules which state legislation did not provide, but in addition, and perhaps more importantly, the importing merchants hoped to escape from state protective tariffs. Those tariffs, like the non-consumption and non-importation agreements of pre-revolutionary days, were designed to check the importation of British goods; yet that importation was of vital concern to most American merchants.

The most vocal group whose interests transcended state boundaries in the new nation were those known as the "public creditors." Perhaps most of the large holders of the public debt were also merchants. Certainly most of them were concentrated in the com-

[42] Copy of letter to Governor Hancock, Cushing Papers, MHS.

mercial towns. As creditors of the states they demanded payments of interest and principal. As holders of and speculators in the national debt, they were solidly behind the movement to grant an independent income to Congress. Cutting across all groups were men who had long wanted a strong central government as a matter of conviction as well as of particular interest.

Throughout the Confederation these groups tried different ways of achieving the ends they desired. Some tried to interpret power into the Articles of Confederation, some tried to amend it, and some hoped and worked for a constitutional coup d'etat. Hence, despite the concern with politics in the states, Americans at the same time focused much of their thought on the central government as it struggled with the problems which faced it. Those who feared a strong central government, or at least feared the uses to which it might be put, insisted that the central government did well. Those who wanted a strong central government refused to give Congress under the Articles of Confederation any credit for its achievements. The truth, as always, lay somewhere between the extremes of political propaganda.

PART FIVE

The Achievements of the Confederation

It is commonly believed that during the Confederation the government of the United States was a weak and incompetent affair, devoid of power and ideas, without a record of achievement, and sinking fast into oblivion. Certain basic ideas are set forth about it: it was difficult to get a quorum of Congress to do business; it had no income; it had no power to handle the country's ills, and so on. The government was "weak," of that there is no question. It had been created that way deliberately because its founders had feared, and during the 1780's they continued to fear, a strong central government as they had feared and fought against the British government before 1776.

Yet one cannot understand the history of the Confederation government if one talks of it only in terms of efforts to remedy its obvious weaknesses. To do so is to miss much of the point of the political history of the American Revolution. One misses also the fact that the central government struggled mightily with problems left by the war and with still others arising from the birth of a new nation. Furthermore, one loses sight of the fact that the government of the Confederation achieved a measure of success, at least according to the lights of those who believed in the kind of central government provided by the Articles of Confederation.

The Congress of the Confederation laid foundations for the administration of a central government which were to be expanded but not essentially altered in function for generations to come. The United States acquired a vast source of future wealth as the states ceded their claims to western lands. The national domain became a fact in 1784. Between then and 1787, in three great ordinances, Congress laid down the basic policies that were to be used as the United States spread westward to the Pacific. At the same time a permanent staff of government employees was built up. These men carried on the affairs of the central government whether Congress was in session or not. When the Washington administration took over in 1789, the members of the new administration in effect moved into front offices staffed with men who for years had handled the details of foreign affairs, finance, Indian relations, the post office, and the like. Many of these employees continued to do the basic work of the central government after 1789 as they had done before. The government under the Constitution of 1787 would have been as helpless without them as the Confederation would have been, yet this "bureaucracy" has been unknown to most of the people who have written of the Confederation.

The government of the Confederation struggled to straighten out the tangled mess that resulted from the financing of the war, and here too made progress. Finally, it faced the basic issue of the relationship of the balance of power between the central government and the states. That issue was before the people of the new nation from the outset of the war. After 1783 the believers in the federal system provided by the Articles of Confederation sought hard to solve its problems. They recognized that the central government needed more power and they sought to acquire that power, meanwhile carefully guarding against any basic change in the nature of the Articles of Confederation.

As one views the achievements of the Confederation, it is evident that the story is not a negative one, but a story of steady striving toward a goal. The "weakness" of the central government under the Confederation was the weakness of any government that must achieve its ends by persuasion rather than by coercion. There was a large group of the citizens of the new nation who believed in persuasion; a smaller but equally powerful group believed in a central government with coercive authority. The triumph of the latter group in the face of the achievements of the

Confederation government was a victory for a dynamic minority with a positive program. It parallels in many ways the achievement of an equally dynamic, but quite different minority, in bringing about the war for independence and in writing the Articles of Confederation.

18

Foundations for the Future

The Creation of the National Domain

THE FACT of expansion into new land loomed even larger in American thought and economy in the 1780's than it had in the colonial period. The dispute over the control of the West contributed to the tensions leading to the war for independence, but independence did not end the dispute, for Americans fought with one another as to whether the central government or the individual states should control the lands claimed by them on the basis of their ancient charters. The reason for the conflict was primer-simple although its ramifications were endless and clouded by constitutional and legal theories that have led later generations to lose sight of the realities upon which eighteenth century men kept a steady eye.

In the conflict over westward expansion before the Revolution, various colonial land speculators had laid out overlapping claims to the region beyond the Alleghenies. As we have seen, the conflict held up the ratification of the Articles of Confederation until March of 1781. At that time Congress had before it several cessions, including the most important one of all, that of Virginia. But Congress did not accept the Virginia cession until 1784. The reason for it was obvious: Virginia, in ceding the Old Northwest, insisted that before the cession became final Congress must declare void all land company purchases in the region, something that Virginia had done several years before. Furthermore, Congress must guarantee Virginia's remaining territory to her: that is, Kentucky. These requirements were aimed directly at the land speculators of Pennsylvania and Maryland who claimed land both north and south of the Ohio and who evolved constitutional theories to prove that Congress had sovereign power and could therefore take the lands from Virginia.

For three years after 1780, the land speculators and their friends fought to evade the conditions attached to the Virginia cession. Stockholders of the Illinois-Wabash and the Indiana companies, such as Robert Morris, Samuel Wharton, James Wilson, and Charles Carroll of Carrollton, were from time to time members of Congress, and still others like Benjamin Franklin were not without influence. In Congress they and their supporters fought hard. They continued to argue that Congress had sovereignty over the region and therefore could ignore the Virginia cession. But at the same time they tried to force an unrestricted cession from Virginia. Neither idea was followed consistently, and sometimes both were urged at once if expediency seemed to dictate.

Some Virginians at first thought that Congress would accept the cession because the "covert maneuvers" of the land companies were so obvious that their abettors would not be "hardy enough" to continue to support them. But other Virginians knew better: "The modes and methods which these artists pursue," said Richard Henry Lee, were well known, and they would stop at nothing to gain their ends. Lee was right, for a few weeks after the cession of 1780 James Wilson, George Morgan, Benjamin Franklin, and others petitioned Congress to exercise its "sovereignty," and thus by implication, to ignore the Virginia conditions and confirm the claims of the Pennsylvania-Maryland speculators.

For a time congressional committees favored the claims of the speculators. They declared that Virginia extended only to the Alleghenies and that most of the land company claims were valid. The Virginians fought such arguments to a standstill. Whenever a report on land cessions came before Congress, the Virginia delegates asked each member to declare just what were his connections with the land companies involved. By the spring of 1783 such tactics, and the fact that the land companies could never get seven states to vote for them, resulted in the consignment of favorable reports to oblivion.

The Virginia delegates told their legislature to do with the West as it pleased, but at the same time they continued to urge Congress to accept the cession. The land companies likewise continued to petition. James Wilson, who was president of the Illinois-Wabash Company, was also a member of Congress and was most eloquent in debate and productive of theories to do away with Virginia's claim.

With the ending of the war in the spring of 1783, the land companies began to lose ground. The need for an independent income was real. It was obvious also that Virginia was selling lands beyond the Alleghenies, and that if Congress did not accept her cession, it would lose one of the surest sources of wealth for the central government.

The result was a new committee report in June of 1783. One by one it took up the conditions attached to the Virginia cession, and while it managed to avoid a definite commitment on any one of them, the effect was a tacit acceptance of the Virginia point of view. The landless states and their speculators failed to block adoption of the report because Congress was facing new realities. One of them was the financial problem of the central government. Another was the old promise that Congress would give land to soldiers if they enlisted for the duration of the war. Army officers were also interested in western lands, and once Washington surrendered his command, he spent time with Congress lobbying for the officers who hoped for land grants northwest of the Ohio. He pointed to an increasingly obvious truth: that while Congress and Virginia debated, people whom he called "banditti" were settling the land. Such people were depriving officers of their "just claims" and above all, were bringing about the danger of Indian war.

The result of such realities and pressures was that Congress asked Virginia to make a new cession of her claims. For a time it seemed that the Virginia legislature would withdraw the cession entirely. Then, late in December 1783, it ceded the Old Northwest, this time without specific restrictions, but with enough generalities to make it plain that such restrictions were implicit in the act.

On 1 March 1784 Congress accepted this cession and the national domain was at last a reality.[1] Congress at once went to work drafting ordinances for the government, the survey, and the sale of the public domain. Military control of lawless inhabitants

[1] The foregoing account is based on Merrill Jensen: "The Creation of the National Domain, 1781–1784," MVHR, XXVI (1939), 323–42.

was provided for. A policy for making treaties with the Indians was established.

The man chiefly responsible for the foundation of the first "colonial policy" of the United States was Thomas Jefferson. He had long been interested in the region west of the Alleghenies, not as a speculator, but as a statesman, a scientist, and a believer in agrarian democracy.[2] Where others wanted to hand the West over to speculators, he wanted it to belong to actual settlers. Where others distrusted westerners as banditti and wanted them ruled by military force, he wanted them to govern themselves. Thus when he brought the Virginia cession to Congress, he had definite ideas about what should be done. He was made chairman of a committee to draft an ordinance for the government of the new public domain. He believed that the land should be given to the settlers, for they would have to pay their share of the national debt anyway. Why should they pay double? If settlers had to pay for the lands, they would dislike the union. Furthermore, they would settle the lands no matter what Congress did. One settler in the West would be worth twenty times what he paid for the land, and he would be worth that every year he lived on his farm.

Jefferson proposed that the domain be divided into ten districts which ultimately would become states. He gave those districts names which were made fun of then and have been ever since, although it must be said that the names he chose are no less musical than some of those given to the states of the Old Northwest in the end. There was to be self-government by the people, not arbitrary government by congressional appointees. Whenever Congress offered a piece of territory for sale, the settlers within it were to establish a temporary government and to adopt the constitution and laws of whatever state they chose. Whenever the territory had 20,000 people, they were to hold a convention, adopt a constitution, and send a delegate to Congress. When the population of the territory equalled that of the free inhabitants of the smallest of the thirteen states, the new state was to be admitted to the union as an equal partner. The new state must agree to remain a part of the United States; be subject to the central gov-

[2] The most recent and best account of Jefferson's relation to the West is Anthony Marc Lewis: "Jefferson and Virginia's Pioneers, 1774–1781," MVHR, XXXIV (1948), 551–88.

ernment exactly as the other states were; be liable for its share of the federal debt; maintain a republican form of government; and exclude slavery after 1800. Thus Jefferson planned a government for the national domain. When the Ordinance of 1784 was finally adopted by Congress, only a few changes were made. The reference to slavery was dropped and one new restriction was added: the future states might not tax federal lands nor interfere with their disposal.[3]

It is too often said, and believed, that the Northwest Ordinance of 1787, which repealed the Ordinance of 1784, provided for democracy in the territories of the United States. The reverse is actually true. Jefferson's Ordinance provided for democratic self-government of western territories, and for that reason it was abolished in 1787 by the land speculators and their supporters who wanted congressional control of the West so that their interests could be protected from the actions of the inhabitants.

Meanwhile, with the Ordinance of 1784 adopted, the next step was to provide for the survey and sale of the lands. Jefferson was on the committee appointed to draft such a plan and here too he had ideas, although his belief that the West should be given to the actual settlers was soon lost sight of in the need of Congress for revenue and in the rise of new speculative groups.

Jefferson left for France to replace Franklin as minister before the Ordinance was completed. In its final form the Ordinance of 1785 provided that the West should be divided into townships, each containing thirty-six square miles. Four sections in each township were to be reserved for the United States, and also one third of the gold, silver, and copper. In each township lot sixteen was set aside for public schools. Once surveyed, the lands were to be sold at public auction by the loan office commissioners in each of the states. The land could not be sold for less than a dollar an acre and payment was to be in specie, loan office certificates reduced to specie value, or certificates of the liquidated debt of the United States. Lands were reserved to provide the bounties promised the army during the war. This Ordinance was adopted by Congress 20 May 1785.[4] At once surveys were gotten under way by Thomas Hutchins, geographer of the United States. It

[3] 23 April 1784, *Journals*, XXVI, 275–9.

[4] *Journals*, XXVIII, 375–81, "An Ordinance for ascertaining the mode of disposing of Lands in the Western Territory."

was a long, slow process. By 1787 Hutchins and his men had surveyed four ranges of townships, starting at the western boundary of Pennsylvania.

But the Land Ordinance of 1785 was soon forgotten. New speculative interests swept down upon Congress and grabbed for enormous chunks of the public domain. The drive was spearheaded by New Englanders and by others who had few if any ties with the pre-revolutionary land companies. No group was more interested in the West than ex-army officers who saw in western lands an outlet for the desires and energies that had been so frustrated at the end of the war. Thus Rufus Putnam wrote Henry Knox in the fall of 1783 that rapid settlement was so certain that it was to the interest of officers and soldiers not only to locate lands but to become settlers "as well as adventurers by purchases [of] public securities." [5] Samuel Holden Parsons wrote from the West in 1785 that if he ever returned East he knew he could convince his friends "that public securities, if Congress a little alter their system, is their best estate." Only give him some government post in the West and "I will make the fortune of your family and my own till time shall be no more." [6]

What these men hoped for was a military colony in the Old Northwest such as they had proposed to Congress from Newburgh in the spring of 1783.[7] But Congress soon made it plain that it was going to sell land, so the officers changed their plans. Early in 1786 Rufus Putnam and Benjamin Tupper issued a call to the Massachusetts officers and soldiers who had served in the Revolution. They proposed county meetings to choose delegates to a meeting at Boston to organize an association to be called the Ohio Company.[8] The company was organized and shares of stock were sold.[9] The leading men, in addition to Putnam and Tupper, were Samuel Holden Parsons, Winthrop Sargent, and the Reverend Manasseh Cutler, an ex-army chaplain.

The Ohio Company asked for a virtual suspension of the Land

[5] 23 Oct. 1783, Knox Papers, MHS.

[6] To William Samuel Johnson, 26 Nov. 1785, William Samuel Johnson Papers, LC.

[7] "A Military and Civil Establishment in the Lands of Congress," Samuel Holden Parsons to William Samuel Johnson, 24 Nov. 1785, William Samuel Johnson Papers, LC.

[8] *Massachusetts Centinel*, 25 Jan. 1786.

[9] Ibid., 11 March 1786.

Ordinance of 1785. Four ranges had been surveyed but had not been put up for sale when the Ohio Company appeared before Congress offering a million dollars for lands beyond the survey. The ultimate success of the Ohio Company was due in part to the fact that once more the balance of power in Congress was shifting, a shift no better expressed than in the election of General Arthur St. Clair as president. But the success of the Company was also due to the remarkably skillful lobbying of the Reverend Manasseh Cutler. Samuel Holden Parsons had made no headway, but when Cutler appeared, things began to move. He found, for instance, that William Duer, secretary to the board of treasury, associated with some New York speculators, was trying to get a million acres on the Scioto River without paying for them. Cutler and Duer joined forces. Cutler dropped the Ohio Company's idea of making Parsons governor and advocated General Arthur St. Clair, president of Congress.

The shift in tactics smoothed the way for the Ohio Company. Congress agreed that it might take up "a tract of land which shall be bounded by the Ohio from the mouth of Scioto to the intersection of the seventh range of townships now surveying; thence by the said boundary to the northern boundary of the tenth township from the Ohio; thence by a due west line to the Scioto; thence by the Scioto to the beginning. . . ." The price was to be not less than a dollar an acre payable in loan office certificates reduced to specie value and in other certificates of the liquidated debt of the United States. Up to one seventh of the total purchase price could be paid in the land bounty certificates issued to the officers and soldiers of the Continental Army. The price, however, was reduced by a third, for that much allowance was made for bad land and for incidental expenses. The purchase was an enormous bargain, for national debt certificates were selling for as little as ten cents on the dollar in the open market. In the final sale Congress held back some of the land. Section sixteen in each township was reserved for education. Section twenty-nine was set aside for "the purposes of religion." Sections eight, eleven, and twenty-six in each township were reserved by Congress for future sale. Not more than two townships were to be set aside for "the purposes of a university." [10]

[10] [Report amended of Committee on Memorial of S. H. Parsons], 23 July 1787, *Journals*, XXXIII, 399–401. The documentary history of the Ohio

While the Ohio Company was making plans to exploit the West, the West itself was boiling with activity. Before surveys could be made, Congress must get the Indians to give up their claims. The result was a series of treaties. One treaty was signed at Fort McIntosh in 1785, but the Shawnee, the most important tribe, refused to come. A second treaty was negotiated at Fort Finney in 1786. The Shawnee attended and gave up some of their claims. There was no alternative to treaty-making except to kill the Indians, an alternative which the westerners tried their best to carry out.

Meanwhile, without regard for Congress or the Indians, settlers were moving beyond the Ohio and squatting on likely looking pieces of land. In 1785 Congress ordered the settlers to stay south of the Ohio. Troops were raised and sent to the frontier. They burned squatters' cabins but they could not kill the dogged hunger of men for land. When the troops moved on, the settlers came back and rebuilt their homes.[11] John Armstrong, an officer given the task of removing the settlers, declared that they were "banditti whose actions are a disgrace to human nature." [12] The settlers were defiant. One of their number issued an "advertisement" in which he said: "I do certify that all mankind, agreeable to every constitution formed in America, have an undoubted right to pass into every vacant country, and to form their constitution, and that from the Confederation of the whole United States, Congress is not empowered to forbid them, neither is Congress empowered from that Confederation to make any sale of the uninhabited lands to pay the public debts, which is to be by a tax levied and lifted by the authority of the legislature of each state." [13] Such men fought both the soldiers and the Indians. South of Ohio the Kentuckians demanded help from both Congress and Virginia and carried on a bloody struggle all the while. Between 1783 and 1790 perhaps 1,500 Kentuckians were killed and 2,000 horses were stolen. No one knows how many Indians or squatters north of the river lost their lives.[14]

Company is to be found in Archer B. Hulbert, ed.: *The Records of the Original Proceedings of the Ohio Company* (2 vols., Marietta, 1917).

[11] 1 April 1785, *Journals*, XXVIII, 223–4.

[12] William H. Smith: *The St. Clair Papers* (2 vols., Cincinnati, 1882), II, 4, n.

[13] 12 March 1785, ibid., II, 5, n.

[14] James A. James: *The Life of George Rogers Clark* (Chicago, 1928), 325.

Frontier warfare and the settlement of the land by more and more squatters convinced many a member of Congress that the westerners should be denied the right of self-government. "The emigrants to the frontier lands," wrote Timothy Pickering, "are the least worthy subjects in the United States. They are little less savage than the Indians; and when possessed of the most fertile spots, for want of industry, live miserably." [15] Pickering's attitude was shared by many important leaders who had long feared the growth of the West and who distrusted all westerners. Very few easterners took much stock in Jefferson's ideal of self-government for the West as expressed in the Ordinance of 1784. By 1786 Congress was once more discussing the problem of government for the West. James Monroe, who had made a tour of the West with troops in 1785, declared that the question with regard to government was: "Shall it be upon colonial principles, under a governor, council and judges of the United States, removable at a certain period of time and they admitted to a vote in Congress with the common rights of the other states, or shall they be left to themselves until that event?" [16]

The reconsideration of the Ordinance of 1784, which arose from the fear of westerners and the danger of Indian war, was given new urgency by the Ohio Company. These men wanted a guarantee of property rights and rigid political control. The result was the Northwest Ordinance of 1787. Richard Henry Lee put the whole case neatly when he said that the new Ordinance seemed necessary "for the security of property among uninformed, and perhaps licentious people, as the greater part of those who go there are, that a strong toned government should exist, and the rights of property be clearly defined." [17] In another letter he said that "the form of this government . . . is much more tonic than our democratic forms on the Atlantic are." [18]

Under the Ordinance of 1787, government was to be carried on by a governor, a secretary, and three judges appointed by Congress. These men were to adopt whatever laws they chose from those of the thirteen states. Whenever a district had 5,000 male inhabitants, the landowners could choose an assembly. The first

[15] To Rufus King, 4 June 1785, King: *Life*, I, 107.
[16] To John Jay, 20 April 1786, Burnett, VIII, 342.
[17] To Washington, 15 July 1787, *Letters of Richard Henry Lee*, II, 425.
[18] To [Colonel Henry? Lee], 30 July 1787, ibid., II, 430.

task of this assembly was to nominate ten men from whom Congress would pick five to act as a legislative council. The assembly could pass laws, but the governor was to have an absolute veto on all legislation. The Northwest was to be divided into not more than five nor less than three districts. Whenever any one of those divisions had 60,000 free inhabitants it was to be admitted to Congress and then be free to write a constitution and establish a state government.[19] The government of the West by Arthur St. Clair in the years after 1787 was an ample demonstration of both the westerners' dislike of eastern control, and of the clear purpose of eastern speculators to get and keep a position of pre-eminence.

So far as the government of the United States was concerned, the sale of land began to pave the way for the payment of the national debt. It was a matter of newspaper comment that such sales "must give an immediate rise to the current value of the securities of the United States, which are received in payment for the lands as specie." [20] Congress was at last in a position to carry out the conviction of many Americans that the sale of the lands was all that was needed to solve the financial burden left by the Revolution. The conflict in policy had been decided in favor of sales rather than of settlers, although even so, the land was cheap by comparison with what lands farther east were selling for. Before 1789 the sales made by the United States amounted to 1,487,986 acres for which Congress got $839,203 in securities. In addition, bounty warrants for another 238,150 acres of land were taken in.[21]

In the years to come the Land Ordinance of 1785 and the Ordinance of 1787 remained the basis for the sale and government of the national domain. By the 1830's the United States had sold more than forty-four million dollars worth of land and thus justified those men in the 1780's who had believed that the national domain alone would pay the foreign and domestic debt of the United States.

[19] 13 July 1787, *Journals*, XXXII, 334–43. The one thing left of Jefferson's original plan was that slavery was forbidden in the Northwest Territory.

[20] *Massachusetts Centinel*, 19 May 1787.

[21] Payson J. Treat: *The National Land System 1785–1820* (New York, 1910), ch. iii, "Land Sales Under the Confederation."

The Creation of a Bureaucracy

A second major achievement of the Confederation was the creation of a bureaucracy which carried on the day-to-day work of the central government. To talk of the Confederation government in terms only of Congress—of its difficulties in doing business, of the failure of some of the states to be fully represented—is to tell a distorted story, for the government continued to function whether Congress met or not. Congress was primarily a policy-making, not an administrative body, although administrative officers were elected by and responsible to it. This practice was reversed after 1789 when administrative officers were made responsible to the executive rather than to the legislature. The creation of a responsible staff of civil servants by the Confederation government is an almost unknown story. These men carried on the work of the departments of war, foreign affairs, finance, and the post office in season and out. Many of them continued to be employed after 1789. The best example of this was Joseph Nourse of Virginia who became register of the treasury in 1779, a post which he held until 1829 when he retired because of old age. He kept books and prepared innumerable reports for Robert Morris, the board of treasury, Alexander Hamilton, and the secretaries of the treasury who followed him. If it had not been for Nourse and men like him, with years of practical experience in the day-to-day affairs of government behind them, the Washington administration would have been badly hampered.[22]

Throughout the Revolution there had been much debate and theorizing as to the way the central government should be administered. The more democratic revolutionaries distrusted executive power of any kind and insisted that members of Congress

[22] A recent example of the failure to recognize how government administration after 1789 was rooted in the years before, is the otherwise useful book of Leonard D. White: *The Federalists* (New York, 1948). Because the author seems to take for granted the idea that the government in 1789 was virtually a new creation, he terms my *Articles of Confederation* an "account of the government of the Confederation" whereas it is in fact a study of the writing and ratification of the first Constitution of the United States, not a history of the government at all. Likewise he slights Sanders: *Executive Departments*, which is a detailed study of administrative history, problems, and theory before 1789.

themselves, acting in committees, should directly control all departments where permanent employees carried on routine business. The conservative revolutionists, on the other hand, argued consistently for the creation of single executives who were not members of Congress. They argued that this would mean efficiency in the conduct of business and leave members of Congress with more time to deal with legislative matters. The opposition to this did not dislike efficiency, but they had a lively fear of unchecked executives, a fear born of their reading of history and their more recent experience with royal governors. Until 1780 they had their way, although the committee work wore them to a frazzle. Then they began to lose ground as the conservative revolutionists gained control of Congress. By the end of 1781 single executives, not members of Congress, were in charge of war, foreign affairs, and finance.[23]

The tide turned once more as the war ended, but the only department to be changed was that of finance, where a committee of three took the place of Robert Morris. The departments of war, foreign affairs, and the post office remained in the hands of single executives. Beneath them, secretaries, clerks, commissioners, accountants, translators, and the like served from year to year without much reward and without any glory.

The one figure who, more than any other, represented continuity throughout the Revolution was Charles Thomson, the Irish-born "Sam Adams of Philadelphia." He was elected secretary of the First Continental Congress by the radical element which had immediately sensed in him a fellow spirit. Thomson kept the Journals and all the other papers of Congress and saw to their printing. He performed every sort of job that Congress wanted done, even to serving for a time as president. His office carried on correspondence between Congress and the state governments; his signature and seal were placed on the official versions of ordinances, commissions, and treaties. At its peak, his office had a deputy secretary, two clerks, and a messenger, and all of them were overworked. Thomson plainly ranked, in the eyes of many congressmen, with the president, and with the heads of executive departments after 1781. In 1785 Francois de Barbé-Marbois, the French consul general, said of Thomson that he was "the oldest servant of Congress, and there has been no one more constant

[23] See *ante*, ch. ii.

in all the revolutions which have agitated this assembly. He is a man wise, uniform, and full of moderation. The confidence of Congress in him has no limits. . . ." [24]

He was faithful and industrious to a machine-like degree. He had a sturdy temper that caused him to insist on his dignity and position in the inevitable clash of tempers among men so closely associated. He had a feud with Henry Laurens when the Charleston merchant was president of Congress. Laurens swore that Thomson refused him access to the papers of Congress. He once threatened to kick Thomson, whereupon the little man doubled up his fist and dared him to try it. Another time Laurens said that he got a reply from Thomson "so very rugged, as had nearly carried me beyond the limits within which every gentleman will confine himself in a public assembly." Thomson defended himself heartily. He said Laurens had not behaved properly as a presiding officer. He had gotten along with other presidents well enough. He said that he was "too proud a spirit to brook indignities" and that he would not court any man "however high in office, by fawning, cringing or servility." There were particular issues between them that Laurens had not mentioned. Thomson had refused to agree to Laurens's attack on Mr. Lynch, and furthermore Laurens had been unable to persuade Thomson "that Moses, the man of God and deliverer of Israel was an impostor and that he deceived the Israelites at Mount Sinai by his having had the knowledge of the use of gun-powder." Plainly the proud Charleston merchant had met his match in the equally proud Irish immigrant. Thomson came through the battle with Laurens with his position as strong as ever, but he was to have troubles again and again. In 1780 a diarist reported that "yesterday Mr. Searle caned the Secretary of Congress and the Secretary returned the same salute."

In 1783, John Jay urged Thomson to write a history of the Revolution so that posterity might have a true account of it. Leave the military story to the "voluminous historians," said Jay. "The political story of the Revolution will be most liable to misrepresentation, and future relations of it will probably be replete both with intentional and accidental errors." [25] No man of his times was better fitted to write such a history, and Thomson

[24] To Vergennes, 25 Feb. 1785, Bancroft: *Constitution*, I, 414.
[25] 19 July 1783, Charles Thomson Papers, LC.

began the task. In 1785 he told Barbé-Marbois that he had taken advantage of his custody of the papers of Congress "to prepare secret historical memoirs of everything which has not been inserted in the published journals; that his work had already more than a thousand pages in folio; and that it would complete the history of the revolution. . . ." [26] If Thomson ever wrote such a history it has been lost. There is only the barest beginning of a few pages labeled "History of the Confederation" in the Papers of the Continental Congress.[27]

When the new government was established in 1789, Thomson was chosen to carry to Mt. Vernon the official notification of Washington's election to the presidency. Thomson turned over the papers of the Confederation to the new government. He expressed a desire to retire, but it is plain that he wanted to continue in a secretarial office such as he had held. But gratitude to loyal public servants was not an invariable characteristic of the new administration, and Thomson's hopes were denied. The Federalists even objected to paying his salary during the period of transition in the spring of 1789 when he continued to keep the records and served as the symbol of the old government. Thomson lived on until 1824, keeping in touch with those people who had early looked upon him as Philadelphia's Sam Adams.[28]

The post office department was established by Congress in 1775. Benjamin Franklin, who had been deputy postmaster general for the American Colonies, was put in charge until he went to France. Beneath him were a secretary, a comptroller, and a growing number of deputy postmasters throughout the United States. The biggest problem was lack of funds because the Confederation Congress, like those of later days, kept rates low for political reasons. The officer who represented continuity was Ebenezer Hazard who held various offices from 1775 until 1782 when he became postmaster general, a post he held to the end of the Confederation. In 1782 the department had twenty-six riders carrying mail, and a variety of officials at headquarters in Philadelphia. Bad roads, poor ferry service, dishonest riders, and highwaymen all led to poor service.

[26] To Vergennes, 25 Feb. 1785, Bancroft: *Constitution*, I, 414.

[27] PCC, no. 9, LC.

[28] Sanders: *Executive Departments*, ch. x. Burnett's *Letters* and the *Journals* bear witness to Thomson's importance on almost every page.

There were constant congressional investigations, charges, and countercharges as to the source of inefficient service. Furthermore, until the Confederation was ratified, the states paid little attention to Congress's desire for a monopoly of the postal business. Even after 1781, however, some states insisted that they had the power to establish postal service within their borders.

In 1785 Congress authorized the carrying of mail by stage and was at once involved in troubles over contracts, for stagecoach owners, like steamship, railroad, and airline owners of later days, sought to get all the traffic would bear. The post office department found it difficult to pay expenses out of income, but so does it now. Meanwhile the postal service expanded. By 1788 there were sixty-six deputy postmasters scattered from Maine to Georgia, and in the same year, Congress directed the postmaster to provide service to the Ohio Valley.[29]

The war department was set up under a single executive in 1781, and General Benjamin Lincoln was appointed its head. He was the only one of the new "executives" who was not a member of the Morris group, and he refused to fall in with their plans. If he had, said one of Morris's enemies, "Heaven only knows what kind of a form our federal government would have assumed." [30] After Lincoln resigned in 1783 Joseph Carleton, secretary in the department, carried on the business. Early in 1785 Congress passed an ordinance clarifying the duties of the department. The secretary was to keep his office near Congress, keep track of public stores, and settle the accounts of the department.[31]

Early in March 1785, General Henry Knox was elected secretary from among several ambitious candidates. The most ardent of them was Timothy Pickering of Massachusetts, an earnest seeker of government jobs after 1783.[32] However, Knox's friends had promoted him ever since Lincoln's resignation, and Knox had the enormous advantage of Washington's support. It was that support which got him the command at West Point at the end of the war and in 1785, "the Great Man," said Pickering, "interested himself warmly in favor of the successful candidate." [33]

[29] Sanders: *Executive Departments*, ch. ix.

[30] Samuel Osgood to John Adams, 7 Dec. 1783, Burnett, VII, 380.

[31] 27 Jan. 1785, *Journals*, XXVIII, 21–4. The secretary was to have the power to appoint the members of his department.

[32] Pickering Papers, MHS.

[33] To General Gates, 31 March 1785, Emmet Coll., Misc., NYPL.

As secretary, Knox had many duties. He was in charge of public stores, the disposition of troops, frontier defense, including the superintendents of Indian affairs who were ordered to obey his instructions, and the administration of the military bounty lands. In 1788 the department consisted of Knox, three clerks, and a messenger. Six hundred and seventy-nine men and officers were in the army. These men were stationed at various posts on the frontier. Arms and ammunition were located at various arsenals scattered from Massachusetts to South Carolina. Knox, both as a private individual and as secretary of war, heartily supported the ideals of the nationalists. He spoke of the "vile state governments" as "sources of pollution" and he worked actively in the suppression of Shays's Rebellion. Thus it was natural for the Washington administration to take him and his department over into the new government without a break in continuity of policy or personnel.[34]

The first "Secretary for Foreign Affairs" was Robert R. Livingston of New York, a man entirely congenial to the Morris group. His resignation in 1782 was greeted with delight by ardent revolutionary leaders such as the Lees and the Adams's and by others who disliked the Morris influence, whatever their political beliefs. There were many candidates to succeed him, but no one was elected for months and the business of the department was conducted by the president of Congress. Then in May 1784 John Jay was elected before his return from Europe. Jay did not accept at once. Congress had been on the move ever since it had left Philadelphia in the summer of 1783. It moved to Annapolis and then to Trenton. Jay said that he had a family, and before he could accept, Congress must decide where it was going to locate.[35] Congress moved to New York late in 1784 and Jay accepted the post. At once he made it clear that he intended to play an important role and that if Congress did not like it, he would resign. Congress soon agreed that all correspondence relating to foreign affairs should go through Jay's office, which was staffed with an undersecretary, a doorkeeper, a messenger, clerks, and three interpreters. Jay busied himself with problems of foreign trade, infractions of the Treaty of Peace, and negotiations with foreign

[34] Sanders: *Executive Departments*, ch. vi.

[35] To Charles Thomson, 20 Oct. 1784, Charles Thomson Papers, LC. Jay also demanded the power to appoint those who were to serve under him.

powers. He attended Congress, served on committees, and debated on the floor. His prestige and power were great, although his popularity was uncertain.[36] He represented, as no other man except Charles Thomson, continuity of policy because of the turnover of membership in Congress and the failure of many states to be represented during sessions. "The little stability of Congress," said Otto, the French consul in New York, "insensibly gives to the ministers of the different departments a power incompatible with the spirit of liberty and of jealousy which prevails in this country . . . Mr. Jay especially has acquired a peculiar ascendancy over the members of Congress." Otto feared that since so much important business went through his office, Congress would "insensibly become accustomed to seeing only through the eyes of Mr. Jay," and this he thought was "hurtful to the freedom and impartiality which ought to prevail in the national senate." [37] Jay, however, did not always have his way. He wanted to war on the Algerian pirates, but Congress refused. Popular opinion defeated his proposal to surrender the navigation of the Mississippi to Spain in return for trade privileges for northern merchants.

Politically he was as much of a nationalist as Henry Knox, and his letters constantly refer to his hope of adding power to the central government. The appointments of Knox and Jay to permanent posts at a time when the opponents of strong central government were in the ascendancy may be only a seeming paradox. Jay had redeemed himself with the Lee-Adams group, temporarily at least, by his opposition to Spain and France while in Europe. Knox had behind him the powerful support of Washington's prestige and also a surface willingness to float with the tide. But far more important, perhaps, was the fact that the antinationalists had for years focused most of their fire on the treasury and in particular on Robert Morris, superintendent of finance.

Robert Morris's name is well known, but the significance of his public life is but dimly realized. As a figure of the Revolution he is perhaps a more important symbol than Sam Adams, for the

[36] Sanders: *Executive Departments*, 119–27.

[37] To Vergennes, 25 Dec. 1785, Bancroft: *Constitution*, I, 473–5; to Vergennes, 10 Jan. 1786, ibid., I, 479. Otto was much alarmed by Jay's anti-French attitude.

latter's work was finished in 1776, whereas Morris's greatness and influence began then and rose to its peak in 1781–3, when he shaped the policies of government and dominated much of the economic life of the new nation. Beyond this, he was for a time the figure around which centered all those men who sought to give the new nation a powerful central government and who, in 1783, contemplated without many qualms the possibility of doing so by force.

Such men had bitter enemies among those who had been active leaders in starting the war for independence and in establishing the independence of the several states. They deplored not only Morris's political ideals, but his business practices also, and kept up an increasing fire against them in public and in private. The most violent of his enemies were Arthur, William, and Richard Henry Lee of Virginia. They were ably assisted by Samuel Adams and James Warren of Massachusetts and by democratic leaders in Pennsylvania such as Samuel and George Bryan. But, in addition, many merchants such as Henry Laurens of Charleston, Stephen Higginson of Boston, and political moderates like Joseph Reed of Philadelphia, also opposed Morris and his group. Reed, for instance, in 1783 lamented the "universal discouragement of the Whigs, who find themselves impoverished and even sunk in credit by the new and rising interests." Morris, he said, was a man "whose dictates none dare oppose, and from whose decisions lay no appeal." [38]

No attack on Morris was more extreme than that by William Lee who declared him a most dangerous man in America. He said that Morris was bankrupt at the beginning of the war, left the country bankrupt at the end of it, but that at the same time "amassed an immense fortune for himself. . . ." [39] The first attack on Morris's business methods came as early as 1775 and continued throughout the war.[40] Henry Laurens got into an open row with Morris over the waste of money by the secret committee which placed war contracts from 1775 to 1777. Laurens swore that men like Morris made "patriotism the stalking horse to their

[38] To Nathanael Greene, 14 March 1783, Joseph Reed Papers, NYHS. See also Rev. William Gordon to Gen. Horatio Gates, 21–2 Jan., 3 Feb. 1783, Gates Papers, NYHS.

[39] Worthington C. Ford, ed.: *Letters of William Lee* (3 vols., Brooklyn, 1891), III, 947–8.

[40] John Adams, Notes of Debates, 25 Sept. 1775, *Works*, II, 448–9.

private interests" and hid behind Washington as they did so.[41] The greatest scandal that broke during the war, and which led to so many charges and countercharges that the truth may never be known, was that over the purchase of supplies in Europe. Silas Deane got most of the blame, but he was a partner and agent of Morris and other American merchants. Benjamin Franklin was repeatedly accused of complicity. The Lees of Virginia carried on the fight on both sides of the Atlantic with the shrill insistence of terriers worrying a mastiff.[42] In the middle of the fight Laurens resigned as president of Congress so that he could carry on the battle from the floor. After Morris became superintendent of finance his enemies forced an investigation of his conduct in office, but nothing came of it.[43] By the spring of 1783, as Morris and his group played off one force against another in an effort to gain power for the central government, the clamor against them rose to a peak. Privately, Morris told Congress that he would resign, and then, without consulting it, published his resignation in the newspapers. He declared that "funding them [the public debts] on solid revenues, was the last essential work of our glorious revolution" but that he was now afraid that it would not be done. He stated that to increase the debts without providing the means of payment "does not consist with my ideas of integrity." [44] Congressmen were furious, for this action was an open attempt to force adoption of his funding scheme. Arthur Lee attacked him in a series of newspaper essays. He charged that Morris had destroyed public credit and had accused Congress and the states with intent to defraud, while he himself had made a fortune out of the war.[45] Arthur Lee was attacked in turn as a disgruntled office seeker who should have had Morris's job except that no one trusted him, which might be an advantage since he trusted no one.[46] Despite his resignation, Morris stayed in office and it was believed by some that he would ruin the chances of anyone

[41] To John Laurens, 8 Jan. 1778, Burnett, III, 20–5.

[42] Arthur Lee to James Warren, 8 April 1782, ibid., VI, 326.

[43] Diary of Robert Morris, 29 Aug. 1782, Wharton, V, 676; Arthur Lee to Samuel Adams, 6 Aug. 1782, Burnett, VI, 429.

[44] *Pennsylvania Gazette*, 5 March 1783, supplement.

[45] Philadelphia *Freeman's Journal*, 5, 12 March 1783.

[46] "Civis," "To the Honorable Arthur Lee Esquire, Delegate from the Commonwealth of Virginia to the Congress of the United States," Philadelphia, *The Independent Gazeteer; or the Chronicle of Freedom*, 12 April 1783.

who tried to take his place. Opposition to the impost of 1783 was in part the result of a belief that if it were granted, it would merely increase Morris's power, not that of Congress, for he would control appointments and the disposal of the money received.[47]

Opposition grew rapidly even far from Philadelphia. General Greene wrote Washington from South Carolina that the people of the state were much prejudiced against both Congress and "the Financier" and that this was leading to more independence of Congress than one could wish for.[48] The legislature of Massachusetts made its objections specific in October 1783. It declared that it had been natural to focus attention on the war and that to have done otherwise "would have been grasping at the shadow and relinquishing the substance" but that now it was time to "examine minutely the principles upon which we are acting. . . ." The legislature complained about the failure to handle the national debt adequately and then instructed its delegates to "use your *unremitting* endeavors to have the office of superintendent of finance abolished, and a board of treasury, consisting of three persons, annually chosen from different states, with proper powers, instituted in its stead; for history invariably evinces, that the public revenue naturally begets influence to the person to whom the disposal of it is committed; and it must be our wisdom to diminish that bane of all free governments, by placing it in such a manner as to have the least possible effect. However pressing and justifiable the reasons might have been for instituting the office of superintendent of finance, and intrusting such extensive powers thereto; or however faithfully and impartially they may have been exercised, we conceive such reasons do now cease, and in a time of general tranquility cannot operate for its continuance. If you should fail in your application for the abolition of that office, you are by all means to endeavor to procure an abridgement of its powers, so far as relates to the great control over public officers, and in the settlement of public accounts." [49] The final story of Morris's administration remains to be told. There is no question but that he was an extremely skilful manipulator of funds and credit and that he brought a measure of system into the chaos of Revolutionary finance. But in the course of doing so

[47] Stephen Higginson to Samuel Adams, 20 May 1783, Burnett, VII, 166–7.
[48] 16 March 1783, Washington Papers, LC.
[49] Massachusetts *Acts and Resolves* (1782–3), 796–8.

it seems evident that he did not distribute available funds with an even hand, that he did use his financial power to reward friends and partners while ignoring the claims of equally worthy citizens. Thus his letter books show that he drew bills of exchange in favor of such partners as John Ross and John Langdon, and Haym Solomon, "my broker." These bills were drawn on Dutch and French bankers where the United States had credits, and on state collectors and loan officers who had funds. Thus Morris's connections got most of the available money of the United States, while other creditors got nothing at all.[50] Dr. Edward Bancroft, the ex-spy, came to Philadelphia after the war. He had been and was to be connected with the private business dealings of Morris, Deane, and others. He wrote as a matter of fact—and not in condemnation—that Morris would resign as soon as he could "extricate some of his friends" and that he was endeavoring to do this "by the money borrowing in Holland. . . ." [51] Barbé-Marbois, the French consul general, told the French government flatly that Morris was a man who expected the French government to pay "all the illegitimate profits that he had taken to himself, and of which he is unhappily in possession." Marbois said that Morris's "avidity can make him capable of very reprehensible irregularities" and, unless bound by Congress, would take few pains to fulfill obligations of the United States to France.[52]

When a man's enemies, his friends, and foreign observers all agree that he is using his office for private gain, even if the charge is completely unfounded, his tenure is apt to be uncertain or, at least, his usefulness slight. After repeated threats to do so, and long after he had lost control of Congress, Morris finally retired 1 November 1784.[53]

As the campaign against Morris mounted, his enemies made plans to take over the treasury. The Massachusetts delegates,

[50] Official Letter Books, *passim*, LC.

[51] To William Frazer, 8 Nov. 1783, Bancroft: *Constitution*, I, 332. Bancroft predicted that this loan would fail when Van Berckel's reports got back to Holland. John Adams actually did negotiate a loan. Evidence of Bancroft's connections with Morris are to be found in a letter of Silas Deane to Jeremiah Wadsworth, still another Morris connection, 14 Dec. 1784, Emmet Coll., no. 593, NYPL.

[52] To Rayneval, 24 Aug. 1784, Bancroft: *Constitution*, I, 379–80.

[53] Official Letter Book F, 331, LC. He published an accounting of his years as superintendent in 1785, but it satisfied no one and there were repeated investigations continuing into the 1790's.

acting on their instructions, moved that the treasury be "revised." The result was a report which in effect slapped Morris, for it declared that if any of the proposed three commissioners engaged in trade directly or indirectly, they could never thereafter hold any office under the United States. Congress at first rejected the report, declaring that there had been "very great advantages" from the administration of Robert Morris. But the very next day the ordinance was passed. It provided that a board of treasury should exercise the powers of the superintendent of finance and suffer only loss of office if they engaged in trade.[54] It took time to elect the commissioners. Those first chosen refused appointment. In January 1785, Samuel Osgood of Massachusetts, Walter Livingston of New York, and John Lewis Gervais of South Carolina were elected. After the latter refused, Arthur Lee of Virginia was chosen. Thus by the summer of 1785 the board of treasury, dominated by two of Morris's leading enemies, was in control of the finances of the United States.[55] Congress, said James Warren, has "got clear of that sink of corrupt influence which so long contaminated some of their measures," of an office "which made rapid strides to dominion. . . ."[56]

The duties of the new board were many. It supervised the treasury officials who were settling the accounts of the military departments, the continental loan officers in the states, the commissioners who were settling accounts between the United States and the states and between the United States and individuals. The multitudes of memorials sent to Congress were turned over to the board for investigation. The board called for documents, heard evidence, and reported back to Congress. There were hundreds of requests, particularly from hopeful souls who saw a chance to make something out of the confusion. The widow of a brigadier general asked for extra money in 1788. The request was turned over to secretary of war Knox who reported back that he was sorry for widows and orphans but that he was not "sensible of any particular services or sufferings performed or sustained by her late husband whereon to justify so uncommon a partiality."[57] In 1776 three speculating merchants of Albany had bought goods

[54] *Journals*, XXVI, 356–7; XXVII, 437–43, 469–71.
[55] Ibid., XXVIII, 18; XXIX, 582.
[56] To John Adams, 28 Jan. 1785, *Warren-Adams Letters*, II, 248–9.
[57] PCC, no. 138, I, pt. 2, ff. 567–8, LC.

in Canada which they sold to the army and lost money in the doing. In 1786 they claimed that they had done so for the United States and should be repaid. The board tracked down the facts and reported back that the merchants had engaged in speculation as private individuals and "though the event proved contrary to their expectations" they had no more claim on the United States than the public creditors.[58] Daniel Gray of Connecticut, a former assistant commissary of purchases, claimed that he had money coming from the government, but the board could find no record that he was entitled to any, and stated that "the general opinion entertained of his character will not justify a blind and implicit confidence in the accuracy and propriety of his charges." [59]

Then there was Richard Gridley of Massachusetts: he told Congress that in 1775 a Major Browne had furnished him with a horse and buggy to carry his surveying instruments. But, said Gridley, "the horse so furnished was killed at the Battle of Bunker's Hill, and the sulky (being kept in the public service 'till the year 1780) rendered altogether useless." Major Browne applied to the state of Massachusetts for payment and was refused. He then sued Gridley and collected fifty pounds of the lawful money of Massachusetts. The board solemnly examined the case and reported back that Gridley was a Massachusetts colonel when he got the horse and buggy and that his claim could not be allowed without "establishing a precedent which would subject the general treasury to a multitude of claims. . . ." [60]

In addition to endless petty claims such as these, the board prepared endless reports to Congress on income and outgo. They paid the troops and the civil employees. They kept up a constant correspondence with state officials urging prompt payments of monies provided by state legislatures.[61] The board worked out careful procedures for the conduct of the business of handling accounts. When Congress referred a question to the board, it examined the merits of the case and reported back to Congress. If Congress then resolved that an indefinite sum be allowed, the claim then went to the comptroller's office in which there were three independent

[58] *Journals*, XXX, 205–6.

[59] Ibid., XXIX, 839–40.

[60] Ibid., XXX, 437–8.

[61] For instance see the Board of Treasury to Gerard Bancker, Treasurer of New York, 13 May 1786, and Bancker's reply, 16 May 1786, PCC, no. 139, ff. 261, 265, LC.

officers. The clerk examined the accounts and reported to the auditor who likewise examined them. If the claimant was dissatisfied with the decision of these two officials, he could appeal to the comptroller whose decision was final, not even the board of treasury having the power to alter it. Whatever amount he found due he reported to the board and it in turn issued a warrant on the treasurer for payment.[62]

There is every evidence that the board was rigorously honest. No complaints against the red tape insisted upon by government accounting officers in the twentieth century are any more querulous than those leveled at the board of treasury because of its rigid insistence on the documentation of all claims.

As the board struggled in the swamps of unsettled accounts and wrangled with the states, its members often sounded like the man whose administration they had so bitterly denounced. As they sat on the inside looking out, they too became concerned with acquisition of more power for the central government. Samuel Osgood declared that the management of money matters was a serious business. He deplored the payment of debt that had taken place as a result of depreciation, and also the millions of dollars that would perhaps never be accounted for because of confusion during the war. But things were different now; there was more time "as well as the experience purchased by the needless expenditure of upwards of fifty million dollars to introduce order and economy in our money transactions." He now believed that Congress either must have coercive power to collect money or to levy an impost. He admitted that the power to do justice would also involve the power to do injustice: "power must be lodged somewhere yet it should be done with a proper degree of caution and such checks" as to prevent misuse. He had once been opposed to such power, but experience had obliged him to change. Patriotism and public virtue "are no match in this country for dishonesty and intrigue. Americans have no more virtue than other people." [63] Osgood had moved far since 1783. Arthur Lee too had moved as he faced the problems of finance, but he was more concerned, as he

[62] Samuel Osgood to Francis Dana, 8 Jan. 1786, Osgood Papers, NYHS.

[63] To Rev. William Gordon, 19 Jan. 1786, Osgood Papers, NYHS. This was in answer to a letter from Gordon, 10 Jan. 1786, in which Gordon asked why Congress did not "accommodate itself to the wishes of many well meaning republicans" and ask for the impost for only fifteen years and allow states to employ their own collectors.

had always been, with the dangers of speculation. He wrote to Sam Adams, "I am afraid my dear friend that we will live to see the noble fabric we have labored so much to rear to liberty, honor, and independence, uprooted from its foundation from the rapacity for speculation which appears to me to have ascended from commissaries and quartermasters to legislators." He denounced the efforts to avoid payment of debts to Britain; the emission of paper money; the purchase of securities by a few, at two to three shillings on the pound. He said that such things were perhaps the reason the states did not contribute enough money to the union. Money was desperately needed to pay interest on the foreign debt and the salaries of the employees of the Confederation government.[64]

Such men as Lee and Osgood, unlike their fellow officers Jay and Knox, did not want a "national" government, but they did want enough power lodged in Congress to maintain the Confederation. Lee perhaps realized that the best defence against the drive of the nationalists would be such power. Meanwhile the board of treasury labored with the financial problems left by the war. Their means were inadequate, as they realized, but by 1789 much of the chaos at war's end had been reduced to a pattern of investigation, evaluation, and settlement.

[64] 14 Feb. 1786, Samuel Adams Papers, NYPL.

19
The Aftermath of Wartime Finance

The Settlement of Accounts

THE GOVERNMENT of the Confederation worked hard at liquidating the financial problems left by the war. Although something had been done before the end of the war, there still remained the vast problem of settling accounts between Congress and the states; the accounts of the five army departments; the granting of depreciation, back pay, and commutation certificates promised the officers and soldiers of the Continental Army; the disentanglement of the muddled affairs of the secret and commercial committees; the adjustment of the records of American agents and diplomats, and of European bankers and merchants, involved in borrowing money and buying war supplies in Europe.

The settlement of all these accounts was enormously difficult because throughout eight years of war so many different people had handled government funds. Some had kept records which could be found, others had kept records and lost them, still others refused to surrender those they held, while many had kept none at all. All sorts of people had been given cash, bills of exchange, paper money, and quartermaster and commissary certificates. The records of what they had received, what they had bought, and what they had turned over to the government and the army were, at best, confused. This was as true of headquarters offices as it was of commanders of small bodies of troops in remote parts of the country. Agents in Europe handled vast sums: loans, bills of exchange, cargoes of tobacco, proceeds from the sales of captures, and the like. When one adds to this the fact that the various forms of money and certificates used declined in value while prices rose rapidly, and that the policy of the government was to settle all accounts in terms of actual specie value, one can begin to understand the task that faced the board of treasury and the various commissioners who settled accounts under its direction during the 1780's.

The biggest problem was the settlement of accounts between the central and state governments. The Articles of Confederation provided the basis. They stated that expenses for the common defense and general welfare were to be paid from a common treasury to be supplied by the states in proportion to the value of granted and surveyed land and the buildings and improvements on such land in each of the states. Such a valuation had not been made by the end of the war. At that time an amendment to the Articles was proposed which divided expenses among the states according to population; this amendment the states refused to ratify.

Meanwhile, lacking any accurate valuation, Congress apportioned expenses among the states according to rough guesses as to their population. Congress issued requisitions on each for its share of the expenses, and the states in turn were credited or debited on the books of the treasury with what they paid or failed to pay on these requisitions. Simplicity ends at this point, for until 1780 Congress had financed itself largely through paper money, the sale of loan office certificates, the issuance of commissary and quartermaster certificates, and foreign loans. The states too contributed to war costs. They raised and paid troops; they supplied the Continental Army with food, clothing, and ammunition; they issued paper money and borrowed money themselves for the common cause. States received continental funds to use as well. In turn, upon requisition by Congress, the states supplied continental money, specie, state money, and specific supplies of food, clothing, and ammunition to Congress. In the course of this interchange most of the states were convinced that they had supplied far more to the United States than their appropriate share. Therefore, when faced with financial difficulties of their own, they told Congress that they had paid enough or too much. They threatened to stop payments, and some actually did so. Let the slack states pay up, they argued, and above all let the accounts be settled. No one knew quite how this could be done equitably.

The nationalist politicians wanted to solve the problem by declaring all state expenses a part of the common debt incurred in fighting the war, the whole to be administered by the central government. This would have been a simple way of avoiding the complex problem of balancing accounts, but another motive was involved as well. Robert Morris was convinced that such action would be as significant a centralizing force as the loan office debt. In 1783 he had the support of men like Jefferson, probably because Virginia had an enormous war debt which would be lightened if assigned to Congress and then redistributed among the states either according to population or land values. However, Congress would not include the idea in the finance plan of 1783 when it went to the states, and the need of balancing accounts remained as great as ever.[1]

One plan had been worked out early in 1782 and commissioners went to the states to do the job. States that were found making overpayments were to be credited with interest; states that had not paid their share were to be charged interest. The commissioners were also given power to settle the claims of individuals who held quartermaster and commissary certificates given by army purchasing agents. Five commissioners were appointed to settle the accounts of the five army departments: quartermaster, commissary, hospital, clothier, and marine.[2]

Some progress was made. Then in June 1784, Congress once more revised policy. Commissioners were given wider discretion. At the same time Congress directed that new certificates be given for old quartermaster and commissary certificates, which, like other certificates, were to draw six per cent interest.[3]

Some of the commissioners had little difficulty as they went about exchanging new certificates for old.[4] Most of them were

[1] Morris to the President of Congress, 8 March 1783, Jared Sparks, ed.: *The Diplomatic Correspondence of the American Revolution* (12 vols., New York, 1829–30), XII, 335–6. During the 1780's, as we have seen, Virginia paid most of her war debt.

[2] *Journals*, XXII, 83–8, 102–4. All such commissioners were to be appointed and controlled by the superintendent of finance.

[3] 3 June 1784, ibid., XXVII, 541–4. The basis for all settlements was to be the scale of depreciation which Congress had adopted in August 1780.

[4] McCormick: New Jersey in the Confederation, ch. vii.

slow and methodical and were damned by commissioners appointed by the states to work with them.[5] The Massachusetts legislature insisted that the rules were too complicated and should be simplified.[6] For their part the commissioners had troubles too. Some states had no documents to support their claims, or state officials refused to supply records. Others simply ignored the men sent out by Congress.[7] Despite such difficulties, men in some of the small states soon finished their jobs and were ready to move on to other tasks.[8]

The difficulties were enormous in states like Virginia which allowed county and state courts to pass on all claims for supplies provided the United States. When such claims were granted by the courts, the claimants were given certificates and the state then charged them against the United States.[9] Such procedure was shocking to the commissioners and to the board of treasury, but Virginia paid no attention.

The complaints against slowness and against meticulous methods finally induced Congress to change procedures in 1787. Five men were given the job formerly handled by one for each state. These new commissioners were given more leeway. Congress also agreed that state expenditures unauthorized by Congress could be included in the final settlement. A board of review was set up in New York to make final decision on all claims, whether supported by adequate evidence or not, and with the power to make allowances "as they shall think consistent with the principles of general equity." [10]

Even the new freedom granted the commissioners of Congress did not make their lot an easy one. William Winder complained that he had to examine no less than 150,000 documents submitted by Virginia. Furthermore, the state would not let him bundle

[5] Oliver Ellsworth and Oliver Wolcott, jr. to the General Assembly [Connecticut], May 1785, William Samuel Johnson Papers, LC.

[6] To the Board of Treasury, 1 July 1785, Osgood Papers, NYHS.

[7] William Winder to the governor of Delaware, 15 Aug. 1785, Nicholas Van Dyke Papers, LC.

[8] William Winder, Statement of Liquidated Claims in Delaware, 31 May 1786, Gratz Collection, PHS. Winder said that he had issued 580 certificates numbered from one to 580 amounting to $43,960.21, and that there were a few unliquidated claims left for which certificates might still be issued.

[9] Andrew Dunscomb, Commissioner for Adjusting the Accounts of Virginia, to the Board of Treasury, 1 July 1785, PCC, no. 139, f. 229, LC.

[10] 7 May 1787, *Journals*, XXXII, 262–6.

them up and send them to New York to speed up the work.[11]

Because of the sheer mass of evidence that had to be gone through, the state accounts were not finally settled by the end of the Confederation, but much of the basic work had been done. Not until 1793 were commissioners, appointed according to an act of Congress in 1790, able to complete the task. When it was done the suspicion of many of the states was confirmed. It was found that, as a whole, they had contributed $114,407,297 to fighting the war whereas the central government had contributed but $36,742,599 to them. When the balance was divided among the states according to their population, the central government owed money to seven states. Much bitterness resulted in the case of states like Virginia which had contributed more than nineteen million and received less than four million and yet was charged with $100,000, a sum which she refused to pay.[12]

The certificates promised the Army were handed out rapidly. By the end of 1786, John Pierce, commissioner of army accounts, had virtually finished the task of issuing the depreciation, back pay, and commutation certificates which had been promised to the officers and soldiers of the Continental Army. Nearly eleven million dollars in such certificates had been issued within three years.[13]

The settlement of the accounts of the five army departments was more complex, for part of them had been settled by the states and part of them by the commissioners of the United States who took up the certificates issued by purchasing agents during the war. The other side of the problem was the settlement of the accounts of the headquarters departments. Untold sums of paper money, cash, and quartermaster and commissary certificates had been handed over to purchasing agents, deputies, sub-deputies, and the like. The board of treasury insisted on an accounting, and well it might; for it turned out that the United States was

[11] 28 May 1788, PCC, no. 138, I, pt. 1, ff. 365–79, LC. See also his letters to Andrew Dunscomb and his trial abstracts, PCC, no. 138, I, pt. 1, ff. 345–55, LC.

[12] Report of Commissioners of the Public Debt, 29 June 1793, Treasury Department, Bureau of the Public Debt, Old Loan Office Records, NA.

[13] List of Certificates issued to the Officers and Soldiers of the Late Army of the United States by John Pierce, Commissioner, to 2 Nov. 1786, Osgood Papers, NYHS. As an illustration of the careful way Pierce worked see his letter to Governor Nicholas Van Dyke of Delaware, 7 Sept. 1786, Nicholas Van Dyke Papers, LC.

often a creditor. The task was virtually complete by the end of 1788.

The man in charge of the marine, clothier, and hospital departments found that most of the unsettled claims consisted of those of the United States against people who owed it money. Nevertheless many men still demanded money despite the records. Thus the firm of Livingston and Turnbull claimed over $2,000, although the commissioner had sued them for $17,000 which his books showed they owed the United States.[14] The man charged with winding up the accounts of the commissary and quartermaster departments likewise found that his biggest task was to collect from former officials who still owed money to the United States.[15]

Many European accounts were destined to remain tangled for decades, particularly those of Silas Deane and Caron de Beaumarchais, but others were straightened out by Thomas Barclay, who was selected by Congress in 1782 to go to Europe for that purpose.[16] American commercial agents, diplomats, and French bankers were among those involved. John Adams, for instance, had received and spent large sums on his own account, and in addition he had joint accounts with Deane, with Franklin, and with Lee and Franklin. Barclay got and examined all such records and reported back to the board of treasury.[17] The accounts of the French banker, Ferdinand Grand, were examined by Barclay. In 1785 he reported the task completed and said he believed that Grand had done the business given him "faithfully and honestly." [18]

The board of treasury, which supervised the work of so many different men after the war, gave its particular attention to the accounts of the secret and commercial committees which had been dominated by Robert Morris, his partners, and his agents.

[14] Benjamin Walker to the Board of Treasury, 6 May 1788, PCC, no. 138, I, pt. 2, ff. 393–5, LC.

[15] Jonathan Barrall to the Board of Treasury, 6 May 1788, PCC, no. 138, I, pt. 2, ff. 397–8, LC. That ardent job hunter, Timothy Pickering, still avoided settling his accounts as quartermaster-general as late as 1797 when he was secretary of state.

[16] *Journals*, XXIII, 728–30, 773–82.

[17] Accounts of John Adams, PCC, no. 138, I, pt. 1, ff. 21–2, LC; John Adams to the Board of Treasury, 26 Jan. 1787, PCC, no. 138, I, pt. 1, ff. 15–6, LC.

[18] Accounts of Ferdinand Grand with the United States, 1777–85, NA. The final settlement showed that Grand owed the United States 75,500 livres.

This attention was perhaps due to Arthur Lee, whose chief desire was to prove that Morris was corrupt. Those accounts had been political dynamite during the war, as we have seen, and eventually the accounts disappeared.[19] In 1783 Robert Morris urged that they be settled, for he said they were "far from inconsiderable" and involved people in the United States, the West Indies, and Europe.[20]

The accounts had been settled in part during the war, but in a manner that aroused suspicion. Much of it centered around William Bingham, agent of the committee in Martinique and a partner of Morris at the same time. He went there as a clerk. He returned to the United States after the war as one of the wealthiest men in the new nation. Before the end of 1781 he had claimed and been paid over a half million livres Martinique, for sixty per cent of which he presented no vouchers. After Morris took over as superintendent of finance he paid Bingham nearly 350,000 livres more.

The board of treasury went into these transactions with a vengeance. After going over the accounts they concluded that Bingham owed the United States nearly two and a half million livres Martinique.[21] Other accounts were examined with equal interest. Among others the board found that Robert Morris and one of his partners, John Ross, owed the United States a vast sum.[22]

While the United States managed to collect some, it by no means got all that was due it during the 1780's. A list of the debtors of the United States in 1790 is a long one and includes most of the men involved in the business of war supply. Of all the long list, the one who owed the government the most money was Robert Morris.[23]

The achievement of the board of treasury and the many com-

[19] They were in existence as late as 1783. See Robert Morris to Mr. —— —— Clark, 23 Sept. 1783, Official Letter Book F, LC.

[20] To the President of Congress, 12 Aug. 1783, Official Letter Book F, LC.

[21] Arthur Lee Papers, VIII, 141, HUL. Lee noted that all of Morris's partners and favorites were paid in specie "while the army was almost mutinying for want of pay." Lee at least proved to his own satisfaction what he had always suspected concerning the Morris group.

[22] Ibid., VIII, 176. The amount stated was 691,584.16 but the kind of money is not indicated.

[23] War Records, Army Branch, Revolutionary War Documents, no. 28,793, NA.

missioners who worked under its direction was a real one. The story is not one of a stricken government unable to function, but the story of a government that worked hard to settle the problems left by the war, despite the obstacles in its way. It was a government to whom merchants, war contractors, politicians, and foreign bankers owed money. The government owed money in turn and it struggled to make payments. Although it needed an independent income, it was not so helpless as is commonly supposed. The balance sheet of its income and outgo, of its credit with Dutch bankers, of the devices used to pay interest, and of the potential wealth resulting from the ownership of western lands, is a record of real effort, some results, and great promise.

The Balance Sheet of the Confederation

Perhaps no clear balance sheet of the Confederation can be created, but the records of the treasury, which have hitherto never been used by men who have written about the finances of the Revolution, offer enough evidence to show that the traditional stories are half truths at best. The achievement of the Confederation government in settling accounts is a partial demonstration of this. The government did not solve all the problems that faced it, but it can be asked, what other government before or since ever did either?

The biggest task of the Confederation government was the liquidation of the national debt. The total war debt of the Revolution was an enormous sum in terms of the paper used, but the vast bulk of it had been cancelled by the end of the war. Perhaps $400,000,000 in paper money, quartermaster, and commissary certificates of the central government, and equally great sums that had been issued by the states, had been wiped out by the middle of 1783. The remaining war debt was small by comparison, although its political significance was enormous.

In the spring of 1783 Congress estimated the remaining domestic debt of the United States at about $34,000,000. This estimate included the loan office debt, the army debt, arrears in interest, and an uncertain amount of unliquidated debt in various forms of certificates scattered throughout the country.[24] The reduction of this estimate to precise figures was the task of the board of treasury and the various commissioners appointed to "liquidate" the accounts of the United States during the 1780's. As the work continued, the treasury reported its progress to Congress. By the end of 1785, $14,578,009 had been liquidated.[25] By the end of 1787, the task was essentially complete. The liquidated loan office debt was $11,412,285. The certificates issued the army and still in circulation came to $8,932,293. Commissioners settling accounts between the states and the United States had issued $3,614,011. The commissioners settling the accounts of the army departments had issued $817,330. An item of $2,680,429 represented credits on the funding books of the treasury for settled accounts and cancelled certificates issued by commissioners and loan officers. Miscellaneous items brought the total of the liquidated debt to $27,995,242.[26]

Hamilton's first report on the public credit in 1790 is ample evidence of the success of the Confederation in liquidating the debt. His figure for the liquidated domestic debt of the United States was $27,383,917, some $600,000 less than Nourse's statement in 1787.[27]

In May 1788 the foreign debt of the United States was estimated at $10,271,561. This included money borrowed from the French and Spanish governments, the Farmers General of France, and the bankers of Holland. The foreign debt grew rapidly during the Confederation. French loans were stopped at the end of the war but Dutch bankers began making loans in 1782. Between then and 1789 they loaned the United States $3,600,000.[28] As in the

[24] 29 April 1783, *Journals*, XXIV, 286.

[25] Statement of the Domestic Debt of the United States, as Liquidated to 31 Dec. 1785, PCC, no. 141, I, ff. 87–8, LC.

[26] Statement of the Liquidated and Loan Office Debt of the United States, to 31 Dec. 1787, by Joseph Nourse, Register of the Treasury, PCC, no. 141, I, f. 361, LC. The army debt had been reduced by nearly two million dollars since John Pierce, Commissioner of Army Accounts had reported his work in November 1786. See Osgood Papers, NYHS. This reduction is perhaps in part the result of the sale of lands in the Old Northwest.

[27] Samuel McKee, ed.: *Papers on Public Credit, Commerce and Finance by Alexander Hamilton* (New York, 1934), 24. Hamilton estimated that there was another two million dollars of unliquidated debt, mostly in continental bills of credit. He estimated the arrears of interest at over thirteen millions.

[28] Report by Joseph Nourse, 6 May 1788, United States Finance, Misc., MSS. Div., LC.

case of the domestic debt, Hamilton was in substantial agreement with Nourse as to the foreign debt. He estimated it to be $10,070,307 in 1790, a smaller figure than Nourse's, but he added to it arrears in interest which he calculated at $1,640,071.[29]

The money borrowed during the Confederation was spent carefully, with the result that excellent credit was maintained in Holland. In the four years from 1784 through 1787, $583,062 was paid in interest, $127,598 was used to pay the expenses of American ministers, $172,087 was spent in the payment of old accounts, and $136,737 was paid in premiums on the loans made. In addition $319,242 was paid by Ferdinand Grand and the American ministers for bills of exchange drawn by Robert Morris and the board of treasury. The failure of a Dutch banking house in which the United States had deposited money accounted for $43,110. The total cash spent was $1,381,836 by the end of 1787.[30]

The United States thus maintained a handsome cash balance on deposit with Dutch and French bankers throughout the Confederation. This was the result of the policy of the board of treasury, of John Adams, and of the cautious Dutch bankers who not only lent money to the government, but who bought up increasing amounts of the domestic debt of the United States during the 1780's. Interest on the Dutch loans was paid regularly. The only interest defaulted was that on a French loan which came due in 1786, whereupon the French government assumed the payments on it until 1790. The faith of the Dutch bankers in the future of the United States was shown in offers to buy the entire debt of the United States to France.

In this they soon found competition from various American speculators and European bankers. It seemed to all the interested parties that the hard-pressed French government might be induced to sell the American debt at a healthy discount, and all of them believed that the United States was a land of opportunity. Interest grew more avid as the Constitution of 1787 was sent to the states for adoption, but it was the unsettled land of the United States that seemed the best justification for speculation in American debt. American land might not always be at the center, but it was always in the near periphery, of even the most cautious

29 McKee: *Papers by Alexander Hamilton*, 23.

30 Joseph Nourse, Register's Office, 31 July 1788, Abstract of Foreign Payments in 1784, 1785, 1786, & 1787, PCC, no. 141, I, ff. 413–5, LC.

banker's hopeful thoughts of the future in the eighteenth century.

When an international combine of French and English bankers and speculators sent Brissot de Warville to America in 1787, one of them told him that the Americans would adopt the new constitution and that thereafter every eye ought to look to America "as being the unfailing road to prosperity" and that Europeans would buy land there. "I know of no period when the spirit of speculation has been so general as at the present," he wrote, "no period which presents a revolution like that of independent America; and no foundation so solid as that which they are about to establish." [31]

When de Warville got to America in 1788 he met Andrew Craigie and William Duer, secretary of the board of treasury. An agreement was soon worked out between de Warville acting for Etienne Clavière, a Swiss banker who had moved to France, and Craigie and Duer. They proposed to buy up the United States debt to France and as much of the domestic debt as they could manage. In addition they hoped to get control of all the loans to be made by the United States. Duer and de Warville were given large shares, in the hope of preventing them from dealing with Robert and Gouverneur Morris, who had similar notions. Duer had as a secret partner Samuel Osgood of the board of treasury, who had indeed traveled far since the days when he had denounced the speculations of Robert Morris.[32]

Duer was not a man to limit his opportunities by loyalty to agreements or partners. Soon he was in touch with Robert Morris and Jeremiah Wadsworth. Then, after Duer "conceived" that Mrs. Henry Knox "had been assailed on the subject," the secretary of war became interested. All these men were aware that the Dutch bankers had the inside track in American finances and that they had offered to buy the debt in 1786. They decided that if the proper man could be sent as minister to Holland, it might help in the competition for the purchase of the American debt to France. Some of them thought that Gouverneur Morris would be the right man, but Knox and Wadsworth suggested Rufus King. Duer therefore approached King. King was coy but interested and said that he was not indisposed to a foreign appointment, and that "if in perfect consistence with the duties and dignity of the

[31] Quoted in Davis: *Essays*, I, 156–7.
[32] Ibid., I, 158–61.

office, I could promote the interest of my friends it would be a great satisfaction to me." [33]

The plans of this group of hopeful speculators were frustrated, partly by their own duplicity toward one another, and partly because the Dutch bankers had laid their grounds well through the purchase of large sums of the domestic debt and through loans to the government of the United States. Eventually they did buy the French debt, and they remained the chief bankers of the United States after 1789 as they had been before.[34] The foreign debt of the United States was thus a matter of lively interest to contemporaries, who had much more faith in its ultimate payment than most of the people who have written about it since that time. Interest mounted after the Convention of 1787, but Europe's most cautious bankers had shown their confidence in the United States before anyone knew there would be such a convention.

The domestic debt was a subject of similar interest, although it sold on the market at far less than its face value. The market value was low because the government was able to pay only part of the interest and that part in indents rather than in cash. Furthermore, as it passed from hand to hand and was consolidated in the hands of relatively few men, there was a persistent demand in the states that when the debt was paid, its holders should be paid what they had given for it and not its face value. That was the practice in the payment of some of the state debts during the 1780's and perhaps only the wildest visionaries among the speculators hoped for what Hamilton gave them after 1789. Despite this the debt was a subject of ever-increasing interest. The states began buying it up against the day of final settlement between them and the central government; the Dutch bankers began buying it; and western lands were opened for sale and could be bought with debt certificates. All these things started the market upwards, and after the Convention of 1787 the boom was on.

Meanwhile the Confederation was not a government staggering along without an income, as is so often assumed. The treasury records for the 1780's are full and often confusing, but at the same

[33] Notes on a Conversation with William Duer, 21 Dec. 1788, Rufus King Papers, NYHS; King: *Life*, I, 623–4.

[34] The best account of these schemes is in Davis: *Essays*, I, ch. iii, "William Duer, Entrepreneur, 1747–99." There is a detailed unpublished account in Robert R. LaFollette: The American Revolutionary Foreign Debt and its Liquidation (Ph. D. Thesis, George Washington University, 1931).

time illuminating. During the administration of Robert Morris the total receipts of the treasury, from taxes, loans, financial operations, and the like, were $8,177,431.[35] Expenses dropped drastically at the end of the war; and so did income. The treasury records, however, show that the central government continued to have a yearly, if fluctuating, income throughout the Confederation. The receipts of the treasury were the following: 1785, $632,389; 1786, $478,491; 1787, $799,556; 1788, $1,557,179; 1789, $422,897. The money taken in consisted of specie and indents collected by loan office commissioners in the states, sales of bills of exchange, collections from debtors of the government, and treasury warrants issued for salaries and expenses in advance of collections.

The largest share of income came from the states. Between 1 November 1784 and 12 September 1789, the loan office commissioners received $1,488,000 in specie and $2,235,000 in indents, a total of $3,723,000, from the state governments. Of this amount over three quarters of a million dollars in specie and indents was still in the hands of the loan officers at the end of the Confederation. The treasury, however, took in over a million dollars more than it received from the loan officers. A large part of this sum came from bills of exchange drawn against balances in European banks. The bulk of the remainder came from the settlement of old accounts.[36]

Of course the government did not get as much money as it needed. Its biggest problem was the payment of interest on the national debt. The treasury managed to pay most of the interest on the foreign debt, chiefly by means of loans from Dutch bankers. The use of indents to pay interest on the domestic debt was a novel device whose effectiveness was defeated largely because of the concentration of the national debt in the North in the hands of a relatively few men. The big holders of the national debt got far

[35] Summary Account of the Receipts and Payments, commencing with the appointment of Robert Morris as Superintendent of Finance, 20 February 1781 and ending with his resignation the 1st of November 1784, in Statements of the Financial Affairs of the Late Confederated Government of the United States from February 1781 to September 1789, MSS. Div., LC.

[36] The above figures are derived from the General Account of Taxes and the Account of Taxes Collected in the Several States and paid into the Treasury. This document is contained in Statements of the Financial Affairs of the Late Confederated Government of the United States from February 1781 to September 1789, MSS. Div., LC.

more indents than they could use to pay state taxes; hence their market value declined. If the debt had been widely held among the people the indents would have served a useful purpose as a circulating medium and carried the debt until the sale of western lands got under way.

However, the rough balance sheet of the Confederation does show certain positive things. It shows that the new nation had a cash income from the states; that it had sound credit with Dutch bankers; that it paid most of the interest on the foreign debt and part of the interest on the domestic debt; and finally, that it had arrived at a position where it could begin to pay the principal as well as the interest on the domestic debt through the sale of western lands. It was "deficit financing," of course, but it can be argued that the Confederation perhaps came as close to making means match needs as many a twentieth century government has been able to do. These have kept going by enormous increases in national debts, whereas the Confederation actually managed to reduce the principal of its debt. Its methods were not "sound" finance by modern standards, but we have yet to see how "sound" the national debts of the twentieth century will be.

The lack of an independent income was the great political as well as the great economic weakness of the Confederation government. This lack, perhaps more than any other single fact, brought about its downfall. If the government had been able to acquire an income of its own, the strongest argument against it would have been shattered. Even so the problem of the national debt was being solved in a different fashion. One state after another during the Confederation assumed the national debt owned by its citizens. This process was the result of the joint pressure of public creditors who demanded better returns on their holdings, and of politicians who feared that national payment of the debt would mean a powerful central government.

The States and the National Debt

Americans in the eighteenth century had an intense awareness of the relationship between economic and political power, as we have seen in the debates over the finance plan of 1783.[37] There was

[37] See *ante*, ch. iii, *post*, ch. xx.

common agreement that the methods used to pay the debt would inevitably affect the balance of power between the states and the central government. The nationalist leaders were convinced that payment by the central government would be a means of adding power to it and hence they demanded an independent income for it. The federalists, believing equally with the nationalists that the result would be a powerful government, opposed the grant of an independent income, and in addition, proposed that the domestic debt be divided among the states and paid by them. During the Confederation, the failure to secure such an income, the clamors of the public creditors, and the political convictions of the federalists, resulted in steady progress in the direction of state assumption of the national debt owing to their citizens.

The first part of the national debt to be assumed by the states was the military debt. After Congress gave up paper money in 1780, arrears in back pay of the Continental Army mounted. The cash that came in went to pay army contractors and holders of the loan office debt, not the soldiers. Congress demanded money of the states to pay the army, but instead the states began paying their soldiers in the Continental Army directly. Robert Morris threatened that if the states did so, they would get no credit when the accounts were balanced, but the states ignored him.[38] When the war ended the soldiers were promised back pay and commutation certificates by Congress. As the soldiers returned to the states and the certificates were issued, the states took over those certificates too. New York and Massachusetts allowed their soldiers to exchange such certificates for state certificates. Pennsylvania, New Jersey, and Delaware paid interest on them; others took them in on taxes.

There was nothing to do except for Congress to face the fact that in one way or another the states were assuming this portion of the national debt. In 1784 and again in 1785, Congress agreed that if the states paid the military debt, they would be given credit on it against the day of final settlement of accounts between the states and the central government.[39]

The other part of the national debt which the nationalists regarded as a "sacred obligation" of the central government and a strong "cement" to the union was the loan office debt. The pay-

[38] To the Governor of Rhode Island, 26 June 1782, Wharton, V, 524.
[39] *Journals*, XXVI, 269; XXVII, 506; XXVIII, 261.

ment of interest and principal was dependent upon a steady income, and requisitions on the states were no guarantee of this. There were those who argued that the future sale of the national domain would pay the debt, but meanwhile there was the problem of the clamoring creditors. The power to levy import duties depended upon the unanimous consent of the thirteen states. If this could be gotten at all, it would take time, and meanwhile many creditors, however much they might yearn for a strong central government, yearned even more for quick returns. Hence, like the soldiers, they turned to the state governments. The forces of nationalism were thus split between their ideals of government and their economic interests.

The entering wedge in the state assumption of the loan office debt was the use of indents for the payment of interest by the continental loan officers in the states. In June 1780 they were directed to refund the loan office debt. All old loan office certificates were ordered brought in and reduced to their specie value as of the time of purchase.[40] Later, all old loan office certificates were exchanged for new ones. By 1787 that task had been completed and a paper debt of about $67,000,000 had been reduced to approximately $11,500,000.[41]

The continental loan officers also had the duty of paying interest on the loan office certificates issued in their states. Until 1782 interest on loan office certificates issued before March 1778 was paid by bills of exchange drawn on France. In that year six million dollars was borrowed in France but Robert Morris told Congress that all this money was "anticipated" and that nothing was left to pay interest on the loan office debt. This step on the part of Morris was actually not the result of his inability to pay interest, but of his desire to have the public creditors put pressure on Con-

[40] Ibid., XVII, 567–9.

[41] On the role of the loan officers see Nathaniel Appleton to Samuel Osgood, 20 April 1785, Osgood Papers, NYHS. The loan officers kept registers of their transactions. See for instance the Virginia Register of Depreciated Loan Office Certificates Canceled and Certificates Issued for the Specie Value thereof, Old Loan Office Records, NA. Such records give the face value, date of issue, and name of purchaser of the old certificate; the rate of exchange and its specie value; and the date, amount, and name of the person to whom the new certificate was issued. It was thus possible despite Hamilton's argument to the contrary, to distinguish between the original owners and the speculative owners. The new certificates, of course, declined in value and were the subject of speculation, but here again it was possible to tell at what time they had been bought and by whom.

gress and the state legislatures in support of his demands for an independent income for the central government. However, the majority of Congress, who knew little or nothing of the actual financial situation, ordered the loan officers to stop payment of interest. At the same time they asked the states to contribute $1,200,000 a year to the loan officers, who in turn were ordered to pay interest with the money received before turning over anything to Congress.[42]

With the stoppage of interest payments by Congress the public creditors started to clamor, as Morris planned they should. They held meetings and sent petitions to Congress and state legislatures. They proposed a convention of creditors from all the states. In all this they had the assistance and guidance of Robert Morris.[43] Their activities lent fervor to the actions of Congress in the spring of 1783, as we have seen. At the same time their pressure on the continental loan officers in the states led to a new device. The loan officers began issuing certificates, known as indents,[44] for interest due. Robert Morris was strongly opposed, for this interfered with his plans, but he was not able to stop the process once it had been started. Soon the states began accepting these indents as part payment on taxes. Thus the states assumed a part of the responsibility for the domestic debt. At first Congress refused to acknowledge what the states were doing, but not for long. In April 1784, Congress agreed that each state could pay one fourth of its requisition in indents and declared that the public creditors must regard the interest as paid whenever they surrendered their certificates.[45]

This decision alarmed southerners, for relatively little of the loan office debt was owned in the South. John Mercer of Virginia guessed that not more than $300,000 was owned in all of Virginia, and that therefore that state would have to make up the

[42] *Journals*, XXIII, 545–6, 554–5, 562–71; John Witherspoon, Speech in Congress on a Motion for Paying the Interest of Loan Office Certificates, Burnett, VII, 464–7; John Taylor Gilman to Josiah Bartlett, 17 Sept., 1782, ibid., VII, 473–4.

[43] Hamilton to Robert Morris, 28 Sept., 9 Oct. 1782, *Works* (Lodge ed.), IX, 293, 296. See also Petition of Public Creditors of Chester County, Penn., *Pennsylvania Gazette*, 1 Jan. 1783.

[44] For examples see Thomas Smith, Receipt Book for [indents] Paid, PHS, and Register of Certificates Issued for Interest—Virginia, Old Loan Office Records, NA.

[45] *Journals*, XXVI, 312–4.

balance of requisitions in specie.[46] But David Howell of Rhode Island was delighted, for he believed the decision was a blow at Robert Morris and his friends. "The charm of remitting all payments to Philadelphia is now broken," he said, "and I hope that vortex will no longer swallow down the treasures of other states." [47]

The next year Congress decided that since two thirds of the requisition for that year was for the payment of interest on the domestic debt, each state might pay two thirds of its quota in the indents paid to their citizens by the loan office commissioners.[48] Thus by 1785 a means of paying interest had been worked out through the assumption of responsibility by the states. By the end of the Confederation the state loan officers had issued large sums and had then taken in over $2,235,000 after the states had collected them in taxes or had received them on their own holdings of the national debt.

Interest payments with indents did not satisfy the public creditors, for both the indents and the loan office certificates declined in value. Moreover, it was doubtful that under this system Congress would ever redeem the principal at face value as promised. Therefore the creditors appealed to the state governments for outright state assumption of the principal as well as the interest of the national debt. Maryland did so even before the war was over. In November 1782 she provided that her citizens could exchange their holdings of the national debt for state securities. Under this act she assumed over $200,000 in loan office certificates.[49]

New Jersey acted next. Her citizens owned about one eleventh of the total domestic debt of the United States, $2,431,845 in 1790, an extraordinary amount for so small a state. Of the total, $1,121,360 were in loan office certificates, $917,968 in liquidated quartermaster and commissary certificates, and the remainder in soldiers' notes given at the end of the war. When Congress stopped paying interest in 1782, New Jersey creditors demanded action by

[46] To the Executive Council of Virginia, 10 April 1784, Burnett, VII, 491.

[47] To the Deputy-Governor of Rhode Island, 31 May 1784, ibid., VII, 538.

[48] *Journals*, XXIX, 768. Loan office commissioners were forbidden to issue indents if their states did not pass legislation to comply with the rest of the requisition.

[49] *Laws of Maryland* (Hanson ed.), ch. xxv; *Votes of Proceedings of the House of Delegates of Maryland*, 2 May, 13 Dec. 1787.

the state. The result was an act in June 1783 levying a tax, part of the proceeds of which were to be given the continental loan officer in New Jersey for payment to New Jersey creditors. Then in December 1783 the legislature directed the state treasurer to pay the interest directly to New Jersey creditors of the United States. When the army notes were issued in 1784 the state started paying interest on them as well as on the quartermaster and commissary certificates which were liquidated by the commissioner sent by Congress to settle accounts. In December 1784 the state announced that it would pay no more money to the United States until all the states had approved of the impost of 1783 and of the plan for supplemental funds. This remained the policy of New Jersey throughout the Confederation, although it weighed heavily on her taxpayers. They agreed to all proposals to strengthen the Confederation and they welcomed the Constitution of 1787, largely because they wanted to shift the heavy burden of payment to the central government.[50]

The outstanding example of state assumption was that of Pennsylvania whose citizens owned a vast amount of the domestic debt. By 1784 they held over $2,500,000 in loan office certificates and over $3,000,000 in other forms.[51] The nationalists were powerful in Pennsylvania, but they were split because many of them wanted cash payments more than anything else. Public creditors met in Philadelphia and demanded that the state government pay interest on the national debt as other states were doing. Robert Morris and his group opposed the demand, but they were slowly beaten down. Support for state assumption came also from federalist leaders in Pennsylvania who believed with their fellows in other states that the states should pay the national debt. By the fall of 1784 the Constitutionalist party regained control of the state legislature. At once it was proposed that the state take over payment of the interest on the national debt owned by Pennsylvanians. Shortly thereafter a bill was printed in the newspapers for public discussion.[52]

The executive council, led by President John Dickinson, objected that the whole scheme would enrich speculators who had bought up large quantities of loan office certificates for a fraction

[50] McCormick: New Jersey in the Confederation, ch. vii.
[51] Brunhouse: *Counter-Revolution*, 131, 283, n. 53.
[52] *Pennsylvania Packet*, 6 Jan., 4 Feb. 1785.

of their face value. The council declared that according to the proposed scheme the speculators would get forty to fifty per cent interest a year in specie, as well as the rise in value of the principal. The original holders who had had to sell because the public did not pay them would now be taxed in specie, and this would be an even greater hardship. In addition, the council objected that Congress should have time to complete its funding plans. The council proposed that the unsettled land of the states be sold and the debt paid in that way; otherwise there would be too heavy a tax load.[53]

The public creditors jumped into the fray in a memorial to the legislature. They were alarmed at the idea of distinguishing between the original and the speculative owners of the loan office certificates. They lamented that there were ways of getting property besides "direct industry," and that while they would not defend speculators, they declared that a man who had bought certificates at their low ebb merited all the profit he could get because of the risks he ran. The plan to pay the debts by the sale of public lands was dishonorable. The lands were worthless. Think of the widows and orphans suffering with hunger and perishing with cold while waiting for the state to pay them for their loan office certificates. The state should pay in cash and at face value.[54]

Satirists joined the executive council in the attack on the scheme. They declared that very few of the original owners had any loan office certificates. The ancient "widows and orphans" argument was scoffed at. "Mr. Startup's arms are to be a triumphal car, drawn by a company of ragged invalids, and the crest a large bottle, full of widows' tears—the motto, 'His Lacrymis!' " said "Harry Holdpost," in a dialogue with "Jack Wantplace." [55] "Centinel" said that most of the debt was in the hands of speculators who had got it for a tenth of its value. Their cry was "public faith" but what of "equal justice?" Those who had suffered from the depreciation of continental bills were as much entitled to justice as the speculators.[56]

The council kept up its opposition to the payment of interest on the national debt by the state, but insisted that if it were done,

[53] John Dickinson, Speech to the Assembly, 1 Feb. 1785, *Pennsylvania Archives*, 4th ser., III, 991–1012.

[54] *Pennsylvania Gazette*, 15 Dec. 1784.

[55] Ibid., 19 Jan. 1785. See also "Andromache," ibid., 9 Feb. 1785.

[56] Ibid., 2 Feb. 1785.

the original holders must be distinguished from the speculators.[57] The forthright opposition did not stop the legislature which was dominated by a group cutting across party lines. Philadelphia merchants like Charles Pettit—who called the funding bill his bill, and by which the newspapers said he would make £6,000 a year in interest alone—joined with westerners in supporting it. The westerners agreed to support funding in return for eastern votes for opening up the West. They proposed to raise the money by a general tax of £200,000 a year, the sale of western lands, and the issuance of paper money. Many Philadelphia merchants were horrified by the paper money part of the bill and protested against it. The nationalists, who had fought a losing battle against the state assumption of national debts ever since 1782, continued their opposition. But the bill went through the legislature 16 March 1785.[58]

Bitterly, a poet wrote of the soldiers who had fought through the war:

> Then ask them for whom in summer's heat they glow?
> For whom they shiver in the winter's snow?
> For whom, if naked, scout from hill to dale,
> Whilst thirst and hunger cruelly assail?
> For us the SPECULATORS answer, sure,
> For us the soldiers all their toils endure;
> For us the state shall special statutes frame,
> Let soldiers, yeomen, be content with fame.

Despite such denunciations, the assembly proceeded to the next step: the outright assumption of the national debt owing to its citizens. Early in 1786 it provided that all holders of United States loan office certificates in Pennsylvania could exchange them for bonds of the state. The Republican party, led by men like Morris, voted solidly against the measure, not because they were not heavy holders, but because they were still fighting to keep intact the national debt which they so firmly believed to be the great unifying force which might in time achieve a national union.[59] Shortly thereafter, the state took over the securities bought by its citizens in the loan offices of New Jersey and Dela-

[57] Ibid., 4 Feb. 1785.

[58] Pennsylvania *Statutes at Large*, XI, 454–86; *Pennsylvania Gazette*, 23 Feb., 9, 23, 30 March, 6 April 1785; Brunhouse: *Counter-Revolution*, 170–2.

[59] Ibid., 185; Pennsylvania *Statutes at Large*, XII, 158–64.

ware as well. Altogether, Pennsylvania assumed over five million dollars of the national debt.[60]

The attack on the Pennsylvania speculators continued and reached a climax in the spring of 1787 when Noah Webster published an essay defending the original holders of the national debt. He said they ought to be compensated for their losses, or exempted from taxes to pay for the debt. Others had continued to argue that the debt should be paid at its market rather than its face value; that the real worth of securities was what they sold for on the open market. They charged that not more than one sixth of the funding tax would go to original holders of the certificates. Such writers, and Webster in particular, were attacked violently. Webster was a "retailer of nouns and pronouns," he was a "Shays," a "traitor." Not only had his ideas produced rebellion in Massachusetts; he had come to Pennsylvania "to propagate his hell-born opinions"; he was "an assassin of public and private justice." Under pretence of asking for justice for the original holders, he was stabbing "the very vitals of our country." [61] Of course Webster's ideas had not produced Shays's Rebellion. It was rather the reverse of them that brought about the revolt of Massachusetts farmers, a revolt which horrified him.

The next state to assume the national debt owing its citizens was New York. In 1786 a New York law allowed the exchange of various forms of state and federal debt for new certificates and provision was made for interest payments by the issuance of paper money.[62] New Yorkers, like Pennsylvanians, held a large portion of the federal debt: an estimated £1,496,000. By 1788 nearly a million pounds of this debt had been assumed by the state and it was said that this amount was more than New York's share of the entire national debt.[63]

The state assumption of the debt was the result of creditor demands for immediate returns and was backed by those political leaders who feared the nationalist program of Robert Morris, Alexander Hamilton, James Madison, and others. However, not all the states looked on the program as a permanent one. Pennsylvania, for instance, provided that its assumption act would continue only until Congress acquired an independent income. By

[60] Ibid., XII, 426–7; *Minutes of the Pennsylvania Assembly*, 12 Nov. 1787.

[61] *Pennsylvania Gazette*, March and April; *Massachusetts Centinel*, 9 May 1787.

[62] 18 April 1786, *Laws of New York* (1886 ed.) II, 253–72.

[63] New York *Daily Advertiser*, 28 Jan., 2 Feb. 1788.

1785, Congress had swung far from the position it held in 1783 when dominated by the Morris group. Its president was Richard Henry Lee.

The assumption of the national debt by the states was in line with such men's ideas, but at the same time it created a real problem, particularly for the South. The Maryland delegates in Congress stated it clearly. They said that the requisition of 1785 would be of enormous advantage to those states which owned the great bulk of continental securities: that is, the states from Pennsylvania and New Jersey eastward to New Hampshire. Those states could pay two thirds of their requisitions very cheaply. The Maryland delegates urged Maryland to buy as many of the final settlement certificates as it could. They took it upon themselves to make arrangements to buy from two to four millions in "continental money," and asked for £3,000 in bank notes to pay for it.[64] A year later a Maryland delegate was still urging the state to buy up public securities, for the other states were doing so and consequently the price would rise. He reported that Pennsylvania already had more than its proportion of the national debt and that other states were nearly in the same position.[65]

By the spring of 1787 Arthur Lee of the board of treasury was urging the governor of Virginia to get into the security market and to buy secretly and rapidly. He said that large quantities were already locked up in the treasuries of several states and that other states were proposing to buy. The purchase of public lands with securities, and an arrangement of the treasury board for calling in some millions more, would further reduce the quantity and raise the price. Furthermore, if the Constitutional Convention then meeting should provide funds, the price of public securities would rise rapidly and greatly.[66] The Virginia legislature followed his advice and appropriated £6,000 in cash and a tobacco fund to buy securities. At the same time the legislature agreed to the most recent requisition of Congress, but with little intention of actually providing funds, "it being the general wish to possess ourselves of a large proportion of the public securities before an appreciation takes place under the new government." [67]

[64] James McHenry to John Hall [28 Sept. 1785], Burnett, VIII, 23; Maryland Delegates to Daniel of St. Thomas Jenifer, 5 Oct. 1785, ibid., VIII, 227.

[65] John Henry to the Governor of Maryland, 30 Aug. 1786, ibid., VIII, 455–6.

[66] 20 May 1787, *Calendar of Virginia State Papers*, IV, 288–9.

[67] Archibald Stuart to James Madison, 2 Dec. 1787, Madison Papers, LC.

Thus not only did some of the states assume the national debt owing to their citizens, but others went into the open market and bought up depreciated securities. When the accounts between the states and Congress were finally settled in 1793, it was found that the state governments owned a vast amount of the national debt, The full story of the role of the states in paying the national debt before 1789 is yet to be told, but its political importance is as great if not greater than that of the individual speculators.[68]

[68] I am deeply indebted to the researches of James Ferguson of the University of Maryland who is doing the work in the sources that is necessary before we can have an adequate understanding of the financial history of the American Revolution. Two further studies in progress at the University of Wisconsin will add much to the research already under way. These are doctoral theses by Whitney K. Bates on The Assumption of State Debts, 1783–93, and by Edward F. Robinson on The Board of Treasury, 1785–9.

20

The Quest for Congressional Power

THROUGHOUT THE Confederation, Congress needed and repeatedly asked for more power. Both the nationalists and the federalists agreed that the central government should be strengthened. There was a fundamental difference, however, between the demands of the two groups. The nationalists sought to change the essential character of the constitution through amendment, interpretation, and finally in 1783, some of them toyed with the desperate hope of uniting the army and the public creditors to acquire by force what the facts of wartime necessity and endless argument could not achieve. The basic nationalist argument that the war could not be won without creating a strong central government was discredited by the winning of the war, and the nationalist leaders left Congress in 1783, largely because most of them had served the three years allowed by the Confederation.

Their federalist opponents, most of whom had been ardent revolutionary leaders before 1776, were thoroughly aroused by nationalist schemes and they gained new confidence with the winning of the war. As they regained power in many of the states, they sent men of their own political convictions to Congress. Such men believed in retaining the essential character of the Articles of Confederation, yet they recognized that the problems that faced the new nation could be better solved by adding specific powers to Congress. Hence most of the men who opposed the nationalists' schemes now supported the various proposals to give Congress the power to regulate trade and to collect an independent income. But there was a profound difference between such proposals and those of the nationalists: most of them were grants of specific powers to

Congress for limited periods of time, not amendments to the Articles of Confederation.

The request for the power to regulate trade failed because the states themselves engaged in the regulation of trade in an effective and profitable manner, and because southern leaders believed that centralized control would mean the exploitation of southern shippers for the benefit of northern shipowners. The question of an independent income was infinitely complex. Its chief purpose was to pay the national debt. All agreed that the foreign debt was a national obligation, but as we have seen, there was sharp division as to how the domestic debt should be paid. The nationalists argued that it should be paid by the central government; the federalists that it should be divided among the states and paid by them. Here, too, a sectional split appeared, for the vast bulk of the national debt was owned in the northern states. Many roots of the antagonism that ultimately led to war between the North and the South are to be found in the era of the American Revolution.

Above all, the controversy over the quest for an independent income was linked up with the ultimate nature of the central government. The thinking of American political leaders was deeply influenced by their knowledge of English constitutional growth and of the development of colonial self-government in the eighteenth century. That knowledge told them that political power and financial power went hand in hand. Both the nationalists and the federalists believed that national payment of the war debt would mean the supremacy of the central government over the states; that state payment would mean the retention of ultimate power in the hands of the states. Thus men on both sides believed, and their actions were consistent with their convictions.

The Power to Regulate Trade

American colonials had objected to British regulation of American trade whenever it interfered with either real or imagined profits and liberties. In the first and second continental congresses many merchants had feared to leave the British Empire and argued for centralized regulation of commerce. Throughout the war those merchants who became Patriots continued to hope for it. After the war ended, the impact of post-war trade problems won widespread support for handing the power over to Congress.

Foreign goods poured in at war's end and American cash poured out to pay for them. Most of the goods came from and most of the cash went to Great Britain. Most men acted as if the golden day would last forever. Some voices were raised in alarm and prophesied doom as they witnessed the fall of prices at the end of the war. Such men predicted accurately what would happen if Americans continued to buy more than they sold. When such predictions came true, as they did by the spring of 1784, Americans tried to avoid both thought and responsibility by damning the British for what had happened. They turned to the governments of the states and of the United States and demanded laws retaliating against British commerce.

A ready-made issue was at hand in the British order in council of July 1783 excluding American ships from the West India trade. Doing something for American economy by doing something to the British became a popular panacea. In practice, as we have seen, American shippers soon evaded British restrictions. Meanwhile, nationalist politicians actually welcomed such restrictions since they gave them new arguments to support their demand for centralized power.[1] Popular antagonism against the British was bolstered by commercial depression. The result was the passage of legislation by most of the states favoring American shipping and products over British.

State legislation was effective but not uniform, and American merchants wanted a uniformity which only centralized control could provide. However, the first concrete proposals for congressional regulation came from the planting states of Virginia and Maryland. In the fall of 1783, Maryland authorized her delegates in Congress to agree to an amendment to the Articles of Confederation giving Congress power to prohibit imports and exports of foreign goods in other than American vessels. She laid a five shilling duty on every ton of British shipping, and a two per cent ad valorem duty on British goods brought in in British ships. These duties were over and above the duties on goods imported in

[1] Ch. xii, "The Conflict of Opinion."

vessels owned by the citizens of Maryland and of the other states.[2] During the same fall, Virginia authorized Congress to prohibit the importation of British West India produce in British vessels, an authorization to go into effect when the other states passed similar laws.[3]

Meanwhile Congress took up the question. In September 1783 a committee suggested that Congress should have the power of regulation. Another committee was appointed to tell this to the states.[4] While this was happening, the merchants of Philadelphia united in sending a circular letter to merchants in other American cities, suggesting that they work for a grant of power to Congress,[5] a suggestion with which merchants everywhere agreed.

Congress soon submitted a request to the states for a grant of power to pass navigation acts: to forbid the import and export of goods in the vessels of countries not having treaties with the United States, and to forbid the subjects of foreign states to import goods from other than their own countries, unless exempted by treaty. Congress suggested that the grant of power be limited to fifteen years. In sending out the request, Congress declared that the prosperity of all was dependent on the prosperity of trade, that British restrictions on Americans entering the West India trade were "growing into system," and that unless Congress got the power, "our foreign commerce must decline, and eventually be annihilated." [6]

Virginia agreed almost at once, for the request was in line with her previous act.[7] In the meantime Virginia had asked other states to join with her in authorizing Congress to prohibit imports of British West India goods in British vessels. South Carolina agreed to this, but when Congress asked for wider power she was uncertain and beset by many fears. Most South Carolina merchants believed that Congress should have some control, but many wanted it limited to the West India trade. Others doubted that England could be forced to do what Americans wanted. Many had a very real fear that centralized control would result in New

[2] *Laws of Maryland* (Hanson ed.), ch. xxix.
[3] Hening, XI, 313–4.
[4] *Journals*, XXV, 621–2, 628–9, 661–3.
[5] Charles Pettit to Joseph Reed, 13 Feb. 1784, Joseph Reed Papers, NYHS.
[6] 30 April 1784, *Journals*, XXVI, 321–2.
[7] Hening, XI, 388–9.

England domination of the carrying trade of the South. With these fears as background, the legislature debated the question in 1785 and not until 1786 did it grant the request of Congress.[8]

As the merchants waited for the states to act on the request from Congress, and as the states went ahead passing laws of their own, the merchants became more and more alarmed. Their demand for centralized control became more fervent as they lost one battle after another in states such as Massachusetts, Rhode Island, and Pennsylvania, to the rising manufacturers who demanded the adoption of protective tariffs. Importing merchants did not want British goods kept out—only British ships. It was clear to any merchant that the impost proposal of 1783, if granted to Congress, would mean far lower duties than those being levied by the states. They said that Congress had not asked for enough power. The request was merely for the power to prohibit certain kinds of trade. What merchants wanted was a general power to regulate trade given permanently to Congress.[9] Newspapers in the commercial towns hammered away at the necessity of a "radical cure," as the *Pennsylvania Gazette* called it. Congress must have power to "counteract those illiberal and impolitic systems, whose influence, like that of a malignant comet, has operated so banefully throughout the states." [10]

Congress took up the question again, this time under the leadership of James Monroe, who was new to Congress. Late in 1784, Monroe was made chairman of a committee to study the question of trade regulation. The result of its work was a report to Congress proposing an amendment to the Articles of Confederation.

The proposed amendment asked for perpetual power to regulate trade with foreign nations and between the states, and power to levy imposts and duties on exports and imports. This power was hedged about to meet the objections of those who feared power in the central government. Citizens of the states were not to pay higher duties than the citizens of foreign states. Any state could prohibit the import and export of any kind of goods whatever. All duties were to be collected by the authority of the states and to go to the use of the state in which they were paid. Congress

[8] Singer: *South Carolina in the Confederation*, 90–100.
[9] Rufus King to Elbridge Gerry, 19 May 1785, King: *Life*, I, 97–8.
[10] 29 June 1785, also 19 July 1786.

was in fact to establish uniform policies which were to be implemented by the states. The whole proposal was in sharp contrast to the impost of 1783 which was before the states for approval.[11]

Many members were for the amendment. One thought it would ensure freedom of commerce among the states. Another was sure it would end the "diabolical trade" in which British ships carried out American goods. Even the Rhode Islanders supported it, for it answered many of their objections to the impost proposal of 1783.[12] In general, the amendment's supporters argued that the union rather than the states could better encourage domestic industry, obtain reciprocity from foreign nations, establish a commercial interest in the United States, keep American councils free from foreign influence, and raise a navy for the public safety.

The opposition reiterated its ancient fear of the corrupting influence of power: of the certain intoxication of those entrusted with it. They asserted that the amendment was an attack on the Confederation and that all such attacks were dangerous, even when they failed.[13]

The proposed amendment was never sent to the states. It was defeated in Congress in part by those with deep "prejudices" against all attempts to increase the power of Congress; even those who saw "the necessity . . . fear the consequences." [14] Its defeat was due, above all, to a sharp division of interest. Southerners feared the northern merchants, an emotion inherited from colonial experience. One member said he did not wonder at their "anxiety to obtain a monopoly of the carrying trade of the Union." Many southern delegates believed that such control would mean that the South could ship only in American ships. The result would be fewer purchasers and hence lower prices for products, while the price of imported goods would go up. Southerners felt that it was good policy to have as many buyers and as many importers as possible. They asked pointed questions: Could the United States afford to enter into a commercial war to open up the West Indies; if such a "war" could be won, would there be enough American ships to carry American produce?

[11] 28 March 1785, *Journals*, XXVIII, 201–5.
[12] Burnett, VIII, 13, 15–6, 18.
[13] Monroe to Madison, 26 July 1785, ibid., VIII, 171–2.
[14] Monroe to Jefferson, 15 July 1785, ibid., VIII, 166.

On the other hand, some members agreed that it was necessary to discourage foreign shipping and favor American, as many of the states were doing at the time, including Virginia and Maryland. But too few men were willing to take a middle ground. James McHenry wrote Washington that "the point of true policy lays between forcing the growth of our shipping and doing nothing that may forward their increase. Perhaps the southern states should give up something, and the other states should not ask everything." He wanted a navigation act that would slowly augment the shipping of all the states without wounding the interests of any.[15]

But the delegates from states with strong shipping interests would have all or nothing, while the agrarian opposition, led by Richard Henry Lee, now back in Congress as its president, would have no act of any kind. The result was an impasse and eventual oblivion for the proposed amendment.[16]

Congress therefore turned to its earlier request for the power to pass navigation acts. In March 1786 it made a survey of state actions on that proposal. It said that three states, Delaware, South Carolina, and Georgia had ignored the plan. Massachusetts, New York, New Jersey, and Virginia had agreed to it except that their enabling acts restrained its operation until all the states agreed. The rest of the states had passed various measures, some setting the date after which Congress could use the power, others limiting or amending the plan. Congress once more asked the states to agree to the grant of power. And there matters stood at the end of the Confederation.[17]

That they stood thus was due to various things. By 1786 the cry of necessity no longer had the power it had had in 1784. Even more important was the division of interest between North and South which could not be ignored as a force in national politics either then or later. The issue was the carrying trade, and not the sale of American products, most of which had a ready market. The merchants of the northern cities were carriers. As a rule the

[15] To Washington, 14 Aug. 1785, ibid., VIII, 183.

[16] Monroe to Jefferson, 15 Aug. 1785, 19 Jan. 1786, ibid., VIII, 186, 286; McHenry to Washington, 14 Aug. 1785, ibid., VIII, 183–4; John Jay to John Adams, 1 Nov. 1785, *Correspondence*, III, 175–6.

[17] 3 March 1786, *Journals*, XXX, 93–4. South Carolina had agreed in February 1786, but word had not yet reached Congress.

planters were not, though merchants were of growing importance in the South.[18]

Outsiders jeered at the Americans, and particularly at the Bostonians. One writer asked if the southern states would again be the dupes of New England which "is denied by nature, any staple commodity; and, being a member of that confederacy that has lately assumed a place among the nations of the earth, is deprived of almost every commercial privilege she enjoyed when her vessels could display the British flag." People there are numerous, poor, enterprising, and now unemployed, and artful and ambitious men are likely to avail themselves of the circumstances, and even if the southern states do not become dupes again, "still some revolution in the American system, is not very remote." [19] The anonymous writer was more prophetic than he realized, for northern merchants were bitter and breathed all sorts of threats. Rufus King, who moved closer and closer to the merchants' point of view as he approached marriage with an ex-Loyalist merchant's only daughter, informed John Adams that the eight eastern states "have common objects, are under similar embarrassments, would vest adequate powers in Congress to regulate external and internal commerce. . . ." He said they would even go so far as to form a subconfederation if the southern states would not agree to vest Congress with the necessary power.[20]

The issue was clear. If Congress could exclude the foreign competition of northern shipowners, the southern states which shipped the great cargoes of tobacco and rice would have to pay whatever freights were charged. Both sides knew this, although too often it was glossed over with talk of national honor and the public good; not always though, for as one merchant told the president of New Hampshire, the state should send delegates to Annapolis in 1786 for it was an offer "that we of New England ought not to let pass unnoticed by any means if we can secure the carrying trade of the southern states. . . ." [21]

[18] David Jackson to George Bryan, New York, 18 July 1785, George Bryan Papers, PHS; Benjamin Lincoln to Rufus King, 11 Feb. 1786; King: *Life*, I, 156–60.

[19] Item in the *Pennsylvania Gazette*, 3 Aug. 1785, from Nassau, Bahama, dated 6 June.

[20] 2 Nov. 1785, King: *Life*, I, 113.

[21] J. Bowen to President Sullivan, Providence, 18 Aug. 1786, Emmet Coll., no. 9334, NYPL.

As important as the southerners' fear of exploitation by northern merchants, was the fear among democratic elements in America that Congress would abuse any power given it. In Virginia it was doubted that the advocates of congressional power would succeed in the legislature because of "the apprehensions, in some minds, of an abuse of the power." [22] In Pennsylvania a democratic leader, Samuel Bryan, agreed that Congress ought to have power over trade, but he felt that the difficulty would be how to regulate it so as to prevent Congress from "absorbing all power and influence within their vortex." He was afraid that Congress "would seize the present moment to obtain dangerous powers, so fascinating is the love of power on the one hand, and the little caution of the body of the people on the other hand when their passions are inflamed." [23]

Many things thus combined to defeat any grant of power over trade to the Confederation. In addition, by 1786 there was less pressure on Congress, for the advocates of centralization were turning more and more to the idea of a complete political revolution rather than to mere amendment of the Articles of Confederation. Perhaps, indeed, they wanted to avoid any amendment for fear it would jeopardize hopes of political revolution. Then too, while men debated measures, the ebb and flow of trade was bringing recovery to the seaport towns. And last but not least, the states themselves engaged in highly effective regulation of trade and collected fat revenues in doing so. These economic facts inevitably meant a decline in the popular support which in 1783 and 1784 was behind the demand for centralization.[24]

The Quest for an Independent Income

Far more important than congressional control of trade was the debate over an independent income for Congress. The nationalists declared that Congress must have it or the union would break up. Late in 1782 General Greene said he feared the "contracted

[22] Edmund Randolph to Washington, 3 Dec. 1785, Bancroft: *Constitution*, I, 470.

[23] Samuel Bryan to George Bryan, May 1785, George Bryan Papers, PHS.

[24] Ch. xiv.

policy" of the states would ruin the Confederation and that it "must be kept together by the national debt." [25] In the summer of 1783, Robert Morris asserted that if the states turned a deaf ear to the appeals of Congress "one of the first effects must be to dissolve the Confederation." Whether a better bond or anarchy would follow, only time could tell.[26] On the other hand, the true federalists believed that the union would break up if Congress became independent of the states. Such a government would be no better than the British control had been.

Such was the conflict of opinion that surrounded Congress as they debated finance in the spring of 1783. The plan Congress finally agreed on, as we have seen, was a compromise among the clashing interests of states, sections, and ideologies, and was agreed on in the end only perhaps because of the threats of the army and the public creditors.

The finance plan of 1783 was sent to the states accompanied by an eloquent address written by James Madison.[27] In June, Washington put all his weight behind the plan and predicted "anarchy and confusion" if the Confederation were not given more power.[28]

The opponents of an independent income for Congress were as alarmed by the plan of 1783 as by the Impost of 1781, even though the new proposal was not an amendment to the Confederation but a grant of power for twenty-five years. Such men were convinced that with the end of the war and resumption of normal commerce and agriculture, the states would be able to satisfy the "constitutional requisitions" of Congress. Yet, said Arnold of Rhode Island, "ideas of the necessity of forming a general system of finance (which will throw a share of the power and strength of Government, now held by the states, into the hands of Congress) seems in the minds of some to prevail over every other consideration. . . ." [29]

The conflict of opinion within Congress was more than matched by that outside. The opponents of the measure formulated clear-cut objections. Rhode Islanders in their attack on the Impost of 1781 had set forth detailed theoretical arguments which were typical of those used after 1783. They insisted that the Confedera-

[25] To Charles Pettit, 21 Dec. 1782, Joseph Reed Papers, NYHS.
[26] To George Olney, 20 Aug. 1783, Robert Morris, Official Letter Book F, LC.
[27] 26 April 1783, *Journals*, XXIV, 277–83.
[28] 8 June 1783, *Writings*, XXVI, 488.
[29] To the Governor of Rhode Island, 28 March 1783, Burnett, VII, 111.

tion was a union of thirteen sovereign states: that " 'each state retains its sovereignty, freedom, and independence,' say the Articles of Confederation; yet Mr. C. with a sovereign smile, informs us that 'we are not to contemplate the United States as composing thirteen sovereignties. . . .' "[30] Another writer said, "let the United States keep then the sovereignty divided among themselves, or at least keep the purse in their own power. . . ." A "bunch of kings" is more dangerous than a single one.[31] The creation of an independent Congress "would change our republics into aristocracies. . . ."[32] "Democritus" declared that "power, among people civilized as we are, is necessarily connected with the direction of public money. . . ." Grant the impost and before we know it we shall become one great republic, instead of a combination of small states. "And as our territory is much too large for a democracy, or even an aristocracy, some Caesar or Cromwell, finding absolute authority within his reach, would presently start up in kingly shape to rule over North America."[33]

In the South, George Mason of Virginia was an outstanding opponent of further grants of power. In 1782 he defended Virginia's title to the West from the attacks of the land speculators in Congress. He denounced the land speculators' argument that sovereignty had "devolved" from the British government upon the Congress. He called it a "doctrine of sovereignty, teeming with oppression and striking at the vitals of American liberty. . . ." He went on to say that "posterity will reflect with indignation that this fatal lust of sovereignty, which lost Great Britain her western world, which covered our country with desolation and blood, should even during the contest against it, be revived among ourselves, and fostered by the very men who were appointed to oppose it!"[34]

In the spring of 1783 the citizens of Fairfax County, Virginia, met to instruct their delegates in the Virginia legislature. George Mason wrote the instructions which reflected his basic convictions. He was opposed to paper money, to any obstacles to carrying out the provisions of the Treaty of Peace, and to any more than necessary delay in the collection of taxes. He was for payment of the

[30] "A Farmer," *Providence Gazette and Country Journal*, 23 March 1782.
[31] Ibid., 24 Aug. 1782.
[32] Ibid., 8 Feb. 1783.
[33] Ibid., 3 May 1783.
[34] To Edmund Randolph, 19 Oct. 1782, George Mason Papers, LC.

public debt and for ample and prompt payment of the soldiers. In such matters he was in complete agreement with the nationalists, but he insisted that they must be handled by the states, and he never wavered in his conviction that they could be.

He was therefore opposed to the finance plan of 1783 and the message sent by Congress pleading for its adoption. The request and the plea, if carefully examined, would be found to "exhibit strong proofs of lust for power." They contained the same arguments that were formerly used in the "business of ship money" and to justify the arbitrary measures of the "race of Stuarts in England." Mason agreed that the duties might be proper, but insisted that only the separate states should have the power of levying and collecting taxes. "Congress should not have even the appearance of such a power. Forms generally imply substance, and such a precedent may be applied to dangerous purposes hereafter. When the same man or set of men, holds both the sword and the purse, there is an end of liberty." [35]

These instructions were attacked violently. It remained to be proved whether the Americans were honest or not, said one writer. "There is now a crisis of the most delicate nature taking place: the crisis of moral and national reputation. . . ." It is a cant phrase of the day to be jealous of power. It is a passion which may possess the bravest or the basest minds: it belongs as much or more to the conspirator as to the patriot. He declared that he had never known a man who had much of this jealousy of power in him "but I could discover a littleness of soul, an enviousness of heart, a fractiousness of temper, and a fondness for himself, at the bottom." Such a man is not jealous of the power of Congress but "wants to play the cheat and probably wants to get into power, by meanly and treacherously undermining those who have been preferred before him." [36]

Some opponents of an independent income had more than argument: they had a specific program to offer. They proposed that the national debt be divided among and paid by the states. They also proposed that this should be done according to a scale of depreciation so that debts would be paid at their real rather than at their

[35] Kate M. Rowland: *The Life of George Mason* (2 vols., New York, 1892), II, 48–52.

[36] *Pennsylvania Gazette*, 9 July 1783.

face value. The expense of the civil list of Congress should likewise be apportioned annually among the states.[37]

The opponents believed that an independent income for Congress would bring an end to the Confederation at some time in the future. Their judgment, often called narrow and selfish, was right enough as of the time, because the supporters of such an income hoped that it would create what its opponents so greatly feared: an all-powerful central government. Only if one recognizes this basic agreement can one understand the struggle in the states where the plan of 1783 was debated and voted upon.

Several states acted rapidly on the impost part of the plan. New Jersey, Connecticut, Delaware, and North Carolina had very little direct import trade, so they were willing enough to have the central government levy an impost. New Jersey approved of the grant in June 1783.[38] The governor of Delaware reported approval by his state and said that any state which did not "must be blind to the united interest, in which that of the individual states are inseparably connnected." [39] Pennsylvania, still in the hands of nationalist leaders, agreed to the impost in the fall session of the legislature in 1783.[40] South Carolina followed in the spring of 1784,[41] as did North Carolina [42] and Connecticut.[43]

There was little opposition in most of these states, but in Virginia, Massachusetts, and New York the story becomes both more complicated and more illuminating of the issues of the times.

Massachusetts agreed to the impost in October 1783, but not without qualms. The "country party" wanted the funds used only to pay the foreign debt, and not for commutation of soldiers' pay.[44] Old revolutionists like James Warren agreed that public credit must be maintained, but felt that there must be an easier way. The impost would harm commerce and be "dangerous to

[37] "A Freeholder," *Providence Gazette*, 26 Oct. 1782, and "Plain Dealer," ibid., 10 May 1783.

[38] *Acts of New Jersey* (Wilson ed.), 329–30.

[39] To Washington, 2 July 1783, Bancroft: *Constitution*, I, 319.

[40] 23 Sept. 1783, Pennsylvania *Statutes at Large*, XI, 162–6.

[41] Ralph Izard to Jefferson, 27 April 1784, *South Carolina Historical and Genealogical Magazine*, II (1901), 194–5.

[42] North Carolina *State Records*, XXIV, 547–9.

[43] Connecticut *State Records*, V, 326–7.

[44] Joseph Pierce to Henry Knox, 20 Oct. 1783, Knox Papers, MHS.

public liberty. . . ."[45] There was, in addition, a group of men led by Stephen Higginson who were deadly enemies of Robert Morris: they were convinced that the "aristocrats" of the middle states were conspiring to achieve power under his leadership.[46] The grant of power was therefore accompanied by instructions ordering the Massachusetts delegates in Congress to abolish the office of superintendent of finance, or at least to limit its power.[47]

The dispute in Virginia was heated and came close on the heels of Virginia's repeal of the impost of 1781. That, according to disgruntled Governor Harrison, had been achieved by the Lees who had used the arguments of Rhode Island.[48] The powerful George Mason, as we have seen, was as much opposed to the new plan as to the old one. Thomas Jefferson disliked the plan because the assumption of state debts had been left out, but he wanted the state to adopt it anyway, and worked with members of the legislature to that end. Among them Patrick Henry was as usual "involved in mystery," said Jefferson, but, "should the popular tide run strongly in either direction, he will fall in with it." However, if Henry could not decide which way the tide was running, he would have a difficult time choosing between his enmity for the Lees and his enmity for an additional grant of power to Congress.[49] But Henry, for once, went against the tide: he came out for the impost, which at least had the effect of making it certain that the Lees would not change their position and favor it.[50]

Despite Henry's support of a scheme which was for the most part the ideal of his political enemies, the Virginia legislature refused to act. There was much talk of the danger of a powerful Congress. But probably the basic practical objection was that collections in Virginia would be so great that her consumers would in effect pay far more than her just share of the national debt. Many Virginians believed the United States would owe the state at least a million pounds when accounts were settled.[51] As in other states, many Virginians wanted the amount to be collected,

[45] To John Adams, 27 Oct. 1783, *Warren-Adams Letters*, II, 232.
[46] Higginson to Samuel Adams, 20 May 1783, Burnett, VII, 166–7.
[47] Massachusetts *Acts and Resolves* (1782–3), 796–8.
[48] To Washington, 31 March 1783, Washington Papers, LC.
[49] To Madison, 7 May 1783, *Writings* (Bergh ed.), IV, 440–41.
[50] Edmund Randolph to Madison, 15 May 1783, Madison Papers, LC.
[51] Joseph Jones to Madison, 14 June 1783, *Letters of Joseph Jones*, 117.

credited to that state's accounts with Congress.[52] There were endless arguments, of course. Randolph even found it necessary to try to refute an assertion that Congress had sent Thomas Paine to Rhode Island to support the impost.[53]

By June the chances of the impost were "lessened exceedingly" and even Patrick Henry was "utterly silent." [54] At the end of the month the whole question was postponed to the next session of the assembly.[55]

Richard Henry Lee summed up the attitude of the opposition. The proposal, he said, was "too early and too strong an attempt to over leap those fences, established by the Confederation to secure the liberties of the respective states. Where the possession of power creates as it too frequently does, a thirst for more, plausible arguments are seldom wanting to persuade acquiescence." The Confederation, which allowed the states to levy and collect taxes as they pleased, would be sapped, and the all-important power of the purse would be vested in an aristocratic assembly. Give the purse, and the sword will follow, and "that liberty which we love and now deserve, will become an empty name." [56] Despite this defeat in the spring of 1783, the supporters of the impost continued to work for it and in the October session of that year, Virginia granted the impost to Congress.[57] Even Rhode Island in time agreed to the impost, but with certain specific changes to suit its convenience. The collectors were to be under control of its legislature rather than of Congress. Eight thousand dollars a year was to be set aside to pay Rhode Island's share of interest on the foreign debt. Surplus sums were to be set aside to pay interest on the domestic debt due within Rhode Island.[58]

During the spring of 1785, Congress surveyed the situation and decided to send delegations to the states of Rhode Island, New York, and Georgia to urge them to agree to the plan of 1783.[59] Then, early in January 1786, the secretary of Congress made a full

[52] Randolph to Madison, 29 May, 14 June, Madison Papers, LC.

[53] Randolph to Madison, 15 May 1783, Madison Papers, LC. As we have seen, it was Robert Morris who sent Paine—without the knowledge of Congress.

[54] Jefferson to Madison, 17 June, *Writings* (Bergh ed.), IV, 443.

[55] Joseph Jones to Madison, 28 June, *Letters of Joseph Jones*, 123–4.

[56] To [William Whipple], 1 July, *Letters of Richard Henry Lee*, II, 284.

[57] Hening, XI, 350–2.

[58] Rhode Island *Acts and Resolves* (Feb. 1785), 23–5.

[59] 15 March 1785, *Journals*, XXVIII, 162.

report on what had been done by the states. The proposal consisted of two parts, he said. The first part dealt with the impost. To this eight states had agreed. He cited without comment Rhode Island's action. Maryland seemed to have reiterated its support of the impost of 1781 but had done nothing about the plan of 1783. Delaware was reported to have agreed to the request, but Congress had never received any official confirmation.

The second part of the plan called for a total contribution of a million and a half dollars a year from the states to be raised in any way they saw fit. Only New Jersey, Pennsylvania, and North Carolina had agreed to this, while Rhode Island had done so in part. The proposed amendment to the Articles of Confederation, which shifted the basis of apportionment of federal expenses from land values to population, had been agreed to by eight states.[60]

This report was handed to a committee of Congress which in turn examined the various state laws. The committee concluded that seven of the states: New Hampshire, Massachusetts, Connecticut, New Jersey, Virginia, North and South Carolina had granted the impost in such a manner that if the remaining six states made similar grants, the impost could be put into effect at once.

The committee agreed that it was natural for the states to be cautious and to investigate the proposals thoroughly, but they had had nearly three years to do so. During that time many changes had taken place in the membership of Congress, yet each successive Congress had approved the plan. The committee went on to list the interest payments that should be made and the need for funds to do so. It agreed that the sale of western lands would pay part of the domestic debt but this process would take time because of the need of surveying. Meanwhile foreign creditors should be paid. Once more the committee promised that all the money received would be used to pay interest and principal on the national debt.

It declared finally that "the crisis has arrived"; to refuse money to Congress would be to "hazard not only the existence of the union, but of those great and invaluable privileges, for which they have so arduously and so honorably contended." They resolved that requisitions from Congress could not be looked upon as "the

[60] 3 Jan. 1786, ibid., XXX, 7–9.

establishment of a system of general revenue, in opposition to that recommended to the several states" in 1783; that requisitions were a temporary expedient. Therefore compliance with the whole plan was recommended anew, and particularly the impost part of it.[61]

At this point, New Jersey declared that it would pay nothing on the requisition for 1786 until all the states had agreed to the impost, or at least until the states that levied duties for their own benefit would give them up. New Jersey had failed in her efforts to build up her trade and she now admitted it. Her legislature declared that the impost duties of certain states drew revenues "from other states whose local situations and circumstances will not admit their enjoying similar advantages from commerce." New Jersey was merely reiterating the position she had taken in December 1784 when the legislature directed the treasurer to pay no more money to the United States until all the states had agreed to the impost of 1783 and to the plan for establishing supplemental funds.[62]

Congress responded by sending a delegation headed by Charles Pinckney of South Carolina. He pleaded with the legislature to rescind its resolution. He said that all the states except New York had agreed to the impost. If New Jersey refused to help supply the common treasury, the union would be endangered. Suppose the Confederation were dissolved and a convention called: would not the large states want a greater share of power? While the central government was weak and inefficient, the states were refractory. The greatest danger of the United States was from disunion. There was no danger from a "federal aristocracy." Pinckney said that the great danger was of "anarchy . . . or rather worse than anarchy, of a pure democracy. . . ." [63] The arguments of Pinckney and his fellow delegates were effective. The New Jersey legislature rescinded its resolution but took another futile sideswipe at New York by creating still another free port.[64]

Meanwhile other states changed their grants of the impost power to conform with the request of Congress. Even Rhode

[61] 13 Feb. 1786, ibid., XXX, 62–8.

[62] *Massachusetts Centinel,* 15 March 1786; McCormick: New Jersey in the Confederation, ch. vii.

[63] Burnett, VIII, 321–30.

[64] Ibid., VIII, 330, n. 49.

Island did so, although it was said that Mr. Howell "belched forth every curse on mankind" in opposition.[65] By August 1786 every state except New York had conformed.[66]

The battle in New York was long and bitter. Agrarian New York, in control of the legislature, was opposed to any change which would mean more land taxes. Virtually all of the delegates from in and around New York City were for it, while the back-country farmers, except for the great landlords, were opposed. In 1785 supporters of the impost had tried hard to get it agreed to. The propaganda on both sides was enormous in quantity, but represented no change from what had been said in other states. In the spring of 1786 the New York legislature once more took up the question. A bill to approve was introduced, but it was soon amended to provide for collections according to the state impost law rather than according to regulations to be provided by Congress. This was bitterly opposed by the New Yorkers, especially those heavily interested in the national debt, who wanted the national government rather than the state governments to pay it. In the senate a determined but futile effort was made to amend the provision for state collection out of the bill. As finally agreed to, the bill granted the United States the duties on imports to be collected by men appointed by and responsible to the state of New York. The collectors were to pay to Congress the whole amount collected. Congress was given the power to sue delinquent collectors in New York courts. The money collected from the act must go to pay the war debt. All other import duties were to be suspended while the act was in force, which was to be for twenty-five years unless the war debt was paid sooner. New York thus did grant an impost, but not on the terms demanded by Congress.[67]

Congress refused to accept the act. Instead, every state in Congress except New York voted to ask Governor Clinton to call a special session to reconsider.[68] The governor refused to do so on the grounds that he had no power to call special sessions except on extraordinary occasions. This was no such occasion. The New York legislature had gone over the question again and again and

[65] Rhode Island *Acts and Resolves* (Feb. 1786), 33–5; *Pennsylvania Gazette*, 22 March 1786.

[66] *Journals*, XXXI, 559.

[67] Cochran: *New York in the Confederation*, 167–75.

[68] *Journals*, XXX, 439–44; XXXI, 513–4.

made its decision. Once more Congress asked that he call a special session, and once more he refused. When the legislature did meet in its regular session, it approved of the governor's refusal. Once more the supporters of a national income tried to get the legislature to agree. But the enemies of congressional control of collections pointed out that they had given the impost and that they should try state collections first before declaring that method a failure.

Two days after the final refusal of the New York legislature to grant Congress control over the collection of the impost, Hamilton moved the appointment of delegates to the Convention of 1787 and both houses shortly approved, moved in part no doubt by the general alarm caused by Shays's Rebellion.[69]

The climax of the effort to persuade the states to give Congress specific powers came during the summer of 1786. During the same time, Congress also discussed the idea of calling a general convention to approve of wide amendments to the Articles of Confederation. The letters of the members of Congress during that summer do not reflect the optimism that was to be found within the states. Members of all shades of opinion were in agreement that something should be done to add power to the central government lest it should fail completely. The board of treasury complained that it had no ready money on hand. The state governments were going about their own business and for the most part ignored the pleas of Congress, except for the grant of power to collect an impost. Within Congress itself it was difficult to have enough states represented to carry on business. Members bombarded the states with demands for adequate delegations; they insisted that members in New York should attend sessions regularly. The situation so concerned Congress that during the summer a committtee declared that no member should be absent without the permission of either Congress or the state government.[70]

When one looks beneath the complaints about general debility and state indifference, one finds basic divisions of greater significance. The delegates of the northern states had been defeated in their effort to get Congress to agree to an amendment giving the power to regulate trade to the Confederation. The Northerners

[69] Cochran: *New York in the Confederation*, 75–9.

[70] *Journals*, XXX, 408–9. The resolution was voted for by only five of the twelve states represented at the time.

breathed threats against the South and some of them talked of setting up a separate confederacy in the North. The "eastern" and "middle" states are of one interest, said Theodore Sedgwick. What, he asked, is the advantage to them of a connection with the South? The northern states give the South protection, but it refuses to give them a part of their commerce, which is all they have to offer.[71]

Meanwhile the southern states felt equally aggrieved. The hottest issue of a hot summer was the question of the Mississippi. As we have seen, John Jay, as secretary for foreign affairs, functioned as a representative of the northern merchants in his dealings with Spain. He was willing to give up any claim to the use of the Mississippi in exchange for commercial advantages in Spanish ports. The five southern states were able to block his every effort, for nine states would have to agree to any such sacrifice of the West. But this success did not lead to happy relations between the two sections in Congress. Neither did the fact that the bulk of the national debt was held in the North. As we have seen, the northern states could pay a large share of their requisitions in indents because they had taken over payment of interest on the national debt owing their citizens, whereas the South had to meet its requisitions, if it met them at all, by payments in specie.

Despite these sectional divisions, there was general agreement among most members that something should be done. As early as March, William Grayson reported that some members believed that a general convention for the alteration of the Confederation should be recommended to the states. Such men declared the Confederation was utterly inefficient, that if it remained in its state of imbecility, the United States would be one of the most contemptible nations on earth. But not all members felt that way: Grayson, for instance, wondered if it wasn't better to bear present ills than to fly to others of which they were ignorant.

Early in May, Charles Pinckney of South Carolina moved that there be a grand committee to consider the affairs of the nation. He argued that Congress must have more power. To get it, either a convention should be called, or Congress should ask the states for power to raise troops, control commerce, and execute the powers given it. James Monroe of Virginia answered that Congress had

[71] To Caleb Strong, 6 Aug. 1786, Burnett, VIII, 415.

the power to raise troops and to compel obedience in every case when acting according to the Confederation.[72]

The discussion of the proposal went on week after week but nothing was done, partly because of lack of representation. More than this was involved, however, for many of the states were concerned only with their own problems and with no others. The "eastern" states were interested only in commercial powers. They would not agree to give Congress power to prevent the use of paper money. New York and Pennsylvania would be "indisposed" when they heard it proposed that the Confederation should "become a national compact." New Jersey, Delaware, and others would not like to vote in accordance with their real rather than their supposed importance in the union. Thus did William Grayson report the situation. He did not think affairs desperate enough to bring about a real reformation and he believed that a partial reformation would be fatal. The only thing to do would be to bring all problems together, and then, by a general compromise, a good government might be achieved. He suggested that since Virginia had gone so far as to call the Annapolis Convention, she should go farther and propose to the other states that they give their delegates enough power to "comprehend all the grievances of the Union, and to combine the commercial arrangements with them, and make them dependent on each other. . . ." [73]

The result of discussions in Congress was the appointment of a committee to prepare amendments to the Confederation. The report consisted of seven articles to be added to the Articles of Confederation for the purpose of making the "federal government adequate to the ends for which it was instituted." Article fourteen gave Congress the power to regulate trade between the states and with foreign nations, with all duties collected to go to the state in which they were paid. Article fifteen provided that states failing to pay their requisitions after a time to be fixed by Congress must pay additional charges at the rate of ten per cent a year on their quotas. Article sixteen provided that if a state did not pass laws to meet requisitions, Congress should have the power, after a

[72] Thomas Rodney, Diary, 3 May 1786, ibid., VIII, 350–1.

[73] To James Madison, 28 May 1786, ibid., VIII, 373–4. Like the good Virginian he was, Grayson declared that Virginia should not forget her own objects, such as a liberal settlement of public accounts.

majority of the states had passed such laws, to assess and collect the necessary taxes in the state concerned, using regular state officials. If a state tried to block such collections, Congress would have power to appoint its own officials to do so. Article seventeen provided that any state paying more than its share should receive interest, and states in arrears should pay interest. Article eighteen provided that whenever Congress found it necessary to establish new revenue for a period of not more than fifteen years, and eleven states agreed to it, it would be binding on the remaining states. Article nineteen provided that Congress should have the sole power of declaring what offenses against the United States were treasonable, and of defining piracy on the high seas. It also provided that Congress could establish a federal court to try and to punish all officers appointed by Congress. The court would also be a court of appeal from the state courts in all cases involving the interpretation of treaties, the regulation of trade and commerce by the United States, the collection of federal revenue, and cases of importance in which the United States "shall be a party. . . ." Trial of fact by juries and also the benefits of the writ of habeas corpus would be held sacred. The court would consist of seven judges from different parts of the Union. Article twenty dealt with the problem of attendance in Congress. It declared that the states should elect delegates at a certain time and that, after their acceptance, they should be at Congress on 1 November, the beginning of the "federal year." If any delegate should withdraw without leave of Congress, when needed to maintain the representation of a state, he should be disqualified from holding office under the United States and in the states.[74]

These proposed amendments did not alter the essential character of the Articles of Confederation but they did provide for adequate power to meet the immediate needs of the central government. The amendments were discussed in Congress for some time, but they were not adopted and sent to the states.[75]

There are very few clues as to why Congress did not act. One can only hazard the guess that by the fall of 1786 the men most anxious to create a strong central government had pinned all their hopes on a constitutional convention entirely apart from Congress.

[74] 7 Aug. 1786, *Journals*, XXXI, 494–8.

[75] Rhode Island Delegates to the Governor of Rhode Island, 28 Sept. 1786, Burnett, VIII, 471.

The calling of the Annapolis Convention by the state of Virginia was the culmination of a long campaign to achieve such an end. The people at large perhaps knew but little of the issues with which their political leaders were so much concerned. But those leaders knew that the supporters of the Annapolis Convention had more than commercial regulations in mind. One member of Congress declared that he had "decisive evidence" that its backers had called it to head off any enlargement of the powers of Congress.[76] Others doubted that commerce was the real concern of its backers and said that "political objects" were also involved.

When the Annapolis Convention met, and then hurriedly disbanded, it declared that the commercial powers of Congress could not be altered without taking other matters into consideration as well. Therefore it recommended another convention to meet in the spring of 1787. This report was sent to Congress and the states. Congress at first ignored it and then, early in 1787, issued a call for a convention to meet to revise and amend the Articles of Confederation. When the states elected delegates to that convention, they in turn instructed their delegates to revise and amend the Articles of Confederation.

But when the convention met in Philadelphia in May 1787, its members decided to ignore their instructions and to create an entirely new government. Thus the government of the Confederation was abandoned. The writing and ratification of the Constitution of 1787 is thus the beginning of a new chapter, not the ending of an old one, in the book of American history.

[76] Theodore Sedgwick to Caleb Strong, ibid., VIII, 415.

Conclusion

The Significance of the Confederation Period

THE FOREGOING pages indicate that the Confederation Period was one of great significance, but not of the kind that tradition has led us to believe. The "critical period" idea was the result of an uncritical acceptance of the arguments of the victorious party in a long political battle, of a failure to face the fact that partisan propaganda is not history but only historical evidence. What emerges instead is a much more complex and important story in which several themes are interwoven. It was a period of what we would call post-war demobilization, of sudden economic change, dislocation, and expansion, and of fundamental conflict over the nature of the Constitution of the United States. Each of these themes is so interwoven with the others that any separation is arbitrary but, taken separately or together, they are better keys to an understanding of the period than the traditional one.

At the end of the war Americans faced innumerable problems arising from it. What should be done with war veterans? Should the Loyalists return to their homes? What should be our relations with foreign friends and foes? Should commerce be free or should there be discrimination, and if so, against whom and for whose benefit? How would peace affect the economy? How should the war debt be paid? What kind of taxes should be levied to pay it, and who should pay them? When the war-boom collapsed, why did it? What should the state or central governments, or both, do about it? Should government encourage one form of economic enterprise over another or should it keep hands off? What about discontented groups: should government ignore them, cater to them, or forcibly suppress those who might revolt?

Such questions or others like them have probably been asked

after every great war in history. They were asked, debated, and given various solutions during the 1780's. The significance of those debates and solutions has often been misunderstood. This is no better illustrated than in the case of the national debt during the 1780's which is usually discussed only in terms of depreciation and nonpayment of interest. Actually much more was involved than this. The debt was fantastically low compared with the national debt of today—about twelve dollars per capita as compared with seventeen hundred—and the nation had vast untouched natural resources with which to pay it. Multitudes of accounts had to be reduced to simple forms so that they could be paid, and this the Confederation government managed to do. But even more important than the economics of the national debt was its politics: should it be paid by the states or the central government? A fundamental assumption of every political leader was that the political agency which paid the debt would hold the balance of power in the new nation. Hence, the supporters of a strong central government insisted that the national debt must be paid by Congress while their opponents insisted that it should be divided among the states and paid by them. The latter group was on the way to victory by the end of the 1780's, for they were supported by clamoring creditors. The result was that one state after another assumed portions of the national debt owing to its citizens. Thus the traditional story is so out of context as to be virtually meaningless. This is true of other traditions as well. Most of the ports of the world were open, not closed, to American citizens. Reciprocity and equal treatment of all United States citizens was the rule in the tonnage and tariff acts of the states, not trade barriers.

To say that many of the pessimistic traditions are false is not to say that all Americans were peaceful and satisfied. The holders of national and state debts wanted bigger payments than they got. The merchants wanted more government aid than was given them. The farmers, hit by high taxes and rigid collection of both taxes and private debts, demanded relief in the form of lower taxes and government loans from state legislatures. Such demands kept state politics in an uproar during the 1780's. However, the often violent expression of such discontents in politics should not blind us to the fact that the period was one of extraordinary economic growth. Merchants owned more ships at the end of the 1780's than they had at the beginning of the Revolution, and they carried a greater share of American produce. By 1790 the export of agricultural produce was double what it had been before the war. American cities grew rapidly, with the result that housing was scarce and building booms produced a labor shortage. Tens of thousands of farmers spread outwards to the frontiers. There can be no question but that freedom from the British Empire resulted in a surge of activity in all phases of American life. Of course not all the problems of the new nation were solved by 1789 —all have not yet been solved—but there is no evidence of stagnation and decay in the 1780's. Instead the story is one of a newly free people who seized upon every means to improve and enrich themselves in a nation which they believed had a golden destiny.

Politically the dominating fact of the Confederation Period was the struggle between two groups of leaders to shape the character of the state and central governments. The revolutionary constitutions of the states placed final power in the legislatures and made the executive and judicial branches subservient to them. The members of the colonial aristocracy who became Patriots, and new men who gained economic power during the Revolution deplored this fact, but they were unable to alter the state constitutions during the 1780's. Meanwhile they tried persistently to strengthen the central government. These men were the nationalists of the 1780's.

On the other hand the men who were the true federalists believed that the greatest gain of the Revolution was the independence of the several states and the creation of a central government subservient to them. The leaders of this group from the Declaration of Independence to the Convention of 1787 were Samuel Adams, Patrick Henry, Richard Henry Lee, George Clinton, James Warren, Samuel Bryan, George Bryan, Elbridge Gerry, George Mason and a host of less well known but nc less important men in each of the states. Most of these men believed, as a result of their experience with Great Britain before 1776 and of their reading of history, that the states could be best governed without the intervention of a powerful central government. Some of them had programs of political and social reform; others had none at all. Some had a vision of democracy; others had no desire except to control their states for whatever satisfactions such control might offer. Some were in fact as narrow and provincial as their opponents said they were. However, the best of them agreed that the central government needed more power, but they wanted that power given so as not to alter the basic character of the Articles of Confederation. Here is where they were in fundamental disagreement with the nationalists who wanted to remove the central government from the control of the state legislatures.

The nationalist leaders from the Declaration of Independence to the Philadelphia convention were men like Robert Morris, John Jay, Gouverneur Morris, James Wilson, Alexander Hamilton, Henry Knox, James Duane, George Washington, James Madison, and many lesser men. Most of these men were by temperament or economic interest believers in executive and judicial rather than legislative control of state and central governments, in the rigorous collection of taxes, and, as creditors, in strict payment of public and private debts. They declared that national honor and prestige could be maintained only by a powerful central government. Naturally, not all men who used such language used it sincerely, for some were as selfish and greedy as their opponents said they were. The nationalists frankly disliked the political heritage of the Revolution. They deplored the fact there was no check upon the actions of majorities in state legislatures; that there was no central government to which minorities could appeal from the decisions of such majorities, as they had done before the Revolution.

There were men who veered from side to side, but their number is relatively small and their veering is of little significance as compared with the fact that from the outset of the Revolution there were two consistently opposed bodies of opinion as to the nature of the central government. There was, of course, a wide variation of belief among adherents of both points of view. There were extremists who wanted no central government at all and others who wanted to wipe out the states entirely. There were some who wanted a monarchy and others who would have welcomed dictatorship. But such extremists are not representative of the two great bodies of men whose conflict was the essence of the years both before and after 1789.

While the federalist leaders gradually moved to a position where they were willing to add specific powers to the Articles of Confederation, the nationalist leaders campaigned steadily for the kind of government they wanted. During the war they argued that it could not be won without creating a powerful central government. After the war they insisted that such a government was necessary to do justice to public creditors, solve the problems of post-war trade, bring about recovery from depression, and win the respect of the world for the new nation. Meanwhile their experience with majorities in state legislatures merely intensified their desire. They became desperate as state after state in 1785 and 1786 adopted some form of paper money that could be loaned on farm mortgages and be used to pay taxes, and in some cases private debts as well. When they were able to hold off such demands and farmers revolted, as in Massachusetts, they were thoroughly frightened.

They looked upon such events as evidence of the horrors of unchecked democracy and they said so in poetry, private letters, newspaper essays, and public speeches. The problem, they said, was to find some refuge from democracy. They worked hard to control state legislatures and they were often successful, but such control was uncertain at best, for annual elections meant a constant threat of overturn and the threat was realized repeatedly.

We may not call it democracy, but they did. Edmund Randolph put their case bluntly in his opening speech in the Convention of 1787. He said, "our chief danger arises from the democratic parts of our constitutions . . . None of the [state] constitutions have provided a sufficient check against the democracy. The feeble senate of Virginia is a phantom. Maryland has a more powerful senate, but the late distractions in that state, have discovered that it is not powerful enough. The check established in the constitutions of New York and Massachusetts is yet a stronger barrier against democracy, but they all seem insufficient." Outside the Convention General Knox was saying that a "mad democracy sweeps away every moral trait from the human character" and that the Convention would "clip the wings of a mad democracy." James Madison in the *Federalist Papers* argued that the new Constitution should be adopted because a "republican" form of government was better than a "democracy."

The debate was white-hot and was carried on with utter frankness. It was white-hot because for a moment in history self-government by majorities within particular political boundaries was possible. Those majorities could do what they wanted, and some of them knew what they wanted. Democracy was no vague ideal, but a concrete program: it meant definite things in politics, economics, and religion. Whatever side of the controversy we take, whether we think the majorities in state legislatures governed badly or well—the fact to face is that men of the 1780's believed that the issue was democracy as a way of government for the United States of those days.

They faced the issue squarely. They thought hard and realistically about the problems of government. They understood that society is complex and that the truth about it is multifold rather than simple. James Madison summed it up as well as it has ever been done. There are, he said, many passions and interests in society and these will ever clash for control of government and will ever interpret their own desires as the good of the whole. Men like Madison and John Adams believed, as Madison said, that the "great desideratum which has not yet been found for Republican governments seems to be some disinterested and dispassionate umpire in disputes between different passions and interests in the state." In the tenth number of *The Federalist*, after citing various origins of political parties, Madison said that "the most durable source of factions [parties] has been the various and unequal distribution of property. Those who hold and those who are without property have ever formed distinct interests in society. Those who are creditors and those who are debtors, fall under a like discrimination. A landed interest, a manufacturing interest, a mercantile interest, a monied interest, with many lesser interests, grow up of necessity in civilized nations, and divide them into different classes, actuated by different sentiments and views. The regulation of these various and interfering interests forms the principal task of modern legislation, and involves the spirit of party and faction in the necessary and ordinary operations of the government."

The constitutional debate of the 1780's was thus carried on by men with a realistic appreciation of the social forces lying behind constitutional forms and theories, by men who were aware of the relationship between economic and political power. This realistic approach was lost sight of in the nineteenth century by romantic democrats who believed that once every man had the right to vote the problems of society could be solved. It was lost sight of too by those who came to believe in an oversimplified economic interpretation of history. In a sense they were as romantic as the democrats, for they assumed a rationality in the historic process that is not always supported by the evidence.

If the history of the Confederation has anything to offer us it is the realistic approach to politics so widely held by the political leaders of the time, however much they might differ as to forms of government and desirable goals for the new nation. Throughout the Confederation men with rival goals pushed two programs simultaneously. The federalists tried to strengthen the Articles of Confederation; the nationalists tried to create a new constitution by means of a convention, and thus avoid the method of change prescribed by the Articles of Confederation. The movement to strengthen the Articles failed on the verge of success; the movement to call a convention succeeded on the verge of failure. The failure of one movement and the success of the other, however we may interpret them, is one of the dramatic stories in the history of politics.

Essay on the Sources

THE MATERIALS for the history of the Confederation are enormous in extent. There are hundreds of volumes of printed records, laws, and letters, vast quantities of newspapers, and untold thousands of manuscripts. These are scattered in libraries throughout the United States. The best of the historical writing is to be found in such magazines as the *Pennsylvania Magazine of History and Biography*, *The New England Quarterly*, *The American Historical Review*, and in many of the old historical magazines published in the nineteenth century. The publications of such organizations as the Colonial Society of Massachusetts, the Massachusetts Historical Society, and the New York Historical Society contain a wealth of printed sources and monographs all too little used by scholars. All such publications, as well as books and monographs, have been given full bibliographical citations in footnotes.

Perhaps the most fascinating of all the sources are the newspapers and magazines of the 1780's. The years immediately after the war saw a rapid increase in the number of newspapers and magazines, and the beginnings of the daily newspaper in the United States. There were perhaps a hundred newspapers in the United States by 1790. Several impressions are made as soon as one opens their yellowed pages, often printed with lovely type, and always on rag paper, so that even today they are more sturdy than yesterday's newspaper, and usually more beautiful typographically. The first impression that one gets is that Americans were very much a part of an "Atlantic Community." Virtually every newspaper gave more space to the seaports ringing the Atlantic from Newfoundland through the West Indies, to Africa, southern Europe, and the Baltic, than they gave to what was happening in the United States. This was natural enough when one remembers that most American newspapers were printed in seaport towns whose acquaintance with Trinidad, Leghorn, Lisbon, Hamburg, Glasgow, and London, and very shortly, Canton as well, was closer than it was with the region a hundred miles west of tidewater. However, the intensity of political life in the 1780's worked a rapid change. More and more the newspapers printed articles on the problems that faced Americans, all the way from arguments in behalf of the merits of American poets and artists to the iniquities of paper money.

One at once gets a sense of the vitality with which Americans debated issues. One is also impressed with the fact that most newspaper publishers believed that it was a part of their public duty to print materials on all sides of a question, even when they were counter to a particular publisher's own views.

The advertisements, the poetry, and the "intimate" news published by the majority of the papers are a never-ending source of joy to the reader and a trap for the man who would do research. Many a poem and news account printed without benefit of asterisks in the eighteenth century would never be printed in a respectable twentieth century journal, even with asterisks.

In using the newspapers I have concentrated on a few papers such as the *Massachusetts Centinel* and the *Pennsylvania Gazette* which are remarkable for the attention they pay to public affairs and the fairness with which they set forth a variety of views on all topics. Editors in the eighteenth century made constant use of scissors so that the same news item or political essay often appears in the newspapers all the way from New Hampshire to Georgia, sometimes with acknowledgment and sometimes not.

The manuscript collections that remain to us offer still another insight into the public and private life of the Americans of the 1780's. Of course much has been printed, but far more remains in a host of libraries. Two striking facts at once appear as one turns over letter after letter. The first is that most of the published letters are those of one side in the political struggles of the period. Some of the outstanding nationalist leaders like Washington, Madison, and Hamilton have had their letters printed, sometimes in many editions. But we do not have the same easy access to the letters of such men as Patrick Henry, George Mason, Samuel

Bryan, George Bryan, and George Clinton. Two volumes of Richard Henry Lee's letters and four volumes of Samuel Adams's letters have been printed, it is true, and scattered letters are to be found buried away in printed collections and magazines. But the task of unearthing them is a real one that is as fascinating as it is difficult. The other striking fact, with a few exceptions, is that we have only the letters written by a man, not the letters written to him. But there are hundreds of unpublished letters to men like Samuel Adams, George Washington, and James Madison which must be read in connection with the printed ones before the scholar can have any understanding of the rich variety of the public and private life of such men.

In quoting manuscripts and newspapers I have modernized spelling and capitalization but I have not tampered with punctuation. To do so would be to launch on a sea of uncertainty. Here and there, as in the case of a letter of Daniel Boone, I have quoted a document as written, for to modernize would be to lose the delightful flavor of the original.

A third basic source for the history of the period is the legislation passed by the states. Such laws have been little used, yet it was state legislation which shaped the economic and political fabric of the new nation during the 1780's, and it did so without any interference from outside. The laws, as always, are a difficult source, for one seldom if ever can be sure how they operated. Nevertheless such laws as those relating to trade, money, debts, and taxes offer much that is vital and new. Anyone who wants to make a sincere effort to understand the life of the times must read the thousands of yellow, finely printed pages of statutes as well as the letters of the men who passed them, and the newspapers which battled for and against them.

The greatest single collection of sources is to be found in Washington, D. C. The manuscript division of the Library of Congress and the National Archives contain thousands of unused, and often unknown, manuscripts. No more striking example of this is to be found than the collection of papers in the Library of Congress containing the quarterly reports of the Register of the Treasury during the 1780's. In them can be found an accounting of the day-to-day work of the government of the United States. Here, and elsewhere in citing statistics, no effort has been made to reduce dollars, pounds, florins, livres, and so on, to a single standard, for rates of exchange varied from year to year, month to month, and from state to state.

A final word should be said in behalf of those who collect autographs. Many a library has collections of the signatures of the generals of the Revolution, the signers of the Declaration of Independence, the Articles of Confederation, the Constitution, and so on. Fortunately for the scholar, such signatures usually are attached to letters. The search through these collections is a constant treasure hunt with happy surprises in the most unexpected places. Two notable collections of this sort are the Emmet Collection in the New York Public Library and the Gratz Collection in the Pennsylvania Historical Society.

In the preface I have listed the libraries in which manuscripts were used; in the footnotes I have cited particular collections. I have not tried to list all the manuscript collections relating to the history of the period. Indeed, it would be difficult to do so, even for only one of the libraries with a major collection. Where guides have been published, even the best of them are an inadequate index to the riches to be found. It would in fact be impossible, short of the expenditure of funds which most libraries do not and probably never will have, to list and describe their collections adequately. Perhaps it is just as well, for the scholar must see and work through the materials for himself, not only for the sake of research, but for the joy of doing it.

List of Abbreviations

AHA,	American Historical Association
AHR,	American Historical Review
APS,	American Philosophical Society
CL,	Clements Library
CSM,	Colonial Society of Massachusetts
HUL,	Harvard University Library
JEBH,	Journal of Economic and Business History
LC,	Library of Congress
MHS,	Massachusetts Historical Society
MVHR,	Mississippi Valley Historical Review
NA,	National Archives
NEQ,	New England Quarterly
NYHS,	New York Historical Society
NYPL,	New York Public Library
PCC,	Papers of the Continental Congress
PHS,	Pennsylvania Historical Society
PMHB,	Pennsylvania Magazine of History and Biography
PSQ,	Political Science Quarterly
WHS,	Wisconsin Historical Society
YUL,	Yale University Library

Index

ALL PLACE AND PERSONAL NAMES
TO WHICH REFERENCE IS ONLY INCIDENTAL
ARE OMITTED FROM THIS INDEX

Index

Index

Index

A NOTE ON THE TYPE
IN WHICH THIS BOOK IS SET

This book is set in Monotype Caslon, a modern adaptation of a type designed by the first William Caslon (1692–1766). The Caslon face has had two centuries of ever-increasing popularity in the United States—it is of interest to note that the first copies of the Declaration of Independence and the first paper currency distributed to the citizens of the new-born nation were printed in this type face.